His Healing Love

His Healing Love

Dick Winn

A Morning Watch book, prepared to assist in the daily devotions of senior youth.

REVIEW AND HERALD PUBLISHING ASSOCIATION
Washington, DC 20039-0555
Hagerstown, MD 21740

Edited by Raymond H. Woolsey
Designed by Richard Steadham
Cover art by Harry Anderson

Printed in U.S.A.

Library of Congress Cataloging-in-Publication Data

Winn, Dick.
  His healing love.

  Includes index.
  1. Devotional calendars. I. Title.
BV4811.W595   1986   242'.2   86-13060

ISBN 0-8280-0353-X

ABOUT THE AUTHOR

When he wrote this book, Dick Winn was president of Weimar Institute in California. He had helped to found the institution and later served as its chaplain. Currently he is on graduate study leave.

Elder Winn studied theology at Andrews University, earning a master's degree and the Master of Divinity degree as well. He is the author of a number of books, including Bible textbooks for grades 7 and 8 in English-speaking Adventist schools, *A New You, If God Won the War, Why Isn't It Over? Into His Likeness,* and *God Is the Victor,* published at Pacific Press. He has had a number of articles published in various church journals.

Elder Winn and his wife, Terry, are the parents of two teenagers, Julie and Jeff, students at Weimar Academy.

BEING FREE IN JESUS

Now the Lord is the Spirit, and where the Spirit of the Lord is, there is freedom. 2 Cor. 3:17, R.S.V.

For thirty-five years Bill had been very careful to live by the minute requirements of a conservative Christian lifestyle. He was convinced he must do that in order to obtain salvation. Suddenly, however, he turned his back on all religion. "I've got to be free to become myself," he complained.

Perhaps Bill had never studied today's text. Probably he felt, as do many Christians, that the Spirit's presence and freedom just don't seem to go together. Such people see God as needing to impose upon them a heavy sense of "ought-ness"—"You ought to do this," "you ought not to be that." Freedom seems a cruel joke, but to admit it would be rebellious, and they "ought not to be rebellious!"

But if there is in one's religious experience such a feeling of oppression, of heavy demands for submission to power, then we can be sure that the Spirit of the Lord is not there. He is not involved in such religion. For the Spirit of the Lord does not work by force.

We must recall that there is more than one kind of force. Far more subtle (and therefore more effective) than physical force is emotional force. And that comes in myriad forms: the threat of withholding love, using past failings to rub the raw nerves of hurting self-worth, and verbal scoldings and harangues, to name just a few.

Our God works not by force but by imparting the principles of truth and illuminating the mind to understand that truth, making it vital to our lives. God doesn't need to use force to support His truths for they are well able to stand on their own merits.

In human structures, whenever leaders become deficient in truth they must immediately compensate with a display of power. Such leaders either do not have truth behind their schemes or they do not trust the ability of their subjects to grasp what truth they may have.

But God has neither problem. Not only is His government rooted in sensible, coherent truth, He also has great confidence in the capacities of His creatures to perceive that truth! To use force is to deny both these principles.

In an atmosphere of freedom, how quickly our minds respond to grasp the principles of truth on which God builds His gracious government. Are you free in Jesus? Then thank His Spirit for showing you how to be free!

7

FREEDOM THROUGH CONFIDENCE

In him we have access to God with freedom, in the confidence borne of trust in him. Eph. 3:12, N.E.B.

A young boy who was crippled in one foot was cautioned by his mother not to run. Indeed, while in fact he could outrun his younger sister, he was told that he was not able to run. Relying on the information given him by the one he most trusted, he ceased this activity, slowly lost what ability he had, and ended up a recluse. This seemed to confirm his mother's assessment.

What a tragedy! And it is equally so with those of us who have listened to the inferences of the evil one. We have a crippled left foot, as it were, and the devil tells us that we cannot run—to the Father! His reasons are all lies.

First of all, Satan tells us that the Father is angry. You rarely run toward someone who is angry with you! Adam and Eve surely did not. To this falsehood he adds a subtle insinuation: God doesn't like cripples in the first place. He tolerates their approach only after they have done something to appease Him.

God deals directly with this misleading information. He gives us better facts, both about us and about Himself. And in order that He can be the most trusted source of information in our lives, He lived out the truth about Himself in the person of His Son. As we see God in Christ, we begin to trust in Him. As our trust grows, we become more confident in our approach to Him until, at last, we know that we have total freedom in our access to Him. Some even start to run toward Him!

If only we could grasp an even greater truth: we do not need to stay crippled! God is the great restorer. In our flight into His presence we find that He "is able to do immeasurably more than all we can ask or conceive" (Eph. 3:20, N.E.B.). For God desires us not only to be able to run but to run and not be weary. He has it in His plans that we shall renew our strength, mounting up with wings like eagles (Isa. 40:31).

Our God is the one we should trust the most. He has the most reliable information. He has only our best interests, our highest achievements, in mind. And He is eager and ready to have us run into His presence. We might even hasten there on wings!

WHOSE OPINION NEEDS CHANGING?

In Christ God was reconciling the world to himself, not counting their trespasses against them, and entrusting to us the message of reconciliation. 2 Cor. 5:19, R.S.V.

The sin problem does not center in God's opinion of man but in man's opinion of God. It was not God who turned away from man, but man who turned away from God. The focus of all true religion is on God's endeavors to get men to change their opinion about God. The focus of all false religion, on the other hand, is found in men's attempts to get God to change His opinion of them.

Christ came to change our understanding of the Father. He died on the cross that we might know something very important about His love and truthfulness, so that—in knowing it—we would change our opinion of the Father. Satan has distorted even the death of Christ on the cross as Christ's act to appease the Father on our behalf. Many Christians believe that Christ's crucifixion allowed the Father to change toward us—to show mercy where previously He could show only wrath.

Sin is the breaking of a relationship with God, but we humans are the ones who moved away. It grieved God that we should go "into a far country." And Jesus revealed that the Father walks by the gate, continually looking down the road for the first glimpses of any returning children. Remember, however, that the wandering son came home when he began to understand who his father really was.

But how will the Father feel about us wanderers when we do come home, still smelling of the pigs and dirty laundry? Will He dress us down for our stupidity? Will He make sure we are not restored to family membership until a pound of flesh has been exacted in payment for our crimes? Paul answers that question explicitly: God's attitude is one of not counting our trespasses against us. No retribution, no groveling for condescending forgiveness. We see that we need to come home to the Father; that is enough.

What is more, the Father does not put us on the provisional membership list in order to rub our face in our crime. He immediately entrusts to us the most important mission a human can carry! He sends us to help change the opinions of still others about the Father. He makes it clear that He holds no grudges. He expects great things from us. Incredible! Couldn't you love such a God?

IT IS OURSELVES WE HURT

But he that sinneth against me wrongeth his own soul. Prov. 8:36.

Another translation says, "He who finds me not, hurts himself" (N.E.B.). If you discover that you have a fatal disease, you seek a physician. If, instead, you decide that you don't need one, give yourself enough time and you no longer will need one. Many grieving widows have exclaimed ruefully that their spouses just wouldn't admit that they needed medical help—to their own destruction.

Our estrangement from God is causing us untold suffering. We are thirsty; He is the Water of Life. We are hungry; He is the Bread of Life. We are sick; He is the Great Physician. However, a very convincing liar, Satan, has made us wary of our wonderful God, saying things that are very misleading and downright wrong about Him. He says that when we sin, it makes God angry. That if we don't shape up, God will wipe us out. (And good riddance, too!)

If God were to be vindictive with anyone, certainly it would be to this perpetrator of falsehood. Instead, God acts with utmost integrity. No artificial shame is cast upon this archenemy. No arbitrary disciplines exacted. Looking on, we can even detect a definite courtesy being displayed on God's part toward this most unsavory foe.

God never changes. We have found ourselves born into the enemy camp. "Condemned!" Satan screams with hellish accuracy. But with infinite tenderness and careful language, God tells us the full story. He tells us how we have been born into a broken relationship with Himself, but that His feelings toward us have always been thoughts of peace and healing. "For I know the plans I have for you, says the Lord, plans for welfare and not for evil, to give you a future and a hope" (Jer. 29:11, R.S.V.).

He tells us the truth about our condition. Our separation from Him damages us. God does not punish us by inflicting hurt. We *are* hurt as a natural consequence of our apartness from the One who is the most loving, caring, truthful, loyal, exciting, innovative, encouraging, et cetera, source of input into our lives. It only makes good sense to agree that He is absolutely correct and to confess our condition. Coming back into right relationship with Him (justification), we begin to experience the total healing that God so desires for us.

JESUS CAME ANNOUNCING FORGIVENESS

Let it be known to you therefore, brethren, that through this man forgiveness of sins is proclaimed to you, and by him every one that believes is freed from everything from which you could not be freed by the law of Moses. Acts 13:38, 39, R.S.V.

Jesus didn't come bargaining with forgiveness; He came announcing it. Jesus didn't say, "I will forgive you *if* you will believe in Me." He said, "I *am* a forgiver—won't you please believe Me?" Jesus came to this earth to proclaim "good tidings of great joy, which shall be to all people" (Luke 2:10). The good news is not that I am forgiven, but that God is a forgiver!

The angels didn't say that the good news was only for the believers, but for all people. Unfortunately, not all of them would become believers in that good news. But the news remains constant, whether or not we believe it. In Christ, God announced forgiveness for all people. The lost will indeed be lost, not because God did not offer them forgiveness, but because they did not accept the Forgiver.

We cannot trust in that which is conditional if we must produce the conditions. Were God to say, "I will forgive you *if* you will believe in Me," we would begin to measure the quantity of our faith, then doubt we had produced enough.

By contrast, were God to say, "I *am,* by My very nature, a forgiver; I cannot be unforgiving, any more than I can be unloving," we would have something upon which to rest our confidence. Then, believing in Him, trusting in that unconditional forgiveness, we would be healed from further need to rebel.

When Jesus cried out from the still-prostrate cross, "Father, forgive them; for they know not what they do" (Luke 23:34), He was not begging for something the Father was unwilling to do. Rather, He was announcing for all to hear that the Father *is* a forgiver. And He hoped those cruel soldiers who were at the moment driving spikes into His wrists would hear that message, for someday they might come to know full well what they had done. And as they staggered under the awareness that they had driven nails through the Creator, He wanted them already to have heard the news "You are forgiven."

What could be more freeing from self-centered concerns than the assurance that our greatest need, freedom from the death penalty, has already been met at the cross of Christ?

11

FALLING SHORT OF KNOWING GOD

All have sinned and fall short of the glory of God. Rom. 3:23, R.S.V.

Jill felt a deep estrangement from her mother, who always seemed to find fault with whatever Jill said. Finally she began to understand the reasons behind her mother's thinking—and to appreciate her obvious love for her. In time Jill and her mother became close friends.

In our growing understanding of the sin problem, we see more and more that it is our lack of knowing God Himself that has always hindered our relationship with Him. This He knows, and in every conceivable way He seeks to win our confidence.

On the mountain with Moses, God passed before His hidden servant and proclaimed His name by declaring the quality of His dealings with mankind, which is His glory. In Jesus He lived before us with such winsome candidness that our hearts have been thrilled. Yet, even for believers, God has seemed somehow a little remote and unreachable. We "fall short" in our understanding of Him, and in the end it perpetuates our inability to relate totally and positively to Him. This results in what we typically call sin.

God understands our need to understand Him! In the most loving and thorough way He has set about to reveal Himself to us. That revelation has taken time, as it does in all lasting friendships. But that need not put us off. It is not a statement of any lack on His part of a desire to have us live eternally with Him. Rather, it is concrete proof that He is most eager to establish a union with us that will endure throughout the fathomless ages of eternity.

Just knowing that God cares so much about the quality of my relationship with Him causes my heart to swell. It means that He believes in my capacity to be that kind of friend. It means that His opinion of me is favorable, that He will go to any lengths to secure me to Himself. I can hold my head high! The great God of the universe values, and is aggressively seeking to establish, my friendship!

As I see Him as He is, I trust Him with my very life and future. I love Him with all my heart. And I know that the break in my relationship with Him will be forever healed. Let us seek Him with renewed assurance, knowing that His eagerness to be one with us far exceeds anything we have imagined before.

FIRST RELATIONSHIP, THEN DEEDS

Formerly you were yourselves estranged from God; you were his enemies in heart and mind, and your deeds were evil. But now by Christ's death . . . God has reconciled you to himself. Col. 1:21, 22, N.E.B.

There is a vital one-two-three sequence in this text. Seldom has Paul spoken more clearly about the real nature of the sin problem. Notice how it happens: (1) you were estranged from God; (2) you were enemies in heart and mind; and then (3) your deeds were evil.

We can hardly say it too often: Sin is a relationship word. I cannot talk about sin without talking about God—about the alienated relationship between myself and God. Having chosen a life apart from Him, all my values become distorted. Being estranged from the lover of my soul, I become insecure and defensive. And that insecurity so readily finds its expression in hostility.

What, then, can result except evil deeds? Since we have been created for fellowship with a loving and personable God, the absence of that friendship is devastating. It is fair to say that virtually everything we do that is unkind, immoral, immature, and otherwise sinful, we do in a frantic attempt to fill that resulting ugly emptiness.

Of course, our God knows that this is exactly what happens. He knows that just as sin is a relationship word, salvation is also a relationship word. If we do sinful deeds because we are estranged from Him, then His first step is to win us back into that healing friendship with Himself.

Satan is also very interested in spelling out a path to God's friendship. He says that if we will do enough good deeds, God will reward us with His friendship. God, however, offers His friendship, not as a reward for our good deeds, but out of the sure conviction that this is the only means that can ever produce good deeds. Only those who are loved can be truly loving.

How much we need to remember that we are not trying to reconcile God to us, but that God is reconciling us to Himself. The hostilities never were His in the first place; they are not His to drop. We are the estranged ones. The cross of Christ is God's act to win us, not Christ's act to placate God.

And God is confident that, having won us to Himself, He can do great things in us, even removing every last blemish that the broken relationship has caused.

WHEN YOU'VE BEEN FORGOTTEN

"Can a woman forget her sucking child, that she should have no compassion on the son of her womb?" Even these may forget, yet I will not forget you. Isa. 49:15, R.S.V.

The closest relationships available to us in this life are supposed to teach us of God's relationship with us. When they fail to do this or teach us just the opposite, we might well wonder if there is any hope.

One of the most agonizing of life's tragedies is when someone who should have loved us, no matter what, fails to do so. It is almost enough to destroy us. Bitterness often pervades the whole life causing every good thing to be discounted, every slight to enlarge like a mountain. "It's not fair!" we cry. And we are right. But that is not the end of the matter.

God sees deeply into our wounded hearts. With utmost sensitivity He lifts us up into His great arms of love and reminds us that though such unthinkable things can happen on this runaway planet, they will never happen with Him. By using a carefully chosen analogy, He helps us to realize that He cannot forget us because He has so identified with us as to make us a part of His own being (see Isa. 49:16).

All of us are damaged by our passage through this life. Some are devastated. Only very tangible evidences of God's love can bring these wounded souls back from despair. But God has a plan to do just this. It includes all of us who have come to know and trust Him.

Jesus showed us how. He lived God's life in very real and reachable ways right in the middle of a very damaged people. He cared, He listened, and He touched them. He cried, and I believe He laughed—warm, genuine laughter of someone who enjoys another person and delights in him. He was honest and straightforward about the problems of life. People were always more important than their current decisions.

Hearts were warmed, hopes renewed. Some even dared to believe that their past life need not hinder them in their future successes and acceptance. And is not this the finest privilege of a mother—to send forth her offspring secure in their potential and innate worth? Perhaps we may cry with the Master Himself, " 'Who is my mother, and who are my brothers?' And stretching out His hand toward His disciples, He said, 'Here are my mother and my brothers!' "(Matt. 12:48, 49, R.S.V.).

IS REJECTION USEFUL?

All that the Father gives me will come to me; and him who comes to me I will not cast out. John 6:37, R.S.V.

Perhaps we've gotten it from each other, this idea that God rejects us when we fail. When we disappoint each other, we know how quickly that cold distance flows in. Almost intuitively we suspect that with His very high standards God has even more reasons to reject us when we don't measure up.

In fact, some are sure that God's giving and withholding of acceptance is the leverage He uses to get us to do good. When we behave properly He rewards us with His smile. When we act selfishly, we are punished by His judgmental frown. (Somehow we overlook the fact that this never works in human relationships.)

But our God knows that the whole problem of sin is centered in our being distant from Him. He pleaded with Adam and Eve not to break that original faith relationship with Him; but they did, and—along with all their children—have been suffering the tragic losses of alienation ever since.

So the Father's plan for saving people requires that they come back to Him. In His great redemption plan He knows that we have everything to gain if He can keep us in constant fellowship with Himself. The Scriptures are full of admonition to abide in Christ. That's where the healing takes place.

What value is there, then, in His rejecting us? Having put such energy into getting us to join with Him, would He ever break the bond? Would He ever cast us out? Even using rejection as a form of leverage to get us to be good ends up in complicating the problem. Rejection always hurts, making one all the more concerned with himself and his needs. It is only loving acceptance that heals.

Furthermore, God has vastly better reasons for obedience than for us to try to earn as a favor that which He has already offered as a free gift. Obedience, which means living in harmony with His spirit and wisdom, carries all its own inherent rewards. In the same way, one who disobeys draws down all manner of terrible consequences upon his own head. Rather than needing the additional "punishment" of God's frown, he is at that point even more in need of tender nurturing.

Why, then, could Jesus say, "Him who comes to me I will not cast out"? Because He knew better than any that absolutely nothing is gained by casting one out, even when he fails.

LOVE HELPS YOU THINK

That you, being rooted and grounded in love, may have power to comprehend with all the saints what is the breadth and length and height and depth, and to know the love of Christ which surpasses knowledge, that you may be filled with all the fulness of God. Eph. 3:17-19, R.S.V.

Feelings of security are a rare commodity in our present chaotic world. We are often incapable of reaching our full potential because of the negative forces at work inside us—lack of self-worth, the unsureness of the solidity of our lives. And most of our inabilities stem from feelings of being unloved.

Our tenderhearted God knows this. He understands that we can never be fulfilled, or fulfill our high calling, unless we come to the realization that we are absolutely secure in Him, that His love for us is without reservation and totally unconditional. And so He gave us Jesus.

Jesus. We have so many mental pictures available to us. Many are of Him healing. God means to be healing to us, very tenderly healing. Many pictures are of Him teaching. God means to teach us, to fill our hungry hearts and minds with exciting themes, expanding ideas and ideals.

Jesus—quietly riding the waves of the Sea of Galilee. Serene in His awareness of His Father's love. Our Father's love, how steadfast it is, how enduring! We see Him in the midst of a throng of children, their dusty little hands clamoring for His arms. They were sure of acceptance. How sure we may be of God's acceptance, His eager enjoyment of all that we are!

Slowly, as the edges of our agonizing souls give way to the soothing reality of our Father's love, our minds awake. Awake to adventure, because we are secure enough in our heritage, our divine heritage in and through Jesus. We find the paths of understanding opening to us. We marvel at His Creation, His plan for us, and ever more so, the inexpressible height, breadth, length, and depth of who He is. We spontaneously worship Him whose ideals for us surpass our knowledge—that we should be filled with His own fullness, that we should one day be restored into His image.

God's love sets us free to think, to explore, to become. We may be sure that He watches our every step of progress with infinite pleasure, encouraging us to keep on growing.

HOW TO STOP SINNING

No man therefore who dwells in him is a sinner; the sinner has not seen him and does not know him. 1 John 3:6, N.E.B.

We may approach today's text at least two different ways, depending on our understanding of the meaning of sin.

Some would approach it thinking, Now, sin is an act that I do, like eating too much supper or snapping at the kids. That means if I am abiding in Christ, I will always be temperate at supper time and always mellow with the children. If I do eat an extra spoonful of beans, however, of course it means I have ceased to abide in Christ. Because of my failure, He has withdrawn from the friendship.

But the situation can also be understood in these terms: sin is, after all, living apart from Christ. It means that I have chosen to alienate myself from Him. So when I choose for Him to become the very center of my life and I resolve to be bonded to Him in loving fellowship, then I am no longer a sinner.

The difference between these two approaches is that the first focuses on sin as an act; the second sees sin in terms of relationship with a Person. But which one did John have in mind when he wrote the passage? The second part of the verse couldn't be more explicit: "the sinner has not seen him and does not know him." No wonder he is a sinner (one alienated from God); he doesn't even know the One who wants to be his finest friend.

How, then, do you stop sinning? Do you concentrate real hard on how much you are eating? Do you bite your tongue when the children have pushed you up against the wall? Do you stand in dread of being judged by God as an inadequate friend? Or do you get to know the One whom to know is life eternal?

The exciting thing is that this second alternative is the one that really works in changing our actions. That close relationship, when maintained, does a great healing work in our hearts. Those who are made secure by God's unconditional love no longer need to defend their parental image by snapping at the kids. Having found real joy in union with Christ, they no longer need to seek cheap pleasure in overindulgence. The great principle By beholding we become changed (2 Cor. 3:18) has come to the aid of one fascinated with Jesus!

RUINED HOUSES RESTORED

You shall be called Rebuilder of broken walls, Restorer of houses in ruins. Isa. 58:12, N.E.B.

Ancient Israel had a problem. The wall of their capital city had been broken through by enemy forces. Their houses had been plundered. Worse still, they lived under the enigma of claiming to be God's chosen people yet had been under siege.

More than literal walls needed rebuilding. The nation needed that deep inner healing that only God could bring. Their houses lay in ruins, even as their hearts had been plundered by the enemy of souls. They called themselves "chosen," but they were estranged from the One who had chosen them. They were as defenseless against those who would take them captive as they were against the thoughts that made them prisoners of unbelief.

In Isaiah 59:1, 2 God explains that His attitude toward Israel had been constant. *They* had brought a separation between themselves and God—because of their stubborn refusal to relate properly to Him. They insisted on fighting battles as their own wisdom dictated, then asked God to put His firepower behind their decisions. Any success made them proud. Any failure they blamed upon God.

Israel fasted in order to induce God to favor them, to get them out of the messes into which they got themselves. God wanted them to face reality. He did not want them to stop eating food; He wanted them to stop being selfish and self-willed. In essence, He told them, "Learn what I am like by experiencing what it is I really want."

God wants us to stop hurting—ourselves and others. To have our lives freed from all that would hold us apart from Him. We have been yoked together with false concepts about God. Consequently we have lived in such ways as to deny ourselves the privilege of friendship with Him. We have feared God when we should have been fed by Him. We have stumbled in darkness, not knowing that He was the light. We have found ourselves homeless when He would draw us into His own family.

The break in the Jerusalem wall was symbolic of the break in the relationship between Israel and their God. As they returned to trusting friendship with Him, not only would their city be restored to safety, but they themselves would be secure against the attitudes and false religious concepts of the surrounding nations. That is no less true for us today.

HOW FAITH MAKES US WELL

He said to her, "Daughter, your faith has made you well; go in peace, and be healed of your disease." Mark 5:34, R.S.V.

Jesus could have spoken to that startled, just-healed woman from the crowd in several different ways. For example, He could have said, "Woman, My miraculous power has just made you well." But He didn't, because that wouldn't have told the whole truth.

Or He could have said, "Woman, your strong convictions have made you well." But that would have confused people about their role in approaching God. They might think that sincerity earns a response from God.

Instead, He was referring to the relationship between Himself and the woman in which she looked to Him in trusting confidence. This was what produced the healing.

This brief encounter with an unnamed woman on the road to Jairus' house was an acted parable of the plan of salvation. The healing of our sin-damaged lives happens as we enter into and enjoy a loving friendship with a great Friend. And that, at the very core, is the meaning of faith.

In all our conversations about "righteousness by faith," we must be careful not to become so absorbed with righteousness that we forget about faith. In the purest sense, we cannot talk about faith without speaking of the Object of our faith. "Faith" does not exist in the abstract; there is only "faith in Christ."

And it is that confident, informed, involved relationship that is, itself, the healing power. O that we could grasp all that Jesus meant when He said, "Your faith has made you well." Was this recorded in Scripture only for women who are hemorrhaging or for those with other physical ailments? What is faith capable of healing? What transformations can vital love effect in one's life?

Consider: would there be any further need to stand on someone else's face in order to stand taller if we already knew we were proudly claimed children of the King? Would we strike back in retaliation against those who threaten us if knew that God Himself is on our side? Such a grasp of the divine-human bond will bring genuine righteousness into one's life.

And that, at the practical level, is righteousness by faith!

ASKING AND EXPECTING

You do not have, because you do not ask. James 4:2, R.S.V.

One of the most painful experiences in life is to have at your disposal the very thing needed by a loved one who does not seek it from you. Worse still is to be rejected when you freely offer the item or service. Either way, you hurt more for this person, knowing that they will go without, than you do for yourself.

God longs for us to ask Him for all that we need and desire. In the most gentlemanly manner He makes known to us that He is well able to satisfy us entirely. When we do not ask, He reminds us with divine sorrow that we do not have simply because we have not asked.

Do we play mental games with ourselves? Have we come to feel that God's invitation is more for the testing of our souls than for the tangible answers available? Do we feel a kind of spiritual high in "having faith" while "waiting on the Lord," while not really expecting an answer? This kind of experience makes testing in and of itself of more value than the individual being tested. Such concepts, whether harbored openly or only in the secret places of a doubting heart, cast an unhealthy shadow upon our heavenly Father.

Should we expect answers? Why would our reasonable God play games with us? He is very straightforward. The more you know God, the more likely it is that your requests will be in harmony with His wisdom. And the more you can be sure that reality will meet expectation. Believing that God will give what you ask can make you feel vulnerable. It is only when you learn that He delights in giving us tangible answers can such feelings be replaced by joyous anticipation.

There is no merit in the act of believing. Our hope lies solely in the One in whom we believe. And asking without any real hope of receiving is to mock the One to whom our requests are made. Not to ask at all is perhaps the strongest statement that we can make about our doubt about God's goodness and His willingness to deal with us realistically.

Perhaps God wants us to test Him more than He desires to test us. And in testing God, we will find that He is absolutely reliable and wonderfully practical.

SAFE IN HIS PRESENCE

Come, see a man who told me all that I ever did. Can this be the Christ? John 4:29, R.S.V.

This woman's invitation to her friends becomes very startling when we recall just what it was that Jesus had told her about her past life. She was only a few moments into a conversation with this total Stranger when He was telling her that she had gone through five husbands and was working on her sixth.

Let's admit it; even with intimate friends, one is usually very reluctant to become so vulnerable as to discuss the failures of a single marriage. But to admit to a whole string of failures to a stranger? Either she was pretty calloused or there was something about this particular Stranger that invited confidence.

We can be sure it was the latter, because she went back home to her friends and invited them to come and stand in the presence of this same Man, running the risk that He might well be able to tell them, too, everything that they had ever done.

She suspected that He was the Christ and named as her evidence His ability to reveal her past. But she was eager to tell her friends about Him because of what He did with that sordid information. He saw it not as a barrier, threatening to His unsullied purity, but as a portrayal of her needs. And He got right to the point of meeting those needs.

Our God isn't just some sanctified palm reader. He holds insights into our past failings, not so that He can shame us into submission or use guilt manipulation to entice us to goodness. His only goal is to heal. In His presence we can crawl out from behind our embarrassment, lift up our tenderest nerves for His healing touch, and even invite other injured sinners to join us.

At times we are inclined to hold a dim view of the work of the recording angels. Perhaps we just aren't sure what God will do with the information that He will get from them. But when we see that His every act is to bring healing, to open the door for self-honesty, our fears diminish.

Some people pay large sums of money to sit in the presence of a professional counselor who, by his accepting manner, makes it easier for them to face painful truths about themselves. Wouldn't kneeling in the safe presence of Jesus accomplish the same thing?

WHEN JUSTICE IS LIKE POISON

Do horses run upon rocks? Does one plow the sea with oxen? But you have turned justice into poison and the fruit of righteousness into wormwood. Amos 6:12, R.S.V.

Whatever would make justice like poison? It seems almost inconceivable. Justice—why, the very word sounds like "equality" and the "rights of conscience." Yet we Christians can make what is very right end up very wrong.

Often we assume to know God so well that we hold Him accountable for the choices that are our own. We say the Lord made this happen or told me to go there, but is the Lord accountable for these things? Some earnest souls claim God's guidance one day for the very things they blame the devil for the next. What are we saying about our heavenly Father with such fickleness? To unbelievers He must look rather capricious.

When we sternly say that God makes bad things happen to teach us lessons, is it no wonder that candid people feel a little sick to their stomachs? Especially when such sentiments are couched in love language. In fact, we make accepting Him just about as easy as it is to plow the sea with oxen.

How we act has a lot to do with this. We raise our children "in the truth" by mouthing doctrines while we try, as it were, to make them run their horses upon the rock-hard evidences of our own misconceptions about God. We tell them that He loves them but that they will be torturously destroyed if they do not serve Him. We reject them when they act disgracefully; or treat them with condescension, thinking that they don't notice, expecting that they should be grateful that we have chosen to do so.

God is not like that! He knows that horses can't run on rocks. He knows that we will never come to trust Him unless we discover how very reasonable are His ways. His justice is not like poison, it is the great celestial antibiotic against the spread of the virus of sin in our hearts and minds. Sin is our predictable response to such twisted concepts about our great God. Justice is His persistent endeavor to reintroduce reality into our lives.

God's justice is not the justice of a judge exacting a price for our injustice, but rather that of a teacher wanting to impart truth to his students. Shall we not all gladly come under His tutorship?

THE (SUBTLE) BATTLE WITH SELF

He died for all, that those who live might live no longer for themselves but for him who for their sake died and was raised. 2 Cor. 5:15, R.S.V.

It has been said truly that the battle against self is the most difficult battle the Christian must fight. But that battle is made more difficult because many do not understand the nature of the battle. Though it has a very overt level—the conflict against the lust of the flesh, the lust of the eyes, and the pride of life—there is a much more subtle dimension, which has proved the downfall of many.

Many see it as a battle, indeed an unending struggle, against selfishness itself. In this battle I try to make myself stop doing selfish things, or even to stop thinking selfish thoughts. And when I fail to achieve as I know I ought, I am burdened with guilt.

But unless I know in my soul that God has pardoned and accepted me, I will find the questing after pardon to be the object of all my works, the focus of all my religion. My concern for what God thinks of me (rather than for what the world thinks of God) will be the flavor of my spiritual life. And thus self, rather than Jesus Christ, is the object of my attention.

This variation of the battle against self is so subtle because it sounds so pious. We can even report our progress in prayer meeting and make it the focus of endless private anguish. But that will only obscure the fact that "self" is still the reigning motivation in my life.

The only cure for this most basic of all forms of selfishness is fully to accept that God has indeed given that which I most deeply crave: His unconditional love, pardon, and acceptance. This gift is not a reward for my accomplishments but an outflowing of His very character.

Having received as a gift that which I previously craved to earn, I am set free from self—free to live for Christ. This is how selfishness is destroyed. To see the sure message of the cross is to tell me that I no longer need to live for myself, but I can live for the One who died to meet all my needs. I can live for His glory!

Perhaps the battle to *believe* is the real battle against self—to believe that God really is so effectively loving!

THE HIDDEN QUESTION

Jesus said to them, "Do you believe that I am able to do this?" They said to him, "Yes, Lord." Then he touched their eyes, saying, "According to your faith be it done to you." Matt. 9:28, 29, R.S.V.

Two blind men, pleading for mercy, approached Jesus. Obviously they wanted to be healed of their malady. But the way in which they asked revealed that they accepted what was traditionally held to be the reasons for blindness. They asked for mercy, believing their blindness to be evidence of God's disfavor (see John 9:2).

Jesus met their request with a question. Did they believe that He could heal them? Surely, they knew He could! They must have seen Him heal others or heard a good report. We might well imagine that their answer came quickly, "Yes, Lord!" But was more involved than His power to heal physically?

Was Jesus gently nudging them into new patterns of thinking? Maybe later, as they lay on their backs looking at the intense blue of the Mediterranean sky, the question came back as softly as the delicate wisps of clouds above. Was there a hidden meaning in His inquiry? As they mused on this were new thoughts awakened in their minds? Did they begin also to see with spiritual eyes?

Jesus came to reveal the truth about the Father to His troubled earthly children, to explain that God loved them and never arbitrarily induced pain as a means of punishment. He came to bring weary hearts back into fellowship with the One who could give them rest. Did they begin to grasp a deeper meaning in Jesus' question? Do you believe that God would *want* to do this? Do you realize how much God wants to be involved with sinners? That it is in keeping with who He is, to bring sight to your eyes?

Surely Jesus was telling them that God is never arbitrary. He never acts out of anger. He deals with reality, even as He desires us to do. He wants us whole. Yet it would be a big step for these humble men to believe such things in the face of all that the priests taught. It would put them at odds with their friends, because then they, too, would have to address similar concepts.

The blind men had believed and went away seeing. I only hope that they had the courage to let that be only the beginning.

CALLING SIN BY ITS RIGHT NAME

When he comes, he will convince the world concerning sin . . .
because they do not believe in me. John 16:8, 9, R.S.V.

She cried as one who would not be comforted. She had just been "labored with" by a fellow church member regarding some sinful thing she had done. He had been "calling sin by its right name," and she freely admitted that she had done it. "The Spirit is really convicting me," she said. "I feel crushed!" She seemed surprised when I suggested that the Holy Spirit might not necessarily be the one behind her convictions.

Strange as it may first appear, Satan is also in the business of convicting of sin. Some people he persuades to care nothing about sin except to find new ways to plunge into it. But he has a special approach for the conscientious. He tells them that sin is fundamentally selfish actions, but he wants them to know nothing of a relationship with a forgiving Saviour who alone can heal this selfishness.

The Bible certainly does address the sinful actions that we humans find so easy to do, but Jesus knows that there is little value in sending the Spirit with an unabridged list of sinful actions to prohibit. Those sinful actions are but the symptoms of a broken relationship with our Creator. To focus on the actions without first healing the relationship would only drive guilt-ridden, intimidated sinners further from a holy God.

Satan's convictions of sin center around behavior, and the aim is to crush with despair. The Spirit's convictions of sin center around relationship, with an aim to reconcile rebels into trusting belief in God.

Perhaps this should give us pause to consider our human endeavors to call sin by its right name. We seldom have problems spotting the outward signs of other people's inward hurting—those things we call sins. It could possibly even minister to our pride to be able to point them out, to "rightly name" them.

But unless we know why people are inwardly hurting, and unless we know how to walk them back to the arms of Jesus, we may well be participating with Satan's crushing endeavors. When we come to the place where we can never talk about sin without talking about Jesus Christ, where sin makes sense to us only in terms of broken relationship with Him, then we are ready to be used by the gentle Spirit.

PEACE BORN OF TRUST

Thou dost keep him in perfect peace, whose mind is stayed on thee, because he trusts in thee. Isa. 26:3, R.S.V.

Is peace the elusive reward we get from disciplined concentration on God? Or is peace a tangible reality that comes from knowing that God is absolutely trustworthy?

The more we find God to be so utterly attractive that we cannot get Him out of our minds, the more at peace we will become. This is no shallow sentimentalism, as when one sighs and pines for an earthly lover. Neither can rigid intellectualism satisfy the cravings of the heart. It is only as we begin to grasp the irrefutable truth of a wise and loving God that we finally come to make the most practical decision of our lives. We trust Him, and in trusting Him we find perfect peace.

The psalmist wrote, "Righteousness and peace will kiss each other" (Ps. 85:10, R.S.V.). Righteousness, that coming into right relationship with God because the misconceptions about Him have been removed, brings us peace as a natural consequence. In fact, they are inseparable. But what is peace, anyway? An absence of trouble? Emotional flatness? Is it God's always being present to keep us from falling into the puddles?

Genuine peace is a statement of faith independent of circumstances. It is unshakable confidence in who God is and how He has chosen to deal with the complexity of the sin problem. It brings inner joy and celebration over the One who has so thoroughly resolved the apparently unresolvable—the blending of justice and mercy.

Peace is also very practical. When you *do* fall into the puddles, you know that God has not forsaken you. You do not spend yourself trying to figure out why He let you get wet. Instead, your settledness about Him and about your relationship with Him enables you to look beyond puddles. You know that puddles go away eventually; God is forever.

Some look only to their feelings for peace. By these feelings they test their spirituality. Consequently, they spend much time thinking about themselves instead of moving forward in fresh understanding about God, the originator of peace. Any negative emotions are quickly denied in favor of the euphoria they think peace should bring. The sad truth is that peace never comes in this manner. God does not give peace; He *is* our peace.

"May the God of hope fill you with all joy and peace in believing, so that . . . you may abound in hope" (Rom. 15:13, R.S.V.).

DEADLY DEVOTION

The hour is coming when whoever kills you will think he is offering service to God. And they will do this because they have not known the Father, nor me. John 16:2, 3, R.S.V.

Jesus' prediction is puzzling. How can people who don't even know God kill someone on behalf of God? Doesn't religious murder imply a consuming devotion to God? Why, then, does Jesus say that such people don't even know God?

These religious zealots, these self-appointed guardians of public virtue, will never admit to not knowing God. In fact, they probably quote Scripture and invoke God's name as they pull the trigger. They might even thank Him for helping them have such good aim, because the "God" whom they worship is the kind of God who believes in using force in the name of righteousness.

Such people may kill in the name of God. The problem is that they have the wrong God. They might use the right names when referring to their God, perhaps even calling Him Jesus or Father. But having the right name doesn't make Him the right one. It's His character qualities, His manner of relating to people, His methods of solving the sin problem, that set the true God apart from every counterfeit.

To have a correct understanding of God's true character is vastly more than just theological icing on the cake. Jesus' comment makes it clear that to worship an oppressive God is to become oppressive ourselves. To worship a vindictive, punitive God is to become such ourselves, for by beholding God, we are changed into His same likeness. If our picture is faulty, the change will also be faulty.

As tragic as it would be that Christians should be put to death for their beliefs, the vastly greater tragedy is that it should be done in the name of God. To see a Christian go to his death-sleep abiding in Jesus brings no satisfaction to Satan. But to see God's reputation blackened in the process brings him a perverse delight, for that is his goal. If there is one thing that is worse than for a person to die, it is for him to die while alienated from God. And nothing could be more alienating than for him to think that God is an oppressive murderer.

Though we will not likely kill in the name of God, may we never in other ways misrepresent Him because we have not known the Father or His Son.

BECOMING GODLIKE

We know that when he appears we shall be like him, for we shall see him as he is. 1 John 3:2, R.S.V.

Many theological discussions center on how a follower of Christ becomes like Him. I wonder how many people go from these discussions discouraged. There are endless lists of outward deeds to do and not to do. They include foods to eat and foods not to eat, clothes to be worn and clothes not to be worn. This might be termed sanctification by lists.

But such deeds do not necessarily make us godlike. That is evidenced by the passage in Matthew 7:21-23, which tells of those who will someday cry unto God to let them enter the kingdom of heaven but will be told that their deeds are evil. This they cannot understand, and they cry, "Lord, Lord, did we not . . . do many mighty works in your name?" (R.S.V.).

Godlikeness will show itself in the way we act, but the things we do can stem from many motivations. The desire to be saved can be one of the most selfish of motivators—in reality, it might be the quest to please self forever.

Working for the salvation of others can still be selfish. We might enter into such activity to be well thought of by others. True Godlikeness goes much deeper, though in fact it is expressed by the way we interface with the world around us.

Our text today offers a real clue to becoming godlike. It is not just at the second coming of Christ that we may become like Him. "And we all, with unveiled face, beholding the glory [character] of the Lord, are being changed into his likeness" (2 Cor. 3:18, R.S.V). By beholding God and all that He is—just, reasonable, long-suffering, loving, forgiving, healing, friendly, creative, and infinitely more—we find admiration and adoration swelling in our hearts for Him. And just as basic as the law that makes water flow downhill and balloons float in the air is the predisposition of my heart to copy what it regards.

Our motivations stem from who we are, from our inner values. When our hearts regard God, this is more than an objective appreciation of His being. It involves a relationship, because to enjoy relationships is the truest essence of God.

To know God is to love Him. To focus upon Him is to become like Him, inwardly as well as in outward deeds.

FRUITLESS BIBLE STUDY

You study the scriptures diligently, supposing that in having them you have eternal life; yet, although their testimony points to me, you refuse to come to me for that life. John 5:39, 40, N.E.B.

When Jesus chides people for studying the Bible, you can guess He has a large concern on His mind. In this straightforward appeal He deals with perhaps the most dangerous of all Bible-oriented delusions. It's the belief that salvation is found in the accumulation of religious data and that the Bible is a warehouse of such facts.

A variation of this belief is that the Bible is filled with requirements that the devout must follow to commend themselves to God. It is true that the Bible does contain much information about how people should live. The deception is one of sequence and of motive.

Since Scripture requires the actions of love, only those who have first become lovers can fulfill its commands in letter and in spirit. And people become lovers only by being in living connection with their loving Father.

Jesus spoke later to these very thorough Bible students regarding their evangelistic approach. He said, "You travel over sea and land to win one convert; and when you have won him you make him twice as fit for hell as you are yourselves" (Matt. 23:15, N.E.B.). On the surface, that was a harsh thing to say to devout folks whose interest was in imparting codes for right living.

But all such behaviors are ultimately meaningless rituals to those who have not first found their Father to be the natural center of their souls. Any religion that appears to impose upon its youth or its new converts a staggering list of lifestyle requirements without first leading them into a personal interaction with God is subject to Jesus' same appraisal.

You can hear the tears in Jesus' voice as He says, "You refuse to come to me for that life." Why should anyone be reluctant to come to Him? to know His gracious welcome? to rest secure in His love? There can be but one reason: the enemy has succeeded in deceiving that person into thinking he or she will not receive a gracious welcome, that there is no security in His love. What a tragedy!

The answers we find in Scripture depend on the questions we ask. If we ask each time we open its pages, "Who *is* He, that I might know Him, love Him, trust Him with my life?" we shall not be disappointed.

GOD'S NAME IS HIS CHARACTER

I will make all my goodness pass before you, and will proclaim before you my name. Ex. 33:19, R.S.V.

A multitude of renegade Hebrew slaves was camped in the desert. Their main activity seemed to be complaining and fighting among themselves. God had worked marvelously for them, delivering them from Egyptian bondage, but they were in bondage still—to misconceptions about the character of God and His intentions concerning them.

Moses, their leader, was deeply troubled over the nation's lack of confidence in their deliverer God. Chosen by God to be His spokesman to this simple-minded people, Moses knew that they would be able to comprehend only as much as he himself could clearly explain. Therefore he longed to know God better. One day he asked God to show him His glory.

Moses was not seeking a mere display of light and power. God's glory signified His presence—as in the pillar of cloud and fire. God understood that Moses desired to be near Him in order to know Him better, both for himself and for the sake of the people he was trying to lead to the Land of Promise. Moses asked, "Show me now thy ways, that I may know thee and find favor in thy sight. Consider too that this nation is thy people" (Ex. 33:13, R.S.V.).

Answering his request, God hid Moses in the rock and passed before him, revealing His glory—proclaiming His name. When Moses described what he had seen, he used words that describe God's character. He proclaimed his assurance that God is merciful, gracious, patient, abounding in steadfast love, faithful, forgiving, and just (verses 19-22, R.S.V.). By this, God encouraged Moses to nurture and guide His people. In essence, God was saying to Moses, "Show them who I am by the way you govern them."

Hundreds of years later, God again "passed before" mankind in the person of His Son. In that wonderful life "we have beheld his glory" "full of grace and truth" (John 1:14, R.S.V.). As we go to teach all nations about Him we might well remember that the best way to show who He is, is by relating to others in the same way that He relates to us. We may be compassionate, long-suffering, constant, and true. And God's promise to us is the same as it was to Moses: "I will be with you." We will be in such close relationship that we will be secure enough to act this way.

MIRACULOUS RELIGION?

On that day many will say to me, "Lord, Lord, did we not prophesy in your name, and cast out demons in your name, and do many mighty works in your name?" And then will I declare to them, "I never knew you; depart from me, you evildoers." Matt. 7:22, 23, R.S.V.

How impressed we are with the miraculous! We give our full attention to that which makes our heart pound and our breath quicken. We remember the spectacular and often drop our powers of discrimination just for the sheer enjoyment of the event.

Is it any wonder, then, that when people come face-to-face with their personal readiness to meet God, they should look to the miraculous to provide the basis for their standing? Jesus spoke of people who could attest to rather impressive acts: prophetic utterances, demonic deliverances, even miracle working.

Most of us may not be able to boast as impressive a "missionary report" as theirs. But we can recall what we might claim as minor miracles. We think of the flood of feeling we had during a Week of Prayer altar call; it even produced tears. We think of the time we prayed for God to help us find our glasses, and we found them (in our pocket). And what about the time we led someone through Bible studies until he was baptized? Don't all these constitute proof that we are among the elect?

But Jesus warns us that all this just doesn't deal with the problem. Miraculous power may *impress* us; but we are *changed* only by a deep personal acquaintance with a marvelous Person. We may put off some bad habits; we may preach some pretty potent sermons; we may even lead people to the church, where they may find Jesus Christ. The only one who will be impressed, however, will be ourselves. What we really need is to be impressed with God. Otherwise we will still be working on that old myth that salvation is rooted in performance rather than in relationship.

But Jesus says it produces workers of iniquity. For even good, miraculous, God-tagged works done apart from a personal relationship with Christ are iniquitous works. Not because the works are sinister, but because they are done by persons who are alienated from God and who, by that fact, are sinners.

Won't it be infinitely better to hear Jesus say on that great day, "Come! We have been intimately acquainted. Let's continue that friendship forever"?

TAKING SIN SERIOUSLY

In the past he was patient and overlooked people's sins; but in the present time he deals with their sins, in order to demonstrate his righteousness. Rom. 3:25, T.E.V.

Members of a congregation were in anguish over their responsibilities toward a member who had fallen into overt sin. Caught in that usual perceived tension between justice and mercy, one finally spoke: "Well, it's nice to be forgiving, but we have to take sin seriously." They took sin seriously, expelled the member, and lost touch with him.

The tragedy is that they felt they had to be unforgiving in order to take sin seriously. They felt that saying "We love you, we accept you; we will not let your failings create a barrier between us" would ignore sin. Sadly, they did not know just how seriously such a response does deal with sin!

In the Garden of Eden, Satan's lie to Adam and Eve was that sin isn't really all that bad. "You can sin and get by with it," he hissed. "You will not surely die." The truth, of course, is that sin (separation from the Life-giver) should indeed have caused death—the second death at that! Then God could have said, "See, I told you so. Sin really *is* all that bad." But Adam and Eve wouldn't have been around to hear the lesson.

So God risked holding off the consequences. For four thousand years Satan taunted, "See, sin doesn't really cause the second death." But when Jesus cried out, "My God, why hast thou forsaken me?" (Matt. 27:46) and died the second death, the universe knew forever: sin really *is* all that bad. God *does* tell the truth; He *is* righteous.

Was God being unforgiving toward Adam and Eve? Had He withdrawn from the relationship as a form of punishment, protesting their affront to His authority? Hardly! The problem of sin is not that they had offended His dignity, but that, through deception, they had departed from Him and from reality. And such departing from reality would bring its own terrible consequences.

Sin does bring its own punishment. Its first consequence—eternal death through separation from the Life-giver—Jesus took seriously on the cross. But the secondary consequences, the broken friendships, the blasted self-respect, the sinking health—these must be taken seriously by the sinner. And they are so painful that neither God nor church members need to add to the pain by punitive rejection. Even though expelled from the garden, God held Adam and Eve close as they suffered those results.

OWNING UP TO DISOBEDIENCE

For God has consigned all men to disobedience, that he may have mercy upon all. Rom. 11:32, R.S.V.

Why is God so interested in pointing out the universal disobedience of the human race? What reason does He have for wanting to make sure that everyone owns up to being disobedient? Is this so that no one will try to sneak away from the smarting pain of His rebuke?

Paul seems to have another purpose in mind in today's text. He recognizes a principle in God's dealings with us sinners: Those who admit their disobedience receive mercy; those who do not admit it receive no mercy. The problem with those who do not receive mercy is not that God has held it back, but that they didn't recognize that they needed it. Those who do not know they have a disease will not reach out to the Physician.

As priceless as the gift of mercy is to all who know they need it, most of those to whom God has made this offer are still suffering outside its gracious benefit. It seems stupid to reject healing when the disease is fatal without treatment. But that reveals the lengths to which all of us go to protect our image. We would rather die championing our innocence than to risk facing seemingly certain embarrassment and rejection should we show up at the clinic door and whisper our disease.

When we know in advance, however, that our admission will be met with mercy it does make the admission easier. When we learn that the Physician knows how to keep confidences and that His cures are effective, we are more likely to risk owning up to our great need.

John said of our Father that if we will confess our sin, He can be counted on to forgive and to cleanse. To confess, in this context, means to agree with God's opinion of us—to say, "Yes, You are right in Your appraisal; I *am* a sinner, very much in need of help." The interesting point, of course, is that God already knows full well what our condition is; we don't confess for *His* sake, but for ours.

It is so true: the goodness of God leads to repentance. It can also be said that this same goodness so surrounds us with security that we are able to admit our need to repent. The personal question for us is How can we stay away from such a warmly drawing Friend?

EXAMINED BY THE JUDGE

Search me, O God, and know my heart; test me and know my anxious thoughts. See if there is any offensive way in me, and lead me in the way everlasting. Ps. 139:23, 24, N.I.V.

David had a marvelous understanding of his heavenly Father, and it spills out almost automatically in this psalm. He is fearlessly opening his inner life without reservation for the careful examination of the King of the universe.

We who wish we could hide the secrets of our hearts wonder at his candor, his vulnerability. The secret, however, is found in his last phrase. He knows that, were the Father to find any offensive ways within him, the result would be instruction and not judgment. He knows the Father's heart and His desire to lead David in the way everlasting.

We hide behind our fig leaves when we fear that our nakedness will become the object of derision and scorn. Adam and Eve hid, leaf-clad, in the bushes of Eden because they had already fallen under the spell of Satan's view of God. They believed God would harshly condemn them for their nakedness. But God went in pursuit of them, holding out an animal skin for clothing—not because His pure eyes were offended by their nakedness, but so their shredded self-esteem might not be further torn.

Many people fear the judgment of God because they see Him as one who can evaluate our performance only for the purpose of condemning our failures. They see Him as bound by a strictly legal system, in which the only thing one can do with wrong is condemn it. But David saw Him as a father, and fathers relate to wrong in their children by nurturing and instructing them beyond such immaturity.

Our greatest need is to admit our great need. But admitting need is not easy. We cling to whatever scraps of adequacy we can find to bolster our bruised self-worth; why be "up front" about our inadequacies? We shall never know God's strength, however, until we own up to our weakness. And so God Himself has every reason to make it easy for us to admit our weakness, that His strength might be perfectly displayed in us.

David knew God, not as the administrator of an abstract legal code or as an offended lawgiver. He knew Him, as we may, as a loving Father and a wise Instructor in the ways everlasting—in the ways that last forever!

HAPPINESS IN KNOWING WE NEED GOD

**Blessed are the poor in spirit, for theirs is the kingdom of heaven.
Matt. 5:3, R.S.V.**

How much better to seek the *Giver* of salvation than to seek the gift! If
you had a generous, rich uncle, would you not value the uncle himself
more than his fortunes? For without the character quality of generosity,
his fortunes would be of no benefit. It would be narrow to value only his
fortunes when the greatest of his gifts is fellowship with himself.

The New English Bible puts today's text this way: "Blest are those
who know their need of God." Their need *of* God; I like that. So often we
become consumed with all the things we need *from* God: forgiveness,
pardon, healing, and so on. We spend our spiritual lives seeking these
things from Him.

When you receive a gift it can make you feel uncomfortably
obligated. Is that God's way of gaining our servitude? If God were to use
His love as a means of obligating us, then to see the full meaning of the
cross would crush us. It is no wonder that so many Christians are somber.
They feel the conflicting emotions of gratitude and entrapment. On one
hand, they know that they should be eternally thankful for the gift of
eternal life, yet they feel somewhat horror-stricken at the thought of
meeting God face-to-face, unsure if they've fully met the obligations
imposed by this gift.

Likewise, how much better it is to know that God is a forgiver by
nature than to seek forgiveness itself? If forgiveness were not a very part
of the character of God, we might expect to encounter situations in which
He would not forgive. If examined more closely, what appears at times to
be His unwillingness to forgive would reveal the fact that He was no
longer being sought as a forgiver.

God has given Himself and all that He is to us, as exemplified in the
giving of His Son. True and lasting happiness comes when we realize
that, in giving Himself, He gave us everything we could ever need or
want. If the King is ours, so is His kingdom. If the Forgiver is ours, so is
His forgiveness. "And this is eternal life, that they know thee the only
true God, and Jesus Christ whom thou hast sent" (John 17:3, R.S.V.).

HAPPINESS OUT OF SORROW

Blessed are those who mourn, for they shall be comforted. Matt. 5:4, R.S.V.

How does God comfort us? Does He play spiritual magic and simply remove sad feelings? And is there more than one kind of mourning?

Even children cannot fully be comforted unless they are reassured in their hearts that everything is all right. The older we get, the less satisfying a pat on the head or overly simple words are to our bruised and troubled souls. As Christians, we find comfort in the death of loved ones when we know that their lives are "hid in Jesus." But what about the father or child who died "unsaved"?

What about all the terribly unfair things that keep happening on this miserable old planet? Who hears us? Who can shoulder our griefs with us as we cry silently in the darkened night, "Why? Why?"

God can. He knows it all, and more. Hear the tenderness of His great heart as He speaks to our need: "I hear you! 'I have seen your tears,' and 'I will heal you' " (2 Kings 20:5, R.S.V.)! That is what the whole plan of redemption is about. God is interested not in just "getting us out of here." He is committed to making us whole. This includes making us more adequate to handle our sorrows while yet on this earth.

Our restoration is top priority for God because He knows that eternity will only be as secure as are the people who dwell there. And He knows that security is the bedrock of our comfort. By healing our minds, by giving us understanding and hope, God makes us fit for heaven. Fit for heaven because we realize that heaven, and subsequently our remade earth, is a fit place in which to dwell. Fit by reason of the kind of God that is sovereign there.

It is a happy thing to discover that God is so much greater than the sorrows of this life, that He relates to us in the most healing ways. He not only gives us answers but encourages us to ask more questions. He offers more than just a change of location at the Second Coming; He offers a change in the quality of life, both now and eternally. He assures us that He does not wish merely to control the circumstances of our lives; He wants to bring resolution.

It will be good to go home to be with such a wonderful Father God.

CAREKEEPERS FOREVER

Blessed are the meek, for they shall inherit the earth. Matt. 5:5, R.S.V.

I like being at home. I also love people and fellowshipping with them. If I had to choose between going to a party and staying home . . . well, I'd have to choose both: I'd have the party at my house!

There's nothing wrong with loving to be at home. In fact, there is everything right about it. And there is everything right about our ties to this earth, in the sense that it is our home. Indeed, it is the home that God Himself chose for us in the beginning.

We often talk about "going to heaven." But God knows that we'd probably enjoy the "party" more if we ended up at our house. Thus, when the great controversy between good and evil is finally over, God plans that we will come home.

Right now our little planet is undergoing terrible stress. Ecologists decry rapid erosion of the earth's resources. Cartoonists depict mankind falling off its overcrowded surface. We are in trouble! All manner of cruelty infests society. Why? To say, "because of sin," is not an incorrect answer, but is it a sufficient one? Sin is a word that has become almost a cliché in modern society.

I believe that God wants us to be more integrated in our thinking about such problems. This is the age of advanced technology. Computers are taken for granted, and the silicon chip may someday make libraries a thing of the past. Along with these unparalleled achievements, people have tremendous access to information of every dimension. They expect answers consistent with such availability. Abstract religious words will not satisfy their desire to understand the world's crises.

Our world is in chaos because those that were given charge over it have become chaotic. In the beginning, man reflected the image of his Creator and was nurturing to his earth-home, developing and replenishing it. Separation from God brought separation from God's methods, and man has hurt the earth ever since.

It will be a wonderfully happy time when our friendship with God is fully restored. Once again we will be like Him who is "meek and lowly in heart" (Matt. 11:29). We too will be gentle and ministering. God will rejoice with us the day we can come home again to our renewed world. He'll trust us once again with its care, because we will have learned to trust and appreciate His way of government.

FULLNESS OF SATISFACTION

Blessed are those who hunger and thirst for righteousness, for they shall be satisfied. Matt. 5:6, R.S.V.

Have you ever eaten without satisfaction? Eaten until you are stuffed, but without contentment? Why doesn't the feeling of fullness suffice? The answer has to do with the way in which we were made in God's image.

We were not created to be mindless. We have been given the equipment, as it were, for very fine tuning. Our potential is staggering! Yet we so often settle for so little. We who were destined to share the throne of the Infinite keep ourselves scarcely above the beasts.

We have to go deliberately against this high calling in order to slide down into the dregs of humanity. Though we are born into the world out of harmony with divine principles, God has placed within us the nagging desire for something better. We plant flowers beside our houses, but not because they help hold up the foundations. We like matching silverware and clean sheets. And we aren't really satisfied with bland, unappetizing food, no matter how nutritious it might be. Scientifically, we now know that food digested without relish is not utilized by the body to the same extent as food consumed with pleasure.

Our wise God knows that we will never be happy with a religion that delivers only the basics—legal standing in the heavenly courts—without the attendant fullness of restored friendship of heavenly beings. It would be like obtaining a marriage contract in order to become a citizen of a country without then entering into the marriage relationship. It might get you in, but in the ensuing days and years how much enjoyment would you have in living with a stranger?

With awakened minds, we may turn our faces toward heaven with eager anticipation. To hunger and thirst after God and that relationship we may have with Him is to be filled with joyous anticipation. It textures our lives with forbearance and sympathy, and stimulates us to new heights in soul winning. After all, we weren't made to keep good things to ourselves, either!

THE HAPPINESS OF SHARING GOD'S REALITIES

Blessed are the merciful, for they shall obtain mercy. Matt. 5:7, R.S.V.

Nothing God does is arbitrary, for He is absolutely reasonable. If we think He is arbitrary, it is only because we have not yet come to an understanding of His ways. One does not teach a child not to hit by hitting him.

In showing mercy, was God being condescending? Is His the attitude of a benign potentate who has for some reason known only to himself decided to pardon the disobedient lackey? Does that fit into your picture of a merciful God? Though we know He loves us, we often think mercy implies a sort of sovereign choice. Those that feel their security lies in a God who has the biggest punch must then live with the possibility that He might obliterate them, too. The fact that He chooses not to is of little comfort. He could change His mind.

When we hold such ideas of mercy, how could we then offer to another any better? We can show mercy only to those who are weaker than ourselves. It brings us to a very basic question: What is mercy?

May I suggest that mercy means not letting another's actions ruin your mutual friendship. It allows that person the freedom to keep on relating to you even though he has compromised the friendship. It means that you value that individual more than you care about his momentarily adverse actions. It means that you are willing to "weather" his misbehavior as a deliberate and calculated move to heal your relationship with him. Mercy is in the service of restoring the friendship to all that it was meant to be.

God relates to us with a deliberateness born of intelligent understanding of our need to feel secure in His presence. He well knows how prone we are to hide from Him. So that we have no need to fear, He explains that He has chosen not to deal with us according to our actions.

The wonderful benefit of our choosing to relate in this way to others is that it works! The more we see how well-designed are God's plans concerning us, the more we appreciate Him. We know that we have not earned mercy by showing mercy. We rejoice that we have discovered the reasons why God deals with us the way He does.

As a matter of fact, it makes us all the more eager to be in relationship with Him!

SEEING IS BELIEVING

Blessed are the pure in heart, for they shall see God. Matt. 5:8, R.S.V.

When you love someone very much, being apart is agony. Then comes that wonderful day when you see each other again. You have only to watch couples at the airport to know that is a happy occasion.

Our love for God causes us to anticipate the day we can be with Him forever. There's only one detail that might spoil our eagerness. We have to be pure in heart. And according to the latest tally, that means sinless! Sinless! Does that give your heart pause? Who of us can claim to be even *close* to such an ideal? Why, I still eat Hershey bars occasionally.

Impurity in water makes it cloudy. Impurities in glass can render it opaque. And so it is with the human heart. We react wrongly because we have things in our hearts that distort our perception of situations. Our emotions are clouded with hurts and angers. Even our best understandings may not be accurate.

"The heart is the most deceitful of all things, desperately sick; who can fathom it? I, the Lord, search the mind and test the heart" (Jer. 17:9,10, N.E.B.).

Our hearts are sick, and God has a solution: "God has not sent his Son into the world to pass sentence upon it, but to save it—through him. Any man who believes in him is not judged at all. It is the one who will not believe who stands already condemned, because he will not believe in the character of God's only Son" (John 3:17, 18, Phillips).

Believing in the character of God's only Son is to believe in the character of God Himself. In Jesus' prayer for His disciples (and us!), He said, "Father of all goodness the world has not known you, but I have known you and these men now know that you have sent me. I have made your self known to them" (chap. 17:25, 26, Phillips).

The misconceptions we have about God cloud our minds. We are only acting accordingly when we relate to life in less than healthy ways. The removal of these misconceptions allows us to see God, full of goodness and truth. And we will act accordingly, because the patterns of our thinking will have been healed. This is what it means to be pure in heart.

Incidently, it's God who is waiting at the "airport" for us to come home!

THE GREAT PEACEMAKER

Blessed are the peacemakers, for they shall be called sons of God. Matt. 5:9, R.S.V.

How I wish I had the tongue of an angel! Perhaps this is what I would say:

"I have been amazed at God's enduring love for you earthlings! Hour by hour He is pained by your lack of response to His tender entreaties. Pained for you! Sometimes God commissions me to do something very tangible for you in order to reveal just how much He wants all of you.

"When Lucifer (you know him as Satan) tricked Adam and Eve into believing that God was trying to keep them from reaching their fullest potential, all of us here in heaven wept. That's what he'd told us, too. Some of my best companions believed him. You should see them now. They fight among themselves for the basest privileges.

"God treated those rebel angels with the greatest courtesy. That should have told them something, but instead they took it to mean that God would not take care of the horrible rift they were causing here. You think that way, too, sometimes. What you both misunderstand is that God *is* taking care of the problem. He is making peace in the universe, but not the way any of us would have suspected at first.

"God's way of making peace is not by removing the ability to make war, but by removing warlike desires. That is why He has chosen the way He has to relate to you on earth. He knows that when you feel the need to defend yourselves, it makes you defensive. When you feel rejected, your first reaction is to reject the rejecter. He knows that when you know you are accepted, you will be accepting.

"What touches all of our hearts up here is that we can see that His approach to you is not contrived for the sake of effect! It is genuinely the way He is and the way He feels about you. He knows how vulnerable you are. He does not condemn you! Ever! But some of you just will not believe this, and you condemn yourselves to a life of defensiveness.

"All of us here are full of hope, though. After Jesus lived there with you for a while, it was easier for you to believe God. He sent Him, you know, to change your minds about Him, and not the other way around. It's happening, too! And you are becoming more and more like His sons and daughters!"

LIVING IN YOUR CITIZENSHIP

Blessed are those who are persecuted for righteousness' sake, for theirs is the kingdom of heaven. Matt. 5:10, R.S.V.

If the only forms of persecution were the dungeon and a sword, we might escape heartache more readily than we do. The agony of today's text is that, for most of us, we don't think it applies to our lives.

At the time Jesus spoke these words, Roman soldiers often made life quite miserable for the Jewish people. Surely He meant to comfort them in their days of bondage. But what about you and me? Unless we live in countries where the practice of Christianity is prohibited, or at least politically unpopular, how much do we know of this kind of persecution?

I believe that everything that Jesus said had this overriding reason: to show us the Father. Surely, as He sat on that Galilean hillside speaking to the throngs of people, it was with careful deliberation that He spoke. Surely He knew that you and I would ponder His words in today's world.

Consider: God openly tells us again and again that He desires that we come back into right relationship with Him, that being friends with Him is what enables us to live life responsibly and accountably. Those who refuse to be convinced that this is indeed the absolute truth have a vested interest in proving that they are right. One way to do this is to get rid of any contradictory evidence. And that does not just mean getting rid of believers. It means making the responsible and accountable choices of believers appear to be irresponsible and unaccountable.

This can be done very subtly. An unbelieving husband becomes irate because his Christian wife didn't get dinner on time. Maybe he couldn't care less about the actual time; he's making a point—she's unaccountable! Or an unbelieving wife makes a wisecrack about her Christian husband's choice of a vacation spot. If he hadn't thought of it, she might have suggested it herself. Her real point is—he is unreasonable!

Down through the corridors of time Jesus says, "Take heart! You are the ones who are learning to live in your Father's kingdom." You are learning to appreciate how just and true are God's ways. These experiences in life are your best teachers. And that is cause for rejoicing!

CHANGED BY BELONGING

Put on the garments that suit God's chosen people, his own, his beloved: compassion, kindness, humility, gentleness, patience. Col. 2:12, N.E.B.

Many people will read this passage and, ten seconds later, remember only the list of qualities that they know ought to be in their lives. "I really must be more compassionate," they might say. And some might even turn the verse around, concluding that when they have succeeded in becoming more compassionate they can then count themselves as "God's chosen people, his own, his beloved."

But Paul's argument runs in the opposite direction. He knew full well that our character qualities do not establish relationship, but that relationship leads to character qualities. Paul's powerful plea is for us to recognize just who we are within this relationship. From God's point of view, as He describes us, He chooses His words with care and meaning. We are His "chosen people, his own, his beloved." That's God's statement of who we are, and it is more than sentimentality. Is our own opinion of who we are more reliable than His?

It is a principle that is so very obvious on the human plane; why do we obscure it on the divine plane? Read any book on family relationships and check what it says about how children become loving, confident, secure, patient people. Virtually all authors would agree: They must be loved securely, wisely, unconditionally, by their parents. Any parent who uses emotional distance as a form of punishment, who shatters the parent-child bond in the interest of the child's present behavior, will only compound the problem. Ask a child to tell you the opposite of forgiveness; his answer in essence will be "condemnation." And condemnation stifles human growth.

Is God less than man? Would He use methods to restore and mature us that are less effective than those used by a wise parent? Oh, that we could recognize how intensely we are loved! How powerfully that would make us whole again.

People who are loved walk tall. They do not do it because someone tells them they ought to. They do it because there comes welling up from inside a solid sense of self-esteem, a sense of dignity, the security to dare and to adventure. With their own needs met, they are free to reach out to meet others' needs—to be compassionate, kind, humble, gentle, and patient.

And that's why God loves us as He does!

WHO SERVED WHOM FIRST?

Who is greater, the one who sits down to eat or the one who serves him? The one who sits down, of course. But I am among you as one who serves. Luke 22:27, T.E.V.

Jesus had a choice: He could come to this earth as a commanding ruler, or He could come as a humble servant. Were the choice up to us, we probably would have argued for the ruler role, simply for reasons of efficiency. He could have drawn more attention, organized His followers more readily, and been documented in history more fully.

We know that He chose the role of the servant, but do we know why? It is often interpreted that He did it to set us an example of humility. That may not set well with us, however, if we see no deeper reason.

Jesus came to this earth to reveal the Father and how the Father deals with us wounded sinners. He knew that no role would tell the truth more accurately than that of being the unwearied servant of man's necessities.

Though the Father is indeed the possessor of all power and authority and can command the galaxies in their orbit, these are not the qualities He uses in dealing with sinners. Were He to lord His rank over us, this would intimidate us but not heal us. He could command our submission but not win our bruised hearts.

The manner in which Jesus came reveals the kind of solution He plans for this controversy. He desires no military conquest of the weak by the mighty. The winner in this contest will not be the one with superior firepower, but the One with the most accurate, winsome truth.

We speak so often of serving God that we think service is only toward Him. The incredible truth is that servanthood began in the heart of God. *He* served *us* first. The night Jesus knelt in front of His disciples with a towel around His waist, washing their dirty feet, He was giving them one of His clearest portrayals of His Father. In effect He was saying, "If you have seen Me as one who will even wash dirty feet, you must know that this what your Father is like, too."

ASKING HARD QUESTIONS

Now when the queen of Sheba heard of the fame of Solomon concerning the name of the Lord, she came to test him with hard questions. 1 Kings 10:1, R.S.V.

The queen of Sheba arrived in Jerusalem to test Solomon with hard questions concerning Israel's God. The nations around Israel marveled at the wisdom of Israel's government, and by this God's name had been uplifted. Determined to understand the reasons behind such success and prosperity, the queen of Sheba sought out Israel's king and "told him all that was on her mind." The record states that he "answered all her questions; there was nothing hidden from the king which he could not explain to her" (1 Kings 10:2, 3, R.S.V.).

There is something very wonderful about this story. Here we see a picture of God that is compellingly attractive. Solomon expressed total openness to any questions the queen might have concerning God. And that openness portrays God as eager for us to ask questions—so that He may answer them!

There is no need to fear that God might detect in us some unsettledness in our feelings toward Him. If He should discover that we still have questions in our minds about Him, He will not condemn us—"How *could* you doubt Me?"—but rather, He encourages us to tell Him everything that is on our minds so that He might then answer all our questions. Not one of them does He consider inappropriate or too hard to answer.

Candidly, have you not had questions in your mind to which you dared not give utterance for fear of denying your faith? I know I have. Even when in prayer I have sometimes tended to avoid the issues that are pressing on my heart. Is it because I fear to show any trace of unbelief, that this would displease God? Or is it that I am afraid to face myself? "I'm not *supposed* to have any questions! I'm supposed to *trust*. I should be thankful; I should be praising God more . . . ."

Yes, we are supposed to trust, to trust that God is absolutely committed to teaching us to live in reality. We need to learn to deal with every issue, inwardly as well as outwardly. He calls Himself our friend, deliberately bringing us up to His level so that we may enjoy the uninhibited communion that real friends share. For this friendship we may be deeply thankful, knowing that He delights to answer all our questions! Trusting Him in this way, we show our praise.

FRETTING CHRISTIANS

The Lord answered, "Martha, Martha, you are fretting and fussing about so many things; but one thing is necessary. The part that Mary has chosen is best; and it shall not be taken away from her." Luke 10:41, 42, N.E.B.

There's no doubt that Martha was a good woman. Religious people enjoyed having her around and never questioned the sincerity of her devotion. But these good, church-going folks weren't as discerning as Jesus was about the nature of the fire that burned inside Martha's heart. What they labeled as religious zeal, Jesus saw for what it really was.

Martha was trying to impress Jesus by earnestly caring for Him. She wanted to be sure He noticed the sincerity of her devotion. She wanted Him to change His opinion of her. In a word, she was a legalist. And legalists are always fretting and fussing, for they are never sure that they have accomplished their goal.

But an even more telling sign of the nature of Martha's religious experience was her attitude toward her sister Mary. You see, one who is filled with anxiety about one's standing with God cannot understand those who are sitting, joyful and relaxed, at the feet of Jesus. Martha was certain that Mary wasn't taking religious matters seriously. If Mary was taking sin seriously, she'd join Martha in her anxious bustle to demonstrate her righteousness. Martha fits my favorite definition of a legalist: "Someone who has a haunting fear that somebody, somewhere, is having a good time."

And was Mary ever having a good time! She basked in the warmth of Christ's friendship, falling ever more deeply in love with Him whom to know is life eternal. Jesus spoke to the real issue when He said, "It shall not be taken away." There is rich security in a friendship, especially when the Friend is constant in His attitude toward us. But when we endeavor to earn that friendship, we shall be perpetually anxious.

When Jesus said that Martha was fretting over "many things," He was talking not only about the beans and potatoes. The legalist lives in constant dread that anything he does, even good deeds, may induce the frown and displeasure of God if they are not done perfectly. Any momentary feelings of peace one may find can be taken away quickly the moment one gets a deeper understanding of God's requirements.

I'm so glad Jesus said there is a better part!

DOING US A FAVOR

He also said to them, "The Sabbath was made for the sake of man and not man for the Sabbath: therefore the Son of Man is sovereign even over the Sabbath." Mark 2:27, 28, N.E.B.

I like to imagine Jesus' face as He was saying this to His disciples, because I'm sure His expression revealed His feelings. I picture a hint of a playful smile at the edges of His mouth, as if to say, "Are you ready for this one? You're going to like it!"

And the tone of His voice—it was straining to open their minds to this precious insight: You think the Sabbath is a ritual you've been doing as a favor to God. But you've got it all wrong. My Father likes to do favors for His friends. And this one's for *you!*

The Sabbath had been such a burden for them as they tried to impress God with their diligence in keeping all the rules. Jesus' point was that His Father was already so impressed with His people that He was making a deliberate appointment to spend special time with them. Of all the things that God could do for the benefit of His people, no blessing could be greater than His personal fellowship with them.

Think of all the things God could be doing with His time! He is, after all, in charge of the whole universe. Yet He counts it no sacrifice from His busy schedule to set aside one seventh of each week exclusively for the benefit of His friends. (We sometimes think that *we* are making the sacrifice from our schedules to do Him the favor of our ritualistic worship!)

Could we fully grasp what Jesus is saying, we would cry with David, "What is man, that thou art mindful of him? and the son of man, that thou visitest him?" (Ps.8:4). The question deserves an answer, too. To see our Father going to such lengths to enjoy fellowship with His creatures should tell us that He views us as capable of bringing satisfaction and delight to His heart through that fellowship.

No one knew better than Jesus the fellowship with the Father that the Sabbath celebrates. That's why He calls Himself "the Lord . . . of the Sabbath." Let's celebrate with Him.

GOD HAS ACCEPTED ME!

He will convince the world concerning . . . righteousness . . . because I go to the Father. John 16:10, R.S.V.

Jesus has always worn two hats, as it were. But, then, doesn't any competent mediator? But with Jesus, both hats are worn for the benefit of the same party.

In the situation of an estranged couple, a good counselor will try to bring reconciliation by getting each party to see the other's viewpoint. To do this he will mediate between the two, standing in the place of first one and then the other. By this gentle substitutionary shifting, the counselor allows the offended parties to work through their animosities and fears without having to deal directly with each other.

In our estrangement from God, Jesus is mediator. God has taken the first step in our direction by stating that He is holding nothing against us. Paul wrote, "Our message is that God was making all mankind his friends through Christ. God did not keep an account of their sins, and he has given us the message which tells how he makes them his friends" (2 Cor. 5:19, T.E.V.).

God doesn't need to have His mind changed concerning us! In every way possible He lets us know that He accepts us. Why, then, do we need Jesus to mediate for us? The answer is simple: *we* feel the need to "test the waters" in our return to God. So Jesus dons the hat of mankind and goes into the Father's presence, not to win over the Father but so that *we* can be convinced of the Father's response.

The other hat Jesus wears is divinity. Coming to us, He portrays our God as warm, forgiving, accepting, and extremely desirous of reestablishing friendship with us. "He who has seen me," Jesus told His disciples, "has seen the Father" (John 14:9, R.S.V.). So He is God's gracious substitute, even as He is ours.

Both hats are for *our* benefit! And the ultimate statement of God's acceptance of us is to have Jesus, our Substitute, living in God's presence today. We can be totally convinced that our relationship has been set right because Jesus has gone to the Father and has been accepted as *us!* No wonder Jesus said later, referring to the time He would once again be with us, "In that day you will ask nothing of me" (chap. 16:23, R.S.V.). It will no longer be necessary; we will be one with the Father, just as He is!

HOW TO BE A SELF-WILLED CHRISTIAN

You must work out your own salvation in fear and trembling; for it is God who works in you, inspiring both the will and the deed, for his own chosen purpose. Phil. 2:12, 13, N.E.B.

Let's imagine a large chart with three positions clearly marked on it. These three positions portray three stages of our Christian walk.

Start down in the lower left corner of the chart with Position 1 and label it "Selfish will." This represents pre-Christian values. It's the independent, "I'll-do-what-I-want" will of the rebel. This needs no explanation; we've all been there.

Next draw a sweeping line (like the arc of a pendulum) to the far right of the chart and mark it Position 2. Give it the title "No will of my own." This is the experience of many new Christians who remember with tears the days of their independence from God. With absolute sincerity they vow never to move outside God's will. When asked what they might wish to do, they would say, "It's not what I want, it's what God wants that matters; I must crucify myself."

For those at stage two, any thought of doing what one wishes to do, brings back painful memories of their pre-Christian days, and they recoil at the idea. Obedience means meekly submitting to whatever God wants, interposing nothing at all of one's own wishes and desires. God originates all instructions and plans. Interestingly, God—and not the individual—is then accountable for what happens!

Once again, use your marker to draw a line to the top and center of the page, and locate Position 3. Give this one the label "Sanctified will." This represents the position of the mature Christian, the one whose values and goals have been edified by Christ, who indeed has the mind of Christ. This is the one who finds, to his sheer delight, that what he most wants to do is the very thing that Jesus wishes for him to do.

God designs Position 2 to be only transitional. He does not wish to do our thinking and choosing for us. Rather, He wishes to equip us to do our own best thinking and to bear accountability for our own choices. Paul was presenting this idea when he told the Philippians to trust the working of God in their own hearts and—with due respect and reverence—go ahead and make their very own decisions.

CONTENDING FOR GOD

Will ye accept his person? will ye contend for God? Job 13:8.

In Job we find a story of four very religious men. One of them, Job, found himself subjected to a series of unexplainable tragedies. To his three God-fearing friends, these signaled that God was punishing Job for having done something extremely wrong. And they wanted him to make it right—if they could just get him to admit what it was! They felt compelled to explain the character of God to Job, who seemed to have forgotten. But he just didn't get the point. Instead, he told them that they made miserable comforters! (Job 16:2).

The fact is, Job had incredible faith in God. Every outward evidence that he was in right relationship with God had vanished, yet he knew that God would not deal with him as his friends represented. In our text today, Job challenges his friends, "Will you accept his person?" That is, will you accept who God really is? [Do you even *know* who He really is?] How can you contend for Him if you don't even grasp what He is like?

Job knew what God was like, in spite of his current circumstances. "If you and I were to change places," he told his friends, "I could talk like you; how I could harangue you and wag my head at you! But no, I would speak words of encouragement, and then my condolences would flow in streams" (verses 4, 5, N.E.B.). That's how God is, even when we have done wrong!

Though Job experienced bouts of terrible weariness and sometimes uttered words of despair, he always cried out *to* God, never against Him. Listen: "If only I knew how to find [God], how to enter his court, I would state my case before him and set out my arguments in full" (chap. 23:3, 4, N.E.B.). He knew that God was reasonable! He was not afraid to talk to Him about his problems, or his feelings and ideas.

"Then I should learn what answer he would give and find out what he had to say. Would he exert his great power to browbeat me [as my friends are doing]? No; God himself would never bring a charge against me" (verses 5, 6, N.E.B.). The King James Version says, "He would put strength in me" (verse 6).

Was Job right? To his friends God said, "You have not spoken of me what is right, as my servant Job has" (chap. 42:7, R.S.V.).

GETTING GOD'S BLESSINGS

Blessed are they that do his commandments. Rev. 22:14

There is no doubt but that God possesses infinite blessings and that He wants to make them available to His people.

But it is not always clear how those blessings become ours. Have you noticed the way in which we customarily pray about blessings? We pray, "Bless this food to our health." But what are we assuming? Is the blessing "sprinkled" down from heaven like holy water until it becomes part of the food? Would God implant that blessing as readily in a green salad as He would in deep-fried squid? Is the food less healthful if we don't ask for the blessing?

Perhaps it would be more fitting to begin praying as we are pushing the cart through the grocery store. We could affirm to God that we are willing to be reminded to select those foods that are inherently healthful. Then at mealtime we could thank Him for such good food and for the wisdom to prepare it healthfully.

There are three general approaches to the question of how we obtain God's blessings. They could be summarized in this way:

Blessings are earned . . . God is obligated to us by our works.

Blessings are coaxed . . . God is enticed by our begging.

Blessings are inherent . . . God is wise in teaching us.

Much of our praying for blessings falls into the second category. We assume that God retains large quantities of "blessings," which He arbitrarily dispenses (as department store Santa Clauses dispense candy to children) to those with whom He is pleased. The flip side of this idea, of course, is that He also can reach into His bag of curses and inflict a few of those upon people with whom He is displeased.

According to either reasoning, God uses His resources to manipulate us. Worshiping a manipulative God, we in turn become manipulative. We try to "stroke" Him with our eloquent prayers or impress Him with our array of good behavior.

Under the third approach to God's blessings, we see God as describing to us the path of inherent blessing. Those who obey are blessed by virtue of the fact that they walk in those paths. This implies that God always asks His people to do that which will, in the doing, bring the best of physical, social, spiritual, and emotional health. Obedience, then, brings its own reward. Thus neither blessings nor cursings are the acts of an arbitrary God.

ASKING THE RIGHT QUESTION

For God sent the Son into the world, not to condemn the world, but that the world might be saved through him. John 3:17, R.S.V.

Read these three questions and see if you can find what they have in common: How many 3-cent stamps are there in a dozen? Have you stopped beating your wife yet? Did Jesus accept Peter when he denied his Lord?

Did you catch what it was that they have in common? In each case the question itself implies a misleading assumption. Being so concerned to give a right answer to the question, we fail to stop and analyze the assumption critically.

It's the false assumption in that third question we need to look at today. It assumes that the only way Jesus can relate to a deliberate denial is through rejection. It assumes that God's condemnation of the sinner is itself the major consequence of all sin; that if God didn't reject the sinner, He wouldn't be dealing adequately with him.

One of the most persistent emotional myths is the belief that love does not deal directly enough with sin. This myth holds that sin needs stern, harsh firmness if it's to be eradicated. It believes that love is too passive, too gentle, to do that. Perhaps we have picked up these ideas from parents or teachers whose discipline methods held only one weapon in the arsenal: harsh rejection. More likely, not many of us have ever really experienced the potent vitality of love, and we resort to rejection simply because we know nothing else. Unfortunately, we expect God to do the same in His dealings with us.

People who study the learning patterns of young children, especially what blocks learning, have agreed on one vital fact: Mental anguish inhibits learning. To condemn as a means of teaching will assure that learning won't take place. People burdened with guilt cannot hear the teacher's message, and to fail to accept is to condemn. Since Jesus came to this planet to teach us about His Father, is it any wonder that He came not to condemn? Would people hear His gracious message if every sermon brought new condemnation? He could not both condemn and save.

Did Jesus reject Peter when he denied his Lord? We should ask, "What purpose would it have fulfilled? Did Peter need more pain in his heart than he had just inflicted upon himself? Did he need an extra burden of rejection?" How, then, could he have learned of his Friend's forgiveness?

DISCOVERING HIS ACCEPTANCE OF YOU

I will go to the king, though it is against the law; and if I perish, I perish. Esther 4:16, R.S.V.

Courageous Esther! Motivated beyond selfish concerns, she entered her husband-king's court to plead for the lives of her people. Without summons from the king himself, her act carried the penalty of death. That is, unless she found favor with him and he held out to her his scepter.

The story reveals that the king was delighted to see Esther! He was willing not only to hear her request, he was willing to share with her his kingdom. Does this tell us anything about our God?

We cannot earn God's favor. And there is no way we can approach Him by reason of any compliance to rules. "No human being will be justified in his sight by works of the law" (Rom. 3:20, R.S.V.). Taken by themselves, the rules condemn us!

We must remember that there was an active relationship between Esther and the king, the love relationship of marriage. Her access to him in privacy was to be expected. However, when she went before him in his court, he was to her as he was to all: the ruler of the Medo-Persian Empire.

It is of no little significance, however, that his response to her was because he loved her. "When he saw Queen Esther standing in the court, he was pleased with her" (Esther 5:2, N.I.V.). She was no stranger to him; she was his wife. And so he held out to her the symbol of his power, for she would be blessed, and not condemned, by it.

God is more than the ruler of the universe; in Christ He portrays Himself as our bridegroom. He is pleased with us, not because we have been able to meet divine requirements but because of our relationship to Him. He holds out to us the scepter of His power and offers us His kingdom.

God sees our trembling hearts. He knows that though He has proclaimed us His bride, we are not yet convinced of His enduring love.

"Fear not, little flock, for it is your Father's good pleasure to give you the kingdom" (Luke 12:32, R.S.V.).

CLEANING THE LENS

Let your light so shine before men, that they may see your good works and give glory to your Father who is in heaven. Matt. 5:16, R.S.V.

My friend Chuck works on a giant fusion research project. In massive buildings that cover acres of staggeringly expensive equipment, brilliant men are trying to reproduce the same process that happens inside the sun: the release of energy through atomic fusion.

In this project a tiny target is blasted with the energy of huge laser beams, focused through an array of unusual lenses. These lenses are made of a special plastic material designed specifically for laser energy levels. One of Chuck's jobs is to make sure that every one of the hundreds of lenses is spotlessly clean each time the target is fired upon. If there is so much as a tiny speck of dust on them, two things will happen: The first problem is that the tiny speck of dust will diffuse light, keeping it from reaching its target. Several pieces of dust will measurably cut down on the efficiency of the whole project. Thus it requires even more laser energy to create fusion in the target.

But the more serious problem is that the speck of dust that stops the light from going through the lens turns the light energy into heat energy. That heat leaves a tiny black burn mark on the lens. The next time that incredibly strong burst of light hits the lens, the tiny burn mark stops even more light, creating a still bigger scar. Before long, a single burst of light will instantly destroy the lens.

Frances Ridley Havergal, in a profoundly insightful hymn, suggested how Christians view themselves: "I, the transparent medium Thy glory to display." Perhaps she had been reading about the fourth angel of Revelation 18 who would lighten the earth with his glory. She knew that the word *glory* applied specifically to the knowledge of the character of God. And she knew that God wanted to use His people as the channels for such powerful truth about Himself to cover the whole earth.

I think that God is cleaning His lenses, for both the above reasons. He wishes for His gracious character to be known, without distortions, through the people who bear His name. And perhaps there is also a hint in this analogy of how the persistently rebellious will be destroyed by the same brightness that brings rejoicing to the righteous.

WHO NEEDS CHRIST'S MERITS?

To the praise of the glory of his grace, wherein he hath made us accepted in the beloved. Eph. 1:6.

The question Who needs Christ's merits? is not a cocky question like Who needs taxes? It is a very serious question. Who is benefited by Christ's merits?

We often hear it said, "God has accepted us by virtue of the merits of Christ." It is good news indeed to find that we are accepted, but just how do Christ's merits fit in? What part do they play in the transaction? Do we assume that God is impressed with merits? Are we suggesting that since God can't see our rebellious past while we "hide" under the perfect record of Jesus we are therefore accepted? Seriously, does God need Christ's merits in any way to relate differently to us?

Or perhaps we are to see His merits as necessary in order to balance some books in the heavenly courtroom. This would suggest that salvation requires a certain amount of merit. We are obviously short of merit, and so we borrow large amounts from Jesus' account since He has a vast surplus. The Father, in this scenario, checks the books to make sure the bottom line comes out even. Is this really the nature of the sin problem?

I would like to suggest that the concept of being accepted in Christ's merits is simply one of heaven's better illustrations of how God views man. Since some people can think of loving acceptance only in terms of its being deserved, God accommodates their concerns by showing them how totally He accepted Jesus. Then He says, I will accept you just as fully, for you are "accepted in the beloved." Jesus stands as a type of all humanity in revealing how much God loves us all.

The concept of merit, then, is for our sake. We are the ones who need every available illustration of God's positive attitude toward humanity. We need to sense His attitude as illustrated in how He relates to the Son of man.

Some might protest, "Jesus was perfect. No wonder God could love Him. But I'm a sinner." Yet this is the exact point where we can best see the meaning of unconditional love. God's love for us is absolutely not influenced by who we are or what we do. And since forgiveness and acceptance are but manifestations of love, they are offered freely to all.

THE GREATEST OF THESE IS GOD

He who does not love does not know God; for God is love. 1 John 4:8, R.S.V.

In our quest to know God, let us explore 1 Corinthians 13 in view of our scripture for today. Since God *is* love, we may confidently use His name in place of the word *love*. Listen to what this familiar passage says about Him:

"If I speak in the tongues of men and of angels, but have not [God], I am a noisy gong or a clanging cymbal. And if I have prophetic powers, and understand all mysteries and all knowledge, and if I have all faith, so as to remove mountains, but have not [God], I am nothing. If I give away all I have, and if I deliver my body to be burned, but have not [God], I gain nothing.

"[God] is patient and kind; [God] is not jealous or boastful; [He] is not arrogant or rude. [God] does not insist on [His] own way; [He] is not irritable or resentful; [He] does not rejoice at wrong, but rejoices in the right. [God] bears all things, believes all things, hopes all things, endures all things.

"[God] never ends; as for prophecies, they will pass away; as for tongues, they will cease; as for knowledge, it will pass away. For our knowledge is imperfect and our prophecy is imperfect; but when the perfect comes, the imperfect will pass away. When I was a child, I spoke as a child, I thought like a child, I reasoned like a child; when I became a man, I gave up childish ways. For now we see in a mirror dimly; but then face to face. Now I know in part; then I shall understand fully, even as I have been fully understood. So faith, hope, [God] abide, these three; but the greatest of these is [God]"—in whom we have faith! (R.S.V.).

It is not enough to say that God does loving things. God *is* love! In today's text God is not making an accusation against us. He is stating the truth, that we might learn the Source of love. He seeks to bring us to the realization that He understands us fully. He knows our past, our upbringing, our education, our failings, and our dreams. But this knowledge is consistently flavored with His love. He knows nothing about us apart from love!

God longs to have us understand Him too. But He knows that this can never be until we are fully secure in His knowledge of us.

HEAVEN'S ACTIVITIES

They shall build houses and inhabit them; they shall plant vineyards and eat their fruit. . . . And my chosen people shall long enjoy the work of their hands. Isa. 65:21, 22, R.S.V.

Jesus told His friends that He would be building mansions in heaven for all the redeemed. It's a comforting idea, knowing that our arrival in the New Jerusalem won't catch anyone by surprise and that our needs will be well met.

But I fear it has given some the idea that in heaven God will do for us everything that needs to be done, that we will enjoy some kind of well-deserved vacation from responsibilities. God will build; we will inhabit. We could even conclude: God will compose the music; we will learn it. God will write the poetry; we will recite it. God will create, and we will observe. "After all," we might say, "God could do a much better job than we could in all these things."

But could God Himself find satisfaction in a heaven full of appreciative spectators? Would it bring delight to Him to have the balconies of heaven full of applauding audiences, while He does what God does, essentially alone? Would God give us the capacity to be creative, only to let it become dormant in heaven?

I have a growing picture of a God who will approach His friends in the new earth and say—with eager expectancy—"Will you show Me the house you have just built? I'd be delighted to see how you designed the landscaping and crafted an appealing life-space."

I can picture Him coming to another and saying, "Please, sing Me the song you have just composed! You've always blessed Me with your music in the past, and your abilities are really soaring into new realms." I can see Him meeting another on a golden boulevard and asking him about the new compounds he has been creating in his experimental laboratories. Or listening to yet another as he finds new ways to express his insights into the history of redemption.

God created His people that He might enter into the delights of two-way interaction with them. This means—incredibly—that we humans are God-built with capacities to satisfy the heart of God Himself! What other reason would He have had for creating us in the first place?

Should it not follow that God takes delight even now in seeing His people develop their creative capacities to think and to do?

FINDING YOUR CONTAINER

Return, faithless Israel. . . . Only acknowledge your guilt. Jer. 3:12, 13, R.S.V.

There's nothing more frustrating than preparing school lunches only to find the supply of lunch sacks depleted. Or to be at the ocean, hands full of shells and other treasures, knowing that there is no way to get them home. Or worse yet, to have the container in which you are bringing home ripe plums rupture just in time to leave your car the recipient of a soggy mess.

"The kingdom of heaven is like treasure hidden in a field" (Matt. 13:44, R.S.V.). Treasure! How can we obtain it? Listen: "Fear not, little flock, for it is your Father's good pleasure to give you the kingdom" (Luke 12:32, R.S.V.).

We ourselves are the containers for this treasure. "We have this treasure in earthen vessels" (2 Cor. 4:7, R.S.V.). The preceding verses explain what this treasure is: It is the truth of who God the Father is, as revealed in the life of Christ.

Since Eden we have been hiding from God. Hiding because we are afraid. We do not need to hide! Our fears have been based on the false report of the deceiver of men. Through Christ we have seen the character of God and how He relates to fallen mankind. We've seen His love for us, His acceptance of us. And this truth is the treasure that God desires to freely give us. He wants to fill our lives with His friendship.

It is up to us to give God our containers. And we won't give them to Him until we realize that they are empty, so horribly empty. "Only admit you need My treasure," pleads the Father, "so that I can give it to you!"

What is our response? If it is one of denial, then He is forced to help us deal with reality. Ever so carefully He begins to explain to us our condition. At first we think He's caught us in the bushes. But as we stand shaking in our nakedness before Him He just covers us with His own robe, His own perfectly loving life. "Here," He offers, "this will make you more comfortable."

And it does. Before long we are more than warm; we are reconciled! It is then that He begins to fill our vessels with the treasure of who He is. Let us quickly acknowledge that we are empty, for empty containers are just what we need in order to get the treasure home!

GROWN-UP PRAYING

Thy kingdom come. Thy will be done in earth, as it is in heaven. Matt. 6:10.

"Dear Jesus," the sweet young voice pleads, "bless me today, and make my puppy come home." Meanwhile her mother is praying, "O Father! You are welcome in my heart. May I be more secure in Your love, and thus less defensive."

As we mature spiritually, our manner of speaking in the Father's presence will change. There will be less begging for blanket blessings, more aligning with His will. The difference comes from our deepening knowledge of who the Father is. Instead of seeing Him as an arbitrary dispenser of blessings, we increasingly see Him as the author of wisdom, the designer of ideal patterns for living. We grasp more fully the inherent wisdom of those ways, and we see that our problems do not stem from God's reluctance to give blessings but from our reluctance to walk in the paths of blessing.

It dawns on us that the purpose of prayer is not to change God's posture toward us but to change our posture toward God. There is no need to beg or grovel before Him, no need to persuade Him to recognize problems He may not know. Such would be insulting—to both of us. When we see how good God has been to us, begging gives way to praise.

Jesus taught us to pray "Thy kingdom come." Later He said, "The kingdom of God is within you," which means that the truest essence of Christ's kingdom is not its physical location but the ideals and values by which its members live. To pray Jesus' prayer, then, is to make a conscious choice to let our minds and values be brought into harmony with the mind and values of God. This represents submission in the highest sense of the word. It represents not a fearful cowering in the face of superior firepower but an intelligent aligning of the mind with superior wisdom.

At this point many of the blunt imperatives of our prayers begin to fade into other forms. Rather than praying, "Bless me today," we might pray, "I give You permission to nudge me should I begin to walk outside the paths of blessing." Instead of "Bless Uncle Charlie," we will likely pray, "Lord, I am willing to be used by You as some means of bringing joy and healing into Uncle Charlie's life."

And isn't that how we would expect two intelligent persons to converse?

HOW GOD DEALS WITH SIN

**To wink at a fault causes trouble; a frank rebuke leads to peace.
Prov. 10:10, N.E.B.**

A teacher discovers that one of his students has been cheating on his exams. Should he ignore this and act as though nothing has happened? Or should he rebuke the student and suspend him from the classroom? From our text today it seems that the latter would be the more profitable choice. Or would it?

In Proverbs 10:12 we read, "But love turns a blind eye to every fault" (N.E.B). Is this a contradiction? Is there a difference between turning a blind eye to every fault and winking at them? In the *Good News Bible,* verse 10 states: "Someone who holds back the truth causes trouble." To wink at a fault is to avoid dealing with the issues entirely—and to leave them unresolved. This holds back reality. And God is committed to teaching us to live in reality—to live responsibly and accountably in every situation.

Yet it says that love turns a blind eye to every fault! For clarification let us read another translation of verse 12: "But love forgives all offenses" (T.E.V). God does not ignore, but forgives, our offenses. The "blind eye" is His chosen attitude of temporarily commuting our death sentence, that we might live to learn a better way. Forgiveness does not hold back the truth; it is not whitewash. Forgiveness is God's intelligent and loving position toward us.

I believe God has chosen this third alternative. He deals with *us,* holding aside the sure consequences of our actions while He gives us the opportunity to understand the problem and make an informed choice as to how we would like to relate to Him in the future.

So often we think we have only two choices in dealing with those who have sinned. To show mercy we ignore the offense. To show that we take sin seriously, we either expel the sinner from our presence or take stern action against him. Either way, we lose any chance we might have in retaining a healing relationship with the person involved.

Let us cherish the third option! Let us gently and intelligently work through the realities of each problem while expressing, every step of the way, that the individual involved is of more value than any of his presently unwise choices. That's how I would want to be treated.

WHY SELL IT ALL?

The kingdom of heaven is like a merchant in search of fine pearls, who, on finding one pearl of great value, went and sold all that he had and bought it. Matt. 13:45, 46, R.S.V.

When Jesus tells a parable, even the little details of sequence and timing are important to the story. In this one-sentence parable Jesus speaks to that all-important issue of why one would choose to be a committed Christian. But notice when it is that a person makes such a choice.

More closely than we might recognize at first, we can identify with the merchant's insistence on obtaining only fine pearls; nothing less than the finest can satisfy the deepest longings of the heart. We who have sought satisfaction in the trinkets and plastic gems of this dusty planet know the emptiness they leave behind when they crumble. Though we stagger at the anticipated price, we know that were we to find the ultimate pearl we would give up every lesser gem to obtain it. Meanwhile, we hang on to what we have, for it seems to us better than nothing at all.

In Jesus' parable the merchant first finds the pearl and perceives its great worth. Then, with a knowledge of what he is about to gain in the transaction, he willingly sells everything that would divide his attention, every investment in something of lesser value, in order to obtain that which would ultimately satisfy. Were you to ask him if he is paying too costly a price, he would laugh and tell you he is getting the bargain of a lifetime.

Jesus is Himself the pearl. He is available immediately to all who will embrace Him as the center of their lives. But we must recognize that He does not ask us to give up all that we presently cling to until we recognize the value of His friendship. This really says something very practical about our Saviour. He does not urge us to step from our sinking iceberg until we know that what we are stepping onto is firm soil.

Jesus has nothing to gain by hiding from us the great value of the pearl, then urging a blind leap in the dark. Nor does He rebuke us as perversely selfish for clinging to the only securities we know. Instead, He persuasively shows us His great value as a friend. Then, on the basis of such evidence, we choose the security of obviously greater worth.

February 25

ARE YOU LIVING THE LIFE OF FAITH?

Examine yourselves: are you living the life of faith? Put yourselves to the test. 2 Cor. 13:5, N.E.B.

Today's text challenges us to explore honestly our ongoing relationship with God. However, it is not meant to motivate us to see how many good works we are performing. As a matter of fact, examining our "good deeds list" may hinder us in our ability to discern candidly the true quality of our friendship with God.

It is like trying to determine how good your marriage is. A husband might reason, "I earn a good living, stay home nights, fix the washing machine, take out the garbage . . ." And a wife might reflect, "I do the laundry, fix meals, keep the house tidy, mend his socks . . ."

While these things are commendable and even necessary, for the most part, they are poor barometers with which to take a reading on your relationship. Really, not many couples end up in court with the complaint "He didn't empty the garbage!" or "She wouldn't mend my socks!" Granted, these things can irritate, but it is not the things we do so much as the way we relate to each other and how we feel we are being related to by the other that makes marriage work or makes it intolerable.

Likewise, our relationship with God is defined not so much by the actions we do as by the attitudes we have toward God as our personal friend. It is defined also by how we perceive He is relating to us. In our efforts to please God we might ask as did the disciples, " 'Then what must we do . . . if we are to work as God would have us work?' Jesus replied, 'This is the work that God requires: believe in the one whom he has sent' " (John 6:28, 29, N.E.B.).

We believe that Christ is representative of all that God is. We know that when Christ healed people God our Father in heaven was showing us that He desires to heal *our* lives from all that makes us hurt and hurtful. When we see Mary forgiven we exclaim, "God has forgiven *me!*" When we witness the look of tenderest compassion on the face of Jesus for Peter, even as Peter denied Him, we understand: God still wants me, even though I sometimes deny Him.

As today's text implies, I should ask myself: "Am I living confidently and securely in my relationship with God? Is God my friend?"

OUT TO GET THE JUDGE

Satan answered the Lord, "Has not Job good reason to be God-fearing? Have you not hedged him round on every side with your protection?" Job 1:9, N.E.B.

The encounter between God and Satan in the book of Job has all the essential features of the final judgment. There is conflict between the two great protagonists in the universe-wide conflict. On the surface it appears their conflict is over Job. God has said that Job is a good man; Satan has countered with another opinion.

However, the conflict has a much deeper dimension. We begin to realize that Satan cares hardly at all what becomes of Job; his real target is God Himself! And Satan has in his countercharge a twofold attack against Him. First, he implies that God really doesn't know what He is talking about. God has placed His confidence in Job as a worthy example of His restorative power, certain Job will remain loyal to Him. But Satan asserts that if God really knew hearts, He would find how fickle Job is, given a change of his pleasant circumstances.

In his second charge Satan is essentially asserting that no one would place his faith in God wholly on the basis of who God is. He claims that we humans are selfish through and through, and that the only way God could ever draw us to Himself would be to appeal to that selfishness. Job, he claims, is an example of purchased loyalty, not of faith. Faith that is rooted entirely in an appreciation of God simply doesn't exist, Satan claims, because God just isn't worthy of such confidence.

What would happen if Job were to crumble under the test? What would the universe think of their God? About His ability to know the hearts and motives of His creatures? About whether anyone really will worship God for God's sake alone? The judgment here is not primarily focused on Job. From Satan's point of view, what's one puny human, more or less! He is out to get the Judge!

It's exciting to see how God handles the charges. He could have said, "You've got no right questioning My opinions. After all, I am God!" But He didn't. Without any defensiveness He simply said, "Let's let the matter be decided on the basis of evidence. Go ahead and take away all those blessings that you assert have purchased Job's loyalties."

We know the outcome. God concluded that Job spoke of Him what was right (Job 42:7). Can He say the same of us?

GIVING THANKS IN ALL CIRCUMSTANCES

Give thanks in all circumstances; for this is the will of God in Christ Jesus for you. 1 Thess. 5:18, R.S.V.

A baby dies by falling out of a speeding car. Can the mother thank God for this? A teenager becomes a quadriplegic when his car is hit by a drunk driver. Are the parents to thank God for his now-limited future? I hear it again and again: Christians are saying Yes to these questions.

And that yes has an edge on it! "If you, as a Christian, do *not* answer Yes, then you do not believe that God is in control of your life. You do not believe today's text. In other words, you are not much of a Christian."

Well, my answer to the above questions is No! God is not drilling us to become unfeeling automatons. We are not to swallow our intelligence and go through the motions of praising God for things that are horribly wrong. God does not expect us to thank Him *for* all circumstances, but to thank Him *in* all circumstances. Thank Him for sustaining us through the crisis that would drive us insane were it not for His abiding presence. Thank Him that we know that this world is not the last statement of what shall be. Thank Him for all that He is, in spite of all the slander that has been heaped up against His name—often in the name of religion and right.

To thank God that your baby fell out of a speeding car is to indict God as a murderer. "But," you say, "I've asked God to take control of my life and the lives of my children! He let it happen!" Remember: We are on enemy territory! And that enemy is the destroyer of souls. We can expect only that he will be allowed to demonstrate that fact until the great controversy between good and evil is ended. In the meantime, God has promised to be with us and to help us make the kinds of decisions that will enable us to live not only responsibly and accountably but confidently and productively as well.

Dear reader, if there are painful circumstances in your life in which you can see little or no good, look beyond them to the mighty God, your tenderhearted Father. His goodness is never-changing, His love for you is unbudging, and His plans for your life and the lives of your loved ones are far greater than your highest thoughts can reach.

Rejoice and be exceeding glad! Our God is larger than any circumstances in our lives.

WHY FEEL BAD ABOUT SIN?

Against thee, thee only, have I sinned, and done that which is evil in thy sight. Ps. 51:4, R.S.V.

Why do you feel bad when you sin? Do you fear that God will think less of you? Or do you fear that someone will think less of God because of you?

That question is far more than just theological nit-picking; it touches on the deepest motivations of the heart. If your incentive for avoiding sin is so that you will not lose face before God, your basic motivation is selfish. If, on the other hand, your reason for avoiding sin is out of an intensely high regard for the reputation of One whom you love, your basic motivation is unselfish.

When we get right down to it, motivation makes all the difference. We shall have the mind of Christ only when the fires that burn behind our eyes are those of unselfish love. The law can truly be kept only by those who love, for it describes how loving people act. Selfishness cannot produce unselfishness. When I have a selfish reason for wanting to become unselfish, it just won't work.

God knows that, and for this reason He gave us totally unselfish reasons for wanting to become like Him. Having entirely met all our needs (and thus healing our selfishness), He then drew us into love with Himself. More than any concerns for ourselves, we become jealous for the good reputation of our Friend. We know that others shall be making eternal decisions about Him, often based on what they see in us. And we want them to think well of Him!

David knew this, too. When he sinned, he knew exactly who had been hurt the most. Beyond the grief his sin would bring to his own life, David knew that many in Israel would wonder whether God was adequate in David's life—if David had to so clearly depart from God's will in order to get his "needs" met.

There is no evidence that David feared to approach God. He knew that his Father does not use the leverage of emotional rejection to bring one's life into line, for such would only deepen the selfish grasping that led him to his sin in the first place. He knew that God desired not groveling self-mortification but "truth in the inward being"(Ps. 51:6, R.S.V.). And God's loving acceptance made it easier for him to face that painful truth about his weaknesses.

THROW OFF EVERY ENCUMBRANCE!

We must throw off every encumbrance, every sin to which we cling. Heb. 12:1, N.E.B.

For many Christians the concept of sin centers on an angry God. "Jesus loves us, but God the Father . . . ? Didn't Jesus have to die to get God to accept us? Sins are those things we do that make God mad—mad enough that someone has to pay the price, even though we stop doing them."

Though not painted with wild berry dye or adorned with carnivore teeth, these ideas belong to the heathen who serve their gods from fear. To obey God because we think He will remove His protective care from us if we don't is only one step removed from offering incense to a wooden idol. To say we obey God because we love Him, and still "know" that our disobedience will incur His certain wrath, is to play a painful game of theological charade.

Realistically, if a branch is severed from the tree it will die, but not because the tree is angry at the branch. When our first parents allowed their doubts about God to sever their relationship with Him, God knew that they had no other means of survival. In order to give them (and us) the chance to understand this reality, God chose to allow that reality to be fulfilled on the cross. But not for a moment was it vengeance.

Why, then, has God used such words as wrath and vengeance in Holy Scripture? I think God meets us where we are. We do the same with our children, explaining things to them in a way they can understand, fully expecting them to grow into far more adequate explanations. To tell your college-age son that he needs to put oil in his car to keep it "happy" would be an insult to his intelligence. (Will his car not run, then, because it is "mad"?)

The problem with sin is not that it makes God angry but that it encumbers *us!* It keeps us from realizing that God is our life Source. More than that, He is our quality of life! More than electricity in our brain, He is our encouragement to reason; more than strength to our limbs, He is our inspiration to climb to the heights.

God is interested in more than our survival; He is interested in the quality of our lives and, in direct relationship to this, the quality of our union with Him—our life source and our friend.

TRUTH IN ADVERTISING

He came to the disciples and found them asleep; and he said to Peter, "What! Could none of you stay awake with me one hour?" Matt. 26:40, N.E.B.

The lush sounds of happy voices singing in close harmony poured smoothly from the Christian radio station. I listened carefully to the lilting lyrics, perfectly matched to the upbeat melody, trying to imagine what a non-Christian might feel and understand were he to hear the song. "Just brush away your tears and forget your foolish fears, and you'll never be lonely again."

It seemed so inviting, so promising: Become a Christian and you'll never again feel sadness or loneliness. If Christianity could always deliver what its "advertisers" promise, who wouldn't want to "buy it"?

But my memory tracked to a recent conversation with a Christian mother who had been abandoned by her husband. Though her faith in Jesus remained strong, she wept tears not easily brushed away. After years of closeness she was experiencing a crushing longing for human companionship. And her grief was being compounded by guilt. "As a Christian," she said, "I know I'm not supposed to feel so sad. I know Jesus still loves me. I'm letting Him down too."

And so we spoke of the feelings Jesus had on that lonely night as He agonized in the garden. We spoke of how He longed to have His disciples join with Him in prayer. Not because He had any doubts about the effectiveness of His own prayers, but because He craved the warmth of caring, supportive friendship, and because He wished for His friends to be strengthened for the raging conflict to come.

He who grieved in the garden that night was none other than He who created us in His own image, and who said, "It is not good that the man should be alone" (Gen. 2:18). He placed within each of His created friends a deep and wholesome longing for each other. The agonizing and groaning of all creation originates in our separateness from God and from each other. There will be no inner tranquillity in any of us who long for closeness with estranged friends while those friends are still outside of fellowship with us.

Our Father does not shame us for being lonely and frightened. We need not be embarrassed to face the very needs that He placed in our hearts. He does not plan to eradicate our humanity but rather to sustain it with His closeness while we walk through this dark planet of broken relationships.

OUR NEXT OF KIN

Now spread your skirt over your servant, because you are my next-of-kin. Ruth 3:9, N.E.B.

A most beautiful story of loyalty, obedience, and redeeming love is chronicled in the book of Ruth. It is also a description of how our loving God deals with us.

Ruth was not an Israelite by birth, but rather by marriage. Widowed while still a young woman, she lived in Moab with Naomi, her mother-in-law, who also was widowed. When Naomi decided to return to her home country in Judah, Ruth journeyed with her, pledging her life to her mother-in-law's people and God. In due time she married Boaz, one of her father-in-law's kinsmen, thereby assuring herself and her family a place in the lineage and inheritance of Israel.

In this story is a touching portrait of God as He deals with us who are born "separate from Christ, strangers to the community of Israel, outside God's covenants and the promise that goes with them." We were "without hope and without God. But now in union with Christ Jesus [we] who once were far off have been brought near through the shedding of Christ's blood" (Eph. 2:12, 13, N.E.B.).

Boaz is an example of God's tender regard for us. We see how deliberately tactful are His ways of dealing with us. We hear His comforting words to us that we need not look elsewhere to have our wants supplied, that we will not be reproached for seeking fulfillment. We are even invited to dine with Him and, in doing so, to discover that there is more than enough to satisfy us. In every way He is gentle.

The most poignant scene in the biblical narrative is Ruth's approach to Boaz the night he winnowed barley at his threshing floor. Her actions were purposeful, his response full of assurance and acceptance. As her next of kin—"one of them that hath the right to redeem" (Ruth 3:9, K.J.V., margin)—he pledged his intentions toward her, symbolically covering her with his robe.

God longs to have us understand that He is *our* next of kin, that He desires to exercise His right to redeem us and will gladly cover us with His robe—His righteousness. His eagerness is portrayed in verse 18, "He will not rest until he has settled the matter today" (N.E.B.).

We need not fear! All we need to do is *ask*.

COMMANDED OR ENABLED?

Love does no wrong to a neighbor; therefore love is the fulfilling of the law. Rom. 13:10, R.S.V.

The military model of obedience seems so promising! If a drill sergeant can bark, "Flank, left!" to his squad and they immediately pivot in unison, then why can't a father yell, "Chew with your mouth closed!" to his kids and never again have to hear them slosh their vegetables? If a colonel can shout, "Over that hill!" and see his troops charge, why can't Mom say, "Wash those dishes!" and see the suds fly?

The military model contains all the ingredients assumed necessary to make obedience happen: a person in charge, a clear command, and submissive people ready to follow orders. What else does one need? If the children aren't ready to follow orders, the parents only have to increase the threat of pain.

If the military model is so popular, then why can't a preacher accomplish marvelous results when he stands in the pulpit and essentially commands his congregation to stop sinning? We may question whether the preacher and the military commander have much in common, since the insubordinate soldier can be court-martialed—a recourse denied to preachers (at least in this modern age). But if you look closely, you will see that the preacher can "pull rank" on even a five-star general, for he can quote Scripture. And we all know what Ultimate Authority is behind Scripture!

But does God Himself use the military model in solving the sin problem? Is the command "Thou shalt not bear false witness against thy neighbour" just the same as the command "Column, left!"? Doesn't instant, unquestioning obedience represent the ideal for a Christian soldier?

The military model breaks down when we encounter today's text. We know that it is possible to command a certain outward behavior. But God promises more for us than mere outward compliance; He intends that we might be deeply and inwardly changed. He wants His people not to be nervously jumping at the commands of a divine drill sergeant. He wants us acting out—with the highest sense of freedom—the glad promptings of our own loving hearts.

And a loving heart is not commanded; it is enabled. It is not ordered into action; it is loved into wholeness. I do not see our Father shouting, "Stop your lying!" I see Him, with warm heart and tender smile, loving my wounded heart into wholeness, making me so secure in His love that I no longer *need* to lie.

March 5

RUINED BEYOND REPAIR

Now at last restore what was ruined beyond repair. Ps. 74:3, N.E.B.

All of us have had the experience of having something we really value ruined beyond repair. Our dismay can be agonizing. A sense of loss can dog our days, incapacitating us. The worst of it is that we have no hope of recovery.

Enemy forces had destroyed the most precious thing known to Israel: the sanctuary. However, more than the tabernacle lay in ruins. Their relationship with God had virtually been obliterated because of their pursuit of the customs of the heathen nations around them. As far as human resources went, it was a hopeless situation on both counts.

Nevertheless, as our text today indicates, the psalmist realized another factor: God! He knew that God was intimately identified with His people, that His love for them went beyond their foolish and evil choices. And because of this knowledge he found hope, not in circumstances but in *God!*

This is an important realization. Many Christians wait for circumstances to improve before they "indulge" in hope. When the worst happens and whatever they have been praying for is "ruined beyond repair," they are devastated. Their faith is so weakened that they lose heart. Some may even give up the whole Christian walk; others simply cease to function vitally, becoming denominational fixtures rather than "fishers of men." Who can "fish" with no bait? Who can hope without faith?

The wise man wrote, "Where there is no vision, the people perish" (Prov. 29:18). In the truest sense, where there is no vision of who God is, people will lose hope. My faith must rest in a Person—apart from circumstances. Circumstances can reveal the workings of God, but they also can cloud my vision of Him. Only when I come to know God—that He is fair and logical, trustworthy and loving, and intimately identified with *me*—will my faith and hope be in *Him* (1 Peter 1:21).

We may ask God to restore what is ruined beyond repair in our lives, knowing that He is well able to do so. But let our hope be cast higher than the things we seek. Let us fix in our minds the truth that God always intends the very best for us. Knowing that the circumstances of our lives can in no way thwart His purposes, let us be full of assurance that He delights in our restoration. Then we will not hope in vain!

70

WHAT PLEASES GOD?

Without faith it is impossible to please him. For whoever would draw near to God must believe that he exists and that he rewards those who seek him. Heb. 11:6, R.S.V.

A young girl works diligently to clean her room before her mother arrives to inspect the results. Mother surveys the handiwork and purrs her satisfaction. "This really pleases me," she says. Daughter later learns that Mother is pleased also by flowers on her birthday and by sweet willingness to obey.

How easy it is, then, for the daughter to draw conclusions about how to please God. She is sure that God requires good behavior, or even special favors, in order to be pleased with her. The word *pleased* implies that she has finally measured up to some standard of performance that He accepts as adequate.

But a mother's heart knows that this is not the case. Mother is delighted not with the clean room, but with the daughter herself. The birthday flowers are special, not just because of their color and aroma, but because of the warm mother-daughter relationship that they express. It is not her daughter's performance, but her loving presence in her life, that brings the mother such delight.

The Father, the Son, and the Holy Spirit were enjoying the most perfect love relationship among themselves. There is only one way in which a perfect love relationship can be enhanced, and that is by increasing the number of people who enjoy it! And so the Father, Son, and Holy Spirit created the human race. They wanted to share the delights of fellowship with more persons who are able to enter into that joy.

This informed, loving, mutually enjoyed fellowship is the essence of the faith relationship. That is what Satan has destroyed in the Fall. And that is what God wants to restore. Nothing short of this will bring Him delight, for nothing short of this meets the purpose in our creation.

While it is not our performance but our fellowship that brings God delight, certainly nothing is more powerful to produce proper performance in His people than the vital reality of that very fellowship!

But Paul has yet another surprise for us in this text. He says that God will reward those who earnestly seek Him. But with what shall He reward them? If they seek a fish, will He reward them with a stone? If they seek God Himself, will He reward them with anything less than the very thing they seek—personal, life-giving fellowship with Himself?

DUST AND WATER MAKE THE RAIN

Let us know, let us press on to know the Lord; his going forth is sure as the dawn; he will come to us as the showers, as the spring rains that water the earth. Hosea 6:3, R.S.V.

I love the spring rains! Usually gentle, they gladden the earth with freshness, bringing moisture and life to dormant seeds hidden in the earth. In today's text our good God likens Himself to spring rains. But there is more to this passage than first meets the eye. There is an invitation to press on to know Him, to understand how He has chosen to work.

What is rain? Is it simply water in the sky? Yes, and more. It is water that has formed a droplet around a bit of dust. That is our first clue: water and dust combined in such a way as to bring moisture to the earth—a parable in nature to teach us the ways of the Almighty.

The elements themselves are simple, and equally simple their metaphors: God has declared the truth about Himself to be like living water (John 4:10); "we are dust" (Ps. 103:14). And His purpose is clear: "For it is the time to seek the Lord, that he may come and rain salvation upon you" (Hosea 10:12, R.S.V.).

The intriguing thing about rain is that it cannot be formed without the presence of dust. The intimation, then, is that God does not bring the truth about Himself (who is our salvation) to this world apart from human involvement. The perfect example of this is, of course, the incarnation of Christ. In Him divinity and humanity were blended into a perfect revelation of the character of God.

In our modern world the most convincing argument in favor of God is our changed lives. Enthralled by the genuineness of His love, we ourselves become more loving. Esteeming His wisdom, we become more judicious. Satisfied by His reasonableness, we are drawn to that which is rational. Inspired by His innovativeness, we seek out discovery and growth.

Indeed, thoroughly persuaded that everything about God absolutely makes the best sense for our lives, we long for all the qualities of His character to become our own. Moreover, we long to be united forever to Him whom we find to be altogether lovely. It is by this union that God brings the truth of who He is to our world. This is His sweet spring rain.

MERMAIDS AND THE TREE OF KNOWLEDGE

But the serpent said to the woman, "You will not die." Gen. 3:4, R.S.V.

Most of us have heard the ancient myth about mermaids. The story has it that these lithe creatures, with the lower torso of a fish and the upper torso of a beautiful woman, would surface in the sight of passing ships. Using their feminine charms, they would coax homesick sailors to join them in the brine for a sporting romp.

According to the old fable, more than one sailor found the appeal overwhelming, plunged overboard, and immediately met tragic results, not necessarily because this kind of romp was labeled as "sinful" but because sailors just aren't made to live under water. To believe the mermaids was more than just an unfortunate mistake; it was deadly.

The problem with Adam and Eve in eating the fruit from the forbidden tree is not that they had offended the dictums of an arbitrary or jealous God. Their mistake was not that they had eaten a fruit that God had labeled as "sinful." Distracted by the promised enticements of the enemy, they (as did the sailors with the mermaids) ignored the fact that they simply could not live apart from union with the Life-giver.

Their mistake was more than a tactical blunder; it was a deadly delusion. Just as sailors cannot breathe under water, so God's creatures cannot live apart from their ultimate Source of Life.

For centuries theologians have suggested that God simply picked two trees in the garden and arbitrarily said one of them was good and the other was bad. Then He told His people that they could prove their obedience by eating only from the right tree. The problem with eating from the wrong tree, of course, was that it offended God, allowing Satan to just sit back and grin while an angry God unleashed His wrath on sinners. Or so the old theologians said.

The mermaid story is just a harmless old myth. There is, however, no more fundamental question in the universe than whether God's creatures can live apart from a relationship with their God. Is sin (that is, separation from God) really all that bad? Will it really produce the second death? Satan said that it would not. God said that it would. Who was telling the truth?

The answer was demonstrated in most dramatic terms on a rugged cross when Jesus showed the universe how bad sin really is.

FRIENDS WITH GOD!

No longer do I call you servants, for the servant does not know what his master is doing; but I have called you friends, for all that I have heard from my Father I have made known to you. John 15:15, R.S.V.

Friends! To call someone your friend is to be willing to be identified personally with that individual. This is different from just being friends *to* someone—that can denote a certain amount of condescension and a definite separation of your persons. To say that someone is your friend is to say that you not only like him, you trust him.

I am Jesus' friend! If He were still here on this earth, He would seek me out so that we could spend time together. I know that, before long, our conversation would center upon the Father, for that is what Jesus likes best to talk about. And as we spoke together He would share with me the things that the Father wants me to hear (John 17:8). He would remind me that the Father Himself loves me (chap. 16:27). As He continued to speak I would begin to understand: The Father considers me His friend, too!

To be Jesus' friend is a wonderful thing. Why, we know that even little children are safe with Him. We know that when Jesus was here He made Himself available to mankind. He was touchable, reachable—but as to God the Father . . .

When I first began to conjure a picture of God in my mind, He was always seated in a heavy oak chair beside an equally imposing desk, with a bookcase full of thick dark books that reached to the ceiling as the backdrop. At my approach He would turn His majestic head in my direction. Though I could never mentally fill in the details of His face, He was not smiling. I knew He accepted me, even cared deeply for me, but I felt it was strictly because of Christ. I'd never stand a chance if it weren't for His intercession. It had nothing to do with God *liking* me.

My picture of God has changed. The heaviness and darkness are gone. In my mind, He is out of doors, the wind gently blowing at His garments. As I approach He moves quickly and eagerly toward me. Though I still cannot fill in the details of His face, He is smiling. Even more, I can almost hear Him saying, ''I've been waiting for you! I've so much to share with you!''

I am God's friend!

FIG LEAVES OR LAMBSKINS

Then the eyes of both were opened, and they knew that they were naked; and they sewed fig leaves together and made themselves aprons. Gen. 3:7, R.S.V.

Fig leaves and nakedness—they seem such quaint concepts, the kind of thing medieval artists would like to paint in dark tones. But what might they mean to us today? Did Adam and Eve's sin suddenly make their bodies unfit to behold? Is there a deeper meaning to these symbols?

Do you know what it's like to feel naked in the presence of another? Do you ever wish that you could hide all the secret fears and regrets, all the past failings and foolishness, that surely would embarrass you should others find out about them? None of us enjoys having our soul exposed and vulnerable to the eyes and judgments of others.

And so we sew fig leaves together. They come in all shapes and sizes too. There is the young woman who has become a skilled flirt. She craves the attention of the opposite sex because down inside she is fearful that she may be unnoticed, unloved, unclaimed. Flirtation becomes her attempt to hide the hurt, to cover the loneliness.

There is the young man who punctuates his language with slang and oaths, hoping in this way to make his words more powerful, his impact on others more stunning. Yet he does not see that he is poorly covering his naked fear of being regarded as of no account.

The devil has a thousand fig leaves, each one promising to cover some nakedness, some gaping fear that is rooted in our separation from the Lover of our souls. They all promise immediate safety from the gaze of others. But they are all ill-fitting and awkward. And we spend all our energies trying to keep them from slipping.

Our God, who is not scandalized by our nakedness, knows the inner longings of our souls. He knows that our dread of exposure arises from Satan's lie that God will be disgusted with our weaknesses—and that we will be rejected by others should they see us as we are. And so the Father comes to us bearing a smile and a hand-tailored garment, prepared at great expense.

"And the Lord God made for Adam and for his wife garments of skins, and clothed them" (Gen. 3:21, R.S.V.). There is only one way you can obtain a lambskin, and that is by sacrificing the lamb. The cross first covers, and then heals, our nakedness!

WHY GOD GAVE US A MEDIATOR

For there is one God, and there is one mediator between God and men, the man Christ Jesus. 1 Tim. 2:5, R.S.V.

We all know it by heart: Jesus stands before the judgment bar of God, pleading His blood for our pardon. He is our mediator. Is there an implied reticence on God's part to accept the likes of us? If Jesus were suddenly to stand aside, would God's face drop into a menacing scowl, His lips parting with words of our impending destruction?

Jesus said that the Father Himself loves us (John 16:27), that because He loves us so much, He sent His Son into the world, not to make sure we know how mad He is with us, but to help us understand that He has made provision for us to be reunited once again with Him (chap. 3:16, 17). That provision is Jesus.

The problem always has been that we are afraid of God. It started in Eden when our first parents hid from Him. Having acted wrongly, they must have thought that He had come "gunning" for them. Their fears were never confirmed. Quite the opposite! God told them of the plan He had to reinstate their friendship. It involved a mediator.

But why a mediator? Consider: We are afraid of God, afraid that when we do wrong He'll come gunning for us. It makes us hide from Him—hide in our life's work, our pretended indifference, our religious pretenses. We have many ways to hide. And all because we do not understand that God's attitude toward us has never changed! Our fears will never be confirmed. Meanwhile, in His loving and practical way, God has addressed the problem that our fear creates. He has kept His distance from us to calm our fears, sending Someone to explain to us the true situation. (That Someone was even born as a totally helpless infant, as if to underscore the "safeness" of His person!)

God is safe! In the judgment the blood Christ pleads is God's message to us that He's taken care of the results of our separation from Him. As we begin to understand that we need not hide from God, Christ can finally step aside. We no longer feel the need of having someone between us and the Father. Christ will then be given another task. He will be sent to bring us back into the Father's actual presence.

Amen. Come, Lord Jesus!

THE LONGINGS OF JESUS' HEART

"I will come back and take you to be with me, that you also may be where I am." John 14:3, N.I.V.

Our understanding of heaven takes its first shapes from the stories and pictures of childhood. I can recall the time when heaven seemed attractive to me for three reasons. I would be able to fly without effort, I would be able to play with a lion without fear, and I wouldn't have to pull weeds.

As I grew older and faced a few more of the realities of this sin-damaged world, I began to be drawn toward heaven because of its promised relief from pain and death. I have found that heaven can be craved as the end of poverty, war, prejudice, and even taxes! Unfortunately, our desires for heaven often fixate at these rather materialistic levels, and we fail to let God stir in us greater longings. We seldom even know what those desires should be.

So let us listen with our hearts to Jesus' own longings about heaven. What about heaven stirred Him to look forward to it with such eagerness? In His well-known farewell conversation with His disciples Jesus told them that He was returning to heaven to make preparations for His friends. But then He made a very personal promise. He said that He Himself would return for us, to "take you *to be with me* that you also may be where I am."

In Jesus' mind the most satisfying joys of heaven are not centered in its lovely architecture, its economy, or even its ecology. For Jesus, heaven is a great place to be with His friends—with *us!* Jesus knows that the greatest need of our hearts is not for a tame lion, quick transportation, or even a weed-free garden. Our greatest need is for a loving, trusting relationship with a close friend. We are, after all, made in His image. Those needs are a reflection of His own heart.

Of course, heaven will be a marvelously exquisite place, with nothing to mar its perfect joys and beauties. But that's just the way He does things for His friends. He did not intend that the tearless bliss of heaven should be a sop for our selfishness. Rather He intended that nothing should be in heaven that would detract from the enjoyment of its truest essence: loving, growing friendships.

Wouldn't you love to spend eternity with such a Saviour?

GOD SPEAKS WORDS OF COMFORT

It was God who sent me ahead of you to save men's lives. Gen. 45:5, N.E.B.

One of the most familiar stories in the Old Testament is that of Joseph. Though sold into Egyptian slavery by his older brothers, his integrity dominates the narrative. He demonstrated unbudging allegiance to the living God and epitomized the triumph of good over evil in the face of insurmountable odds. In his tumultuous life is portrayed the essence of who God is and how He relates to fallen mankind.

As our text today expresses, Joseph, as a type of Christ, was sent by God into Egypt to act the part of savior to His people. It is important to note, however, that physical relief, welcome as it may have been, was only the most obvious evidence of God's marvelous dealings with Israel. For in the person of Joseph was expressed some of the most sublime characteristics of our great God.

With all the power of the Egyptian monarchy behind him, Joseph's attitude toward his brothers, those hateful betrayers of his youth, was extraordinary. Certainly he would have had every reason, every "right," to extract from them at least some retribution for their treacherous act in selling him to Ishmaelite merchants. At the barest minimum, he could have justly reprimanded them severely for their heartless wickedness. Instead, Joseph *comforts* them! He invited them to "come closer" to him, to be assured that he did not want them to fear him because of what they had done. "I will take care of you," he told them with tears of gladness.

Joseph deemed it a privilege to nurture those that he undeniably could have counted as his enemies! Why? And in the same breath we might well ask why God would ever consider it a privilege to nurture *us*, rebels and conivers that we are! Why has God chosen humility instead of the potential use of His power? The answer is simple: *love*.

Love is its own reason. Why does a mother treasure any opportunity to look after the needs of her wayward teenager? Would she not speedily forget all past grievances in favor of a renewed relationship? Similarly, God joyfully counts our restored friendship with Him of supreme value. Like Joseph, He speaks comfortingly to us: "For I know the plans I have for you, says the Lord, plans for welfare and not for evil, to give you a future and a hope" (Jer. 29:11, R.S.V.).

WHAT IS GOODNESS?

Whoever wants to be first must be the willing slave of all. For even the Son of Man did not come to be served but to serve, and to give up his life as a ransom for many. Mark 10:44, 45, N.E.B.

The noted German philosopher Friedrich Nietzche defined *goodness* as that which enhances the sense of human power. Something is good if it gives one strength to dominate another. This is what enables one to survive in the evolutionary contest. The weak who are dominated and destroyed by the strong have no right to survive, according to the evolutionary scheme. Thus their destruction, said Nietzche, is good.

Jesus Christ held that goodness is found in serving the weak, in ministering to the struggling, and in nurturing the hurting. Jesus regarded people as of great value—products of His own creative act, not of mindless evolutionary processes. To neglect or downgrade the disadvantaged not only hurts these persons, but also dehumanizes the ones who so treat them, for it shreds our common humanity.

The philosophy of Nietzche laid the foundations for Dachau, Auschwitz, and Ravensbrück. The philosophy of Jesus Christ laid the foundations for hospitals, orphanages, and schools. People like Hitler and Goebbels counted themselves as disciples of Nietzche. People like William Carey and Albert Schweitzer count themselves as disciples of Jesus Christ.

We read our history books, and we find it easy to loathe the spirit of domination when we see its excesses and extremes. No one would defend the extermination of millions of Jews. Yet television violence is based on the same philosophy, and it has millions of devotees during prime time every week night.

What is more, the spirit of competition is one that prizes the domination of the weak by the strong. Rivalry leads one to care far more about the thrill of winning than about the hurt in the heart of the loser. As such, it is alien to the spirit of servanthood.

Jesus was not content just to sound a warning against the spirit of conquest and domination whenever He saw it happening. He spent His lifetime acting out the spirit of servanthood. Knowing full well that He was the King of kings, He knew also the spirit of His kingdom. He knew that He wanted the struggling to be aided, the injured to be healed, and the bashful to be made bold. And so He came as the servant of all.

Aren't you glad that He did?

NEW COATS FOR OLD WOUNDS

He provided each of them with a change of clothing. Gen. 45:22, N.E.B.

It is human nature for us to retaliate when we feel that we have been mistreated. Even as Christians, we might find our hearts struggling against "forbidden" emotions such as anger and defensiveness. To withdraw from the offender provides, at best, only temporary relief. And it leaves us to deal with the guilt we experience at having felt such negative emotions in the first place.

Does God understand? Or does He merely "keep score"—grimly noting when we fail or stoically approving our stiff-upper-lip "successes"? After all, He's God! What can He know of our miseries? Plenty! Acted out in the life of His Son, we behold our mistreated, misunderstood, and maligned God not just telling us how we should behave, but showing us Himself.

Another portrayal was through Jacob's son Joseph. Joseph had a beautiful coat of many colors. That coat was taken from him by his brothers, who callously sold him as a slave. Later they dipped his coat in blood and presented it to his father as proof of his demise. Far from dead, however, Joseph grew to be second only to Pharaoh in the land of Egypt. Years later famine forced his brothers to unwittingly seek sustenance from the very one they had so mercilessly mistreated. Joseph held no grudge against them. He not only gave them the food for which they asked, but he arranged for all their needs to be supplied in the coming years. And he "provided each of them with a change of clothing."

For the beautiful coat that had been taken from Joseph and dipped in blood, those brothers received coats, as it were, for themselves. Joseph could have supplied them with funds to purchase their own garments. Instead, in a gesture of sublime forgiveness, he himself clothed them. It was more than they had asked for, more than they expected or deserved. But by doing so, Joseph demonstrated his unconditional acceptance of them. They did not have to deal with his offended feelings. And so their relationship was healed.

What wondrous love! What inspiring sensitivity displayed in service of restored friendship! When I realize that this is exactly how God relates to me, my heart is tempered toward those who do me wrong. In them I see myself; and in me, I can only desire that they might see God.

GOD'S DISCIPLINE

They disciplined us for this short life according to their lights; but he does so for our true welfare, so that we may share his holiness. Heb. 12:10, N.E.B.

Imagine a father about to spank his misbehaving son. The distraught boy pleads for his dad to explain why this is necessary (probably more as a stalling tactic than as a quest for understanding). But Dad takes him seriously and tries to explain.

What would you think if the father were to say, "Son, I'm spanking you because you deserve it"? Or, "The law of the household requires it . . . and you have it coming"? Or worse yet, "You really annoyed me, and I'm getting it off my chest"?

Though we suspect that many parents do indeed spank their children for these reasons, we intuitively know that they just aren't adequate. None of them relate to the needs of the child. True discipline is done for the sake of imparting righteousness to our children—to help them walk in the paths of wholesomeness and blessing. It is not done for the sake of retaliation or merely upholding some abstract code of justice.

And since God is so much wiser than any of us, wouldn't we expect that God is redemptive and educative in all that He does as well? In all His dealings with us as His "misbehaving children," there is no hint of His being merely punitive or retaliatory. His actions are not spurred on by His annoyance with us or with our attitudes. Nor is He indignantly upholding "justice."

God's every action is specifically designed for our benefit. Righteousness (or rightdoing), embraced within our hearts, is His goal for us, and He wisely sets out to teach us how to live in harmony with His very real world. He is not content only to legally pronounce us as righteous; He wants us to think and choose and act in harmony with the principles of righteousness.

The central core of the sin problem is that we have turned God out of the center of our lives. Any remedy that does not restore that is just not equal to the problem. Our wise heavenly Father is not interested in "settling accounts" or "defending His dignity." He is interested in restoring a relationship with each one of His children. Discipline rises to its highest form in His hands: "disciple-ing," winning our free, thoughtful allegiance to Himself.

Should we be content with anything less?

WHEN GOD LAUGHS

Then our mouth was filled with laughter, and our tongue with shouts of joy; then they said among the nations, "The Lord has done great things for them." Ps. 126:2, R.S.V.

Somewhere, somebody started a rumor that God doesn't laugh. Once I heard some astute Bible students heatedly discussing this issue. In all earnestness one young man solemnly declared, "The only time God laughs is when He scorns the wicked!"

I could easily have dismissed his statement but for the haunting awareness that there are probably many others who share his opinion. And I'm just not convinced that if you trade the "stern judge" image of God for a straight-faced Redeemer you gain much ground. Either concept leaves one feeling nervous about actually meeting Him face-to-face someday.

Nothing stifles laughter more than being in the presence of a power figure who is straight-faced. Often these figures use their solemnity to control situations. There is the high school teacher who is sure that if he mingles mirth with instruction his classroom will become unruly. And there is the board chairman who feels that any levity will hinder progress in getting through the agenda.

In other words, to keep control, don't laugh. So, since God has to keep us in control, He doesn't dare laugh. Wrong! God's preferred method of "keeping control" includes our coming to feel absolutely comfortable in His presence again. He doesn't need to manipulate us by His solemnity. He transforms us by His love. And (ask any child) laughter is that warm canopy that allows two hearts to tug the relationship closer and closer because they are so secure.

When God's people reflect that security, the nations will know it! One of the "great things" God has done for us is to restore in us that secure and joyful friendship with Him that our first parents knew in Eden. And we won't be the only ones who will be filled with laughter and shouts of joy! Listen: "The Lord, your God, is in your midst . . . ; he will rejoice over you with gladness, he will renew you in his love; he will exult over you with loud singing ["a shout of joy," N.E.B.] as on a day of festival" (Zeph. 3:17, 18, R.S.V.).

Renewed in His love! Rejoicing and singing! Mouths full of laughter at the sheer pleasure of knowing God not only as our redeemer but as our friend! And it's mutual! Restored into His image, we will once again reflect His joy.

COMMANDING RELATIONSHIP

"Which commandment is first of all?" Jesus answered, "The first is, '. . . Love the Lord your God with all your heart, with all your soul, with all your mind, and with all your strength.' " Mark 12:28-30, N.E.B.

There is such an incredible contrast of ideas in this verse that most people just don't grasp it in the first reading! So try to imagine the setting for this dramatic encounter.

Jesus was talking with a group of devoutly religious people. They were awesomely intent on doing absolutely everything that was required of them lest they miss out on salvation. And since the list of required actions was becoming quite long, allowing the chance that something might fall through the cracks, they wanted to make sure they at least mastered the most important requirement. So they asked Jesus which one that was.

Jesus' reply was completely unexpected. He said, in essence, "Your most important focus is not upon a thing to be done, but upon an intense, total, all-consuming relationship with a Person, whom one could indeed love."

Behavior versus relationship. We are still too often hung up on that distinction. For example, we might enter into a brisk discussion on the question Is it a sin to go hiking on the Sabbath? Some might want to consider how far we would walk, what we might wear, where the walk would take us—wanting carefully to avoid doing a wrong act.

But I suspect that Jesus would want us to ask, "Will it add to, or detract from, my relationship with my Friend?" And I am sure that Jesus would want us to be so enthralled with our heavenly Friend that we wouldn't regard the protecting of that friendship as an imposition upon our desires.

From Jesus, a "command" is not a do-it-or-else threat but rather an expression of His very strong desire for His people. And that desire is not just for actions we can "paste on" the outside of our lives. Rather it is for a relationship with Him that will produce an inner change—which in turn will produce the right outward actions.

When God "assembled" Adam in the garden, He breathed right into Adam's soul an intense longing for his Creator—a longing rich with trust, love, and dependence. Then God woke Adam and entered his life as the fulfillment of that very desire. Jesus now admonishes each of us to return to that original, rightful state for all mankind.

POWER TO TEACH

Jesus came and spake unto them, saying, All power is given unto me in heaven and in earth. Go ye therefore, and teach all nations. Matt. 28:18, 19.

The morning newspaper states that a very criminal person has been "let off the hook" because of some legal technicality. And taxes have been raised again, to support government spending. You do not approve. Under your breath you mutter, "If I were in control, things sure would be different!"

Each of us has experienced, to one degree or another, such sentiments. In the days of Christ it was the overriding consensus of the Jewish nation. Roman control was galling. But God had promised a Deliverer! He would rid them of their heathen rulers! He would come with *power!* Yes, things surely would be different then! So they waited, and they hoped. And One walked among them in the common garb of the day. His feet were as dusty as were theirs. He paid taxes. His hands were the hands of a lowly workingman. Yet . . .

In His eyes were the fires of nobility. His voice was strong, certain. He neither flinched from the piercing reproaches of the Temple priests nor recoiled from daily contact with the Roman guards that ever intruded into Jewish affairs. His unstated authority was worn as naturally and as unpretentiously as was His homespun mantle. Excitement mounted among the people.

When would He assert Himself? When would He take over? Even as He rode triumphantly into Jerusalem, such questions were exploding in the hearts of those who shouted and praised God along the way. The disciples felt it all. Perplexed, they whispered among themselves. What was He waiting for? And then came Gethsemane. Then Calvary. "Use Your *power!*" He was taunted.

Beloved Master, You were using Your power! In the most prudent ways, You revealed God's choicest use of power—to enlighten darkened minds and heal the sin-weary spirit of mankind. Rather than simply controlling the sin problem with divine firepower, You revealed that God desires to resolve it by giving us truth. The truth about Himself.

Later, just before You left this earth to take up Your continuing ministry in the courts above, You made it absolutely clear. As if to dispel any lingering doubts as to the quality or quantity of the power available to You—and, in turn, to us—You assured Your disciples that all power had been given unto You. Then You said, "Go ye therefore, and teach . . . ."

JUDGED FOR TRUTH-REJECTING

There is a judge for the man who rejects me and does not accept my words; the word that I spoke will be his judge on the last day. John 12:48, N.E.B.

So often we are prone to think of the final judgment in terms of God's examination of our sinful acts. We think of the books of record in heaven as having noted every wrong deed of our lives, with the intent that none of them will escape God's righteous reckoning on that fateful day.

But some are puzzled by the promise that God has forgiven our sins, casting them into the depths of the sea. That seems to be a contradiction with their view of the final judgment. Why bring them up again if they've already been forgiven? The dilemma is so distressing that some reject the idea of final judgment altogether. Others, feeling that it is only right that God condemn actual wrongs, doubt that God has indeed forgiven sins.

The problem, however, stems from assuming that the judgment (indeed, the whole plan of redemption) is focused upon the deed done, the act of sin. In today's passage Jesus is seeking to shift our attention from the deed to its cause. Jesus sees the sinful deed as being caused by people who have rejected Him, and thus His Father. He knows that people have rejected Him because they are enshrouded with darkness—the darkness of Satan's deceptions about God.

And so Jesus says, "I have come into the world as light, so that no one who has faith in me should remain in darkness" (John 12:45, N.E.B.). Jesus wanted to turn on the lights, because "when a man believes in me, he believes in him who sent me" (verse 44, N.E.B.). Obviously Jesus' interest was not in keeping track of deeds but in healing the cause of those deeds.

Jesus offered forgiveness, not only for sinful deeds but even for the broken relationship that led to the sinful deeds. But when people reject His revelation of truth, truth about His Father, which alone can heal the broken relationship, they are now guilty of a new offense. They are confronted in the judgment with the question of what they have done with truth.

And since Jesus is the light that lights every man (John 1:9), each person shall identify how he has responded to Jesus' gracious, reconciling revelations of His Father. Should the judgment reveal that I have rejected winsome truth, Jesus needs to say nothing more.

GOD'S OBLIGING LOVE

He said to him, "I grant your request: I will not overthrow this town you speak of." Gen. 19:21, N.E.B.

A young Christian once told me that she secretly was terrified that God might let something terrible happen to her so as to test her faith in Him! God does not condemn us for such fears. He just tenderly comforts us and sets about to better win our confidence.

We find an example of this in the story of Lot, Abraham's nephew. God counted Lot a righteous man despite the fact that he evidently was not resting wholly in God's providence. Even though Lot basically cared about God and others—otherwise he would not have put himself in such dire circumstances to protect two strangers from degradation at the hands of the local townsmen—he felt a need to watch out for himself.

Nonetheless, when it came time to destroy Sodom, the city in which Lot lived, God sent two angels to lead Lot and his family to safety. He was directed to flee quickly to the hills. Lot replied, "You have shown your servant favour and you have added to your unfailing care for me by saving my life." Sadly, though, he finished, "But I cannot escape to the hills; I shall be overtaken by the disaster, and die" (Gen. 19:19, N.E.B.). He pleaded to be allowed to escape to a nearby town ("it is a little one" [verse 20]) in order to save his life!

How shortsighted! As if to say that if he couldn't run fast enough, God might allow him to perish after all!

God knew that condemning Lot wouldn't solve his problem. It never solves anyone's problems. So God's obliging love met Lot where his felt needs were. "I grant your request," the angel said. Then, trying to nudge Lot out of his misconceptions concerning God's intentions toward him, the angel again told him to hurry, "because I can do nothing until you are there" (verse 21, N.E.B.). In other words, "God isn't playing games with you! He wasn't going to have me do anything, anyway, until you were completely taken care of."

God was not indulging Lot. He was pointedly seeking to win Lot's confidence and, by doing so, encourage him to allow his relationship with God to deepen. God understands that only as we come to know that His loving ways for us are altogether adequate will our fears finally be resolved (1 John 4:18).

UPWARD MOBILITY

To him who is victorious I will grant a place on my throne, as I myself was victorious and sat down with my Father on his throne. Rev. 3:21, N.E.B.

Many years ago a television comedy series featured a family of backwoods hillbillies who had struck sudden wealth and moved to Beverly Hills in California. As they fed their pigs in the marble fountains and wore overalls in the velvet-and-lace dining room, the humor unfolded. It was humor based on the absurdity of people relocated into a palace, yet bearing the mind-set and style of the "sticks."

Though the plot was all a spoof, it does suggest one important insight for many in Western society who are "upwardly mobile," who are seeking to upgrade their status in life. True nobility is based not on the lavishness of one's residence, but on the spirit and values of one's mind.

Many writers have scoffed at upward mobility, the quest for wealth and position, because it usually leads to greed and exploitation. Yet, in its truest spirit, I believe that upward mobility was God's idea for us right from the start. He created us for fellowship with the King of the universe! Even after the Fall He still fully intends that we should once again be restored to sit with Him on His throne. Now, *that's* upward mobility!

But that incredible "rise" in social status is not simply a relocation into a magnificent palace. People will not inhabit the palace above who have not here on earth learned the language and spirit of the palace. And this will not be found by shopping at the palace-makers of earth, but rather by giving attention to the matters of the heart.

The English writer John Ruskin said it well: "He only is advancing in life whose heart is getting softer, whose blood warmer, whose brain quicker, whose spirit is entering into living peace. And the men who have this life in them are the true lords or kings of the earth—they, and they only."

Perhaps we should question why we so often hold such a dim view of ourselves when God has such a settled opinion of our destiny and our worth. Nor would a proper appraisal of our destiny lead us to pride or arrogance, for pride, when seen for what it is, is but a cheap compensation, a thin cover-up, for a low self-esteem. But we are children of the King!

FOOLPROOF SALVATION

The faith that leads to righteousness is in the heart, and the confession that leads to salvation is upon the lips. Rom. 10:10, N.E.B.

Most of us become a little suspicious when we hear or read of "foolproof" claims, such as the money-back guarantee that you can lose from two to six inches from your waistline in just one hour if you wear a special body wrap. Or that foolproof plan whereby you can make more than $10,000 a year without ever leaving your home. We know there's a catch somewhere.

In a similar way, "just believe" has almost become a cliché among Christians. Yet many are sucked heartachingly into this oversimplified injunction. They *do* believe, but find themselves relying on their own emotional discipline in order to sustain the assurance of salvation promised. And since everyone has "down" days, the assurance comes and goes like the morning mists. That's the catch.

It seems like a cruel trick. Misgivings about God's part in all this can easily give way to outright skepticism and eventual disenchantment. And if not disenchantment, then hopelessness. What is left if God's own foolproof plan has failed?

The problem is not with God's plan, but in our understanding of it. When we put the emphasis on ourselves, our belief, we will fail. It makes a contest of our emotions. To decide, instead, that the contest is with our intellect makes the problem only more complicated, for the intellect can easily serve a selfish heart.

The passions of the heart are unreliable if unguided by the integrity of our rational thinking. Many a child has been nearly ruined by the ill-measured indulgence of his parents. Our great God would have our hearts and minds balanced so as to bring wholeness into all our actions and interactions.

Therefore, He has ordained that with our minds we apprehend Him and with our hearts we hunger after Him. In so doing, we are led back into right relationship with Him. And this is our sure salvation.

ARE WE SAFE IN JESUS' PRESENCE?

So Mary came to the place where Jesus was. As soon as she caught sight of him she fell at his feet and said, "O sir, if you had only been here my brother would not have died." John 11:32, N.E.B.

A young wife and mother was sobbing her anguished prayer. "Father! Why did You let my husband die? Where were You? Did he not ask You to be with him the very day of the accident? Surely You would not have let this happen had You been there!"

There is a sentiment in that heart-wrenching prayer that is not far from many of us. Do we not start most every day with a prayer for God to be with us? And what is it that we wish to experience by His presence? Isn't it assumed that if He is present we will not face tragedy or heartache?

Certainly this is what Mary assumed when she confronted Jesus following Lazarus' death. She was certain that had He been there, nothing bad could have happened. Can't we identify with those feelings?

But what happens when tragedy does indeed happen to God's people? We quickly conclude either that God was not there or that He was powerless or uncaring while there. Seldom do we question our basic assumption about the effects of His presence.

You see, God's physical presence isn't the issue. Safety is assured not by being in His presence, but by being in His will. The focus of our prayers need not be that He should go with us but that we should walk in His paths, in harmony with His wise will.

Furthermore, the safety for which we should be the most concerned is not safety from disease, or even the first death. Lazarus himself was walking in Jesus' will, yet he died. But in the highest sense of the word he was safe. He was safe from the second death. As for that first death, Jesus simply called it a "sleep" and woke him up!

To long to be in Jesus' presence must mean so much more than wanting Him to be within shouting distance, or even being able to look Him in the eye. It must mean being united with Him in spirit, to sense the joy of harmony with Him in one's basic values. For only those who are close to Him in their souls will one day rejoice when He returns.

FROM RESTRAINT TO FELLOWSHIP

Now before faith came, we were confined under the law, kept under restraint until faith should be revealed. Gal. 3:23, R.S.V.

The quest for freedom begins in the cradle. It seems inbred in us to resist that which would inhibit our desires. Deep inside each of our hearts lives that passion for independence. Does the gospel mean to destroy that passion? Don't answer too quickly, for God Himself hails a certain kind of independence!

Certainly we are not talking about the independence that seeks to live contrary to God's government. That kind of freedom is always destructive to self and others and needs restraint. Notice, however, that our text today says, "kept under restraint *until*." The "until" implies an end to restraint, but does it imply an end to independence? Let us read on, using the Phillips translation of Galatians 3:24: Or, to change the metaphor, "the Law was like a strict tutor in charge of us until we went to the school of Christ and learned to be justified by faith in him."

Ah! There's the first key! Restrained until we have learned to be justified by faith in Him. And, as the text says, we shall learn this by going to the "school of Christ." What is taught in the school of Christ? Jesus Himself testified that He came to reveal to us the Father (John 17:4; Luke 10:22).

Therefore, we shall come to know the Father by studying the life of Christ. And in coming to know Him, our relationship with Him will be healed, or "set right," as the word *justify* implies. Having learned how good, how reasonable and adequate, are His ways, we will joyfully adhere to His counsel. As it was Christ's, it will be our meat and drink to do the will of God. Not because we *have* to (restraint), but because we *desire* it ourselves.

We desire it ourselves! That is the second key. What restraints need be applied to the driver who *wants* to drive safely? The restraints are in himself. Even so, his choices are still his own as to where he will travel. His independence is not at variance with the law; it is served by the law! For the law is not to abort independence but to guide us safely in our choices.

God created us to be more than restrained children. He created us to have fellowship with Him (1 John 1:1-3). By our own independent choice we may do just that.

THE WRONG ONE COMES FIRST

Then he will be revealed, that wicked man whom the Lord Jesus will destroy with the breath of his mouth, and annihilate by the radiance of his coming. But the coming of that wicked man is the work of Satan. 2 Thess. 2:8, 9, N.E.B.

Around this world millions of earnest, Bible-believing Christians are looking forward to the soon return of Jesus Christ. They are anticipating a dramatic pattern of events surrounding His coming: a time of terrible trial, the resurrection of the righteous dead, and the destruction of the wicked. But most important, these Christians are letting this blessed hope shape their daily lives. And I would hope that every reader of these pages would be included in this group!

Sometimes, however, Christians seem almost to compete with one another in asserting how quickly they believe Christ might return. It's as though the ones who believe He could come in a year are more devout than those who suspect ten years to be more likely.

There is a great risk involved for those whose primary concern about Christ's coming is its "soonness," and that is that the wrong "Christ" will get here first. Paul describes the fact that Satan, claiming to be Christ, will make a dramatic, deceptive appearing just prior to Christ's actual second coming. He will employ all his demonic, miracle-working power to sway the emotions of eager believers.

Satan is no fool; he will seek to approximate as closely as he can those qualities that many have hoped to find in Christ. He will heal the sick and even appear to raise the dead. And he will align himself with political powers to seek to enforce peace and unity in a fractured world. Those Christians who have believed all along that this is how God should solve the world's sin problems will gladly give their allegiance to him.

Every emphasis on the nearness of Christ's coming should be matched with a strong emphasis on just who it is who is coming. The manner and methods of Jesus should be so clear in our minds, in clear contrast to the manner and methods of Satan, that we shall be able to spot the impostor in spite of his drama and power. Every message to the world that Jesus is coming soon should include such a clear and attractive picture of His character that people will indeed be glad to see Him when He arrives!

THE COSTLIEST FREEDOM

By the open statement of the truth we would commend ourselves to every man's conscience in the sight of God. 2 Cor. 4:2, R.S.V.

Those of us whose families for several generations have been United States citizens too often take for granted the wonderful freedoms guaranteed to us by our Constitution. Our cradles were rocked by the great-granddaughters of the American Revolution—whose own cradles were made secure by established precedents of civil and religious liberty.

We have forgotten (or perhaps we never really understood) the price of our nationally celebrated freedoms. Undeniably, there was bloodshed and loss of life. However, there was something equally costly, something inherent in the framing of our Constitution. It is what made our nation unique among all other nations. In a nutshell, it is the concept that freedom of conscience should be guaranteed to all people, even though we recognize that some would misuse that very freedom.

Think about it! Would you, *should* you, give a person or people freedom when you know that they will possibly misuse it? It is not an easy question to answer, especially when it means the potential hurt of other innocent people. Yet in order to preserve the dignity and value of individuals, it is expedient that such freedom be allowed. In fact, it is for this very reason that God Himself has chosen freedom rather than force as the foundation of the government of heaven.

As our text today indicates, God desires our intelligent response to truth and our genuine allegiance to His kingdom. He is interested in the quality of our relationship with Him, not merely proper behavior. In order to preserve our ability to be open and candid in our friendship with Him, He has given us the real option of not agreeing with Him. The fact that He is our only source of life is revealed to our minds only because it is reality. It is not a threat; we may choose not to believe this.

What a testimony of God's faith in our ultimate destiny! We were created to enter into genuine, spontaneous friendship with Him and with all the other created beings of the universe. The cross of Calvary is an eternal testimony of the extent to which God has been willing to go to preserve that quality of friendship. Only as we begin to appreciate what it costs God to continue to guarantee us such freedom will we cherish every opportunity afforded us to improve our relationship with Him.

GOD DOES A GOOD JOB

Your beauty should reside, not in outward adornment—the braiding of the hair, or jewellry, or dress—but in the inmost centre of your being, with its imperishable ornament, a gentle, quiet spirit, which is of high value in the sight of God. 1 Peter 3:3, 4, N.E.B.

A friend once introduced me to a young woman with the following request: "I'd like you to meet Julia; will you please explain to her why your church discourages the wearing of jewelry?" It wasn't exactly the topic I would have chosen as a way of getting acquainted or of introducing her to my church! But the request had been made, and she seemed eager to know.

So we spoke of today's text and of the deeper issues Peter had in mind when he wrote it. It seems true that Satan is always seeking to destroy our self-worth. Every time we follow his path, we end up feeling less valuable, less lovely, less sure of our inner worth and true esteem in the eyes of others. Feeling so empty on the inside, we try to compensate by hanging decorations on the outside.

I suggested, however, that Christ's dealings with us are designed to restore and build our true sense of worth and dignity. To rest in His accepting love, to walk in His wise paths, to enjoy His kind of quality relationships, and to know the grand destiny He has for us all—these lead to a rebirth of true inner worth.

"And so," I concluded, "for a Christian to still be hanging the shiny little decorations on the outside would be to advertise that Christ hasn't done a very good job on the inside. Christ deserves better credit than that. He does a good job of restoring our self-esteem."

She nodded in understanding. "Do you know what my job is? I'm the representative for a leading costume jewelry company. My job includes teaching sales personnel how to sell jewelry. And that is exactly our pitch. Jewelry helps an insecure woman feel better about herself."

The Lord says, "You are my witnesses" (Isa. 43:10, R.S.V.). It is our privilege to portray in the most attractive light the quality of the work that our Father does as a skilled craftsman of the soul. No longer do we feel a need to resort to baubles, bangles, and beads to draw people's attention away from the gaping inner holes and frayed edges of the soul.

WEARING SUITABLE ARMOR

Put on the whole armor of God, that you may be able to stand against the wiles of the devil. Eph. 6:1, R.S.V.

Everybody has seen her. Her hair is always a little unkempt, her lipstick just a shade too bright, and her clothes too youthful for her mature years. Her eyes wander the room as she enters, as if she is looking for someone. She is.

We all know that she's "no good." She hasn't followed the rules and is now paying the price. If we could see into her past circumstances, perhaps we would see that she has been trying for all her years to compensate for deep feelings of inadequacy. Granted, it isn't the acceptable way to handle her problem, but it is evidently the only way she understands.

Our text today talks about standing against the wiles of the devil. The Phillips translation says it this way: "So that you can successfully resist all the devil's craftiness." So much of our bad behavior is really human caulking in the cracks of our hearts. Satan has access to us because of our broken relationship with our heavenly Father. He has totally misrepresented God's attitude toward us, leaving us susceptible to his suggestions as to how we may best cope in life.

There is an answer! We do not have to fall prey to the devil's trickery. We may put on "the whole armor of God"—*truth,* the truth about God and His attitude toward us, to gird the loins (figuratively, our vulnerability); *righteousness,* the restored right relationship between us and our God, as a breastplate (to cover our emotions); *the gospel of peace,* the good news of how God deals with fallen man, to shod our feet (to guide our way of dealing with each other); *faith,* that unshakable confidence we have in who God is, as our shield against the darts of the devil (to guard our right concepts about God); *the helmet of salvation,* that protective reality that we are safe with God (that necessary security in order for us to be able to make rational decisions); *the sword of the Spirit,* the Word of God (that divine, outside-of-us testimony to all these things).

Only as we allow God to cover us with His protective armor—with the truth about Himself, and by our restored relationship with Him—will we find no need to try to compensate for the endless emptiness of life apart from Him.

HOW TO FIGHT SIN

Come to your right mind, and sin no more. For some have no knowledge of God. I say this to your shame. 1 Cor. 15:34, R.S.V.

With her chin resting in her hand and with a scowl on her face, a young woman blurted out her perplexity about her boyfriend. "Why is it that he spends so much time in prayer and yet still does such stupid things? He's so immature, yet he is certain that we ought to get married! I don't spend nearly as much time in prayer as he does, yet I can see all kinds of reasons why we shouldn't get married. Doesn't prayer make a person think right?"

That's not a silly question. Though every Christian is soundly in favor of praying, we still know of too many times when we prayerfully made a decision we later knew to be the wrong one. And it's easy to think at those times that God let us down—that He didn't tell us what to do. Does prayer, in itself, lead to correctness and maturity of action?

Spiritual maturity is not something that God shoves into our minds. He does not wave His hands over our brains and infuse us with some type of spiritual magic by which we suddenly think only righteous thoughts of the highest quality. He made our minds to be educated. He created us with the capacity to process truth, and to handle it with clarity and integrity. And then He gave us the Holy Spirit to aid us in apprehending the deeper, spiritual meanings of truth.

Paul's invitation to come to our right mind is most specifically tied to his next sentence: "For some have no knowledge of God." That is the central core of the sin problem. To know God's great love for us is to trust His forgiveness, His caring, and His plans for our future. To know the Father's wisdom is to trust the total adequacy of His will, His law, and His guidance.

In essence, sin is the condition of being separated from the Father. It is alienation from God, which comes from believing that He is either hostile, indifferent, or irrelevant. To believe such things about God (and thus remain distant from Him), especially in view of all that Jesus has shown us about Him—that is the ultimate stupidity. Let's come to our right minds!

THE STORY THAT STARTS AT THE END

I have swept away your transgressions like a cloud, and your sins like mist; return to me, for I have redeemed you. Isa. 44:22, R.S.V.

At sometime we've all turned to the end of a book to discover how the story ends before we've read the whole narrative. There is something in us that can't wait! We've got to know! Does it turn out all right? Perhaps the deepest longing in our hearts is reflected in such acts of "peeking"—the longing to know that life is going to turn out all right for *us!*

Have we been left helplessly adrift in a chaotic universe? Is there any hope, any answer to the dilemma into which we were born—that is, our estrangement from God? God Himself has turned to the end of the book, as it were, that we might be comforted in the knowledge that life *will* turn out all right. We have only to return to Him.

Simple as this may sound, returning to God is not that easy if you feel very guilty about the choices you've been making in life, or if you are not at all sure what God will do with (or to) you when you return to Him. I believe many so-called atheists are not really rejecting the existence of God; they are rejecting the concept of a God with whom they could never feel secure. How, indeed, could everything turn out for the best if your concept of God leaves you wondering if you'd even *want* to spend eternal life with Him?

Is heaven just a place where there will be no more pain or sorrow or crying? a place where good food is never lacking and endless tomorrows are assured? Is eternal life merely the absence of death? Do we secretly wish we'd never have to face God, that somehow we could just get "lost in the crowd" on the sea of glass? Or is heaven a ceaseless approaching in sweetest fellowship to the One for whom our hearts long?

If we could but catch a glimpse of our greathearted Father sweeping away our misconceptions (the true source of our misbehavior) about Himself as He proclaims that He has made every provision for counterbalancing our years of separation from Him, would we not eagerly allow our lives to be reunited to Him?

In fact, God announced His intentions toward us even before we knew He cared! And He assures us, "I've made everything right. You can come *home!*"

MORE THAN SHED BLOOD

Indeed, according to the Law, it might almost be said, everything is cleansed by blood and without the shedding of blood there is no forgiveness. Heb. 9:22, N.E.B.

> There is a fountain filled with blood,
> Drawn from Emmanuel's veins;
> And sinners plunged beneath that flood,
> Lose all their guilty stains.
> —William Cowper

Dozens, perhaps even hundreds, of Christian hymns exalt the shed blood of Jesus Christ as the key to salvation. It is a constant theme in Christian literature, the central metaphor of many a sermon.

The blood of Christ, flowing from His hands and feet, His torn back and pierced brow, as He hung on the cross, is a symbol of a larger reality. Jesus' shed blood is a poetic metaphor, a graphic way of saying that He died for me, for shed blood leads to death.

Yet it is worth remembering that when the Roman soldier thrust the spear into Jesus' side (as recorded in John 19:34), there came out a flow of water and blood, indicating that He had already died of other causes. The blood had already separated into serum and platelets. Though blood is a symbol of Jesus' death, to know that His death was not caused by the loss of blood is important. The blood on Jesus' body revealed the cruelty of sinners against their Saviour, but it did not reveal what had caused His death.

For you see, the death that Jesus died in my place was the second death—that death that is caused by separation from the Life-giver. This is the consequence of sin that He bore in my place. The cross of Christ—or more accurately, the death of Christ on the cross—saves me from the second death, not necessarily from the first.

Jesus did not die because of the Roman soldier's spear. He did not die because of the nails in His hands and feet. He did not die because of the extreme agony of the cross, which was intended to be a slow torture leading to death after several days. He did not die from a loss of blood. Jesus died when His Father withdrew His life-giving presence from Him, thus verifying for all the universe just how deadly it is to separate from God.

GOD'S GREAT CONFIDENCE

But while he was still a long way off his father saw him, and his heart went out to him. He ran to meet him, flung his arms round him, and kissed him. Luke 15:20, N.E.B.

Sheila's mother's eyes were wide open as she lay in the darkness. At every new sound she held her breath and listened. The time was well past midnight, the weather was cold and rain was falling. Finally she arose, wrapped her bathrobe closely around her, and took up a position at the front room window. Straining her eyes into the darkness, she sat watching for her tardy teenage daughter.

Long ago a father watched for his wayward son, a son who had left for more than a night out on the town. In fact, he had asked for his inheritance and, upon receiving it, had left the country. It is doubtful that his father had even heard anything from him since then. Though our text today does not actually say that the father was watching, we know that he was by the description of what happened. "While he was still a long way off his father saw him." In the context of the story, there is only one reason for his father to be looking "a long way off."

Why did the father keep watching? Hope and love, of course, made him scan the horizon day after day. However, I believe there was something more: a sureness, a confidence born of knowing that he had dealt well with his son, and the faith that his son would someday remember his father's goodness and come home. And remember he did! Only he underestimated it! Perhaps if he had fully comprehended his father's virtues, he would not have left in the first place.

Dear reader, in this touching parable we have a picture of our heavenly Father that should both comfort and delight our hearts! We can safely surmise that God knows His goodness has power to draw us back to Himself; He need not threaten to yank us back by the scruff of our necks. In His very act of watching for us He reveals His faith in us that, given a chance to "come to our senses"—and in the parable that happened when the son began to think correctly about his father!—we will gladly return to Him.

Like the prodigal son, in returning to God, we find that He runs out to meet us with acceptance—with a crown!

THE BEST GIFT

He did not spare his own Son, but gave him up for us all; and with this gift how can he fail to lavish upon us all he has to give? Rom. 8:32, N.E.B.

There comes a Christmas in each person's life when, in spite of his youthful inexperience, he must make that bold step of purchasing gifts for the other members of the family. I think I was about 7 years old when my mother guardedly slipped several dollars into my hand and whispered that I should try to find a present for my dad.

While she busied herself at a dress shop I walked down the block to where my dad seemed to enjoy shopping. It was a hardware store. I was too bashful to ask for help from the clerk, so I found something colorful that I guessed I could afford, ignored the inquisitive look of the cashier when I paid for it, and took it home to wrap.

Dad was courteous when he opened it on Christmas morning, even when he asked me what it was. I didn't know. My family later figured out that it was a cloth band to put around cold steering wheels for comfortable early-morning driving. I was too embarrassed to ask why Dad never used it.

What would our infinitely wise heavenly Father choose to give us on Christmas morning? Imagine: the ultimate gift from One for whom money is no object and who perfectly knows our needs! He could have given us treasures of exquisite value—works of art, palaces, creature comforts unending.

But instead, He walked down the staircases of heaven with a baby in His arms. He gave us a Person! The perfect gift, designed to meet the deepest need of the heart, the need for a close, loyal, loving Friend. On the surface it would seem to have been far easier for our Father to have given from His treasury of things. But all parents know that the greatest joys on Christmas morning come from having given a gift of the finest quality, matched exactly to their children's needs.

And our God, who created us for fellowship with Himself, knows that we could be satisfied with nothing less than the object of that fellowship. He revealed a pattern at Bethlehem: His best gifts come in the form of people. Jesus was not isolated in the sumptuous wrappings of some elite palace. He lived among us in humble, believable form, an authentic life. And He showed us the One whom to know is life eternal.

THE POWER OF GOD

Yea, I have loved thee with an everlasting love: therefore with lovingkindness have I drawn thee. Jer. 31:3.

Power! You see it in the latest television commercials: four-wheel drive pickups soar into the air with the blazing sun as a backdrop. Powerful nations meet at summit conferences to eye each other and consider the extent of negotiable weaponry. Five-year-old Billy wilts when Dad begins to slip his belt from his waist.

Christians pray, "Thine is the kingdom, and the power, and the glory." Sometimes we rejoice at the thought of God's power. (He can shut lions' mouths and make the sea like dry land!) At other times we wish we could hide from Him. (He can destroy wicked people with fire and brimstone!) Depending on our need and how we feel about ourselves, we cry to God for His power or we run from it.

While not wanting to diminish the quality of power in God (indeed, one of God's own names for Himself is El Shaddai, the Almighty), may I suggest that our human obsession with muscle power has distorted our view of God? Remember the six blind men from India, each of whom had hold of an elephant? Asked to describe the beast, the one who had hold of the trunk said that it was like a huge snake. Another argued that it was like a tree trunk, while yet another thought it was like rope, and so on. The point is that while all were partially accurate, none could conceive of the true nature of the animal.

Jesus said, "Father, the hour has come; glorify thy Son that the Son may glorify thee, since thou hast given him power over all flesh." *Power* over all flesh! But He goes on, "to give eternal life to all whom thou hast given him" (John 17:1, 2, R.S.V.). Power to *give!* And lest there be any doubt as to what He meant, He finished, "And this is eternal life, that they *know thee* the only true God, and Jesus Christ whom thou hast sent" (verse 3, R.S.V.).

To know God is to be drawn to Him. Jesus, in showing us the Father, drew all men unto Himself and, consequently, to the Father. In today's text, God declared through the prophet Jeremiah that He draws us by His lovingkindness. That is the greatest definition of God's power: drawing love!

And by this He has given *us* power—to become children of God (chap. 1:12)!

MAKING ENEMIES FOR GOD

Alas for you, you scribes and Pharisees, play-actors! You scour sea and land to make a single convert, and then you make him twice as ripe for destruction as you are yourselves. Matt. 23:15, Phillips.

Evangelism is for most Christians what apple pie, motherhood, and the flag are for most Americans. The value of evangelism seems almost unquestioned. Oh, it is true that some evangelism is apparently more successful than others—perhaps because of personalities or planning. But no one should be found opposing it! For to tell people about Christ and to invite them to give their lives to Him should be the goal of every Christian.

Yet that was the apparent goal of these scribes and Pharisees whom Jesus so soundly rebuked in today's text. Intensely eager to gain converts, they covered oceans and continents to find names to add to their list. In the broad outlines, their doctrines seemed correct, too. They spoke out against idolatry, evil associates, and religious indifference. And they advocated Sabbathkeeping, tithing, and a healthful diet.

Though Jesus Himself was an evangelist, He pronounced their work to be worse than ineffective. It was outright destructive. Their converts, rather than being more likely to be saved, became twice as likely to be lost—even though they had joined the "religion of the true God." How could this be? How could those who set out to make people followers of the true God actually end up making enemies for Him?

The answer may have much in it for us as well. The apostle Paul labels their zeal an ill-informed zeal (Rom. 10:2). For example, they were driven with zeal to see that no one broke the Sabbath. In service of that goal, they composed thousands of detailed commands, requirements, and prohibitions about Sabbathkeeping. But somewhere in all the paperwork they lost the Lord of the Sabbath.

Their converts ended up with lots of information about the Sabbath, but they were converted to an arbitrary view of Sabbathkeeping. Therefore they saw God as an arbitrary God. And those who worship an arbitrary God become arbitrary themselves—which is the activity of Satan.

Salvation is not assured by the quantity of information one has about God but by the accuracy of that information—because false information about God does just exactly what Satan wants it to do: it makes people enemies of God.

LIVING LIMITLESS LOVE

There must be no limit to your goodness, as your heavenly Father's goodness knows no bounds. Matt. 5:48, N.E.B.

Ours is a world of limits. Speed limits, social limits, limits imposed by stress or handicaps; the list can become annoyingly, if not painfully, long. "Do I *have* to be home at midnight?!" implores your teenage daughter. "Why can't I just win a sweepstakes, or something?!" wishes the dog-tired executive facing the monthly stack of bills that outbalance his income. "If only I were beautiful, like Marilyn Monroe." "If I were better with my hands, I could fix it myself."

We all continually face our own limitations and those imposed on us by society and circumstances. "Oh, to be free!" we sometimes sigh. Teenagers long to become adults. Adults long for retirement. The aged long for their youth. Christians long for the Second Coming. But is that the best for which we can hope? Are our limitations immune from the gospel assurance of freedom and abundant life?

Of course, many limitations are those protections we might not choose for ourselves. Many are not. However, the irony of our lives is that most of us do not use more than 2 percent of our potential! And this may indeed hold the key to our frustrations. Perhaps our surest happiness and our greatest productivity lie in those areas that we pass by in pursuit of our desired goals. This is not to say that our chosen goals are necessarily wrong. Is it possible, though, that we have allowed the ideals we hold to rob us of very real and tangible accomplishments?

I like today's text because it implies an open window in our world of many closed doors. Rather than an impossible command, I see promise and potential. The central issue is not obedience but sonship, as noted in verse 45 of the same chapter. Sons and daughters have the privilege of upholding and extending their father's reputation. And this is our heavenly Father's coronation: limitless love!

Let us make a conscious effort to allow God to develop in us the glorious potential of living limitless love!

SINNERS BEFORE A HOLY GOD

One called to another and said: "Holy, holy, holy is the Lord of hosts; the whole earth is full of his glory." Isa. 6:3, R.S.V.

I was in the ninth grade when my father arranged for me to meet Billy Graham. Knowing that I was thinking of becoming a minister, my father assumed that contact with an evangelist of such stature might inspire me. Following Dr. Graham's crusade meeting, as we stood in the crowd pressing near him, waiting for a chance to shake his hand, I can remember feeling great apprehension. How does one act in the presence of an important person? I was sure my voice would crack. When he finally grasped my hand, what a relief it was to find how genuinely interested he was in making me feel at ease and valued in his presence.

If we feel apprehension about standing in the presence of important humans, how should we feel about standing in the presence of our magnificent, holy, glorious, sovereign God? If the holy angels continually celebrate His holiness and show Him great respect, how should we acknowledged sinners feel about being in His presence? Isn't there good cause for a great chasm between us?

Some have suggested that His infinite holiness is intended to keep us sinners "at bay," intimidated by such grand righteousness, lest we presume to step lightly into His presence. Such holiness would certainly frighten sinners. But would it ever draw sinners? Would it ever make us glad that He is stepping across the chasm to be near us? Would Emmanuel—"God with us"—be heard as good news, or as a signal for alarm?

Jesus came to reveal to us every aspect of the Father's glory that was important for us to know. Yet it did not intimidate, frighten, or repel us. For God's glory does not center in His consuming power; it centers in the qualities of His character. And His character is compellingly attractive.

Jesus came to show us that the gulf between us and our Father is not of His choosing, nor does He wish for it to remain. It is true that God stationed an angel with a flaming sword at the gate of the garden to bar the way for Adam and Eve to return. But this was to prevent them from thinking that a mere physical return to God's presence—short of a complete, informed return of their loyalties—would solve the sin problem.

SUBMISSION TO UNREASON

I do not whisper obscurities in some dark corner so that no one can know what I mean. And I didn't tell Israel to ask me for what I didn't plan to give! Isa. 45:19, T.L.B.

"The discipline man needed most was to learn his submission to unreason. And that for man's own sake as well as Mine, so he won't find it hard to take his orders from his inferiors in intelligence in peace and war—especially in war." From *A Masque of Reason*, by Robert Frost.

In the lengthy narrative from which the above quote was taken, a dialogue between God and Job takes place. Job, a little disgusted with God's apparent capriciousness, is trying to corner God into giving an answer for sending seemingly unreasonable trials. Frost's whole account was certainly written to be humorous, and it is—except that many believers hold similar concepts with utmost sincerity.

"Submission to unreason"—is that God's desire for us? There are many instances in Scripture in which God asked people to do apparently unreasonable things—such as march around a hostile city seven days in a row, or wash in a dirty river in order to be made clean. Instances that certainly seem to bear out such sentiments.

However, closer examination of these kinds of events reveal that God always was working with a stated purpose, i.e., deliverance. He sometimes used unusual methods in order to get peoples' attention or to remove any doubt in their minds as to who was dealing with them. Never did He do anything deliberately unreasonable just for the sake of making people blindly obey Him. It has never been His intention to "whisper obscurities in some dark corner so that no one can know what I mean."

It is my contention that God is *always* reasonable, that it would be contrary to His very nature to be otherwise. He may use "strange, mysterious ways" (Isa. 45:15, T.L.B.), but His desire is that we should be able to sing praises to Him "with understanding" (Ps. 47:7). Or, as *The Living Bible* puts it: "Yes, sing your highest praises to our King, the King of all the earth. Sing thoughtful praises!"

To praise God with our understanding is possible only when we have been encouraged to think. Rather than learning submission to unreason, let us learn to exercise intelligent faith—that unshakable confidence that God is utterly reliable and reasonable. And that He would have us be the same!

FAITH-SURVIVING

They were stoned, they were sawn in two, they were killed with the sword; they went about in skins of sheep and goats, destitute, afflicted, ill-treated. Heb. 11:37, R.S.V.

I have just returned from the home of close friends whose 3-year-old son is dying of leukemia. A precious, well-formed blond with a tender personality like his mother's, he played contentedly on the floor among us as we discussed his death. One would search long to find a more openhearted, Christ-centered couple than his parents. As we spoke of the unspeakable, with many tears, no hint of bitterness or doubt of our Father crept into their words. Their main perplexity was whether to subject his fragile body to painful treatments to forestall his death or let the disease take its sure course.

We knelt in a circle, and I held his restless little hand as we prayed for God's active mercy. Afterward his father walked with me to my car. "I've been studying again the lives of the great people of the Bible," he said, "and I've come to the conclusion that there is no connection between the quality of a person's faith and his protection from tragic death."

What great faith! I remember another who grieved, "If only I had had more faith, my daughter would have been healed." Christians speak much—perhaps too much—of faith healing. Often the assumption is that the more faith one has, the more likely that healing will take place. I would wish for an emphasis on "faith surviving"—on learning how one's faith in God can survive even if one is *not* healed. In the long view, faithlessness is a far more serious tragedy than death!

Satan urges us to believe that our faith is a sacred life-insurance policy; if we invest adequate "faith premiums," God is obligated to protect us from death. Those who hold this view find every life-threatening event to be a faith-threatening event, for the loss of faith is the loss of eternal life. It leads to the second death.

Jesus insisted, however, upon calling the first death but a sleep. To His faithful ones who sleep He will one day soon say, "Awake!" And a tenderhearted little boy—in perfect health—shall be placed in the arms of his glad parents. Together they shall rise, to look into the face of the Life-giver and to pour out their gratitude.

"BOXHOLDER, PLANET EARTH"
Father, glorify thy name. John 12:28, R.S.V.

In my mailbox I found a little brown package labeled "Boxholder, Route 1." Inside was a sample of shampoo and a flier describing its virtues. The product's name was unfamiliar; in a few minutes I had all but forgotten about the sample. It wasn't until discovering I was low on shampoo that I remembered and decided to make use of it. Retrieving it from the "odds and ends" drawer, I stepped into the shower.

I had done what thousands of consumers have done. Not only had I tried a new product; I actually found myself weighing its potential. That was exactly what the promoters wanted. And really, what better way to introduce to the public an unknown product? Whether they knew it or not, their methodology was not only a good idea, it was God's idea first! Wrapped in the coarse swaddling cloth of a peasant woman, Jesus was delivered to this world, a sample of God. He is often forgotten and tossed aside into the "odds and ends" drawer of our minds, then one day we find our supply of life's stability running low. And we remember . . .

However, there is something incredible about this Sample: it fits *all* needs! Coming to show us the Father, Jesus desired that God's name be glorified, honored, and extolled (John 12:28, Amplified). Crying out, "I need someone stronger than I am!" I learn I have as my strength El Shaddai (the Almighty). "No one sees or understands me!" and I discover "El Roi" (the Seeing God). Spinning in a world of no absolutes, I find solid ground in Adonai (Lord, Absolute Authority). It has all been "home-demonstrated" in the person of God's own Son.

"It was there from the beginning; we have heard it; we have seen it with our own eyes; we looked upon it, and felt it with our own hands; and it is of this we tell. Our theme is the word of life. This life was made visible; we have seen it and bear our testimony; we here declare to you the eternal life which dwelt with the Father and was made visible to us. . . . Here is the message we heard from him and pass on to you: that God is light, and in him there is no darkness at all" (1 John 1:1-5, N.E.B.).

God, the I AM—the Way, the Truth, the Life, Bread, Water, Rest, Righteousness, Peace. Whatever we need, God has named Himself! Therefore, "I shall not want."

CHANGE VERSUS CHAINS

He has sent me to bind up the brokenhearted, to proclaim liberty to the captives, and the opening of the prison to those who are bound. Isa. 61:1, R.S.V.

Is it possible to tame a wild animal? Certainly some have done so. Others have tried and failed. But I am sure of one thing: If the animal has its leg caught in a crushing trap, taming is out of the question, at least until the beast has been freed and brought to some degree of comfort.

What about the vicious German shepherd tied at the end of a fifty-foot chain in the neighbor's yard? "Good thing!" you might express. "He's just plain mean!" Then one day you notice he's gone. "Sold him," your neighbor tells you, "to a boy's ranch." The wisdom of such a decision leaves you reeling! "How could you!" you exclaim involuntarily. "Aren't you afraid he'll chew somebody up?" Then you learn that the dog has the run of the ranch, sleeps on the boys' beds at night, and is as tame as a yearling. You go away shaking your head. But it was not natural for the dog to live at the end of a chain. He was meant to be free. All the energy that could not escape in wholesome ways displayed itself in ferociousness.

Are we any different? Bound by the guilt we feel for the wrongs we have done, our behavior may be only slightly more acceptable than the shepherd's. God knows that we cannot respond to Him until we are loosed. So He sets us free from the crushing weight of our guilt, binds up our broken hearts, and tells us that we need no longer be chained to our sins. Then He draws us to Himself. Well might we exclaim with David, "Set me free from my prison, so that I may praise thy name" (Ps. 142:7, N.E.B.).

It isn't a trade-off or bribe; it's reality. We are no more able to praise God while crushed with a sense of guilt than is the wild animal able to be tamed while caught in the trap! Chained to our sins, we snarl and lunge at life. God comes to take our guilt upon Himself, and He says, "I do not condemn you. You may go; you do not need to sin anymore" (see John 8:11). And because He does not demand "taming" before healing, we know we can trust Him. Even more, we are free to love Him!

HOW TO BE GROWN-UP

Let us speak the truth in love; so shall we fully grow up into Christ. Eph. 4:15, N.E.B.

"Grow up, will you!" Have you ever heard these words? Have you ever spoken them? They carry a sting and are usually meant to shame the individual to whom they are addressed, for the message they bring is clear: "You are not acting your age!"

Paul, in his letter to the believers at Ephesus, talks about Christian maturity. But his words entreat and exhort; they do not harangue and humiliate. He deals strictly with reality, yet his expressions are full of grace. Even as he urges the people to "live up to your calling" (Eph. 4:1, N.E.B.), he cautions them to "speak the truth in love" (verse 15, N.E.B.).

Unfortunately, people tend to fall one way or the other: They either hold back truth in order to keep from hurting someone or they indiscreetly "tell it like it is," regardless of the consequences. Much of what passes for frankness is bluntness, yet often our deference thwarts resolution and growth in our lives and in the lives of others. How can we learn to be discriminating, sensitive, and still absolutely committed to reality?

Listen: "Give up living like pagans with their good-for-nothing notions. Their wits are beclouded, they are strangers to the life that is in God. . . . Were you not as Christians taught the truth as it is in Jesus? . . . You must be made new in mind and spirit, and put on the new nature of God's creating, which shows itself in the just and devout life called for by the truth" (verses 18-24, N.E.B.).

"The truth" referred to here is "the life that is in God" as portrayed in Jesus. And only as we allow this truth (about God) to change our thinking and ways of relating to others will we "fully grow up into Christ" (verse 15, N.E.B.). Whatever we say, we can speak "the truth" as Christ did—we can represent God accurately. We do not have to feel the need to avoid hard realities, because we have come to understand how God Himself deals with us. He always speaks to us forthrightly, but with compassion. He honestly addresses our condition, yet He knows what we can become.

We have a lot of living to do in this world before Christ can come to take us home. "In a word," let us "try to be like him, and live in love as Christ loved [us]" (chap. 5:1, N.E.B.).

WHO DUG THE CHASM?

Your iniquities have made a separation between you and your God, and your sins have hid his face from you so that he does not hear. Isa. 59:2, R.S.V.

The position of Jonathan Edwards on the subject of hell and salvation is useful as an object lesson in what not to believe. For example, he believed,

"The God that holds you over the pit of Hell, much as one holds a spider, or some loathsome insect, over the fire, abhors you, and is dreadfully provoked; His wrath towards you burns like fire; He looks upon you as worthy of nothing else but to be cast into the fire; He is of purer eyes than to bear to have you in His sight; you are ten thousand times more abominable in His eyes than the most hateful venomous serpent is in ours."

Though hidden behind gentler language, these same emotions of abhorrence of sinners are ascribed to God by many Christians today. Often they will quote today's text to support themselves. They explain Isaiah as meaning that God "digs a chasm" to keep from being contaminated by sinners, that they must stop sinning before God will condescend to listen to them. They fail to see that Isaiah was taunting a group of people for their arrogant hypocrisy. They were making bold claims to be religious (Isa. 58:1-3), yet were engaged in all manner of oppression and strife. Isaiah affirms that God knows better than to take seriously their double-talk.

Edwards and other "gentler spirits" of the same persuasion are forgetting that the chasm between God and man was of man's choosing, not God's. His children walked away from Him and then as a result got into doing sinful things. God did not catch them doing sinful things and then in disgust walk away from them.

Who would wish to come back into the presence of such a God as Edwards saw? Though Edwards might argue that God would mellow considerably once His people start behaving, to be in the presence of One who is even capable of such explosive anger brings no comfort.

Tragically, Edwards missed the point of Jesus' life. He who touched lepers, who ate supper with prostitutes, who announced forgiveness to men who were pounding nails into His wrists, and who said, "I have come to show you the Father"—He had a better way of dealing with sinners. He decided to love them into wholeness. And—praise God—it works!

SECURE AND INTRIGUED!

Now to him who by his power within us is able to do infinitely more than we ever dare to ask or imagine—to him be glory in the Church and in Christ Jesus for ever and ever, amen! Eph. 3:20, Phillips.

When I first began to use a home computer, I was amazed at what I could do with it. Now I am even more amazed, because I realize that it can handle far more than I will probably ever know how to initiate. Its capacity makes me feel both secure and intrigued. Today's text makes me feel the same way about God.

There are probably two basic things most Christians worry about when they think about heaven: Will they be there, and what will they do once they get there? Much is spoken about the assurance of salvation. Perhaps it is time to mention the promise of Paradise, remembering that heaven begins here.

First things first: God has set about to assure us that "he destined us—such was his will and pleasure—to be accepted as his sons through Jesus Christ" (Eph. 1:5, N.E.B.). Indeed, the whole gospel story is that of our forgiving and accepting Father. What we may have overlooked in our haste to experience security is that, for God, that is only the beginning! While it is thrilling to learn that we are secure in His wonderful salvation, it is even more exciting to become aware that His plans for us exceed anything we could ever imagine! Now and eternally!

It is imperative that we move from clinging to our assurance of salvation to soaring with thoughts of God's fantastic declaration of His plan for our development. The way I read Ephesians 3:20, "infinitely more" means that we should unabashedly anticipate an incredibly close relationship with God as well as confidently aspire to ever greater heights of attainment in personal achievement and growth. Having laid the foundations, God declares the good news that there is no ceiling!

I feel wonderfully secure in God's ability to fulfill His intentions concerning me, and I am delightfully intrigued as to the consequently endless potential involved! I know that His desire is that I "attain to fullness of being, the fullness of God himself" (chap. 3:19, N.E.B.). And so I find myself excitedly "reaching out for that which lies ahead" (Phil. 3:13, N.E.B.).

Perhaps God is encouraging us to lead expectantly positive lives on earth in order to prepare us to live in the unimaginable excellence of His presence.

TRUSTING YOUR DESIRES

Take delight in the Lord, and he will give you the desires of your heart. Ps. 37:4, R.S.V.

He was a conscientious young man, eager to leave behind all the habits and attitudes of his pre-Christian life. Having been very self-indulgent before his conversion, he knew that giving in to his desires could plunge him back into the hedonism he was trying to leave behind.

The result, however, was that making decisions as a Christian became an anguishing task. Any time he had any personal feelings involved with a choice, he was certain that those feelings had to be denied, since they were assuredly selfish desires. Yet most of the time the course of action he desired seemed to be good. And so he froze in indecision.

What freedom and joy he began to experience, however, when he discovered the essence of today's verse! He began to trust the promise that one really is changed by beholding Christ, and that the change includes basic desires of the heart. And he cherished the gem insight that God is not One who will forever tell us that we cannot have what our heart desires. Rather, He changes what we desire!

A new Christian is often rightfully distrustful of his wishes, for the habits of the old life die all too slowly. That which has for years brought him delight is not easily forgotten. But the Psalmist introduces a new ingredient into the believer's life—a new source of rapture. "Take delight in the Lord," David says. Be excited about your God. Be enthralled with the qualities of His person. Be drawn toward this magnificent Friend. Be fascinated with the way He does things for His family members.

The transforming power of a new affection will fundamentally change the kinds of things that bring delight to one's heart. God is too wise to give us the desires of our confused, darkened, self-serving hearts. But He is also too wise—and too loving—*not* to give us the desires of our transformed, enlightened hearts.

For what does a person desire who is enraptured with God, but deeper fellowship with Him, deeper involvement with His lifestyle, deeper interaction with His people? No wonder, then, that those whom God takes home with Him to enjoy eternal fellowship will do—throughout eternity—just exactly whatever their hearts desire. They will walk in perfect freedom, for there will be nothing in their hearts that needs to be denied!

LET'S MAKE IT MUTUAL!

Hope deferred makes the heart sick, but a desire fulfilled is a tree of life. Prov. 13:12, R.S.V.

Mutuality: it's the key to all successful and productive relationships. It prompts you to say, "I feel the same way!" or "I've been there!" and allows you to "rejoice with those who rejoice" and "weep with those who weep" (Rom. 12:15, R.S.V.). It is tremendously comforting when someone shares your grief and immensely satisfying when they understand and applaud your goals. As a matter of fact, life isn't much fun, and is scarcely endurable, without some degree of reciprocity.

There is an interesting component in the issue of mutuality. It did not originate in the heart of man. We read in Genesis 1:26, "Then God ["Elohim," plural] said, 'Let us make man in our image' " (R.S.V.). The very creation of man was a cooperative undertaking of the Godhead. The need for mutuality was "built in" to mankind in that we were made like God.

Conversely, one of the greatest centerpieces of the gospel is that Jesus was made like us in every way (Heb. 2:17), and therefore sympathizes with us in our fallen condition (chap. 4:15). God is virtually saying, "I understand how you feel! I've been there!" He says it in a thousand different ways all through the Scriptures. And if we read very carefully, we shall also understand God.

We hear Him in Proverbs 13:12 when He says, "Hope deferred makes the heart sick, but a desire fulfilled is a tree of life"—I know how sick at heart you feel when your expectations are thwarted. In creating mankind, I intended for you to reveal to the watching universe what I am like! That hope has been deferred, but My desire shall still be fulfilled. And when it is, we shall all rejoice together.

And in 2 Corinthians 1:4: "He comforts us in all our troubles, so that we in turn may be able to comfort others in any trouble of theirs and to share with them the consolation we ourselves receive from God" (N.E.B.)—thereby revealing His comprehensive understanding of our need not only to be comforted, but to give comfort and share experiences.

Perhaps one of the most poignant texts is Isaiah 1:18: "Come now, let us reason together, says the Lord" (R.S.V.).—I'll listen to you, and you listen to Me. It's important to Me that we work out our problems together!

We matter to God! He understands how we feel! Let's make it mutual!

BEING SURE OF ETERNAL LIFE

This letter is to assure you that you have eternal life. It is addressed to those who give their allegiance to the Son of God. 1 John 5:13, N.E.B.

It was a New Year's Eve, and we were sponsoring a restless group of church youth on Colorado Boulevard in Pasadena, California. The plan was for us to try to stake out some sidewalk space for the Rose Parade. We ended up being jostled by countless thousands of people with the same idea but who were more aggressive than we. It was an education in itself.

One sheltered youth, fresh from his first exposure to a "street preacher," laughingly reported that someone had just asked him if he was saved. He told how he had brushed the man aside with a terse comment, then he looked for my approval. "Well," I asked, *"Are* you saved?" He looked stunned, sure that I was jesting.

So we spent the next hour of that very cold night exploring whether one could indeed know that he had entered into life. These passages from John's Epistle became very precious to us that night, for the young man truly did want to know of his salvation. John said that eternal life belongs to those who have given their allegiance to Jesus Christ.

Some people may see this verse through different eyes. They see the sin problem as fundamentally one of legal standing, of one smarting under the legal condemnation of the law, guilty as charged. In their eyes the solution to be sought is a pronouncement of innocence. To be justified, then, is to be saved. I suspect that is what the midnight street preacher had in mind.

But John's words draw our attention clearly in another direction. As J. B. Phillips translates verse 12: "It follows naturally that any man who has Christ has this life; and if he has not, then he does not possess this life at all." The issue is relationship, not legal standing. The key to eternal life is not in hearing a pronouncement of innocence but in knowing the One behind such a declaration.

"Genuine contact with Christ" is a Person-to-person experience, not just a nod toward God. It means finding one's highest satisfactions in thinking about, talking to, and speaking of your well-known Friend. It means that we can approach God with confidence (see verse 15), for the Life-giver has taken His rightful place in the center of our lives.

113

UNLAWFUL RIGHTEOUSNESS

Have you not read what David did when he and his men were hungry? He went into the House of God and ate the sacred bread, though neither he nor his men had a right to eat it, but only the priests. Matt. 12:3, 4, N.E.B.

Walking through grainfields on the Sabbath day may not have been considered inappropriate in Jesus' day, but plucking and eating the grain as one went along certainly was. Pointing to the offending disciples, some Pharisees who had noticed what they were doing asked the Master why this forbidden activity was taking place. Jesus' answer must have shocked them. It might shock us, enlightened even as we are in the twentieth century.

He reminded them of the time that David and his men ate sacred bread from the Temple. In essence He gave them an example of an "unlawful" act as a precedent for His disciples' innocence. He added, " 'If you had known what that text means, "I require mercy, not sacrifice," you would not have condemned the innocent' " (Matt. 12:7, N.E.B.). *The New English Bible* translation of Hosea 6:6 reads "Loyalty is my desire, not sacrifice."

It might be easy to explain Christ's logic by making light of the Temple rules, except that as far as the sacred bread was concerned God made the rules! And Jesus came to fulfill the law, not to abolish it (chap. 5:17)! May I suggest that what the Master was trying to do was to get the Pharisees to look past the rules to the Rule Giver. The intent of the law is to draw us back to the Father. It was our "custodian until Christ came" (Gal. 3:24, R.S.V.), at which time the Father would be fully revealed. Sacrifices were offered because men continued to be misinformed about God, and consequently they behaved badly. "How much better," Christ was saying, "to know the Father well enough to be loyal in the first place!"

When David and his men ate the shewbread, David revealed that he understood that God's ultimate purpose in setting up the Temple services was to nourish Israel back into healthy relationship with their God. So secure was David in his knowledge of God that he did not hesitate to appropriate "God's bread" to alleviate his men's immediate need for physical nourishment.

David was righteous (in right relationship with God), though eating the sacred bread was technically unlawful. Think about it. Both God and His rules are for the sake of His people.

THE REAL TEST OF RELIGION

The king will answer, "I tell you this: anything you did for one of my brothers here, however humble, you did for me." Matt. 25:40, N.E.B.

My students have learned through the years that I do not give academic credit for religious clichés. Even the most conscientious students can easily fall into the pattern of thinking that spiritual success is found in putting together the right string of religious phrases. So when I hear them talking about being "cleansed by the blood," or "broken at the foot of the cross," or even "justified by the propitiation made as an atonement for our transgressions," I ask a question: "Can you describe that same experience without using any religious words?"

Many people have become skilled religionists, experts at "God-talk" and pious phrases. For many of them, religion is a thing talked about in a realm apart from that which is lived and experienced. They see the world divided into two distinct parts: the real and the religious. Since neither God nor heaven have been observed, conversation about them seldom needs to be verified in the common, actual world.

But Jesus knows that heaven is a very real world, as is all His creation, and that its future residents will be real people who have learned to take heaven's principles into their daily relationships. So when He described the test of genuine religion, to be applied to those anticipating entrance into heaven, He did not measure how many nice things they could say about God or their smooth doctrinal statements. He spoke instead of the way in which people relate to the common, unspectacular, not-too-impressive people around us.

Have the principles of the kingdom become such a real part of us that we will express them to those who will give us no honor for doing so? Will our own family members (whom we have long since ceased trying to impress) be treated with the same respect and deference as the wealthy corporation executive who could do us a favor? Can we spot a stranger in a crowded market and consciously regard him as a valuable person, in spite of his evident status in life?

The unguarded, impulsive responses, scattered through a busy day of ordinary pressures, really are the most valid measure of the shape of our souls. They are the unconscious reflection of the Object of our affection.

April 20

MORE THAN COMFORT

This is the word of the Lord the God of your father David: I have heard your prayer and seen your tears; I will heal you. 2 Kings 20:5, N.E.B.

Picture this scene in the emergency room of a hospital: A doctor is standing over an accident victim, comforting her. "There, there!" he soothes. "I see your tears; I understand how badly you are hurt!" As the hemorrhaging woman, calmed by the reassuring words of the physician, ceases her crying, he slowly backs out of the room, satisfied that he has brought solace to the injured woman. Meeting her distraught husband in the hall, he smiles warmly. "Your wife's fine! She's stopped crying!" Ten minutes later she is on her way to the morgue.

"Ridiculous!" you say. And yet do we sometimes credit God with such misprocedure? Do we believe that He is more interested that we stop "crying" than He is that we stop "bleeding"? Do we think that our profession of faith is of more value in His sight than is the restoration of our friendship with Him?

We have much to unlearn about our wonderful God. Even those of us who hold "enlightened views" concerning Him have clung to ideas about Him that keep us tethered to fear and/or a poor self-image. It's time to reevaluate every concept we have that casts a shadow upon free-flowing communion with Him.

In our text today we see God listening, watching, understanding. We believe that; we count on it. We even believe that He wants to heal us. But sometimes we fail to grasp *how much* He desires to do just that! We argue about how healed we can expect to be. Yes, He can take away the cigarette habit. He can reform us and realign our priorities. But can He make us perfect?

"Whoa!" you say. "Nobody's perfect!" (See what I mean?) But, then, what do we mean by "perfect"? In the usual sense, *perfect* means you never do anything wrong again, and we have to reexamine the whole idea of growth throughout eternity. However, if you understand *perfect* to mean fully won back to loyalty to God . . .

Can God fully win back our loyalty? Can our misunderstanding about Him be fully healed? Can we dare hope that our misgivings will be fully assuaged as He thoroughly and finally dismantles our misinformation? In fact, what else could establish our undying loyalty and love to Him?

Friends, I'm counting on just that!

HE HEALED ALL TEN

At this Jesus said, "Were not all ten cleansed? The other nine, where are they?" Luke 17:17, N.E.B.

It is very hard for us fully to understand what it meant to be a leper in the time of Christ. Today leprosy is a disease that can mostly be avoided; if contracted, it can be somewhat successfully treated. But then it was more than a dreaded fatal disease, more than an awful malady that shattered every cherished human contact. Most horribly, leprosy was firmly held to be the judgment of God, His public punishment for sin, the mark of His sure rejection.

And so the leper endured his bleak existence, bereft of all hope in this life and sentenced to eternal destruction after the release of death. In the eyes of the people the incurable condition of a leper was proof that God would never reverse His judgment.

Then Jesus came, full of truth about His Father. He longed to show people that His Father does not inflict diseases as punishment for sin. He wanted them to know that all sinners will find forgiveness when they come home to the Father. Were He ever to walk past a leper without healing him, He would be confirming the people's fear that God will not forgive grievous sinners. No wonder the Scriptures indicate that Jesus healed every leper He encountered!

He even healed ten of them at once, there on the borderlands of Galilee. Ten filthy, isolated, begging men—He made them whole and clean, acceptable to their families, publicly innocent. But only one sensed that his healing, though incredible, was not as important as the Healer. And he came back to worship at Jesus' feet.

The last we see of the other nine is their backs, for their eyes are fixed on their freshly made skin as they scamper off to enjoy the benefits. The gift became the end in itself, and they had no time for the Giver! But Jesus didn't "curse" them by making the leprosy return.

Even in this disappointing outcome Jesus was remaining true to His Father. Though forgiveness is freely offered to all, only those who come back and fall at the feet of the Forgiver have entered into life. The others do not have their forgiveness canceled. But that does not matter. They are lost just the same, not because they are unforgiven but because they indulge the gift, ignoring the Forgiver!

April 22

SOGGY-CAKE FAITH

Let us fix our eyes on Jesus, the author and perfecter of our faith. Heb. 12:2, N.I.V.

Few things are more unpalatable than cake that is not thoroughly cooked. Though tempting-looking on the outside, the inner sogginess can gag you. No amount of frosting will suffice; one bite, and the rest is for the dog (if even he'll eat it!).

At one point in Israelite history God referred to Ephraim as "a cake half-baked" (Hosea 7:8, N.E.B.). In verses 13 and 14 He says, "I long to deliver them, but they tell lies about me. There is no sincerity in their cry to me; for all their howling . . . they are turning away from me."

Insincerity. Can it be cured? It depends, of course, on the root cause. Some insincerity stems from having been backed into a corner with a decision that one isn't ready to make. In that case the only remedy is to be allowed to remake the decision while being given sufficient information to do so. Of course, if a person thinks he already knows enough, the problem becomes immensely complicated. Such was the case with Israel.

God saw that the root cause of the problem was Israel's lack of faith in Him. That was the source of their "lies" about Him. In chapter 14:4, He outlines His plan for their restoration: "I will heal their faithlessness; I will love them freely" (R.S.V.). They were only half convinced about God's goodness. He would love them to wholeness. But first He would have to persuade them that though "they cry to me for help: 'We know thee, God of Israel,' " they were, in fact, "utterly loathsome" (chap. 8:2, 3, N.E.B.). Like soggy cake.

God's methodology hasn't changed. He desires to love us to wholeness, too. So He gave us Jesus. In Jesus we see the Father's love in action; we see forgiveness, acceptance, salvation. Faith springs up in our hearts. We believe! But this is only the beginning. If we stop there, however wonderful the experience, we will end up living in a half-truth. And only half the truth about God can be as harmful as an outright lie.

The answer to this potential dilemma is found in Hebrews 12:2—we need to keep our "eyes fixed on Jesus" (N.E.B.)! Because our understanding of who God is not only began in Jesus; it will also be made complete as we behold the *whole* truth in Him.

`118`

DOES GOD USE DISAPPOINTMENT?

Love your enemies, and do good, and lend, expecting nothing in return; . . . and you will be sons of the Most High; for he is kind to the ungrateful and the selfish. Luke 6:35, R.S.V.

Parents are always looking for an available arsenal of methods to use to get their children to obey. If you are a parent, you probably recognize most of the methods: coaxing, stern commanding, sweet enticing, lengthy sermonizing. Sometimes in sheer desperation we resort to badgering and belittling. I can remember the time I looked coldly at my daughter (following what I considered to be a major infraction) and said, "Julie, after all I've done for you, I am so disappointed in you!"

I was even more disappointed when it didn't lead her to immediate repentance and transformation. But later, when our feelings had calmed, she told me how she felt when I said that. She described the feelings of crushing hopelessness, rejection, loss of self-esteem, and of impossible indebtedness. And—as usual—I found myself reviewing my methods of parenting as well as my understanding of God.

Does God manipulate us with goodness? Does He say, "After all I've done for you, what are you going to do for Me?" What does it mean to "expect nothing in return"? For us to expect something in return means we do good to another, expecting a returned favor, and then feel disappointed if the favor is not returned. Then that disappointment is often used (through subtle comments, glances of the eye, or sullen moods) to make sure that, next time, the favor is returned.

If one is not grateful for all the good things we do, then, in human terms, the kindnesses stop, for they were done to induce gratefulness. But if Jesus called us to come up higher than this, wouldn't we expect His Father not to stoop to such methods?

Our Father does good because He *is* good, not as a means of leverage upon us. He keeps on being kind, even to the ungrateful, because His kindness was not a conditional kindness in the first place. Even His acts of discipline are expressions of kindness, for He wants His friends to live within the boundaries of reality.

God's great kindness to us is intended to inspire us rather than to control us, to heal us rather than to crush us with impossible indebtedness. Unconditional love draws us into wholeness; conditional love drives us to despair.

THE SUICIDE OF SEPARATION

Then Jesus cried with a loud voice, "My God, my God, why did you forsake me?" Matt. 27:46, Phillips.

Thousands of people die every year in traffic accidents. Though the auto makers install seat belts in every new car, many people will die anyway, simply because they did not use the belts. They felt no need to "buckle up," because they never identified with the possibility of being in an accident themselves. Unfortunately, they did not live to benefit from learning that devastating possibility.

Ever since Eden, people have believed that they have life independent from God. The theory of evolution is simply an elaborate explanation to that effect. And the daily existence of atheists and churchgoers alike seems to substantiate such thinking. To find out that God is our only life source may be like discovering too late that we are not immune to traffic accidents.

Man should have perished in Eden. But God wasn't looking for statistics to prove Himself right. He desired that we might live! So He devised a plan whereby we could see what happens to us when we are separated from God yet live to benefit from the lesson. Incredibly, God would become one of us (2 Cor. 5:21)! By beholding Jesus, our substitute, we would discover that sin—separation from God—kills!

Men did not kill the Son of God. He hung upon a crude cross but He died because He experienced the consequences of sin for us. He cried out, "My God, my God, why did you forsake [leave] me?" However, He died knowing that He had accomplished what was needed. For He cried again with a loud voice, "It is finished!" (John 19:30, Phillips).

May I suggest that God did not kill Jesus, either? He simply allowed Jesus to bear the results of man's choice when he withdrew from God. As this happened Jesus cried out, and moments later He was dead. In the sacrificial services the sinner who brought a lamb offering killed it himself. The priest only caught the blood. The staggering truth is, man ultimately kills himself!

God pleads with us to come to our senses. "As I live, says the Lord God, I have no pleasure in the death of the wicked, but that the wicked turn from his way and live; turn back, turn back from your evil ways; for why will you die?" (Eze. 33:11, R.S.V.).

WHY GOD REQUIRES FAITH

**As it is written, "He who through faith is righteous shall live."
Rom. 1:17, R.S.V.**

"Did you know that modern medical science is destroying faith?"
The man's question was absolutely serious, so when he saw the puzzled
look on my face, he tried to explain. "God revealed to us many principles
of health in the Bible," he said. "And we've just had to take them on
faith. But now the scientists are proving them all to be true, and pretty
soon we won't have any more need for faith."

"Does this mean," I asked, "that the less we know about a subject,
the more faith we can have?" "Yes," he replied hesitantly. "Then those
who know the least about Jesus can have the most faith in Him?" He
looked perplexed. "That doesn't sound quite right, does it?" he
responded.

What we understand faith to be certainly shapes our picture of why
God requires it. If faith is a "blind leap in the dark," then God requires us
to be superstitious. He rewards us for our gullibility.

Or if faith is merely assent to the meritorious value of Christ's life and
death outside of oneself, then faith becomes our legal entitlement to
forgiveness. It becomes the means by which God is entitled to change
toward us.

But what if we view faith to be an informed, trusting friendship with
the Lover of our souls? What if it means the reuniting of God's creatures
in a loving bond with their Creator, the restoring of the kind of intimate
fellowship that Adam and Eve enjoyed with their Father in Eden? Then
God requires faith because nothing else can heal the essential sin
problem—the alienation between God and man.

Faith is the response of our hearts to God's gracious appeals for our
fellowship with Him. It is the healing relationship with the One who is the
source of all life, health, and happiness. Faith restores us to our rightful
state, to the condition in which we were created to live: union with our
Creator.

Faith does not change God toward us; it changes us toward God. It
does not coax Him to forgive us; it is our response to the discovery that He
is a forgiver. Faith does not appease God's wrath toward sinners; it heals
the sinner's hostility toward God. No wonder, then, that Paul could
repeat that great scriptural theme: "He who through faith is righteous
shall live"! For faith is connection with the Life-giver.

BEYOND VICTORY

"We have been treated like sheep for slaughter"—and yet, in spite of all, overwhelming victory is ours through him who loved us. Rom. 8:37, N.E.B.

I remember listening to the radio the day the American hostages came home from Iran in January of 1981. The waiting crowd broke into cheers when the men and women stepped through the door of their plane. A huge bubble of camaraderie rose inside my chest, and I found myself cheering with them, celebrating the victory of those returning captives over defeating circumstances.

How good it is to witness human victory in a world terribly twisted with unfair wars and famine! There is so much senseless suffering and loss, so many injustices. At times one is almost compelled to wonder, Is it worth it all? Will the final triumph over evil ever make all that we've gone through here on earth worthwhile? Unless we understand the true nature of the victory God intends for us, we may lose heart.

Victory in itself is not enough. A returning prisoner of war who has to be institutionalized for permanent mental disorientation can bring more agony to his family than when he was thought to be missing in action. At least then they had hope. Likewise, God knows that it is not enough for us to be "saved." It is not enough for there to be no more sorrow or crying, wonderful as that is. It is not enough for us to walk on streets of gold and live in mansions. It is not even enough that we live eternally.

And so God assures us "overwhelming victory." This implies something beyond victory. God not only desires to deliver us from the perils and destruction of this life, but He wants us to live eternally with Him as His sons and daughters. He wants us to know Him well enough to call Him "Abba! Father!" the affectionate equivalent of "Dad" or "Daddy" (see Rom. 8:14-16, N.E.B.). He has "ordained that [we] should be shaped to the likeness of his Son, that [Jesus] might be the eldest among a large family of brothers" (verse 29, N.E.B.).

Jesus knew the Father and was one with Him. In John 17 He prayed that we might share that knowledge and oneness. He said, "I made thy name known to them . . . so that the love thou hadst for me may be in them" (verse 26, N.E.B). This is our overwhelming victory: to know God and be one with Him throughout eternity!

IS GOD PUNITIVE?

In love there can be no fear, but fear is driven out by perfect love: because to fear is to expect punishment, and anyone who is afraid is still imperfect in love. 1 John 4:18, Jerusalem.

More than sixty times in the Bible we read about God punishing people for their iniquities, and then in one verse John says that people who are afraid of punishment are imperfect! Whom are we supposed to believe? What's the real truth about punishment? Is God punitive?

We're dealing here with two different understandings of "punishment." In one sense of the word, *punishment* means the inflicting of pain on someone because of wrong behavior. We envision someone in a position of power or authority (such as a parent, policeman, or teacher), whose job is to monitor the behavior of others. When others in his charge have done wrong, he must deal with that wrong. And so he spanks, levies fines, or makes the offender stand in the corner.

This usage sometimes also carries flavorings of retaliation, emotional vengeance, or getting even. It reveals the assumption that the wrong act will not have inherent consequences that are so very bad and so some sort of pain must be invented and artificially supplied. This is to make sure that the person being punished will fear the lawgiver and thus be more obedient. Some folks simply can't think of a better way to get people to obey than to scare them into submission.

But not so with our God! He has better reasons for us to obey than to fear His wrath. His law presents such vital realities of living that He does not need to "throw His wounded ego on the line" in defense of it. And He is so confident of His ability to instruct us that He wants us referencing to the truthfulness of His ways rather than to the fear of His negative emotions.

Punishment, however, does have a proper function. We are not always quick to grasp how hurtful it is to depart from His ways; and—lest we begin to live in a fantasy—He mercifully brings us face-to-face with the tragedy of our foolishness. Also the destructive effects of a sinful pattern often are not immediately evident. Rather than let us become locked into crushing patterns, He warns us with a sampling of the pain to come. Surely this is what those Old Testament authors meant when they spoke of God's punishment.

THE TRUTH ABOUT SELFLESSNESS

He it is who sacrificed himself for us, to set us free from all wickedness and to make us a pure people marked out for his own, eager to do good. Titus 2:14, N.E.B.

She was pretty, intelligent, and poised; the young man with her was arrogant and sloppy. As I watched them move through the cafeteria line, I wondered what she saw in him. Later I began to wonder if there was something about herself she didn't see.

A low self-image tends to perpetuate unfortunate circumstances that seem to verify that individual's evaluation of himself. Tragically, we Christians often succumb to the same thing! One wonders what it is we do not see in God that allows us to have such a low opinion of our potential.

We often say, "Nobody's perfect!" What we mean is that we have failed to reach a certain standard of behavior. Furthermore, many are convinced that no one can. "Only Christ could," they say. "He was, after all, our Substitute. Even God knew we couldn't!" Such thinking precludes success.

What we must understand is the difference between salvation and restoration. It is absolutely true that we can never merit salvation. But in areas of Christian growth we are not talking about salvation! We are talking about God's adequacy to fulfill our needs. Take selflessness, for example.

Christ was a totally selfless person. Now, do we conclude that because we cannot be selfless enough to atone for our sins that selflessness is beyond us? Our text today says that by His sacrifice Christ "set us free from all wickedness." Selfishness is our attempt to grasp after completeness apart from God. In Christ we are once again at one with God (at-one-ment). Consequently, there is no more need to be self-serving. All our needs are met.

It is time we stopped confusing character development with merit! God knew that as long as we felt unworthy of His company we would continue to live lives that denied us His friendship. Therefore, He redeemed us, and by doing so He enabled us to begin to take hold of "the full wealth of his splendour upon vessels [us!] which were objects of mercy, and which from the first had been prepared for this splendour" (Rom. 9:23, N.E.B.).

Let us be "eager to do good"—not to win Him, but to reveal Him to others that they, too, might learn of their completeness in Him!

GETTING LOST TO GET SAVED

Whoever cares for his own safety is lost; but if a man will let himself be lost for my sake and for the Gospel, that man is safe. Mark 8:35, N.E.B.

Ever since Eden we've thought that we have the best ideas on how to take care of ourselves, how to meet our needs, how to reach our goals. In many cases we are convinced that we can take better care of ourselves than even God can. For example, the lonesome teenager who longs to be loved may seek for it in illicit sexual relationships rather than wait for God's longer, slower, but more satisfying methods to accomplish the goal.

A young business executive seeks for professional success and security— certainly worthy goals in themselves. But if, in his haste to get there, he compromises his health, integrity, and relationships, the goals are no longer worthy of him. When Jesus was being tempted in the wilderness, nothing was wrong with His wanting to be fed, to be sustained by His Father, or to be victorious in His mission to win the earth back from Satan. What *was* wrong with each of the temptations was that they involved shortcuts to the goal, do-it-yourself methods apart from the Father's wise perception of what was necessary.

Virtually every sinful thing that we do has an understandable motive behind it: we are acting to fulfill a legitimate need. We need love, enjoyment, successes, security, sexual release, food and shelter, and freedom from pain. The thing that makes our sinful act so wrong is not the need itself but the fact that we have gone about meeting it by our methods rather than God's.

A 26-year-old woman, fearful that she was about to become an "old maid," was seriously dating a non-Christian. He was eager to enter matrimony, but she was sufficiently apprehensive that she came for advice. She was terrified at my suggestion that she break off the relationship because it appeared she would never have her need for companionship met. After much anguish she cast her full confidence in God and broke up with the suitor. A short time later she met and happily married a fine man of her own faith.

Real victory over sin, then, means coming to have such a practical confidence in God's ability to meet our needs that we will not be prone to meet them on our terms. "Lost" in Him, we are safe.

DOES LACK OF FORCE EQUAL PASSIVENESS?

God loved the world so much that he gave his only Son, that everyone who has faith in him may not die but have eternal life. John 3:16, N.E.B.

Americans no longer call state prisons penitentiaries; they are "correctional institutions." This reflects a move away from the idea of strict retribution, toward the concept of rehabilitation. In the past, criminals were to be punished. Period. This was in service of society: a fearsome warning to dissuade other potential offenders from a similar course of action. It seldom worked. Once released, the ex-convicts were often more a threat to society than they were when first incarcerated.

Something had to be done. And so the concept of rehabilitation came into being. The goal is to bring restoration to the offenders so that they are able to integrate acceptably back into their respective communities. Because this ideal is not always reached, some people cry out against what they call the passivity of law-enforcement officials.

In a similar way, some Christians cry out against the concept of a God who chooses not to deal forcefully with injustice—a God who would rather educate and restore the sinner than to inflict pain upon him for his bad behavior. They fear that anything less than just retribution leads to chaos and anarchy. The understanding that God's justice fits not only the crime but also the criminal is lost under a barrage of text quoting and the solemn warning: "You're making God out to be too passive!"

To the contrary, God is anything but passive! In Eden He arrested the destruction of the human race by putting into effect a plan by which fallen man could be not only rescued but rehabilitated and restored. His is not a posture of weakness but of confidence in better methods. It is, in fact, a posture of impregnable strength! Only an insecure ruler needs to resort to force. By giving His Son, God demonstrated that He is capable not only of controlling the sin crisis but of resolving it.

If we obey God because we believe He will kill us if we don't, our loyalty to Him is tainted with suppressed rebellion. If, however, we understand that God is offering us the option to be integrated back into reality so as to avoid certain disaster, our hearts will be filled with wonder and love that He has gone to such great lengths to provide us that expensive remedy.

TIME: A POOR MOTIVATOR

Hold yourselves ready, therefore, because the Son of Man will come at the time you least expect him. Matt. 24:44, N.E.B.

An ancient story has it that Francis of Assisi was approached by one of his parishioners as he was hoeing in the garden.

"Brother Francis," the man asked, "what would you do if you knew that the Lord would be returning tomorrow?"

The wise old churchman leaned for a moment on his hoe, and then spoke with assurance. "I do believe," he said, "that I would finish hoeing my garden."

In what way would you live your life differently if you knew that Jesus would be coming in two months? Or what if it were but two days? Or even two hours? Is Jesus' lifestyle worth living only because He is coming soon? Or would you continue to live just as you do, even if you knew that Jesus wouldn't come for a hundred years?

Think with me for a moment: if what I am doing at the moment is improper, unhealthy, or otherwise unwise, I should cease doing it immediately, regardless of how soon Jesus might return. On the other hand, as long as what I'm doing is valid and useful, then the length of time I spend doing it isn't relevant.

Jesus pointedly refused to tell His disciples the time when He would return, because He didn't want that to be the reason for their obedience. He didn't want them keeping an eye on the calendar rather than on Him. Rather than being moved by fear that the clock would run out, He wanted them moved by love for Him and the magnificence of His ways.

Though we have heard it so often that some will be shocked to hear me call it into question, I believe it is a flawed argument to say, "Jesus is coming soon, *therefore* get ready!" Jesus is *Himself* good enough reason to live like Him. The real argument should read, "Live like Jesus for His sake; therefore the world will know Him, and He *can* come."

Our verse today does not read "*Get* ready." Rather, it reads, "*Hold* yourselves ready." It means that this very day it is possible for me to *be* ready, to be in a saving relationship with Him. Then my concentration is upon remaining, abiding, persevering, in that close friendship. While it is true that an understanding of prophecy and of last-day events can get my attention, only intimate, sustained fellowship with Jesus can teach me righteousness.

BECOMING PART OF THE DEMONSTRATION

Therefore, my brothers, I implore you by God's mercy to offer your very selves to him: a living sacrifice, dedicated and fit for his acceptance, the worship offered by mind and heart. Rom. 12:1, N.E.B.

Thumbing through a magazine, I came across a classic "before and after" advertisement. On the left side of the page was a picture of a very large woman. To the right was pictured the same woman, considerably thinner. "I was overweight for twenty years!" went her testimony. "But with ——— I lost sixty-three pounds!"

People who are sales promoters admit that two very successful means of convincing the consumer of product worth are visual demonstration and personal testimony. Demonstration alone may leave the viewer apprehensive, but when endorsed by an everyday person, the claims become more believable.

Two thousand years ago God sent His Son as a demonstration of Himself. The Scriptures offer human testimony: "We have seen for ourselves, and we attest, that the Father sent the Son to be the saviour of the world. . . . Thus we have come to know and believe the love which God has for us" (1 John 4:14, N.E.B.).

Christ's life revealed the truth about God: He is tangible, loving, responsive. He's a forgiver, a healer, a teacher. And He accepts us. We no longer need to be afraid. He assures us that He is able to make all things right and that we are of utmost value. Taking our sins—the evidence of our separation from God—upon Himself, Christ died at Calvary, thus exemplifying that God is our only life source.

The witnesses of Christ's day left their testimony in the writings of the Bible. Each succeeding generation of believers has the privilege of bringing fresh confirmation to that confession of faith. In addition, we have been given an invitation to become a part of God's magnificent demonstration. We may become a "living sacrifice," offering our whole selves—body, mind, and heart—to God, so that He might cause "his light to shine within us. . . . We are no better than pots of earthenware to contain this treasure, and this proves that such transcendent power does not come from us, but is God's alone" (2 Cor. 4:6, 7).

As God's children, we can be tangibly lovable and responsive, forgiving and accepting. And by this we not only tell our world today that God accepts them and considers them of utmost value, but we demonstrate it.

THE RISKS OF BEING RIGHT

You, sir, why do you pass judgment on your brother? And you, sir, why do you hold your brother in contempt? We shall all stand before God's tribunal. Rom. 14:10, N.E.B.

It would be hard to imagine that, among all the people reading this book, there would be a one who would wish to be found on the side of wrong. Virtually all of us want to understand and live by the principles of right. To think otherwise would be to deny all that we hold as real and vital as Christians.

Yet to be on the side of right has some very real risks. Consider, for example, what happens when you put a person who is "in the right" into a relationship with a person who is clearly "in the wrong." There will likely be two distinct sets of unenviable feelings.

The one who is in the wrong will likely feel, *I've been a real fool. I feel embarrassed. How can I hold my head high in the presence of this person who can so readily tell me what I've done wrong? I'd escape if I could. Am I of any real value?*

The one who is "right" also runs the risk of certain feelings. He may be thinking, *I'm so glad that I'm right. Being right is the fulfillment of my goals, the foundation of my self-esteem. I'm greatly relieved that I am not among the wrong!*

This relationship would not likely be pleasant or enduring. It would be rife with intimidation and avoidance. Yet Jesus walked this planet as one who was constantly, absolutely right, and He mingled daily with those who were clearly wrong. To our amazement, the Bible reports that sinners heard Him gladly and found Him to be a favorite dinner guest. For Jesus not only spoke the message "I don't condemn you"; He lived it.

The one who is in the wrong cannot make the first peaceful move toward the one who is in the right. He is too intimidated. So Jesus' first goal was to break down the "I'm up, you're down" interchange, so that all of us who are in the wrong might let Him become our friend and transform us into those who love and do the right.

The more "right truth" a Christian grasps, the more essential it is that he have the "right spirit" as well: genuine compassion toward those who are in the wrong.

CONVERTED FROM INTROVERSION

This people's heart has become calloused; they hardly hear with their ears, and they have closed their eyes. Otherwise they might see with their eyes, hear with their ears, understand with their hearts and turn and I would heal them. Acts 28:27, N.I.V.

I'll never forget the first time I looked through the wrong end of a pair of binoculars! Instantly, everything looked miles away. It was especially startling since I had expected just the opposite. Later, I got to thinking about it: many people view life in a similar way. Their relationships with others evolve from a sheltered self-centeredness. Consequently, everything has a smallness about it.

It's like having part of your perceptions shut down. Instead of seeing more, your horizons become pinched. A kind of deafness sets in; you tend not to hear what others are really saying. The more people demand from you, the less capable you feel you are of giving. You become more and more protective of yourself until your heart seems frozen. What can be done to remedy this frustrating state of affairs? How can you learn to see things differently?

God has a way! We read in Romans 12:2, "Let your minds be remade and your whole nature thus transformed" (N.E.B.). And how is this accomplished? "And we all, with unveiled face, beholding the glory of the Lord, are being changed [transformed] into his likeness from one degree of glory to another" (2 Cor. 3:18, R.S.V.). We call it conversion.

Looking at life from a self-centered point of view is like looking through the wrong end of a telescope. "Beholding the glory of the Lord"—the character of God lived out in the Son—has a transforming effect of the mind. In the first place, the reasons for self-centeredness begin to drop away in light of the affirming message of God's acceptance and healing forgiveness. A larger view of life becomes evident as the pageantry of the great controversy between good and evil comes into focus. The eyes begin to see and the ears hear; the calloused heart is softened and revived.

How God desires to do this for each of us! But we are turned inward, afraid and self-protective. For this we are not condemned. As our text today conveys, it is only if we refuse to accept His healing that we are bound to live out the consequences of our spiritual introversion. For if we allow Him to, God will love us into wholeness!

TWO LOOK-ALIKE HOUSES

He is like a man building a house, who dug deep and laid a foundation upon the rock; and when a flood arose, the river burst against that house and could not shake it, because it had been well built. Luke 6:48, N.A.S.B.

Now, if I had been telling this parable, I would have given it an entirely different treatment. Instead of telling about two houses built near each other on the river's edge, as Jesus told it, I would have pictured only one house. I would have told about one man building a magnificent edifice with the finest craftsmanship, and about the other man refusing even to lift a hammer. After all, when it comes to religion, you either have the real item or you have nothing at all, right?

But it's a good thing that Jesus didn't leave it to me to compose His parable, because—as usual—He had something much deeper and more pointed in mind. Jesus told of two look-alike houses, each claiming to be fit for human habitation. In each case, as His hearers painted mental pictures to match His words, they saw people moving into these homes, settling down, and feeling secure from the threatening elements. And then, with consternation, they imagined the human casualties as the foundationless home crumbled under the press of the flood.

Tragically, the people didn't know the secure home from the fragile home until the time of testing came. The edifice looked safe enough—if one didn't inspect the foundation!

From the point of view of outward actions, many religious people look strikingly similar. They speak the same words, go to the same church, and sing the same hymns. Each would seem to have a religious experience of adequate security, for each has settled down in its apparent comfort. Listening to Jesus' parable, however, warns us that unless one's religious experience is rooted on the right base, it will crumble under pressure. And someone will get hurt!

When Jesus says that He is the foundation stone (1 Peter 2:6), He is not speaking a cliché. Those whose religion is a personal adoration of, and fascination with, Jesus Christ have a foundation, a root motivation, for their whole spiritual life that is powerful and unchanging. They are not depending on fellow Christians (who may prove to be false); they are not resting on a creed (which they may find to be inadequate); they are not building on feelings (which often change). They are grounded on the Changeless One. And they will not fall.

THE BANNER OF THE LORD

Who is this that looks forth like the dawn, fair as the moon, bright as the sun, terrible as an army with banners? S. of Sol. 6:10, R.S.V.

One of the most fascinating biblical portrayals of the bond between God and His people is found in the Song of Solomon. The narrative is rich with expressions of mutual delight that the bride and the Bridegroom find in each other. And when the bride experiences the torment of separation from her beloved, she expresses no doubt in their relationship. "I am my beloved's and my beloved is mine," she says confidently (S. of Sol. 6:3, R.S.V.).

Her statement is most revealing when the preceding circumstances are understood. The Bridegroom had come to her in the night, asking to be allowed in. Incredibly, her response reflected feelings of being inconvenienced at his request! "I have stripped off my dress; must I put it on again? I have washed my feet; must I soil them again?" (chap. 5:3, N.E.B). Putting his hand through the latchhole and finding the door bolted, he departed, making no further demand.

Hastening to open the door, she went out into the night in a desperate search for him. She was beaten and wounded by the watchmen of the city walls, who took away her veil, the symbol of her respectability. It should have been enough to make anyone give up! But something comforted her and gave her the confidence that he would return for her—even though she was aware of her disappointing behavior toward him: she trusted the quality of his love!

Her bridegroom was a king. He, like other monarchs, had an emblem that represented his power and dominion. As a banner, it was carried into battle for a rallying point and went before his army when they victoriously marched back into the city. Reminiscent of this, the bride described the king's posture toward her by declaring, "His banner over me was love" (chap. 2:4, R.S.V.). When the Bridegroom returned for her, he rejoiced in her understanding of their relationship. In spite of her failings, he saw her as a returning, victorious army carrying high his banner!

Though we have not always been consistent in our response toward God, we can be sure that His attitude toward us is unchanging. We are His, and He is ours! "May we shout for joy over [our] victory, and in the name of our God set up our banners!" (Ps. 20:5, R.S.V.).

MORE THAN MY SALVATION

If a man's building stands, he will be rewarded; if it burns, he will have to bear the loss; and yet he will escape with his life, as one might from a fire. 1 Cor. 3:14, 15, N.E.B.

Some very interesting names are registered in the Faith Hall of Fame. We're not at all surprised to see the names under the portraits of Abraham and Enoch. We would expect to see Noah, Moses, and even David. But as we walk down the hall of Hebrews, chapter 11, we are surprised to see a sketchy portrait of a burly looking fellow with long hair and deformed eyes. His name is Samson.

Samson—the God-selected deliverer of Israel, who seemed to spend less time fighting Philistine men than he did flirting with their women. The physical giant and the moral pygmy, more apt to swing jawbones than to lead men into prayer. The champion of freedom who died in chains under a pile of Philistine-carved temple stones, who destroyed more of the enemy in his death than in his whole life. What a strange incongruity that he should be selected as a great man of faith.

We must realize that we are dealing with two somewhat separate issues: salvation and effectiveness in witness. Though Samson came to a saving trust in God, his usefulness in bringing others to that same trust was, at best, a very mixed report. And while we have cause to believe that Samson will be saved, it is certain that Samson died in deep chagrin that his life had been so essentially wasted.

Before we are too hard on Samson, however, we should ask whether our own spiritual life is fixated on our own salvation, or whether—with that issue settled—we are enthralled with the bigger issues! What could be more satisfying than to learn to live beyond just our own salvation.

In these final days of earth's history, the giants of faith will not be those who will be "barely" saved, as though out of a fire. Our Father is longing for people who will stand tall in a turbulent world. At a time when every earthly means of support shall be stripped away, when there is a time of trouble such as never was, only those who are sure of their salvation, who are sure of God's attitude toward them, will be able to take their minds off themselves and help others reshape their attitude toward God.

A LESSON IN FRUSTRATED COMPASSION

"O Jerusalem, Jerusalem. . . . How often have I longed to gather your children, as a hen gathers her brood under her wings; but you would not let me." Matt. 23:37, N.E.B.

I had no intention of bringing home a kitty. But there she was, curled up into a tiny ball in a box in front of the Lucky supermarket, two little points of ears distinguishing her head from the rest of her. I paused. She was mostly gray with little streaks of gold. I knew how much my kid wanted a kitty . . .

We called her Lucky, not only because that was where I found her but because that's what she'd have to be in order to survive with all the various dogs in our neighborhood. And survive she did, with spunk and coyness. Barely eight months later she had her first batch of kittens. Though she was a particularly good mother, only three lived.

Midsummer I began to notice how painfully thin Lucky had become. When I discovered that she was still allowing her kittens to nurse from her, I began to take measures to discourage them. Soon after, she looked fatter but became somewhat bad tempered. It wasn't long before I realized that she was pregnant again. Her weight gain was strictly around her girth.

The chill of fall was in the air. Lucky refused to eat much. I prepared a place for her, as I had the first time she'd had kittens. One day she reappeared, thin again. Her kittens were nowhere to be found, and she showed no signs of going to them. I finally located them in the old deserted doghouse. They were scattered and dying. Every effort I made to save them was to no avail. Lucky wanted no part of them. It made me think of today's text.

Lucky couldn't understand how much I wanted to help her and her kittens. And though, of course, her situation did not accurately parallel that of Jerusalem, it did give me an awakened sense of frustrated compassion. It made me realize, if only fractionally, how God must feel when we get ourselves into deep trouble, yet will not permit Him to help us. To force His goodness upon us would only produce terror and resistance. How heaven must marvel at His divine restraint!

The next time someone wonders out loud, "Why doesn't God *do* something?" I think I'll tell him about Lucky.

SAVED BY FEAR?

[Noah] and his wife, and his sons and their wives, went into the boat to escape the flood. . . . Seven days later the flood came. Gen. 7:7-10, T.E.V.

For more than a century Noah had been pleading for people to flee from the coming Flood and enter the ark. They had known for 120 years that it was big enough for them and that the door was open to them. Preoccupied, skeptical, peer-captured, they would have none of it. Even the stunning animal procession, in the end, could not move them. And when an unseen hand shut the big door and locked it, they went on with eating, drinking, and planning weddings. They were only mildly curious.

Until the rain came. Suddenly startled, they watched in mounting terror as the waters rose around their ankles. They began to pound desperately on the doors of the big boat, begging entrance. All at once they genuinely wanted to do the very thing that Noah had wanted them to do for all those decades. They wanted in!

But it was too late. Noah couldn't open the door, and God wouldn't open it. Had He changed His mind? Or was He simply aware that a motive of frantic fear is not a saving motive?

If God could save people who come to Him out of fear, then He could have reopened the doors of the ark and welcomed them in. He could have saved Achan as the stones began to fall, or Korah and his friends as the earth opened to swallow them.

But while fear is a great motivator, it is a very poor teacher. While it tells us that there is great pain in living apart from God, it does not describe God. It pours adrenalin into the heart, but not love. It terrifies, but does not win. The dripping people outside the ark were impressed with the rising waters but not with the One who had so graciously provided them a way of escape. Any selfish person would just as soon not drown. But salvation is not the avoidance of drowning; it is adoration and trust of the Saviour.

God did not send the Flood in order to scare people into salvation but to stay in touch with the bare handful of those who were still open to Him. "Believers" were an endangered species, well-nigh extinct. And He moved boldly to create a new "reserve" in which they could once again prosper and grow.

KEEPING UP WITH GOD'S GOODNESS

"If you have raced with men on foot, and they have wearied you, how will you compete with horses?" Jer. 12:5, R.S.V.

We "work up" to things. We take algebra before calculus. We try the beginners' ski slope before the more challenging course. Many times, as in the case of young children, just growing up helps. In a similar way God first invites us to walk with Him before He challenges us to run. It is only when we allow everyday circumstances to hinder us that we begin to lag behind. It happened to Jeremiah.

God called Jeremiah to plead with Judah to turn from their corrupt practices that were ruining the nation. He prophesied the destruction of Jerusalem at the hands of Babylonian invaders. However, the people ridiculed him, believing that God would never allow Jerusalem to be destroyed because the Temple was there. The worst of it was that these idolaters were prospering!

Worn down and confused, Jeremiah spilled out his complaint to God. In essence he said, "Why are You blessing these people? Why don't You shake them up? You told me to tell them they're doomed, and then You prosper them! I feel like a fool! It only makes them mock You" (Jer. 12:1-4). In response, God gently chides him, "If you have raced with men on foot, and they have wearied you, how will you compete with horses?" In other words: "If you can't keep up with Me now, how will you catch up later?"

Jeremiah had lost sight of God and His methodology. He'd become bogged down by seeing God bless apparently unworthy people. He had forgotten that God has a better way to reach His people. "Let him who glories glory in this, that he understands and knows me, that I am the Lord who practice steadfast love, justice, and righteousness in the earth; for in these things I delight" (chap. 9:24, R.S.V.).

God tried to help Jeremiah understand that in showing Judah kindness and tolerance, He meant to lead them and the neighboring nations to a change of heart (chap. 12:14-17; Rom. 2:4, N.E.B.). "I bound all Israel and all Judah to myself, says the Lord, so that they should become my people to win a name for me, and praise and glory; but they did not listen" (chap. 13:11, N.E.B.). Consequently, the surrounding nations that might have been blessed by them became instead their destroyers.

Jeremiah might have looked to the Lord and never gotten weary (Isa. 40:31)! May we learn this lesson.

THE POLITICS OF HEAVEN

None of them will have to teach his fellow citizen or tell his fellow countryman,"Know the Lord." For they will all know me, from the least to the greatest. Heb. 8:11, T.E.V.

The assignment was to decide on the most ideal form of government. Our college history professor, with a faint twinkle in his eyes, was arguing for a benevolent dictatorship. "After all," he said, "you don't have to wait for the people to go through that cumbersome process of deciding what to do. You trust the good intentions of your leader and do what he says."

Several students, however, were stoutly affirming that the best form of government was a theocracy. "This was the form God chose for Israel," they argued, "and this is how it will be when we get to heaven. God will be the unquestioned leader, and the redeemed will simply do what He says." There was no twinkle in their eyes.

Before you cast a vote, may I raise a few questions? Why would God go to such lengths to teach His people how to make moral decisions here on earth if in the new earth we won't need to make decisions any longer? Is the most important type of decision the Christian can make one of simply saying Yes to God's power? Does a decision to submit to authority represent the highest expression of Christian maturity?

Or is God seeking to get His people intelligently to align their minds with the great principles of His universe? Does He not wish for us to become mature? Paul says that the mature are those who "have their faculties trained by practice to distinguish good from evil" (Heb. 5:14, R.S.V.). To become mature, then, means that people must have opportunity to struggle with important moral choices and to bear accountability for their own acts.

A democracy is a slow, cumbersome, and inefficient form of government. It's not the recommended approach if people want to get a project done in a hurry. But Christians have cherished democracy because they realize that getting a task done isn't as important as what happens to the personhood of the citizens in the process of doing the task.

Since a democracy assumes the right of all people to be involved in making moral choices, to accept accountability for those choices, and to defer to the needs of the larger group, it often prepares people well for the loving, responsible freedom of heaven.

May 12

LIKE A ROARING LION

For I am God and not a man, the Holy One in your midst; I will not come with threats like a roaring lion. Hosea 11:9, 10, N.E.B.

Many of our concepts about God are reflections of how we have been treated by others. Some people are like the little girl who grew up feeling that God is not friendly—because she had been warned repeatedly during church service to "straighten up and sit still! You're in God's house!"

Perhaps the one most common denominator in our misconceptions regarding God is the element of our feeling threatened by Him. Certainly there seems reason to be! After all, He can inflict pain upon us or bless us; surely the best policy is to keep on His good side. And so we sing "Trust and Obey"—all the while trusting that we'd better obey!

Does God need to cash in on our trepidation? Is it possible that we have translated as threats His warnings regarding the sure outcome of our rebellion? To caution someone about the results of putting his hand into the fire is not the same as saying, "If you do, I'll burn you!" Listen as God describes His true feelings toward His wayward people:

"When Israel was a boy, I loved him; I called my son out of Egypt; but the more I called, the further they went from me. . . . It was I who taught Ephraim to walk, I who had taken them in my arms; but they did not know that I . . . led them with bonds of love—that I had lifted them like a little child to my cheek, that I had bent down to feed them. . . . How can I give you up, Ephraim, how surrender you, Israel?" (Hosea 11:1-8, N.E.B.).

Ephraim was about to go into captivity as a result of their wickedness. "Foreigners fed on his strength, but he was unaware" (chap. 7:9, N.E.B.). But God's love was unchanging. "I will not turn around and destroy Ephraim; for I am God and not a man, the Holy One in your midst; I will not come with threats like a roaring lion." His was not the threatening roar of an angry lion ready to attack and devour his adversary. His roar was meant to call His erring children back to Him. "No," He says. "When I roar, I who am God, my sons shall come with speed out of the west" (verse 10).

And that makes all the difference in the world!

SATAN'S CRY FOR JUSTICE

"In the Law Moses has laid down that such women are to be stoned. What do you say about it?" They put the question as a test, hoping to frame a charge against him. John 8:5, 6, N.E.B.

Politicians seeking election have a special knack for playing up one particular issue in society: criminals who are not brought to justice. These vote-seekers tell vivid stories of common thieves and muggers who are let off the hook by liberal courts and maneuvering lawyers, not getting the punishment they justly deserve. A vote for them, we are told, is a vote for certain punishment of all deserving offenders.

It is, of course, an appeal to that part in each of us that says the only thing one can do with a sinner is to punish him, and that to do less than punish is to support lawlessness. It is very similar to the pitch the Pharisees used against Jesus that day they brought a caught-in-the-act sinner before Jesus to see if indeed He would support their "law and order" agenda.

It's a good thing Jesus wasn't running for election, because He was intent on doing more than upholding justice. His goal was to transform that bruised, confused, frightened woman into one who could again walk among her friends without embarrassment.

Strange, isn't it, how the enemy of Christ—whom we usually think of as steeped in lawlessness and injustice—can appear to turn and cry out for justice! Interestingly, this showdown in John 8 is a foretaste of the very conflict that will explode in the final judgment. For as God stands up on behalf of His people (Zech. 3:1, 2), the "accuser of our brethren" (Rev. 12:10) will accuse God of being unjust in not doing to sinners what "justice" requires—destroying them.

But God does not break the law when He acts in a redemptive, loving way, for the ultimate imperative of the law is that of love. The law defends love; it does not make it captive. And so when Jesus poured out a message of healing forgiveness to this guilty woman, He was acting entirely in harmony with the law of love. Yet that aspect of law is the one Satan and his followers are incapable of understanding.

Man's plan for criminal justice frightens people into external compliance. It should never be confused with God's plan for healing sinners. Jesus did not ignore that woman's sin. First He healed her. Then He died for her.

TURNING ON THE LIGHT

I always do what is acceptable to him. John 8:29, N.E.B.

Many believers trace their misgivings about God to the Old Testament accounts of His dealings with people. They wonder if the God of the Old Testament and Jesus Christ are even compatible. Yet Christ Himself said, "I do nothing on my own authority, but in all that I say, I have been taught by my Father. He who sent me is present with me, and has not left me alone; for I always do what is acceptable to him" (John 8:28, 29, N.E.B.).

Christ's life and teachings *are* compatible with the God portrayed in the Old Testament. In fact, Jesus explained that He was the "I am" of the Old Testament (verse 58)! Though it may not immediately appear so, Jesus—as the Christ or as the I Am—"is the same yesterday, today, and for ever" (Heb. 13:8, N.E.B.). And His mission has always been to reveal the Father to mankind.

"But," you exclaim, "the God of the Old Testament was so severe! Jesus was nothing like Him!" This may be a case of seeing shadows in the night, like the child who was sure there was a burglar in her room. When her mother turned on the light, she saw that it was only her bathrobe hanging on her closet door. Similarly, we can chase away the shadows of the Old Testament by "turning on" the light of the New Testament.

Also, it helps to let clearer passages of Scripture illuminate those that are more ambiguous. For instance, God says, "Loyalty is my desire, not sacrifice, not whole-offerings but the knowledge of God" (Hosea 6:6, N.E.B.). We need not struggle over the idea that God is more interested in balancing the account of sins than He is in our coming to know Him. The ministry of Christ to people such as Mary Magdalene demonstrates this truth.

Again we are told, "Yet the Lord is waiting to show you his favour, yet he yearns to have pity on you; for the Lord is a God of justice" (Isa. 30:18, N.E.B.). This certainly puts a different slant on the concept of a just God being sternly ready to punish the wicked! Jesus echoed this expanded understanding of justice when He stated, "It was not to judge the world that God sent his Son into the world, but that through him the world might be saved" (John 3:17, N.E.B.).

Let's "turn on" the light and rejoice!

DON'T MAKE THEM MAD, DAD!

Fathers, do not provoke your children to anger, but bring them up in the discipline and instruction of the Lord. Eph. 6:4, R.S.V.

Try thinking back to your own childhood. Can you ever remember a time when you got up in the morning, looked yourself in the mirror, and said, "I think that today I shall be rebellious"? Can you recall a time when you made a simple, perverse choice to be angry with your parents?

It is a principle that most children would rather be peaceful and happy than be angry and grim. Paul's premise in today's text—though painful for parents to admit—is that when a child is angry, it is quite possibly the parent's fault if the parent has dealt with the child in a way that reveals lack of respect for his rightful sense of freedom and individuality.

Quite often we parents want so badly for our children to obey that we goad them, badger them, even belittle them, in the name of discipline. Then when they respond as Paul predicts they will, we often add our children's anger to their list of crimes. We fail to recognize that rebellion is the inherent result of such an approach.

But that raises a serious question about why there are so many rebels against our heavenly Father. He has never acted toward us in a way that would goad us into anger. Even as He has dealt with our most serious sins, He has done so in a way that reveals respect for our self-esteem and protects our individuality. He has not sought to shame us into submission or overpower us with towering threats of retribution. Why, then, are so many people hostile against our gracious Father?

Jesus put His finger right on the problem when He said, "An enemy has done this" (Matt. 13:28, R.S.V.). Rebels are not hostile against God per se, but against the view of God that Satan has portrayed. And they have fallen for it, thinking that it is the real item! I can scarcely count the number of times I have spoken to persons who appear to be scampering out the back door of the church; yet as we talk about their reasons, they unfold a picture of God painted in dark, oppressive lines by the enemy himself. And they feel they have just cause to be angry with God.

Amazingly, God does not chastise His people for feeling that way about Him. Rather, He illumines them!

THE GOD OF POSITIVE PROMISE

Every promise of God finds its affirmative in him, and through him can be said the final amen, to the glory of God. 2 Cor. 1:20, Phillips.

"I'll be there to meet you." His promise was so reassuring! She would be flying some two thousand miles across the country to a large metropolis where she then needed to make a closely timed connection with a bus line in order to arrive at her destination. Having not traveled much, her unfamiliarity with airport terminals caused her no little anxiety. Her friend's quick response filled her heart with warmth. At the airport two days later, however, the last vestiges of comfort had long vanished when her friend arrived, an hour and a half late. "I'm sorry!" he said too quickly. "I got tied up. Can you catch another bus?"

Making promises comes easily. However, our performance may not always be as good as our intentions. And few things are quite as frustrating and potentially hurtful as broken promises. Besides generating the irritation of being inconvenienced, when someone you have counted on fails you, your relationship with that person can sustain significant damage. Doubts of self-worth can creep in; trust may be replaced with wariness. A hesitancy to take people at their word may develop.

Unfortunately, these attitudes and feelings easily carry over into our relationship with God. Though we don't mean to, we may have hidden feelings of wariness regarding His promises concerning us. Then, since we know we shouldn't feel that way, we also struggle with guilt. What is God's posture toward us in these things?

In our text today we read of "The God of Positive Promise." He understands our need for affirmation, especially since often we do not immediately see the results of His promises. Indeed, that is why He sent Jesus to live among us: to give visual confirmation to His pledged covenant with us. "For all the promises of God find their Yes in him. That is why we utter the Amen through him, to the glory of God" (2 Cor. 1:20, R.S.V.). God has shown us through the life of His Son that He *has* forgiven us. He *has* accepted us. He *has* made an end to sin—that separation between Himself and us, His troubled children.

God's positive attitude toward us, lived out in the life of Christ, is meant to enable us to express confidently, "Amen! We believe it! Let it happen!"

FEELING COMFORTED IN HIS PRESENCE

This is why we are bold enough to approach God in complete confidence, through our faith in him. Eph. 3:12, Jerusalem.

Try to imagine how you would feel if you were a misbehaving student who had just been sent by your teacher to see the principal. Guilty as charged, you stand staring up at his belt buckle, sweaty hands clasped behind you. His voice seems to tumble down from the lofty spaces above. You would probably wish to be just about anywhere else!

Or imagine yourself to be a groom on your wedding day. You have just watched your soon-to-be father-in-law escort the most magnificent young woman in the world down the aisle and place her hand on your arm. Now, staring into her radiant eyes, you stand in the presence of the minister and the wedding party. Can you think of anywhere else in the world you would rather be?

Whenever we approach a person, we feel some definite emotions about being in that person's presence. Some meetings we would like to avoid; others we would like to repeat. It depends entirely upon the interplay of feelings between the two parties. And most of these feelings center around whether we will feel enhanced or diminished in the presence of the other.

Judging from today's verse, how would Paul likely feel in the presence of God? Would he feel tense, restrained, and intimidated before his Lord? Would he come reluctantly to his Father, wishing that he could be almost anywhere else? Paraphrasing his comment to the Ephesians, perhaps we could hear Paul saying, "I feel freedom in my God's presence . . . because I *know* Him. I trust His ongoing love and acceptance. I feel no need for impressive pretense, for mental game-playing, for anxious endeavors to endear myself to Him, for I am certain of His attitude toward me. It was portrayed in Jesus."

Some would object to such a view, asserting that sinners have no right to feel comfortable in the presence of a holy God. They fear that such comfort will result in laxness in our endeavors to overcome sin, or that it lessens our perception of God's great abhorrence of sin. But there is a difference between feeling comforted as a sinner by God's presence and feeling comfortable while sinning in spite of God's presence. For He "who comforts us in all our affliction" (2 Cor. 1:4, N.A.S.B.) heals us by that warm closeness so that we no longer need to sin.

THE PURPOSEFUL GIFT

But the fruit of the Spirit is love, joy, peace, patience, kindness, goodness, faithfulness, gentleness, self-control; against such there is no law. Gal. 5:22, 23, R.S.V.

When it's time to give someone a present, we usually have to decide between getting something that person would use or something he or she would really like. How exciting it is to find a gift that fits both categories. This is especially true when it comes to giving to our children.

We read in Luke 11:13, "If you then, who are evil, know how to give good gifts to your children, how much more will the heavenly Father give the Holy Spirit to those who ask him!" (R.S.V.). One of the best gifts that God could give us is His Spirit. And it is both useful and wonderfully pleasing.

First, let us examine the usefulness of this extraordinary gift. Speaking of it, Jesus said, "I will send him to you. When he comes, he will convince the world of the meaning of sin, of true goodness and of judgment . . . for he will draw on my truth and reveal it to you" (John 16:7-14, Phillips). How wonderfully practical! And we are even told how it works. The Spirit will draw on the truth in Jesus and reveal it to us. What is the truth in Jesus? "He who has seen me has seen the Father" (chap. 14:9, R.S.V.).

What revealed qualities of the Father are inherent in the gift of the Spirit? Paul enumerated them: "love, joy, peace, patience, kindness, goodness, faithfulness, gentleness, self-control." In these very qualities we find the second aspect of God's incredible gift: delightfulness.

Not only is the fruit of the Spirit a positive statement of God's posture toward us, it is a remarkable declaration of His intention to share Himself with us! When that revelation begins to penetrate our hearts, what tremendous delight begins to flood our being! Our God is so good, so unendingly kind and gentle, so awesomely patient and loving, so deliberately restrained when we act foolishly, that we cannot doubt His love. We bask in His joy over us. We trust in His faithfulness. And share in His peace.

That astounding gift that the Father has so sensitively chosen for us is meant to become a very part of our own being. We may partake of its richness. We may, in fact, continually share its abundance with others—which makes it all the more delightful!

Thank You, Father!

KITCHEN THEOLOGY

For even though the desire to do good is in me, I am not able to do it. I don't do the good I want to do; instead, I do the evil that I do not want to do. Rom. 7:18, 19, T.E.V.

On the surface it seemed a tranquil, domestic scene. The aroma of savory cooking drifted from the kitchen, while the Guest of honor was being politely entertained in the living room. Yet there was a poorly hidden tension crackling through the house: the spoon being slammed too hard on the table; the taut voice as the older sister invoked religious authority to get her younger sister to take life more seriously.

Jesus saw it as far more than a domestic squabble or sibling rivalry. He saw in Martha and Mary two markedly different approaches to spiritual life and to Him. And He left no doubt as to which He saw as lastingly useful.

Martha was a prototype of the Romans 7 style of religious experience. Though Jesus had been "received into her house," her experience was still one of distraction, anxiety, and trouble. Martha was tyrannized by the "oughts" of religious life. Though her mind consented that she ought to do many things to please Jesus, the doing of them was strained by fears of inadequacy. The joylessness of her manner revealed that her actions were not her free-flowing native breath.

Mary, on the other hand, had discovered the Romans 8 experience. She was enthralled by the union of her spirit with that of her Saviour, crying out "Abba! Father!" She had discovered that the essence of spiritual life was centered on relationship rather than performance. She was freed from the spirit of slavery and fear, free to know life and peace—because she was enthralled with the Life-giver.

Jesus approved Mary's choice, because He knew that her choice was the opposite of that made by Adam and Eve in the garden. He knew that just as separation from God brings every curse in its train, so personal attachment to God brings every blessing. Far from becoming a passive mystic, Mary, we know, went on to become a vigorous worker in the young church. And that is because the motivations blooming in Mary's heart could not be taken away!

Nothing can more effectively meet our deepest inner needs than to sit at Jesus' feet, absorbed in His healing revelations of His Father and in His personal affection for us.

BAND-AIDS AND NEW-HEART SURGERY

The love I speak of is . . . the love he showed to us in sending his Son as the remedy for the defilement of our sins. 1 John 4:10, N.E.B.

Hippocrates said, "Extreme remedies are very appropriate for extreme diseases." In other words, you do not apply a Band-Aid to someone who has just had open-heart surgery.

As Christians, we talk a lot about getting rid of sin in our lives. We rejoice that the blood of Jesus covers our sins. But what are we really saying? More important, what do we believe regarding the atoning sacrifice of Christ? To conceive of the death of Christ as a way to appease an angry God is to diminish the whole process of redemption. It makes Jesus a divine Band-Aid over the "new-heart surgery" God is performing for each of us.

The way in which we view sin determines how we approach the Surgeon. If sin is bad behavior, we come expecting Him to replace it with better behavior. Unfortunately, as in the case of literal open-heart surgery where harmful habits caused degeneration, corrective surgery isn't enough. Even as physical health is ensured only with a lifestyle change, "new-heart surgery" is successful only to the degree our opinion of God has changed.

Our God saw as appropriate in dealing with the disease of sin the extreme remedy of sending "his only Son into the world to bring us life." Notice: "And his love was disclosed to us *in this*" (1 John 4:9, N.E.B.). May I propose an important clarification? It was the *love* revealed in the sending of the Son, not the physical death of Christ on the cross, that was the primary remedy. "The love I speak of is . . . the love he showed to us in sending his Son as the remedy for the defilement of our sins" (verse 10).

Let me explain further. In Hebrews 3:12, Paul counsels, "Take care, brethren, lest there be in any of you an evil, unbelieving heart, leading you to fall away from the living God" (R.S.V.). Unbelief in God is what makes the heart evil—not unbelief that He *is,* but unbelief in *who* He is. It would do no good at all to remove the results of that unbelief from our lives (sin) if we retain the hurtful opinion of God that is causing the problem in the first place! Therefore, God showed us Himself in His Son. He showed us all that we need to change our minds about Him.

That is the "new-heart surgery"!

SECURE ENOUGH TO DARE

The first came before him, saying, "Lord, your pound has made ten pounds more." And he said to him, "Well done, good servant! Because you have been faithful in a very little, you shall have authority over ten cities." Luke 19:16, 17, R.S.V.

Imagine an investment counselor coming to you with a surefire deal to get a two-to-one return on an investment. You would no doubt be keenly interested and would begin reaching for your checkbook. If he were to offer a five-to-one return, however, you would probably feel rather apprehensive about the risks involved and ask for time to think over the proposition.

But if the investment counselor were to offer you a ten-to-one return, you would probably think, *That's far too risky! I wonder if this fellow is in trouble with the Securities and Exchange Commission. People lose their shirts on this kind of daring speculation. I'm going to play it safe.*

Yet in Jesus' parable, this is the man who received the most lavish affirmation! He was bold enough, with broad enough vision, to venture into a project of major proportions. It held the promise of being a stunning success . . . or a monumental failure. And the money belonged to someone else!

Perhaps that is the key. He had been asked to invest that money on behalf of another person: his Master. Certainly he asked himself, "What if I invest it in a daring project, and something goes wrong? Will He be outraged at me, and condemn me for making an honest try? Or will He at least be glad that I was willing to reach for something of consequence?" In the end, it was his confidence in his Master that led him to manage the money boldly. He was not only commended; he was given the responsibility of managing ten cities.

But Jesus' parable isn't primarily about money. It's about people who feel that the surest way to retain God's favor is to live tiny, conventional, risk-free lives. It's a message about a Master who wraps His people in such intense security that they will be willing to make big plans for Him. If something goes wrong, He will say, "I'm delighted that at least you were willing to try. Here! I have more resources for you; try again!"

The Master called the servant "good and faithful" because he understood the heart of the Master—which made him secure enough to dare!

THE VEGETABLE LAMB OF TARTARY

"Away with you, Satan," he said; "you think as men think, not as God thinks." Mark 8:33, N.E.B.

The legend of the vegetable lamb of Tartary, half plant and half animal, originates from the Middle Ages. When European travelers to the Far East were first introduced to cotton, a plant they knew nothing of at that time, they took it for wool—a substance they did know. Since wool came from sheep, they deduced that cotton came from lambs that grew from a tree to which the lambs were attached by their navels. It was said that the lambs grazed as the plant bent to the ground. The lambs and plant died after all the grass around had been eaten.

We laugh at such preposterous ideas. Yet such legends often survive for centuries as accepted fact. It was no different in Jesus' day. The coming of Messiah had been so cloaked with Jewish tradition and legend that when Jesus "began to teach [His disciples] that the Son of Man had to undergo great sufferings, and to be rejected by the elders, chief priests, and doctors of the law; to be put to death, and to rise again three days afterwards . . . Peter took him by the arm and began to rebuke him," even though Jesus "spoke about it plainly" (Mark 8:31, 32, N.E.B.)!

We marvel at Peter's attitude. He had it all wrong! So wrong, in fact, that Jesus was prompted to utter one of His most startling rebukes: " 'Away with you, Satan,' he said; 'you think as men think, not as God thinks' " (verse 33, N.E.B.). May I suggest that our ideas of why Jesus had to die might be as far off the mark as was Peter's resistance to its even happening?

Jesus addressed Satan directly not to scold or humiliate Peter in front of his friends, but to dramatically draw attention to the originator of such thinking. Our first parents accepted the fatal deception that they had life apart from the Creator. When Peter cried out, "No, Lord, this shall never happen to you" (Matt. 16:22, N.E.B.), he was actually reaffirming the serpent's lie, "Of course you will not die" (Gen. 3:4, N.E.B.).

The death of Christ as the Son of man was to demonstrate once and for all what separation from God brings. To imply that God requires death as a penalty for not believing Him is little better than presuming wool to grow on trees—no matter how many people think so.

"YOU ARE A SEVERE MAN"

Then another came, saying, "Lord, here is your pound, which I kept laid away in a napkin; for I was afraid of you, because you are a severe man." Luke 19:20, 21, R.S.V.

Most authors writing in the field of human personality classify extreme shyness as a type of emotional disorder. The withdrawn, fearful, passive person who seldom finds the courage to assert himself into any social interaction is not enjoying his full personhood. Many authors trace this pattern of excessive shyness to a very strong, overbearing person (usually a parent) in the person's earlier life.

The usual pattern is of one who is often harshly rebuked for doing something wrong. The emotional risks involved in making a mistake become so great that one withdraws into the safety of doing nothing at all. As the pattern continues, one increasingly cowers into solitude, risking no mistakes, no new approaches to friendship, no new adventures in life.

How grievous it was to Jesus, then, when His earthly friends held His Father to be "a severe man." So He told them a parable of a man who took his life—his talents, energies, even his personhood—and hid it inside the handkerchief of fear. His whole existence became flat, "safe," and unproductive. No new friendships to broaden his horizons, no new methods of witnessing, no new dimensions of self-development. Why? Because he saw the Master as one who would pounce on him with severe judgments should he endeavor and fail.

Though Jesus' parable ends with strong dissatisfaction for all who hold such a view, it is a bright beacon of hope for all who hold the Father to be the "Infinite Eavesdropper" who lurks in the corners of your mind, ready to catch you in some little flaw. You can almost hear Jesus shouting, "My Father is not like that! In His friendship, you are safe to risk, to dare, to grow, . . . and yes, even to stumble and then try again. My Father will help you."

In Jesus' parable the servant was condemned not for doing anything wrong but for holding such an unnecessarily tragic view of his Master. It is not a parable about financial stewardship or about helping with the missionary activities of the local church. Rather, it is one of Jesus' most potent means of pointing out just how deeply our view of God shapes the quality of our entire life. "In My Father's friendship," He says, "you are free to dare!"

EVER ASCENDING

Do not lose your own safe foothold. But grow in the grace and in the knowledge of our Lord and Saviour Jesus Christ. 2 Peter 3:17, 18, N.E.B.

Mountain climbers understand how important it is to find a safe foothold before continuing upward. Only the reckless will move before they are sure of their position. Caution, however, does not imply inertness. In fact, to be cautious suggests that movement is anticipated. Fear produces inactivity. It is altogether a different matter to yell "Stop!" than it is to warn "Be careful!"

In the area of Christian growth, three distinct attitudes pervade: recklessness, caution, and fear. I believe our view of God will decide which attitude we adopt. In 2 Peter 3:4, we read of the reckless approach to God: "Where now is the promise of his coming? Our fathers have been laid to their rest, but still everything continues exactly as it has always been since the world began" (N.E.B.). Such people believe that God is uninvolved in the affairs of men—either because He doesn't exist, doesn't care, or is so indulgent that He won't react.

God cares a great deal! Verse 9 tells us, "It is not that the Lord is slow in fulfilling his promise, as some suppose, but that he is very patient with you, because it is not his will for any to be lost, but for all to come to repentance" (N.E.B.)—to experience a healing change of mind concerning Him.

We may be cautious without being afraid. Though warned, "Do not lose your own safe foothold," because of potential error, we are urged to "grow in the grace and in the knowledge of our Lord and Saviour Jesus Christ." The coming of the Day of the Lord need not paralyze us with fear. We can "look eagerly" forward to it because "we have his promise" (verses 12, 13, N.E.B.). Our picture of God can be reassuringly and excitingly clear in Jesus! And Jesus promised that special preparation is being made in the Father's house for our homecoming.

We've only just begun to know the Father through Christ! By His warm and ready acceptance of us, we can be sure that God desires us ever to be ascending in our approach to Him. New insights will thrill our souls as we climb higher and higher, away from the delusions of this world. And should we slip, we know that underneath us are His everlasting arms.

And some clear day we shall see forever!

THE BEST EXAMPLE OF FAITH

I am crucified with Christ: nevertheless I live; yet not I, but Christ liveth in me: and the life which I now live in the flesh I live by the faith of the Son of God, who loved me, and gave himself for me. Gal. 2:20.

I have often asked groups of people to nominate whom they believe to be the best example of "faith" in the Bible. Most people favor the familiar heroes of faith: Abraham, Job, Moses, or Elijah. Some mention John the Baptist or David.

When asked to explain their choices, people usually speak of those events, such as Abraham's offering of Isaac, in which people do remarkable things that don't appear to make any sense. For many Christians it appears that faith has more to do with blind incredulity than with a life-changing relationship.

This is revealed by the fact that virtually no one ever nominates Jesus Christ as the best example of faith. It seldom occurs to us that He lived the life that He did only by His faith relationship with His Father. It is common to think of Jesus as an example in terms of proper behavior for us to follow. But the primary way in which Jesus is our example is in the trusting, depending, informed friendship with God that enabled Jesus' own proper behavior.

Jesus spoke explicitly of His faith relationship with divinity outside of Himself: "I do nothing on my own authority, but in all that I say, I have been taught by my Father. He who sent me is present with me, and has not left me alone; for I always do what is acceptable to him" (John 8:28, 29, N.E.B.). The divinity that charged Jesus' life with power and purpose was not His own, but His Father's.

Watching the way Jesus lived His life charges the word *faith* with explicit meaning. As He fell dying to the ground in Gethsemane, crushed by the most difficult decision any person had ever been called upon to make, He cried out three times, "Not my will, but thine be done." Hours later, as the clouds of the second death began to surround Him, His last words spoke explicit confidence: "Father, into thy hands I commit my spirit!" (Luke 23:46, R.S.V.).

When Paul describes the means by which he lives the new life, he says it is through a very special kind of faith relationship—Jesus' kind of faith. And that same relationship is available to us!

FOOL'S GOLD AND BLIND FAITH

So I advise you to buy from me gold refined in the fire, to make you truly rich. Rev. 3:18, N.E.B.

In the gold rush days of the mid 1800s, many people set their sights on California. Often selling all they possessed, they migrated west in hope of striking it rich. Some did strike it rich, most did not. Perhaps the saddest stories told are about those who thought they had when, in fact, their claims consisted of pyrite—fool's gold!

In the book of Revelation are chronicled the seven different phases of the Christian church since the days of the apostles. To Laodicea—those who live in the very end of time—God says, "You say, 'How rich I am! And how well I have done! I have everything I want.' In fact, though you do not know it, you are the most pitiful wretch, poor, blind, and naked" (Rev. 3:17, N.E.B.).

How many times I have heard this passage read through clenched teeth, as if God could barely restrain His anger and disgust! Yet He clearly says in verse 19, "All whom I love, I reprove and discipline" (N.E.B.). With the concept of discipling, we understand that it is with urgency that He would teach us our error in order to save us from being exposed and shamed. He even offers a solution: "I advise you to buy from me gold refined in the fire, to make you truly rich" (verse 18, N.E.B.).

What is this preciously genuine gold He offers us? "These [trials] have come so that your faith—of greater worth than gold, which perishes even though refined by fire—may be proved genuine and may result in praise, glory and honor when Jesus Christ is revealed" (1 Peter 1:7, N.I.V.). It is our faith in God, as it is tested in the fires of personal experience, that brings us "all the riches of assured understanding and the knowledge of God's mystery, of Christ, in whom are hid all the treasures of wisdom and knowledge" (Col. 2:2, 3, R.S.V.).

God does not desire us to have a blind faith in Him. If what we believe about Him does not integrate realistically and effectively into every facet of our lives and dealings with others, it's as good as fool's gold. The solution involves fellowship with Him. In essence He says, "I understand, and I want to help you. Let Me come have supper with you so we can talk!" (see Rev. 3:15, 20).

Let's hear Him out!

JESUS IS A GENTLEMAN

"Here I stand knocking at the door; if anyone hears my voice and opens the door, I will come in and sit down to supper with him and he with me." Rev. 3:20, N.E.B.

Jesus can invade the vast emptiness of space, speaking but a word and thrusting in worlds, solar systems, and galaxies. He can invade a deep-rock tomb, penetrating even the ears of the dead with the command "Lazarus, come forth!"

He can invade the cells of a disease-ridden body with the simple command "Be whole!" Without asking permission, Jesus commands the armies of heaven, the stars of the galaxies, and the electrons in the atoms.

But when He approaches the loyalties of the human mind, the "invasion" stops. He makes no commands, implies no threats. He does not force the door. The Scriptures portray Him standing, with utmost courtesy, outside the door, knocking. And were the door to be opened, He would enter, not to deliver a scathing rebuke for being left outside but to enjoy a pleasant meal with His new friend.

Could Jesus have commanded a solution to the problem of errant loyalties, He could have skipped some six thousand years of controversy and pain. But He knew that a commanded solution is no solution. And so, even though the Laodicean condition is a deadly one, He still only knocks.

He knocks through that aching emptiness of the heart that only He can fill, through crushing problems that only He can solve, through longings after new horizons that only He can satisfy. He knocks through direct convictions of the Spirit while reading the Scriptures, through a nagging awareness of spiritual dullness, and through the winsome appeals of a genuine friend.

Many leave the door closed to His gentle knocking because they suppose that, like a door-to-door salesman, He is simply "peddling goods." New behaviors to adopt. More things to do, and new lists of things not to do. Additional burdens to add to an already weary life. They fail to notice that the open door welcomes the Person Himself—in warm, healing fellowship. Dear reader, do you have any valid reason to say No to Him?

THE UNANSWERED QUESTION

Jesus said to them, ''Then neither will I tell you by what authority I act.'' Mark 11:33, N.E.B.

Shortly after Jesus fed a huge crowd of people with seven loaves of bread and a few small fishes, He was approached by the Pharisees who ''came out and engaged him in discussion. To test him they asked him for a sign from heaven. He sighed deeply to himself and said, 'Why does this generation ask for a sign? I tell you this: no sign shall be given to this generation' '' (Mark 8:11, 12, N.E.B).

These religious leaders wanted Jesus to show them a sign to prove His authority and messiahship. Why didn't Jesus comply with their wishes? Wouldn't it have saved Him the agony of rejection by the spiritual fathers of Israel, making His mission on earth so much easier? Certainly it would have made life simpler for the disciples. Maybe that's why Jesus warned them to beware of the leaven of the Pharisees (verse 15)—to avoid their line of reasoning.

The Pharisees wanted to see firepower! After all, the Messiah was going to free the children of Israel from Roman bondage, wasn't He? Settle a few scores! Make all the surrounding nations think twice before they trespassed onto the Promised Land! But no such sign was to be given. It would have been profoundly misleading. Jesus came to reveal that God desires to love people to wholeness, not browbeat them into submission—*all* people, including citizens of Rome!

On another occasion, as Jesus was walking in the Temple court not long after having chased away the money changers, ''the chief priests, lawyers, and elders came to him and said, 'By what authority are you acting like this? Who gave you authority to act in this way?' '' (chap. 11:27, 28, N.E.B).

Jesus understood that they desired to force Him into a corner, hoping that His answer would make Him utterly vulnerable to their destructive designs on His life. Instead, Jesus countered by asking them about the authority of John the Baptist. Afraid to expose their own devious minds to the people, they declined to answer. ''And Jesus said to them, 'Then neither will I tell you by what authority I act' '' (verse 33, N.E.B.).

Again, for Jesus to say that God was His authority would have implied overtones of muscle power in His earthly mission. In no way would Jesus misrepresent His Father's character! Power gets people's attention, but it is a poor teacher of God's truth.

TWO KINDS OF SUFFERING

He was despised and rejected by men; a man of sorrows, and acquainted with grief. Isa. 53:3, R.S.V.

A young mother looks tenderly into the eyes of her terminally ill child. She fights back the tears; the lump in her throat is too large for her to speak. Oh, how she cherishes that little life with a love measured by her suffering.

An insecure teenage girl rushes to the window to watch through hot tears as her first boyfriend walks toward the road. He has just broken up with her, and she is sure the world will end before sundown. His attentions to her were the center of her very existence to a degree measured now by her suffering.

To the extent that one loves, to that same extent one is vulnerable to suffering. To the extent that one is self-centered and insecure, to that same extent one is also vulnerable to suffering. But they are two different kinds of suffering! The first kind is rooted in the hurting of the ones who are loved. The second kind is rooted in the failure to be loved.

The suffering of one who is able to love produces character growth as he struggles in every way to bring healing and hope to another who is hurting. He longs for larger capacities of the heart, deeper sensitivities of the soul, more perseverance in prayer. But the suffering of the one who is not loved often inhibits character growth, as he grasps, manipulates, and maneuvers to get other people to reduce the hurt in his heart.

There is a flippant view of the Christian life that suggests that becoming a Christian means launching into a trouble-free life—walking on the sunny side of the street, whistling bright tunes, with the wind at our backs and a smile always on our faces. People who succumb to this view of Christianity are always stunned (and then disappointed in God) when they have to suffer the realities of this grubby planet.

Those who walk with their Master do not escape suffering; rather they exchange the nature of their suffering. They move from destructive suffering to constructive suffering, from energy-draining hurt to stretching and growing hurt.

Jesus is a man of sorrows and acquainted with grief—because He loves so much! He grieves for the emptiness, the hurt, the confusion, and the self-deception in the lives of all of us encompassed in His great heart of love.

WHY JESUS CLEANSED THE TEMPLE

He went into the temple and began driving out those who bought and sold in the temple. Mark 11:15, N.E.B.

To many people the picture of Jesus in the Temple turning over the money changers' tables and driving out the pigeon sellers and other traders is somewhat puzzling and "out of character" with the gentle Master of the Gospels. But is it?

One thing stands out in Jesus' ministry: the picture He gave of the Father. Everything He did and said revealed God as reasonable, compassionate, and approachable, so much so that it made the Israelite rulers very uncomfortable. Their position of authority gave them their hold over the people, and they played their roles to the fullest. In the process they gave a very distorted and sinister picture of God.

That is the basis of Jesus' act of cleansing the Temple. Not only had the people been left untaught as to the true meaning of the sacrifices they were required to bring, but they were scandalized by the way in which they were made monetary victims in the process. Bringing a perfectly acceptable lamb, they ran the chance of having an officiating priest reject it for some obscure reason. They were then directed to the licensed vendor of "acceptable" lambs within the Temple, who would provide them with an animal—at a higher price than one would pay elsewhere. But on the other hand, they were spared the problem of going out and purchasing another animal that also might not pass the scrutiny of the priests.

The fact that the very lambs rejected by the priests managed to be "recycled" into the pens of the "acceptable sacrifice" vendors was not unknown to the people. But they couldn't beat the system. They had to have a lamb that passed the priest's inspection. Needless to say, the whole process brought reproach upon God and His dealings with helpless mankind.

Jesus reacted! Why? Because God was grieved that He should be viewed in such a light. It was like saying that He was willing to take advantage of the needy, that He was unreasonable and arbitrary, that the whole business was in service of cold legality. So God showed the people, by the measure of passion displayed by His Son, how heinous the Temple business was in His sight. When He turned the money tables over, God proclaimed, "Money is not what is important to Me. Sheep aren't important to Me. People are!"

I'm glad that God set the record straight!

FEARLESS RIGHTEOUSNESS

Hearken to me, you who know righteousness, the people in whose heart is my law; fear not the reproach of men, and be not dismayed at their revilings. Isa. 51:7, R.S.V.

Why is the disapproval of others so terrifying to us? Often we will do almost anything to avoid having others regard us as in the wrong. Do you recognize in your own heart that intense desire to be correct, to be known as "in the right"?

Perhaps we doubt our own convictions, our own values, when they differ from the accepted values of others. Yet the fear of standing alone can make us fragile, vulnerable, easily manipulated. And in these times of confused values and intense conflict, that is not a healthy condition to be in.

How can our Father prepare a people who will be able to stand for the right in the final conflicts, against the forceful opinions of what will appear to be the entire world? How can He make us essentially unmoved by the pressures, even the outrage, of people who are themselves threatened by those "who know righteousness"?

God does not do this by barking orders at us with greater force than does the threatening world around us. His people do not trade fear for fear. Rather, we heed His invitation to listen while He instructs us in the ways of righteousness. By wise and patient teaching He writes His law in our hearts. More than that, His powerful and unchanging love works to heal that emptiness and insecurity that plagues us all. In this way He gives us the emotional strength to say, "World, it doesn't matter so much what you think of me. The God of this universe counts *me* as precious!"

God's dealings with us are complete. He begins by showing us the difference between righteousness and wickedness. Taking a second step, He helps us "internalize" the principles of righteousness; He writes them on our hearts so that they represent the very things we most want to do. Finally, He makes us so inwardly secure, so properly self-confident in Him, that we become fearless of the hassles and pressures of the unrighteous.

Paul said, "God did not give us a spirit of timidity but a spirit of power and love and self-control" (2 Tim. 1:7, R.S.V.). What greater strength is there than to know that one is fearlessly standing right in the center of God's will and His love!

SOMETIMES PRESERVATION COMES FIRST

"The Lord commanded us to do all these statutes, to fear the Lord our God, for our good always, that he might preserve us alive, as at this day." Deut. 6:24, R.S.V.

Many people have lost their lives needlessly in a fire either because they did not get out of the burning building while they had the opportunity to do so or because they went back in to retrieve something. Firemen have had to forcibly drag such people from burning buildings. That was not a time for discussion. That would come later.

When God brought Israel out of Egypt, at first they were relieved at no longer being slaves in an alien land. It didn't take them long, however, before they wanted to "go back in" to retrieve their familiar lifestyle. This was no time for discussion. God dealt forcibly with them, binding them around with His statutes and ordinances. There would be time to talk about it later.

"When your son asks you in time to come, 'What is the meaning of the testimonies and the statutes and the ordinances which the Lord our God has commanded you?' then you shall say to your son, 'We were Pharaoh's slaves in Egypt; and the Lord brought us out of Egypt with a mighty hand. . . . And the Lord commanded us to do all these statutes, to fear the Lord our God, *for our good always, that He might preserve us alive,* as at this day' " (Deut. 6:20-24, R.S.V.).

It is important to realize that fire-rescue methods are not the preferred way of dealing with people! Under ordinary situations we don't go around dragging people out of buildings. Nor do we bind them with commands and restrictions in order to preserve them alive. Life-threatening situations call for drastic measures. To the degree that one is removed from such situations, the manner in which he is dealt with changes. There is more time for talking, for explaining, for exploring all the reasons.

God's dealings with us are no different. There are times when "fire-rescue" methods are necessary in order to ensure that we will be around later to enter into dialog with Him. But God does not desire that we remain in a dragged-out-of-fire posture! To do so is not only unsatisfactory, it is unnecessary. Our Father has much to talk to us about! But He preserves us until we are ready.

Let's get started!

TEACHABLENESS

The Lord God has opened my ear, and I was not rebellious, I turned not backward. Isa. 50:5, R.S.V.

There is probably no word in theological circles that can start an argument more quickly, or raise blood pressure more surely than the word *perfection*. Too often perfection is viewed as a level of performance that one must achieve, beyond which there is no more need for growth. That challenging goal, however, always seems to be just beyond the reach of even the most earnest. And this is where the controversy arises. Should one keep on striving? Or should one just claim forgiveness . . . and rest content?

Any concept of perfection that focuses upon our performance, or holds to some plateau of goodness which then earns God's approval, is bound to run into these conflicts. In seeking for a more adequate (and thus more trouble-free) understanding of this nebulous goal of Christian growth, I have been impressed with Isaiah's assertion that God has opened his ears to hear truth; Isaiah, in turn, is entirely free from resistance or rebellion. Isaiah is teachable!

God has many things to teach us—about Himself, His plans for us, His paths of blessing. Since truth is the means God uses to draw us back to Him, our response to that truth becomes an extremely vital issue. What is more, God intends to keep on telling us the wonders of His character, of the plan of salvation, and of the mysteries of nature, throughout the ceaseless ages of eternity. What better preparation for heaven than to become the kind of person right now who will eagerly be open to the Divine Teacher?

Furthermore, when God knows that it is time to work on the next "round" of character development, He will find the task either easy or difficult (or even impossible), depending on whether He finds us to be teachable. Those who, like Isaiah, can say, "I was not rebellious," will find growth into His likeness to be both rapid and accurate.

But teachableness is not something one simply chooses to wear, like a grin. It isn't a matter of one's casually saying, "I think that today I shall become teachable." To be teachable means to trust the Teacher! It means trusting that He will not lead us into a life of drudgery. It means experimenting in our lives with what He has taught us, seeing that it is very good, and returning for more. It means knowing Him!

TOLERANCE OR INTELLIGENCE?

To be patient shows intelligence. Prov. 19:11, N.E.B.

Patience is often thought of more as a virtue than a sign of intelligence. Take, for example, the poor mother of five who does not lose her temper during the chaotic tug and pull of her offspring's growing-up years. Marveling at her ability to endure patiently, we go away impressed but not taught.

Patience is more than control over upset feelings. As our text today states, "To be patient shows intelligence." Now, that changes the picture! It moves us away from the mere exercise of tolerance toward a more reasoned and chosen posture. The mother of five probably has no more inherent emotional strength than any of us. She chooses to retain her patient bearing with her children because she understands that by doing so she is demonstrating to them that difficulties are worked through more effectively in the absence of agitated feelings. Her demeanor is thought through and deliberate.

We read in 2 Peter 3:15: "Bear in mind that our Lord's patience with us is our salvation" (N.E.B.). To many Christians, that means we are walking on eggshells! Someday, according to their thinking, God is going to get tired of the whole mess and destroy the world with fire. And He might lose patience with us even before then—and send calamities upon us! We've all heard of "the judgments of God"!

The redeemed, standing on the sea of glass, will sing a song of their experience with the Lord God. They will praise Him for His dealings with them, announcing that they worship Him because He has revealed His judgments to them (Rev. 15:2-4). God's judgments are not the outpouring of His bad temper; they are His carefully weighed and executed decisions. Sometimes they involve allowing men to experience the results of their own bad choices.

God's patience is divine intelligence. He is demonstrating to us that anger never solves problems; it only complicates them. He knows that we need to learn to deal with correct information without feeling a need to appease His inflamed temper. He desires us to choose to function thoughtfully and reasonably, without imposing our frustrations on others. Impatience is a form of pressure to make others comply with one's wishes. Conduct achieved in this way is meaningless in the process of character development.

Frankly, I respect God! I think His manner of handling the chaos of this rebellious planet (me included!) is downright praiseworthy. For me this equals worship.

WHOSE FAULT FOR FEELING BAD?

"I hold on to my integrity and will not let it go; my conscience does not accuse me, not one single day." Job 27:6, Berkeley.

A teenage boy spends the whole evening watching a lightweight television program rather than doing his homework. The next morning, in an innocent gesture of caring, Dad asks him if his assignments are ready for school. Junior explodes in touchy self-defense. He sulks off to school, wondering why everyone is always "down on his case."

Those of us who have survived the testy years " 'tween 12 and 20" know why he feels that way. We know that, in truth, it is his own conscience, his own sense of self-esteem, that has judged him the most severely. Dad simply touched the raw nerve, calling him to have to reckon with the obvious.

Self-worth stands, as it were, on a three-legged stool. The first leg is built on God's opinion of us—His prizing of us as His bought-back friends. His forgiveness, His caring involvement, His constancy, all stand like pillars in our lives. Though this leg of the stool is as strong as carbon steel, it has the disadvantage of also being the most abstract or intangible, especially for a young person.

The second leg of the stool is made up of the opinions of other people toward us. Few things can shape our self-image more powerfully and immediately than concern for how we are valued by others. The potency of this support in our lives is counterbalanced by the fact that we often have little control over how others view us—since they are usually consumed with protecting their own self-image!

The third leg of the stool is very largely under our own control. It has to do with our own appraisal of our abilities to live a useful, purposeful, controlled life. If we spend our days in lazy indulgence, dissipating our energies into frivolous thrills, we can't feel good about ourselves. Our own conscience will be active in condemning us.

Yet how quick we are to blame those feelings of condemnation on God! Or, realizing that the church upholds principles of usefulness and rightness, we feel that the church is a condemning power in our lives—and avoid it. But it is not fair to blame God, religion, or the Bible for the reproach of our own hearts. Rather our hearts should cherish God's righteous ways.

PRAYING BY FORMULA?

Keep on praying and never lose heart. Luke 18:1, N.E.B.

Why do I have to keep praying the same thing over and over? Doesn't God hear me the first time? If I don't pray enough times, does that disqualify me from getting an answer? How many times is "enough"?

Have you ever had such thoughts, when prayer seems like an exercise in frustration? Do you feel guilty because, secretly, you feel manipulated by God? It seems as though He doesn't answer your prayer because He wants to keep you praying. What a way to develop a friendship!

Let me tell you right now that God doesn't need to utilize such methods to invent relationship. It would be like a mother who wanted to teach her young child that she could satisfy his hunger at dinnertime by allowing him to see her prepare a lovely meal. And as he cried to her to feed him, she kept it from him because she so enjoyed hearing him call to her!

Neither is there some divine formula whereby God's blessings are dispensed, such as Blessings = Prayer × Intensity − Doubt. Though you may have heard the expression "the science of prayer," it does not refer to mathematics. It means, as Paul so aptly puts it, "Persevere in prayer, with *mind awake* and thankful heart" (Col. 4:2, N.E.B.).

Mind awake to what? To *Whom* you are praying! And let me suggest that prayer will take on a totally different meaning in our lives as we focus on the person of God rather than on His "treasure chest." Our text, "Keep on praying and never lose heart," is simply a reminder to keep focusing on our wonderful Father because He'll never let us down! In the parable of the importunate widow and the intransigent judge, Jesus was not teaching that we have to beg God day after day in order for Him to bless us! He was teaching just the opposite: God is *not like that!*

Our good God wants us to be comforted as we wait for an answer to our prayers. He assures us that He hears us and that He "is able to do immeasurably more than all we can ask or conceive, by the power which is *at work* among us" (Eph. 3:20, N.E.B.). Yes, He *is* "at work"—and is willing and able to do more for us than we think He'll do. We need never lose heart!

HOW FAITH WORKS

What matters is faith that makes its power felt through love. Gal. 5:6, Jerusalem.

I know this is a bold assertion. But the longer I live with it, the more I believe it to be true. I believe that virtually everything we do that is illegal, immoral, unkind, unethical, insensitive, or otherwise sinful, we do in a frantic and futile attempt to bolster our self-worth, protect our self-image, or defend our self-esteem. In varying degrees, we are all lonely, frightened people, trying to cling to our little scraps of self-worth.

We are in this wounded condition because all of us have been out of relationship with the Lover of our souls. Viewing ourselves as unloved, we have gone about in the best way we know how to cope with our emptiness. Forgetting that the script was written by Satan himself, we follow the actings of a hundred generations before us. We gossip, exaggerate, boast, manipulate, ridicule, and scorn. But no one applauds. Like a thirsty man drinking saltwater, we cannot quench our thirst. If you want to speak of sin in psychological terms rather than theological terms, this is it!

The inner emptiness of one out of union with God is so full of craving, so powerful, that its longings cannot be stifled by any amount of pressure or commands. Only a loving friendship can heal the heart of an unloved person. And faith does just that. Faith, in fact, is the reestablishing of a loving relationship with God. It puts us into fellowship (indeed it is the fellowship itself) with our divine Lover. And does that ever make a difference in our lives!

In this context, take another look at today's verse. Paul recognizes that the essential ingredient in our lives is that healing bond with our Sustainer. And that relationship is in fact so powerful that the apostle James could say, "By my deeds I will prove to you my faith" (James 2:18, N.E.B.).

Perhaps we hold faith in such low esteem because the real item is so rare. Most people speak of faith as though it were a self-generated opinion about something one can't know for sure but would very much like to believe. Others can talk about faith for pages—even whole chapters—and never mention Jesus Christ. But have you ever found someone who is enthralled with Jesus and who fellowships with Him often who hasn't begun to become like Him?

That is faith's power!

FROM BLESSINGS AND CURSES TO FRIENDSHIP

I offer you the choice of life or death, blessing or curse. Deut. 30:19, N.E.B.

When my daughter was little, she liked cleaning her room because I rewarded her with hugs and kisses. As she grew older she began to appreciate the inherent benefits of having a tidy room. It was a triumphant day when she came to me announcing, "It's so much nicer living in a clean room. I think I'll keep it neat all the time!"

Small children cannot comprehend the deeper reasons for principles and actions. So we reinforce their experiences with praise or discipline that teaches them that "this will make you happy" or "this will bring you sorrow." These external teaching aids become less and less necessary as the child discovers the built-in pluses and minuses of his actions. If I hugged and kissed my daughter today for cleaning her room, she'd consider it unnecessary. But we'd both laugh—because we've become friends.

Just before the Hebrew nation went up to possess Canaan, God spoke to them through Moses. They were given many laws and ordinances to govern their personal and corporate lives. And they were told, "I offer you the choice of life or death, blessing or curse." The blessing of life or the curse of death was inherent in their choice. If they chose to follow God's outline they would benefit from the built-in pluses of doing so. If they preferred the lifestyles of heathen nations they were bound to reap the results.

Only one generation removed from Egypt, however, the people were like little children, unaccustomed to reasoning from cause to effect. Therefore, God reinforced their understanding with promises of His pleasure and warnings of His censure. Had Israel come to appreciate that the lifestyle God desired for them was simply the most sensible and productive way to live, not only would they have prospered, but they would have seen that God was more than a law-giver. He was their friend.

The way God chose to deal with postslavery Israel was not His most preferred method. He met them on the level at which they functioned. The relationship I had with my daughter in her younger years was not my ultimate goal for us. I looked forward to the day she would look beyond my role as parent and see me as her friend.

Today God desires you and me to see Him as more than one who blesses or curses. He wants us to see Him as our dearest friend!

THAT EXTRA OIL

For when the foolish took their lamps, they took no oil with them; but the wise took flasks of oil with their lamps. Matt. 25:3, 4, R.S.V.

Two people are praying about the second coming of Christ. The first prays, "Lord, I have waited for You so long! Come soon and save me from this miserable world." The other person prays, "Lord, use me to enlighten others about who You are so they can choose aright, even if it means You need to delay Your coming."

Both persons want Jesus to return. Both want to see an end to the reign of sin and the beginning of the eternal kingdom. But if you listen closely, you will spot quite different motives as to why they want Jesus to return. And that is precisely the point of Jesus' parable about the ten young maidens who were asked to lighten the way for the coming of the Bridegroom.

Both groups of women had oil in their lamps—the Holy Spirit in their minds to illumine them. Specifically, all ten wanted Jesus to come. They all knew the approximate time and sought to be ready. But five of them were concerned only for the light adequate to get themselves in. The other five (whom Jesus identified as wise) were prepared to lighten the way for the coming of the bridal party. Knowing that they themselves would find entrance, they wanted to lighten the way for others as well.

The sobering part of Jesus' parable, however, is the fact that the five whose concern was narrowly self-centered did not enter into the wedding feast with the Bridegroom. Though they had enough light (truth) to know that the Bridegroom was coming, they were not prepared for the essential privilege of their calling. They were unable to hold the lamp of truth high so that others could appreciate His coming as well.

I find myself confronted with probing questions. Am I more concerned about the "soonness" of Jesus' coming than I am about the One who is coming? Am I more eager to be rescued from this planet than I am to be prepared to tell others about the Rescuer? Is my attention centered upon slipping away from the cold darkness of this world into the warm light of heaven? Or do I find great delight even now in watching the light dawn in someone's eyes as he gets to really know Jesus Christ?

THE RIGHTNESS OF HONEST WRONGNESS

Never despise what is spoken in the name of the Lord. By all means use your judgment, and hold on to whatever is good. 1 Thess. 5:20, 21, Phillips.

Americans love their freedom. However, conservatives contend that too many citizens are turning liberty into license. The "back to God" movements springing up everywhere are an outcry against such permissiveness. People are calling for "men of God" to take the helm of government and "get tough on crime." To many Christians this all sounds very good. Certainly getting "back to God" can only bring relief. Who wouldn't want fearless, Bible-believing statesmen? But wait! Might we trample on the vital principles of freedom of choice?

The Scriptures counsel us to "use your judgment" and "hold on to whatever is good." Another version says "test everything" (R.S.V.). The testing process in which we exercise judgment is absolutely vital in developing strength of character—even when we're wrong, *very* wrong! Take Paul, for example.

Paul was "convinced that I ought to do many things in opposing the name of Jesus of Nazareth. . . . I not only shut up many of the saints in prison, by authority from the chief priests, but when they were put to death I cast my vote against them" (Acts 26:9, 10, R.S.V.). Paul had honestly weighed the situation in Jerusalem and had taken a terribly wrong course of action! What changed him?

Paul was confronted with the person of Jesus Christ. His conscience was not forced, but from this encounter he discovered his error and made an abrupt about-face, becoming the single most powerful witness in early Christendom. To this day God utilizes Paul's strength of character—his rock-firm stand on conviction—as an example to believers everywhere.

Paul's strength of character was not developed that day on the road to Damascus. It had been growing a long time. It was growing even when he was wrong, because he was wrong honestly! Only God knows when that is the case. We cannot know for sure. Therefore, it is better for us to preserve an individual's sense of integrity than to destroy it in the name of right.

JESUS HAS CLAIMED ME

Not that I have already obtained this or am already perfect; but I press on to make it my own, because Christ Jesus has made me his own. Phil. 3:12, R.S.V.

Almost everyone who has studied a course in basic psychology has read about all those babies who died in an orphanage at the close of World War II. The infants all had proper nutrition, plenty of fresh air and sunlight, and clean clothing as needed. There was no evidence of any diseases among them. Yet many of them simply gave up on living. The management, suspecting they might know the reason, hired a number of women to simply pick up the surviving babies, hold them close, and talk warmly to them. The babies' condition improved markedly.

My psychology textbook listed this as concrete evidence that human beings have needs that go beyond biological necessities. We need to be loved. Without love, we are damaged; with the genuine item, we are healed. It is interesting that wise observers in the field of human behavior are verifying what Scripture has been telling us all along. Every human on this planet is made to be bound together in a union of love with God and with each other. We cannot survive without it.

We are not speaking here of warm sentimental niceties; we are talking about the fundamentals for being functional persons. Except as we know how precious we are to our Lord, we spend our days consumed in petty, grasping selfishness, groping somehow to earn or deserve His favor. Such an inward, anxiety-ridden experience cannot foster the true works of righteousness, the works of selfless love.

In the message to the Philippians quoted above, Paul forcefully shares a priceless insight: relationship produces righteousness; righteousness does not produce relationship. In essence he is saying, "Jesus has *already* claimed me, and because of that, I have the inner strength and incentive to become all that He wants me to become—within the nurturing security of the relationship."

Paul is not saying that our relationship with God is a reward for our perfect performance. Indeed, he is emphatic that he does not himself possess such perfectness. Rather, he longs to press toward that wholeness, *"because* Christ Jesus has made me his own."

If Jesus Christ can draw His people upward so powerfully through the impact of a loving relationship, shouldn't we in His family pass on that same love to each other?

GIVING GOD A BLACK EYE

He said to them, "Listen to me, you rebels. Must we get water out of this rock for you?" Moses raised his hand and struck the rock twice with his staff. Num. 20:10, 11, N.E.B.

The children of Israel were murmuring again, this time about the lack of water. " 'Why did you fetch us up from Egypt to bring us to this vile place, where nothing will grow?' they complained to Moses. 'There is not even any water to drink' " (Num. 20:5, N.E.B.).

Since the smitten rock in Horeb, God had miraculously provided water to the Hebrew host wherever in their journeyings they went. It gushed out of the clefts of the rock beside their encampments. The smitten rock represented Christ, "smitten of God"—from whom flows the stream of salvation for a lost race. But they had forgotten how ready God was to satisfy their needs.

Moses took his position in front of the assembled multitude. He had been instructed by God to "speak to the rock and it will yield its water" (verse 8, N.E.B.). Instead, with his voice full of anger and impatience Moses yelled, "Listen to me, you rebels. Must we get water out of this rock for you?" (verse 10, N.E.B.). Then he raised his rod and struck the rock twice with his staff.

"Water gushed out in abundance, and they all drank, men and beasts. But the Lord said to Moses and Aaron, 'You did not trust me so far as to uphold my holiness in the sight of the Israelites; therefore you shall not lead this assembly into the land which I promised to give them' " (verse 12, N.E.B.).

Why such horrible consequences? After all, the people *were* rebellious, and God had told Moses on another occasion to strike the rock! But this time Moses virtually gave God a black eye, a bad reputation. Moses' lack of self-control was evident. And he included God in his display of anger by saying "must *we* get water"—implying that God was reluctant to help them.

Something had to be done. God could not allow Himself to be viewed as an angry, capricious deity. He gave the people water as He had always done. Then He set Moses apart from Himself by disallowing him to enter Canaan with Israel. The reason He gave made it crystal clear: Moses did not "uphold My holiness in the sight of the Israelites."

But God wasn't mad at Moses. Fourteen hundred years later Moses stood with Christ on the Mount of Transfiguration!

WORSHIPING A HOLY GOD

Holy and awe-inspiring is His name. Ps. 111:9, Berkeley.

I must confess to a strong personal prejudice. Will you listen as I share it with you? Though I have rather broad-ranging musical tastes and am willing to grant people their own latitude in this subjective area of experience, I simply cannot handle one style of music. That is the style known as "gospel rock"—religious words or sentiments set in the musical idiom of a rock beat.

While it is true that my temperament does not enjoy heavy drums, strained and highly stylized voices, pounding electronic amplification, and the earthy connotations of traditional rock, I don't think this is my basic problem. My distaste centers, rather, around another matter. That is the picture of our God that is projected through religious rock.

Worship is centered in the adoration of God. Any form of worship, including its music, is shaped by who we believe God to be. The writers of religious music hold a particular understanding of the God about whom they are composing music, and it molds their musical style. I have come to know God as a Being of great dignity, nobility, and grandeur. This does not mean that He is distant and stuffy, or terrifyingly awesome. But I cannot be at peace hearing Him exploited for the sake of private entertainment.

Our understanding of God's character is the basis for our attitudes of reverence toward Him. Satan has successfully portrayed God through many centuries as somber, abusively powerful, and with a very short fuse when it comes to people who misbehave. As a result, much religious music wore dark tones, alien to joy and freedom of spirit. Loving to swing pendulums, Satan then told religious people they could bolt over into the opposite alternative. He presented a God who was a trite, lightweight "pal in the sky." His name could be ritually dragged through just about any style of music, and thus He would presumably sanctify it.

Rather than letting our music shape our understanding of God, I believe that our clear and growing understanding of God must shape our God-centered music. Though our experience in Christ is joyful, even the texture of that joy derives from the Person who brings the joy rather than the joy itself.

Don't you long to hear how the angels—who behold Him face-to-face—adore our holy and awe-inspiring God?

PEOPLE: GOD'S HIGHEST PRIORITY

When a man has two wives, one loved and the other unloved, if they both bear him sons, and the son of the unloved wife is the elder, then, when the day comes for him to divide his property among his sons, he shall not treat the son of the loved wife as his first-born in contempt of his true first-born, the son of the unloved wife. Deut. 21:15, 16, N.E.B.

Has God changed since the days of Moses? Do we read with amazement laws such as the one in today's text? Maybe even despair? Was God permitting polygamy? How do you explain such scriptures?

Many Christians simply throw out the Old Testament. That's the easy way out. Others stammer uncomfortably, "There are some things we can't understand" and try to change the subject. A few support polygamy! Knowing that "every inspired scripture has its use for teaching the truth and refuting error" (2 Tim. 3:16, N.E.B.), what can the serious seeker for truth do with such texts?

Dear readers, God has much to tell us about Himself! And I believe that not all He has to say is wrapped in clean white tissue. Some is wrapped in the soiled understandings of people who have tried to live as best they could in this confused world. Does it surprise you that God "gets down on His hands and knees"—even when it's muddy—to talk to us, His beloved children?

You see, God has priorities, and you and I are at the top of the list! When we have muddy ideas of how life should be, He does not yell at us from millions of light-years away. He joins us where we are, not in approval of our actions but in total identification with our personhood. Like working out a splinter, He starts on the open end of our wounded relationships and slowly works out our wrong concepts and dealings with others.

The law quoted in today's text is not aimed at defining marriage. It is meant to protect the unfortunate offspring of relationships that should never have happened in the first place. But happen they did. And while God carefully worked on getting the "splinter"—polygamy—out He applied "antiseptic" to the situation: He showed His love for the people involved by giving some interim ground rules. In essence He said, "Until you learn a better way, let Me tell you how not to hurt each other so badly."

I'm glad that God hasn't changed!

THE GOD WHO ASKS QUESTIONS

When they had finished breakfast, Jesus said to Simon Peter, "Simon, son of John, do you love me more than these?" He said to him, "Yes, Lord; you know that I love you." John 21:15, R.S.V.

The poet T. S. Eliot once wrote, "Oh, my soul, be prepared for the coming of the Stranger, be prepared for Him who knows how to ask questions."

A good teacher is full of questions. He keeps drawing out of his students deeper awarenesses of their own feelings and convictions. And every time he asks them a question, he is in essence telling them that he prizes hearing their values.

Jesus was constantly asking people questions. "Who do men say that the Son of man is?" (Matt. 16:13, R.S.V.). "Who do *you* say that I am?" (verse 15, R.S.V.). "Do you want to be healed?" (John 5:6, R.S.V.). "Woman, where are they? Has no one condemned you?" (chap. 8:10, R.S.V.).

There was a pattern in Jesus' queries. They were not merely rhetorical questions, designed to make an obvious point. Each one was designed to stimulate self-understanding within His hearers. He wanted their minds to be brought into an informed posture of trust in Him.

So often our prayers become times of frantic talking to God, as though He needed edifying. Or we are busy asking Him questions about details in our lives as though our greatest need is to have the future figured out. But if we will discipline our souls into reverent silence in His presence, we just might hear Him asking us questions. Tender, probing, solicitous questions, designed to help us know ourselves better.

Perhaps we should often, while on our knees, express this message to God: "Father, I know that it is safe here. I know that—together—we can face any issue. I can admit my hidden, dark resentments, my foolish fears, even my cherished sins, and know that You will deal wisely and gently with me. I give You permission to probe me with Your questions. I know that these questions will guide my understanding into the most needed areas of my life. Father, I trust You. Now show me myself!"

Some people pay psychiatrists large sums of money to guide them toward self-understanding. The psychiatrist is skilled not only in asking the right questions but also in providing a supporting, noncondemning atmosphere in which painful answers can be faced. But many have found such a trusting union with God that He Himself guides their self-understanding.

GIVING OUR KIDS REASON TO HOPE

Tell to the coming generation the glorious deeds of the Lord, and his might, and the wonders which he has wrought. Ps. 78:4, R.S.V.

His eyes held a sadness his years could not bear. One leg draped over the arm of an overstuffed chair, he looked languid yet brittle. His mother sat helplessly nearby. "Son," she began tentatively, "is there anything I can do?" Her boy had just come home from juvenile hall, where he had been charged with drunken driving. He was failing his courses at the local high school. "Do?" he responded tonelessly. "Mom, I just don't care anymore."

Across the city, in a type of house that most people can only drive by but can never afford, a teenage girl was being accosted by her mother: "I said, turn it *down!*" The mother referred to the stereo in the girl's room that was blasting out one of the Top Forty tunes. "Why?" the girl asked sullenly. "What else is there?"

What else *is* there for these kids and so many others like them? Their parents' affluence? The Establishment and all its double standards? The threat of annihilation by nuclear war? Honestly, why should our kids hope for anything more than they can grasp quickly today? Look at our world! It's not exactly a place where happiness is the rule of thumb!

But our kids *can* have reason to hope! In our text today we see the answer. We can "tell to the coming generation the glorious deeds of the Lord, and his might, and the wonders which he has wrought." The result of their hearing about their wonderful Father is that they will "set their hope in God" (Ps. 78:7). Notice, it says *in* God. If our children are given a chance to know who He is, *He* will be their hope!

Can we share the right things about God if we ourselves do not hope in Him? If our believing is more theology than a warm, fresh relationship, they won't buy it! Why should they? Why should they hope that it will do for them what it hasn't done for us? If we expect, even demand, that they accept such a belief, we only increase their feelings of hopelessness by adding another requirement to their already long list.

The "wonders which he has wrought" are told best in the context of relationship. If you find that accepting the friendship of God has given you hope and courage, the chances are good that your kids will too.

HOW CLOSE IS GOD?

**They were to seek God, and, it might be, touch and find him;
though indeed he is not far from each one of us. Acts 17:27, N.E.B.**

I have been told since I was a little child that Jesus will descend
through the "open space" in the constellation of Orion at the time of the
Second Coming. And so, of all the countless millions of stars visible in
our heavens, my eyes always search out the middle star in the "sword" of
the supposed warrior figure.

Telescopic photographs of the constellation reveal that this star really
isn't a solid object but is actually a gaseous cloud. Some are certain that
they see in it a large opening, or corridor, going into infinite space
beyond. Somehow it was comforting to me as a child to know that, just
possibly, this is where God lives! But then, I was dismayed to learn that
the constellation of Orion is more than five hundred light-years from
earth. Though I had no way of understanding just how far that was, I felt
despondent that God kept Himself at such a distance that I couldn't even
write the number.

Through the years, then, as I have heard people say, "I just don't feel
very close to God," my mind has translated this into geographical terms.
As I have matured, of course, I have recognized that it really doesn't
matter whether God is six inches away or 6 trillion light-years away.
Geographical distance isn't the issue for an infinite, omnipresent God.

But isn't it just as irrelevant for the one who says, "I don't feel very
close to God," to base that conclusion on flighty feelings as to base it on
geography? The point is that feelings and emotions are a very unstable
basis for measuring one's closeness to God.

Jeremiah complained to his Father about the attitudes of his people
toward God: "Thou art ever on their lips, yet far from their hearts" (Jer.
12:2, N.E.B.). Jeremiah knew that closeness to God was measured not by
people's feelings, by their religious statements, or even by geographical
distances. It is measured rather by the alignment of the mind with the
values of God's kingdom. Jesus said, "Men cannot say, 'Look, here it
is,' or 'There it is,' for the kingdom of God is inside you" (Luke 17:21,
Phillips). It means having the values of Jesus Christ cherished in our
deepest inner loyalties. You can't get any closer than that, can you?

WAYS IN WHICH TO VIEW THE FATHER

The rest of the dead did not come to life until the thousand years were ended. Rev. 20:5, R.S.V.

"I believe in God, but I don't want to belong to any church! Doctrines just make people haggle over the Bible!"

Unfortunately, it is true that doctrines often divide people. Especially when being "right" is viewed as a thermometer of one's Christian experience. We've all heard people piously say of those who do not agree with their particular explanation of Scripture: "They'll understand when they get closer to the Lord!"

Why has God given us doctrine? How important is it that we have the right understanding of, say, the Trinity and the millennium? Will we be saved only if we manage to grasp correctly the articles of faith set forth in Scripture? How much scholastic theology must one master before he or she qualifies as an honest seeker for truth?

May I suggest that doctrine is primarily God's way of giving us varied pictures of Himself. If we approach the study of the Word of God with the purpose of coming to know Him better, we will find ourselves being drawn away from dissension and division. Our desire will be to get a clearer view of the Father, not to add to our "arsenal of truth."

How can a doctrine such as the millennium illuminate our understanding of God? Without getting into a major discussion, I believe that the fact that "the rest of the dead [will] not come to life until the thousand years [are] ended" reveals God's supreme regard for people—even those who have finally and forever rejected Him. During the thousand years when the saved of all ages reign with Christ, those who are lost will be spared the agonies of having to spend that time with Satan without the benefit of God's protection, the protection that they themselves have spurned.

The doctrine of the Trinity teaches me that the essence of the Godhead is relationship. This brings me great comfort, because I know that since I have been made in Their image, it is in God's plan that I experience rewarding friendships. Even when I feel alone in the crowd, I never lose this confidence.

There are so many pictures of God in the Bible! We need not haggle over any of them. They aren't there for rightness' sake—they are there so that not one of us might fail to come to know Him.

GIVING AWAY THE KINGDOM

Fear not, little flock, for it is your Father's good pleasure to give you the kingdom. Luke 12:32, R.S.V.

In a wave of growing appreciation for human rights and democratic principles, most Western countries have adopted representative forms of government. Yet several nations have also retained many of their traditional forms of royalty. It seems that the trappings of royalty have a marvelous way of capturing the imaginations of us common folks.

Have you ever savored in your imagination being in the place of attractive Queen Esther as she approaches King Ahasuerus? This incredibly wealthy potentate, who rules 127 provinces from India to Ethiopia and is able to hold sumptuous feasts lasting 180 days, looks fondly at his young queen and says, "What is your request? It shall be given you, even to the half of my kingdom" (Esther 5:3, R.S.V.).

What sovereign authority, to give one more than one could ever use in a lifetime! And just for the indulgent fun of it, we let our minds explore: "What would I have asked from Ahasuerus? Would I have wanted a nice home, or even a whole seaside resort of my own?" Our imagination surveys the kinds of things earthly kingdoms are prone to accumulate—and that we are prone to covet!

Perhaps this is why our response is often so flat when we hear Jesus' bold promise, "It is your Father's good pleasure to give you the kingdom." Are the treasures that He has accumulated in His kingdom the ones we are inclined to long for? Do we long for the lifestyle of this Servant-King who has freely offered us a share of His kingdom?

The world is full of people who have amassed fortunes at the expense of others. But history remembers fondly the ones whose values centered around a deep love for people. The world has seen enough of royalty who have crushed the masses for the dubious benefit of the slender few. But Jesus was advocating the formation of a new royalty: kings and queens with hearts that are tender and large, whose treasury is made up of people made whole through love.

Our Father takes no delight in giving us a kingdom that would burden us with the anxieties of materialism. He would not countenance any joys other than the ones that bring pleasure to Himself—the joys of loving people into wholeness. The treasures He imparts are those of a transformed heart, and they are eternal!

PRAYER AND BUMPER STICKERS

Tremendous power is made available through a good man's earnest prayer. James 5:16, Phillips.

The car just in front of me on my right began gliding into my lane without signaling. As I jammed on my brakes, I noticed that this unperplexed driver had a prominently placed bumper sticker on his car that read: "When you pray, wonderful things happen!"

I can't help but wonder what a nonbeliever would have thought of this driver's irresponsible actions in view of his obvious advertisement that he was a follower of God. Should prayer make us careless? You've heard the expression "They're so heavenly minded that they're of no earthly good!" What a sad indictment of what knowing God is supposed to do for people!

What about prayer? If "tremendous power is made available through a good man's prayer," what can we honestly expect in our own lives? Is labeling everything "God's will" (because, after all, we've "prayed about it") the only way we can claim God's activity in our lives? Unfortunately, this kind of attitude tends to produce careless living patterns.

Prayer is entering into intimate fellowship with the most awesome Mind in the universe! It is our privilege to "think in His presence"—to work through any and every facet of our lives while consciously interfacing with God's wisdom. It is accepting the accountability for how we live, fully awake to His guidance, without fear of condemnation, because we know that it is not His purpose to belittle or browbeat us. In communion with Him we are set free to look squarely at our lives, meeting the challenges with head held high. We are rescued from mediocrity—we are yoked with divinity! We are released from pettiness—our inspiration is infinity!

I believe that the tremendous power available in prayer is the power to live intelligently and reasonably. It is not a power attained by the waving of a magic wand; it is gained by being in the presence of One who is wonderfully reasonable and realistic. And our prayers are effectual because *we* ourselves are being made more effective through companionship with Him!

As God's friends, let's make sure we do not give unbelievers the wrong impression. We are not exempt from the grubby realities of everyday living. And we are not beyond forgetting to signal when we change lanes! Perhaps someone ought to design a bumper sticker that says, "There's hope! God and I are still talking!"

FAITH: HAVING A GOOD MEMORY

The man who lacks them is short-sighted and blind; he has forgotten how he was cleansed from his former sins. 2 Peter 1:9, N.E.B.

I've finally figured out why it has been so easy for me to be so hard on the children of Israel. I used to become so annoyed at them for so quickly forgetting God's miraculous acts among them and resorting so soon to the faithless murmurings and rebellions of their recent past. I have often wondered how people could be so dense, especially in the face of such astounding miracles. But now I have come to the painful conclusion that I am not all that much different from them. The difference is that the Old Testament packs several lifetimes of history into a few paragraphs, and I'm still forgetting my way through one short lifetime.

Oh, how much we need a good memory! If faith is a relationship of confidence in God, based upon His reliable dealings with us in the past, then Satan can work havoc with our faith just by getting us to forget. The enemy can stunt our growth by getting us to forget our heritage, our own spiritual pilgrimage with our Father, for God's favorite way of revealing Himself to us is through active interaction with us.

Peter puts all these concepts into a very important setting in today's verse. He has been explaining some of the character qualities that Christ wants for His people: faith, virtue, knowledge, self-control, fortitude, piety, brotherly kindness, and love. He knows that as we look at this list of qualities, we will notice that we have not fully incorporated them into our lives. So he explains why: We are shortsighted, blind, and forgetful that we have been cleansed of our former sins.

You see, if we still doubt that God has forgiven our sins, then any quest for Christlikeness will be flavored by desires to earn that forgiveness, and we will be groveling for His favor. To keenly remember His forgiveness is to be set free from selfish clamoring for it—set free to turn toward Christ for His own sake.

In listening to the public prayers of others we more often hear people praying ''Please forgive our sins'' than we hear ''Thank You for having forgiven our sins.'' Could this mean that too many Christians have forgotten the message of a forgiving Lord? Or, worse yet, that they never heard it in the first place?

SEEKING GOD'S FACE

Thou hast said, "Seek ye my face." My heart says to thee, "Thy face, Lord, do I seek." Ps. 27:8, R.S.V.

In the most fundamental way, your face is *you*. At the sight of it, the parking lot attendant will wave you through the gate and the teller at your bank will cash your check without asking to see your driver's license. Can you imagine how you'd feel if one day you were arrested—because someone whom you supposedly looked like had committed a crime? It has happened to others. Some innocent people have spent years in prison because their face was thought to closely resemble the face of a wanted criminal.

What usually happens is that the apparent "look-alike" is picked up by the police and subsequently is "positively identified" by the victim or eyewitness to the crime. Traumatic excitement, coupled with an intense desire for personal safety, is often an underlying factor in such procedures. Not until the real culprit is apprehended is the ill-convicted person cleared. Upon seeing the real criminal, the victim or eyewitness suddenly realizes that the wrong person has been sent to prison.

God calls out to us, "Seek My face! You are mistakenly identifying Me with that criminal, the devil. By sophistry and deceit he has convinced you that I am like him, that I am tyrannical, exacting, and full of displeasure for you. You have been victimized by him, yet blame Me for your sorrows. If only you will seek My face—seek to know Me as I am—you will no longer fear Me. Cleared of the false charges against Me, I will be allowed the freedom to become your friend."

Let us answer Him, "My heart says to You, Your face, Lord, do I seek. In my anxiety and trauma I saw You as one whose anger had been kindled against me. I thought it was You who beat me severely with Your law. And though Your Son came to lift me up into newness of life, I thought You were lurking in the shadows, ready to strike me down again should I not follow precisely after Him.But I see now that this is not true. Your face I will continually seek, so that I will never again be mistaken about who You are!"

Jesus summarized it: "This is eternal life: to know thee who alone art truly God, and Jesus Christ whom thou hast sent" (John 17:3, N.E.B.).

SIN IS A GOD-CENTERED WORD

Any man who believes in him is not judged at all. It is the one who will not believe who stands already condemned, because he will not believe in the character of God's only Son. John 3:18, Phillips.

"Is it a sin to wash dishes on the Sabbath?" a young student asks. For him sin is an act that one does in violation of an authoritative code. Another person laments, "Oh, I am such a sinner!" He implies that sin is somewhat like a disease in one's bones. Still another talks at length about the removal of his sins from the heavenly sanctuary, giving the impression that sin is similar to a block of wood, or an entry in a book, that can be moved around like so much cargo.

The interesting thing about each of these comments is that none of them make any reference to God. Which is not surprising. Many Christians can talk at length about sin (including how to avoid it) without ever mentioning God or Jesus Christ.

That's why Jesus gets right to the point in explaining just what the problem is that we sinners are facing. He doesn't talk about people's actions, their physical condition, or their legal records in heaven. Instead, He hinges it all on their trust relationship with Himself and His Father. Thus He does not discuss sin without discussing God and one's relationship with Him.

Sin is a relationship word. That should make sense, because its opposite, *faith,* is also a relationship word. It makes little sense simply to talk about faith. The word can't stand on its own. It becomes accurate only when we speak of "faith *in* Jesus Christ" or "faith *in* God."

In the same way, we speak and think accurately about sin when we view it as the breaking of that faith relationship with God. The sinner is one who is acting and thinking as though he can live apart from God. The Bible labels his behavior as sinful. But such behavior is simply the result of the broken relationship with God.

If Satan can get us to thinking about sin without ever thinking of it as broken relationship, then he can get us to start tinkering with our behavior without ever returning to God in total dependence and trust in Him. And, frankly, the devil would be delighted to have us trying to stop sinning by that method. What better delusion to keep us occupied—apart from God!

THE PUNISHMENT OF GOD

But he endured the suffering that should have been ours, the pain that we should have borne. All the while we thought that his suffering was punishment sent by God. Isa. 53:4, T.E.V.

There Jesus was, hanging unceremoniously upon an instrument of shame and torture, mocked by Roman guards. Worse still, He had "entered his own realm, and his own would not receive him" (John 1:11, N.E.B.). Then, to underscore His poverty of spirit, He cried out loudly, "My God, My God, why have you forsaken me?"(Matt. 27:46, N.I.V.).

As our text today states, "He endured the suffering that should have been ours, the pain that we should have borne." However, we need not draw the wrong conclusions as to what this means. We need not think that "his suffering was punishment sent by God." We have the privilege of understanding that it was "because of our sins" that "he was wounded" (Isa. 53:5, T.E.V.). In simple language, we can know that He died because He took upon Himself the result of our being separated from our only source of life, God.

Friends, we need not allow the concept of a punishing deity to dominate our thinking. Christ came to portray God as a loving Father. And though it is true that a loving father will at times punish his children, he does this for the express purpose of teaching them reality. The irrevocable death of the wicked is not instruction; it *is* the reality. On the cross Jesus demonstrated the consequences of eternal separation from God. To see it as punishment is to see God as actively taking the lives of unbelievers, rather than their perishing because they have rejected their Life Source.

It is a tremendously vital issue! It has to do with the quality of our relationship with our heavenly Father. No matter how you cut it, if you think that God will eventually kill you for not believing in Him, your posture toward Him is tainted with fear. Remember, He is "not willing that any should perish, but that all should come to repentance" (2 Peter 3:9). The final destruction of the wicked is God's "strange act" because it is so against His will to allow any of us to reap the eternal consequences of separation from Him.

The cross is a statement of reality—of the sure outcome of sin *and* of God's desire that we never experience it! May we all accept such costly evidence, and *live*.

MORAL REALITIES

Make no mistake about this: God is not to be fooled; a man reaps what he sows. Gal. 6:7, N.E.B.

A young boy creates such a disturbance in the classroom that his teacher sends him to the principal's office.When his mother finds out about it, she is irate. But not at her son! She takes it out on the teacher. Later, when this same son spends all of his allowance on candy and has nothing left for an offering at church, she quickly replenishes his supply of money. "I don't want him to feel bad," she says.

In her misguided love for her son, this mother is actually teaching him to live in a fantasy world. She is shielding him from the hard realities that reveal the facts, the cause-and-effect realities that underlie all of life on this planet. She thinks she is keeping him from hurting by not letting him face the consequences of his choices, but in fact she is setting him up for unending hurts in the future.

Another child misbehaves seriously at home. His mother tells him that as a result he will lose his privileges for a period of time. After tears of repentance he begs to have his "sentence" revoked. When Mother holds firm, he pleads, "What's the matter? Don't you forgive me?" She explains that of course she forgives him, but forgiveness isn't the issue. He still needs to learn about moral realities, the sure consequences of bad choices.

Large numbers of Christians today are living the behaviors of this sinful world, yet they fully believe that because forgiveness is available, they will be exempted from all bad consequences. They misunderstand the whole meaning of forgiveness. They think that because the ultimate sentence of the second death has been lifted through the forgiveness provided on the cross, all consequences of bad choices are also lifted.

This widely held belief can be turned over and viewed from the other side as well. It suggests that what is wrong with sinning is that God is resentful and hostile toward the sinner, even inflicting punishment upon him as an expression of His displeasure. The goal of man's religion, then, is to get God to change that attitude toward the sinner, to offer "forgiveness." When the Father says, "I forgive you," they think one is free to disobey God's law. But our Father loves us too much to stand behind this kind of moral fiction!

June 25

LET'S HELP SHOVEL AWAY THE SNOW!

Build up a highway, build it and clear the track, sweep away all that blocks my people's path. Isa. 57:14, N.E.B.

During the night more than a foot of snow had fallen, blowing into two- and three-foot drifts. All traffic had come to a standstill, and snow removal equipment was out in force. The workers were reinforced by many in the community who cheerfully volunteered their help, bringing with them shovels and mugs of hot drink. By noon the highway had been cleared enough to allow vehicle passage again.

Few things are more frustrating than not being able to get where you need to go. Waiting for someone to arrive can be equally disconcerting. If anything can be done to alleviate the problem, it is done—gladly and with no thought of remuneration. There is great satisfaction in being a part of the solution. All the more so when the solution brings you together with someone whom you desire to be with.

God built a "highway" between heaven and earth in the person of His Son. Too often the "highway" is so cluttered with misconceptions that we are prevented from having free access to the Father. We become "snowed in" and wearied in our journey to the kingdom. Of one thing we can be certain: Our anxiety is more than matched by the longing of the One who awaits our coming.

God is in the process of clearing the track and sweeping away all that blocks our path. Not only may we benefit from His actions; we may be a part of the solution. We may bring our own "shovels"—our willingness to share what we are learning about our Father—and "mugs of hot drink"—our genuine compassion and caring involvement with other "snowbound" travelers.

For example, when we learn how reasonable and realistic God is, we become reasonable and realistic with others. God does not expect us to float mystically over the top of this troubled life, our "faith" some sort of invisible magic carpet that will transport us to an ethereal kingdom. His desire is that we live where the "rubber meets the road." If our concept of God leaves us concealing sweaty palms, there is no use pretending that we are anxious to live in His presence forever. Nor can we ever adequately "clear the way" for another.

We need "down to earth" religion. That's where God's "snow plows" are at work!

WHAT DOES THE LAW REQUIRE?

God did this so that the righteous demands of the Law might be fully satisfied in us who live according to the Spirit, and not according to human nature. Rom. 8:4, T.E.V.

A young man travels a great distance from home and falls in love with a delightful young woman. In order to win her hand in marriage, he works years for an unpleasant employer—who happens also to be the girl's father. In the end, the father pulls a classic dirty trick and switches daughters on the young man.

Not one of us today would think that what happened to Jacob was fair. You just cannot substitute one relationship for another. Laban may have argued that one wife was as legally proper as another, but that argument would have been wasted on Jacob. He knew the effects in his own heart of being in love with Rachel.

I am just as unhappy with any picture of God that suggests He is satisfied with a substituted relationship. Our Father created each one of us for a unique and personal relationship with Himself. The central purpose in our creation can be fulfilled only as we enter into that relationship. Would the Father be satisfied by substituting His relationship with Jesus in place of our own, claiming that this fulfills a "legal" requirement? Wouldn't that ignore the personhood of God and of His friends?

To be in a confident, trusting union with God, as the branch is to the vine, is the only right and proper condition of man. This is righteousness; there can be no substitute for it, for it references to the hearts of God and man, not to a legal code.

Many people think of righteousness by faith strictly in legal terms—seeing it as God legally substituting Jesus' righteous record in place of our own, and thereby being content that the sin problem has been solved! But we deal better with the real problem by seeing faith as that deep, trusting, submitted friendship with God, which alone is our rightful state.

God deals with us in order to end the separation rather than to deal with legal "as ifs." His concern is with restoring relationships, not with balancing books. No wonder Jesus was eager to present Him to us as a father rather than as a judge. The "just requirement of the law" (Rom. 8:4, R.S.V.) is union with the Father. Thus Jesus is the way to the Father, not a substitute for it!

WHAT IS GOD WAITING FOR?

Or do you think lightly of his wealth of kindness, of tolerance, and of patience, without recognizing that God's kindness is meant to lead you to a change of heart? Rom. 2:4, N.E.B.

We were discussing the starving children of Ethiopia. "How can God let them suffer like that?" someone asked, his voice betraying alarm. "Why doesn't He do something? Why doesn't He put an end to all of this?"

"We have to see how bad sin is," another explained. "The devil has to be given enough time to expose himself for what he is."

My question is Will seeing how bad sin is bring an end to the sin problem? Has evidence that smoking causes lung cancer brought an end to people using cigarettes? The second coming of Christ is not being delayed because not enough people think the devil is bad. So what *is* God waiting for?

The apostle Paul wrote that God's kindness, tolerance, and patience are meant to lead us to a change of heart. Our opinion of God can remain devastatingly wrong despite the fact that we know how bad off we are in our sinful condition. God knows that only as we see His goodness will we begin to think differently about Him.

We need to focus on the revealed goodness of God rather than the ongoing badness of the devil. The sin problem cannot be settled physically until it is settled mentally. God's heart nearly ruptures with the sorrows of mankind. But were He to continuously intervene to relieve earthly tragedy, we would have a distorted picture of what happens when we are separated from Him.

God is waiting for us to be utterly enthralled with Him. Not emotionally hyped up but totally and intelligently satisfied with who He is. To rescue us from this sin-infested planet prior to that would be to carry some of our misgivings about Him with us to heaven. It would be like cutting off the flank of a cancerous cow and calling the remainder healthy even though the cancer virus was in the bloodstream. Ultimately it would be futile to do so. And dangerous.

God's commitment to reality is in our best interests. The exceedingly high price He continually pays to ensure our total deliverance from the virus of sin should fill our hearts with awe. Rather than cry out, "What is God waiting for?" let us say to one another, "What are *we* waiting for?"

JESUS AND REALITY

Learn all you need to know from his initiation, which is real and no illusion. As he taught you, then, dwell in him. 1 John 2:27, N.E.B.

Reality and illusion. The great controversy centers so much in these two contrasting words. Jesus says, "You will live only when you are connected with the Life-giver." That's reality. Satan says, "You can live apart from God, and I can sustain you." That's an illusion.

Jesus says, "Seek me first, and I will take care of all your other needs." That's reality. Satan says, "Get your own needs met first, by whatever means you can, because no one else will be looking out for you." That's an illusion.

Jesus says, "True satisfactions and pleasures are found in living for others, seeking their wholeness and happiness. This will bring you the greatest joy." That's reality. Satan says, "Real satisfaction is found by plunging into whatever brings you the most intense feelings of pleasure; let other people worry about themselves." That's an illusion.

Jesus says, "I can equip you to live—with your head held high—right in the middle of a demanding and complex world. I'm preparing you to face reality squarely." That's affirming reality. Satan says, "The real world is so terrible, so overwhelming, that you can face it only when your perceptions are chemically altered, your awareness numbed through drugs, or your senses dulled through headlong flight into frivolity." That's denying reality.

Jesus invites us to behold the world of reality—to read books about real accomplishments, to view sane perspectives of human relationships, to imagine life's sober realities and tranquil pleasures. He wants our minds to become accustomed to dealing with His universe as He made it—that is, with reality. Satan entices us to immerse our brains in silliness, lightweight banalities, artificial and hyped-up excitement, and other fantasy pictures of life.

This is why, in the end, God will win the great controversy. Illusion cannot survive in a real universe!

EXPECTING GOOD THINGS

My soul, wait thou only upon God; for my expectation is from him. Ps. 62:5.

Have you ever had a time in your life when everything goes wrong? Your friends admonish you to "pray about it." You do. And even more goes wrong?

Wait a minute! you think. *Wasn't prayer supposed to make things better again?*

It's like going to the bank to cash a check that you know is good. The teller hands the check back to you, saying, "I'm sorry, I cannot give you the money." Astonished, you question, "Aren't there sufficient funds available?" The teller smiles broadly, "Oh yes! This account has limitless funds!" You examine the check closely. The date is correct, your name is there, the signature is authentic. "I don't understand," you stammer. "What's wrong?"

At this point the teller reassures you that there is absolutely nothing at all wrong. "Come back tomorrow," she suggests. But the next day brings no better results. After a time you may be tempted to throw away the check, that is, unless you are absolutely sure that the signer meant for you to have the money and that it *is* available to you. Ultimately the trustworthiness of the person who issued you the check will be the deciding factor as to whether you discard the check.

Prayer can be like having a "good check" that you just can't seem to cash. Having made sure that everything is in order, you sometimes still find yourself without the "funds" you feel are coming to you. God has promised us many things. When the day arrives that these promises apparently cannot be "cashed in," you are left with one thing: who God is.

The psalmist said, "My soul, wait thou only upon God; for my expectation is from him." Our good Father is leading us to green pastures. He promises that we shall walk beside peaceful waters. Can we trust Him when we pass through a valley as dark as death? Through silence as impenetrable as granite? If we are trusting more in the person of God than what we can obtain from His storehouse of blessings, we shall never lose hope.

The primary purpose of prayer is not to make things better. It is a means by which we may improve our relationship with the Father. In reality, what better thing is there than friendship with Him, for He is Himself all, and in all. And having Him, we shall desire nothing else on earth! (Ps. 73:25, N.E.B.).

GOD DOES NOT FRUSTRATE

For this commandment which I command you this day is not too hard for you, neither is it far off. . . . But the word is very near you; it is in your mouth and in your heart, so that you can do it. Deut. 30:11-14, R.S.V.

My fourth-grade teacher will never know how resentful I felt at what she had explained to me. I had just taken a standardized achievement test, and I was smarting under the awareness that many of the questions on the test were utter mysteries to me. My teacher kindly told me that in order to measure the upper limits of even the most brilliant some questions that I wasn't even expected to answer had to be included.

After cooling down for a few hours, I decided I could forgive this calculating piece of academic frustration, in view of its purposes. Yet the same feelings have sometimes surfaced in the years since then as I have thought about the ''testing'' requirements of God's law. It has seemed manifestly unfair that God should require of me that which He knew I was unable to perform.

What is more, it has seemed even more unfair that He should then judge me so severely for failing to reach that impossible standard. More than a scaled score on a national norm was at stake; my eternal life was on the line! How comforting to realize that I am not the first to have struggled with these feelings, and Moses' message is as potent for us as for his hearers. And what a wisely comforting understanding of God he brings!

God is not testing our upper limits that He might judge us; He is expanding our upper limits that we might enjoy Him. He has no reason to frustrate us by commanding the impossible; He has every reason to transform our inner motives that we might love His commands. His relationship to us has never been that of the distant Judge, handing down endless dictums beyond our capacities to perform. It has been that of a nurturing Father, healing and transforming our inner motives that we might enjoy doing right.

So often we have seen victory over sin as similar to sitting on a keg of dynamite, holding down the lid and hoping that it won't blow. We do endless battles with our unchangeable inner drives, gritting our teeth, clenching our fists, and making new resolutions ''not to do that one more time.'' But God's plan for us is to change what it is we really want to do.

What hope there is, then, for all of us who have struggled with the untamed mind-habits of the old life! The victory is not preserved for those stiff-backed few who can take cold showers without gasping. It is free to all who will let God write His law on their hearts.

PERFORMANCE VERSUS RELATIONSHIP

Then they said to him, "What must we do, to be doing the works of God?" Jesus answered them, "This is the work of God, that you believe in him whom he has sent." John 6:28, 29, R.S.V.

Is the message of who God is, only another theological issue that adults may discuss in groups? Or is it a tangible and relevant concept that even youth may embrace? Let my teenage son, Jeff, give you the insight of his own feelings:

"A lot of kids are brought up in settings where they must perform in order to be accepted and loved. They are expected to get good grades in school in order to keep Mom and Dad happy. They feel they have to be funny or good-looking in order to be popular. They know their teachers will like them if they are well behaved in the classroom. Though this is supposed to provide the incentive to do well, it can be very discouraging when they fail to measure up.

"The problem is that when these same ideas are carried over into relating to God, you know you can *never* measure up, and it makes you feel like giving up. *It's impossible!* you think. *I might as well not even try!* Of course all this is covered up by an 'I don't care!' attitude.

"Jesus understood the problem. When He was here on earth He was asked, 'How are we supposed to do good?' In other words, how can we please God? The Jews were hung up on all the requirements and expectations of the Pharisees. With all the countless rules and duties, they were totally discouraged and thought it was impossible for God to accept them. Jesus set things straight. He told them that what pleased God most of all was for them to develop a personal friendship with Him.

"Over the past few months I have been coming to understand that instead of trying to do good, which is useless, we will naturally want to become more like Jesus when we behold Him. When I acquired this new sense of understanding, my view of God was changed. I feel much freer in His presence. Now I want to grow to improve the relationship instead of trying to meet requirements.

"I think there would be fewer discouraged Christians if they had this understanding. God accepts us, not because of anything we do, but because He created us to be His friends. That's what makes living worthwhile."

A STUNNING GIFT

For what is mortal must be changed into what is immortal; what will die must be changed into what cannot die. 1 Cor. 15:53, T.E.V.

You are the manager of Tiffany's Jewelry Store, having in your charge the most lavish inventory of gems and jewelry in the country. And you are interviewing people for the position of head clerk.

One applicant seems to have extensive knowledge of premium jewelry and evident confidence in handling it. Naturally, you ask if he has a criminal record. Sheepishly, he nods the affirmative. "I've served fifteen years in prison," he admits. "For jewelry theft." Would you hire him and hand him the keys to the store? Or would you suddenly worry about that priceless inventory?

Paul tells us that God alone has immortality (1 Tim. 6:16). And yet in today's text he says that God is putting the finishing touches on a plan to begin distributing that Godlike quality to human beings! And what a stunning gift!

Stunning, not only because of the mind-jolting implications of living forever, but also because of the ones to whom God will give it: *Sinners!* Some would view it as similar to giving the keys to Tiffany's to a convicted jewelry thief, for the people to whom God will entrust eternal life will not be placed in solitary confinement. They will be free to travel the universe, openly sharing their values and convictions, acting out the longings of their hearts.

Why, then, will God give eternal life to sinners? Some see it as primarily an expression of love—that God is too generous to withhold such a treasure from those He loves. But loving can be indulgent if it grants treasures to those unable to handle them. For that matter, God loves the wicked, who will not receive eternal life, just as much as He loves those who will.

The gift of eternal life is profoundly an expression of trust. It is God's announcement that He trusts His own abilities to restore His people to complete loyalty. He has confidence that His methods surely will work. Therefore, when He gives out the gift of eternal life, He is announcing that He trusts His people to be fully restored. Former jewel thieves, murderers, liars, and the rest—He will trust us all!

If our God will have ample reason to trust "sinners" with eternal life, shouldn't we sinners, even now, have ample reason fully to trust our God? For that *is* eternal life.

HOPE FOR HOPELESSNESS

Now we find that the Law keeps slipping into the picture to point the vast extent of sin. Yet, though sin is shown to be wide and deep, thank God his grace is wider and deeper still! Rom. 5:20, Phillips.

Two couples shared a duplex in suburbia. On one side lived Mary and her husband, Steve, who was in the Navy. Their relationship flourished in spite of extended times of separation when Steve was away at sea. Rhonda and Joe were quite another matter. Though rarely apart for more than a day at a time, the distance between them seemed wider than the Atlantic and Pacific oceans combined.

Much of the tension in the Christian experience is a result of an awful sense of distance between heaven and earth. God is just too far away! If only we could actually *hear* Him. Or catch a glimpse of Him as did Moses. Or if not of God Himself, at least of an angel!

Such longing can wreak havoc in our sense of peace if we allow the fact of our physical separation from God to override the counterbalancing reality of our union with Him. God's friendship with us is far greater than our physical separation from Him! We read: "Now we find that the Law keeps slipping into the picture to point the vast extent of sin. Yet, though sin is shown to be wide and deep, thank God his grace is wider and deeper still!" Let's stop and think about what this text is saying.

We are born into this world separated from God both in body and in spirit. In order for us to recognize how serious is this condition, God gave us His law. It continually shows us the vast extent of our estrangement from Him—mentally, emotionally, and spiritually. However, there is *hope* for our otherwise hopeless condition! God's love, which we did not ask for and do not deserve, is so wide and deep that it far outreaches *any* distance between us! To be reunited with Him physically while still alienated spiritually is not the key to eternal life. The physical distance is an expression of God's love to us. Only when the spiritual relationship has been restored will we feel totally comfortable in His presence!

The gulf of separation between God and me is actually only as wide as my unbelieving heart. How glad I am that He has bridged this distance with His matchless love!

LEGALISTS ARE REBELS

I am the Lord, and I do not change. And so you . . . are not yet completely lost. Mal. 3:6, T.E.V.

Our usual picture of the religious legalist is of one with permanent worry marks on his brow, collecting endless lists of good things to do and bad things to avoid doing. His religious vocabulary is heavily spiced with words such as "duty," "obedience," and "perfection." And he dreads nothing more than that he might do something that would incur the disfavor of a hypersensitive God. To speak of him as a rebel against God would be, in his eyes, grounds for a libel suit.

But consider again the root motivation of the legalist. His most intense desire is that his diligent efforts at goodness might persuade God to change toward him and to grant favors of grace or kindness He might otherwise not offer. The legalist assumes that he knows exactly what he most needs and wants. Indeed, he knows better than God does, and were he not coaxing those gifts from God, God would not likely grant them.

As such, the legalist is saying that he is better off in his own hands than in the hands of God. He is convinced that he can take better care of himself than God can, were he given the controlling vote. His life is a protest that the gifts of forgiveness and acceptance are held in the hands of a niggardly God who is not inclined to part with them except when coaxed or obligated. The legalist, then, believes himself to be higher, wiser, and more loving than God. And surely that is the ultimate rebellion!

Any time I approach God with a desire to change His attitudes or actions toward me, I am reverting to the postures of a legalist. When God said, "I am the Lord, and I do not change," He was not making a petulant remark or announcing a closed mind. Our Father does not change toward us, because there is nothing in His perfectly loving and wise attitude toward us that needs changing.

God said, "I am the Lord, and I do not change. And so you . . . are not yet completely lost." We dwell in grace, every one of us. Though each of us has sinned, we have each been granted life—and a lifesaving opportunity to change *our* minds. We have not died, not because we have begged for our lives but because our unchanging God is gracious by nature.

WHAT MAKES OUR JOY FULL?

These things I have spoken to you, that my joy may be in you, and that your joy may be full. John 15:11, R.S.V.

Jesus was in the upper room with His eleven remaining disciples. He knew that in just a few short hours their lives would be turned upside down. And so He sought to comfort them ahead of time and to teach them precious truths that they would consequently take to the whole world.

He began by telling them that He was to be taken from them but that His departure signaled preparation for their being with Him forever afterward. Meanwhile He would send the Comforter to help them remember all that He had said to them. He told them that He was going to the Father, that it was to their advantage that He go. He understood that because of His telling them these things, sorrow had filled their hearts. How much more He wanted to explain to them, but they could not bear it right then. "So you have sorrow now," He said tenderly, "but I will see you again and your hearts will rejoice, and no one will take your joy from you" (John 16:22, R.S.V.).

Then He gave one of the most wonderful promises ever recorded in Scripture: "Truly, truly, I say to you, if you ask anything of the Father, he will give it to you in my name. . . . Ask, and you will receive, that your joy may be full" (verses 23, 24, R.S.V.).

As always, Jesus pointed His friends to the Father. "He who has seen me has seen the Father" (chap. 14:9, R.S.V.). "All that I have heard from my Father I have made known to you" (chap. 15:15, R.S.V.). The place He was going to prepare is in the Father's house. Even the promised Comforter "proceeds from the Father," He reminded them (verse 26, R.S.V.). And the joy that was His—that total oneness with the Father (expressed in His prayer for them)—was to be theirs for the asking! "The Father himself loves you," He emphasized (chap. 16:27, R.S.V.).

Jesus knows that there is only one way for us to have total joy. It is not in living where there is no pain or suffering. It is not in having a mansion or walking on streets of gold. It isn't even in living eternally. It is in being restored fully to fellowship with our Father in heaven, for "in [His] presence is the fullness of joy" (Ps. 16:11, N.E.B.).

IT'S HOW YOU PLAY THE GAME

An athlete is not crowned unless he competes according to the rules. 2 Tim. 2:5, R.S.V.

If I had been writing today's verse, I would have written what seems so obvious: "An athlete is not crowned unless he *wins*. He who gets to the finish line ahead of the others wins the prize. It doesn't matter who gets hurt or snubbed along the way. Winning is itself the goal."

In Paul's mind, playing the game by the rules is more important than simply winning the game. For it is the day-by-day, practical matters of life that must be brought within the boundaries of God's will. *This* is what will, in the end, prepare one to wear the crown.

As with the athlete, the Christian never forgets the finish line. But it is a crude athlete who regards his personal victory as more important than the humanity of his fellow-runners. Were he to shove or trip other runners to gain an advantage over them, he would be disqualified.

"Winning," in our usual context of rivalry and competition, implies that someone else must lose. It is an ego-oriented activity in which the self-worth of many is crushed so that a few can supposedly think better of themselves. As such, it damages the very fabric of human respect that is so vital to the healing of persons.

Our Father does not use enticements of selfish rewards to get us to live the Christian life, for living "according to the rules" is itself the reward. We do not embrace those inner qualities of tenderness, compassion, and sensitivity in order to win a crown. They are themselves the crown, the Christ-life within. And heaven is but the marvelous opportunity to enjoy this whole-life forever.

An old bromide says, "It's not whether you win or lose, but how you play the game." In the unstudied moments of life we reveal who we really are. We "play the game" of life by the game rules—the values and attitudes of the soul—that we have internalized through our fellowship with our Lord. If it is natural for us, in the race-pace of our daily course, to have our hearts tuned to the unspoken hurts of those running with us (and especially those lagging behind us), then we shall receive crowns with our names on them at the finish line.

July 7

MORE THAN LEGAL REINSTATEMENT

I will restore to you the years which the swarming locust has eaten, the hopper, the destroyer, and the cutter. Joel 2:25, R.S.V.

"I'll make it up to you!" Mother consoled her little daughter after telling her that a proposed trip to the ocean had been canceled. "We'll go another time."

Still distressed, the child wiped at her tears, hiccuping slightly as she spoke. "Will all the pretty shells still be there?" Assured once again by her mother, she toddled off to her sandbox, muttering under her breath, "Mommy and I will build castles. And we'll feed the sea gulls . . ."

Life in this world can be shattering. We may sustain losses that are far worse than postponed trips to the ocean, losses that are as forever gone as yesterday. Who can replace the loss of a son or daughter who died "out of the Lord"? Having grown up in a home filled with drunkenness and strife, who can go back and experience a happy childhood?

I believe that the wicked indulgences so prevalent today are stark evidence that people are trying to "make it up" to themselves for all the losses, great and small, sustained in their lives. The call to chaste living and to right concepts of Biblical doctrine draws relatively few from the masses. Why? Because the inherent message of self-denial threatens to further increase their sense of loss. Often those who do come to embrace Christianity accept forgiveness for their past sins in exchange for the hope of eternal life. Surely, *that* would "make it up" to them!

But is legal reinstatement into the community of heaven enough? Let's look again at the situation of the little girl mentioned above. Would she have been happy at the beach without her mother there to enjoy and participate in her activities—even if many other children were present? Was not the companionship with her mother what she hungered for more than mere permission to go to the ocean?

Friends, God has more to offer us than legal reinstatement into heaven. His plan is to "restore to [us] the years which the swarming locust has eaten"—and He knows our going to heaven is not enough in itself to accomplish this. We need *Him!* His companionship alone can heal our brokenness and relieve our sense of loss.

God's message to the world is that He has given us Himself! And having Him, we shall desire nothing else on earth (Ps.73:25, N.E.B.).

194

DRESS FOR SUCCESS

Then put on the garments that suit God's chosen people, his own, his beloved: compassion, kindness, humility, gentleness, patience. Col. 3:12, N.E.B.

Everything we choose to wear is a statement of who we see ourselves to be. If we wear the latest designs from *Gentleman's Quarterly,* or Sak's Fifth Avenue catalog, we are saying that we see ourselves to be current, aware, artistic, and not a little affluent. If we choose to wear well-worn khaki or denims, and very "familiar" shoes, we are projecting an image of casualness, a laid-back disregard for the highbrow expectations of society, and a penchant for personal comfort.

Employers have learned to gauge their prospective employees by seeing how they dress. When considering subordinates for promotions, executives note, among other things, how they dress. It is no wonder that the book *Dress for Success* is selling in the millions of copies.

A young man of a royal line—destined to sit on a monarch's throne—will have a dignity, a bearing of self-confidence and poise, that will be evident to others. This will be revealed to a large degree by the clothes he will choose to wear. They will express who he knows himself to be!

Paul says that if we will recognize who we really are—chosen, claimed, and loved by the King of the universe—we will "dress" accordingly. That Spirit-interpreted understanding will impart to us a dignity, a self-image, that will be expressed naturally by those character qualities with which we clothe ourselves.

Each one of the qualities that Paul mentions in today's verse is an expression of a person dealing from a position of strength. He whose own needs for love have been met is set free to be compassionate to the needs of others. A secure person can come out of himself enough to let kindness flow to others. Humility (or teachableness) will mark the life of one who knows he already belongs to God. Beholding our gentle Father and seeing how powerful He has been in our lives through His gentleness will give us the courage to be gentle with others. And one who has benefited from God's patience will be quick to grant others time and space to grow.

"Dressing" with these character qualities, as Christians, is more than a self-chosen statement about our tastes and preferences. It is an accurate statement to the world of who our Father is and how wonderfully He adorns the lives of His people!

HAVING THE RIGHT PERSPECTIVE
And having thee, I desire nothing else on earth. Ps. 73:25, N.E.B.

"It's just not fair! They break all the rules and get all the privileges!" Roger's eyes burned with a mixture of anger and amazement. At 15 he felt things should be cut and dried: the guys in the dorm who messed around should not be having it so good. Yet they were the very ones who seemed able to appropriate every loophole to their advantage. "What good does it do to try to play fair!" The muscles in his cheeks were tense.

Probably every person on earth has, at some time or another, had such sentiments. David certainly did. He lamented, "My feet had almost slipped, my foothold had all but given away, because the boasts of sinners roused my envy when I saw how they prosper" (Ps. 73:2, 3, N.E.B.).

He continued, "And so my people follow their lead and find nothing to blame in them, even though they say, 'What does God know? The Most High neither knows nor cares.' So wicked men talk, yet still they prosper, and rogues amass great wealth." David then indulges in a bit of self-pity: "So it was all in vain that I kept my heart pure and washed my hands in innocence. For all day long I suffer torment and am punished every morning" (verses 10-14, N.E.B.).

However, David knew God too well to remain in such a state of agitation. Catching himself before going any further with his feelings, he admits, "Yet had I let myself talk on in this fashion, I should have betrayed the family of God. So I set myself to think this out but I found it too hard for me, until I went into God's sacred courts; there I saw clearly what their end would be. . . . I am always with thee, thou holdest my right hand; thou dost guide me by thy counsel and afterwards wilt receive me with glory. . . . They who are far from thee are lost" (verses 15-27, N.E.B.).

Only as we are totally satisfied in our relationship with the Father can we accept that God's continued blessing of the wicked robs us of nothing! His choice to love people to wholeness instead of "giving them what they have coming"—even when they take advantage of this posture—can never diminish the fact that "God is [our] possession for ever" (verse 26, N.E.B.).

Having Him, we shall desire nothing else on earth.

THROWAWAY PEOPLE

Even if a man should be detected in some sin, my brothers, the spiritual ones among you should quietly set him back on the right path, not with any feeling of superiority but being yourselves on guard against temptation. Gal. 6:1, Phillips.

You reach for the paper cup in a dispenser and pull it down. You fill the cup and drink from it. When it is empty, it seems cheap and worthless. So you simply throw it away. Keeping it for later use would be too much bother. Furthermore, there are plenty more where this one came from.

You have a number of employees under your supervision. Jobs are scarce, with a dozen applicants for every opening. One of your employees, overwhelmed with personal problems, becomes ineffective on the job. To deal with his problems would demand too much of your time, and the names of a dozen apparently problem-free applicants are on file in the personnel office. So you fire him.

You discover that a church member has succumbed to some dark sin that is embarrassing to the congregation. You begin to weigh the personal demands—in time and energy—involved in helping him to set his life in order once again. Yours is a large congregation, and he isn't a particularly prominent member. What is more, you have *Church Manual* grounds to disfellowship him. What will you do?

How very easy it is to become indignant with troublesome people and to use their failings as an excuse to pass them by in favor of more "promising" people. It is so time-consuming, so taxing of our interpersonal skills, to confront in a redemptive manner the brooding and confused victims of this sin-blasted planet.

Jesus never looked upon anyone as a throwaway person. Even the most unpromising could not hide their true potential from the eyes of One who knew how powerfully His love could affect them. He never cast them aside to go in search of more promising prospects.

Jesus was fond of conducting experiments in love. Nothing brought Him greater delight than to find someone whose personhood had been crumpled, who had been tossed aside as a throwaway by the rest of society. Then He would take on the challenge of seeing how much difference He could make by loving that person wisely and unconditionally.

We represent our Father best when we cherish each person we meet as of great worth.

CREATION, EVOLUTION, OR INSTRUCTION?

A disciple is not above his teacher, but everyone when he is fully taught will be like his teacher. Luke 6:40, R.S.V.

"Do you believe in creation or in evolution?" As he asked the question, I saw a look in his eye that told me there was a catch in it somewhere. But being a Bible-believing Christian, I of course voted for the divine sudden act rather than for the long, slow process of gradual change.

With an "I've got you now" tone in his voice, he asked, "When it comes to obtaining a Christlike character, is it a long, drawn-out process, or is it a sudden, divine act? Is it creation, or evolution?" It sounded good. Not wanting to be thought of as an evolutionist or be seen as faulting God's miracle-working power, I almost fell for it.

But a clear-thinking friend commented, "Instant creation is fine for trees and whales; but our God doesn't instantly create mature characters. Neither Jesus nor Adam had that benefit. Christlikeness of character comes from hearing His word and making choices accordingly."

Jesus spoke clearly to the issue of how one becomes like the Teacher: "Everyone when he is fully taught will be like his teacher." Jesus made us with minds capable of understanding—through the Holy Spirit's enlightenment—the principles of His kingdom. These same minds then can make choices to act in harmony with those principles. And these are the building blocks of character. Character is revealed through the habitual acts that are in harmony with one's internal value system.

I have known several people who have tried to hold to the theory that character is created instantly mature. They believe that their position is a testimony to the miracle-working power of God, and to anticipate a slower process is to make allowance for sin. But they are boxed into that all-or-nothing position that says that, should they detect immaturity within themselves, they must doubt that God has indeed done His miracle in their lives. And they are crushed with the haunting fear that perhaps they are not even converted!

Jesus said, "I am the way, and the *truth,* and the life." His power to change us is rooted, not in enthusiasm, mystic ritual, or incomprehensible acts, but in truth. The longings of the heart after Christlikeness find their highest expression, then, when we say, "Jesus, teach me! Show me Your will, and I will gladly respond."

TELLING IT LIKE IT IS!

Fear God and give him glory, for the hour of his judgment has come; and worship him who made heaven and earth, the sea and the fountains of water. Rev.14:7, R.S.V.

Have you ever been scared to death of someone—until you got to know him? A college dean, a company president, maybe even your first-grade teacher? His rank, his potential power over you, left you feeling vulnerable and nervous until you discovered he liked you. From that point on, his exalted position became your garland—you were *friends!*

Did he change, or did your perception of him change? Most likely, you simply learned to know him for who he was. And your respect for him grew as you experienced the genuine warmth that housed his genius, his accomplishments. If the occasion arose for you personally to defend him, no doubt you found it richly rewarding to be able to say, "No, he's not like that at all. Let me tell you about him!"

Our text today contains a word that many honest seekers of God have misunderstood. To them, to "fear" God means to be rightfully afraid of Him: He's *God!* And He destroys sinners! What happens then, when you learn that He *likes* you? That you no longer need to be afraid of Him? Does He expect you to return to fear so as to give Him due respect? Let me say right now that if you are fearful of God, you *cannot* glorify Him properly! (See 1 John 4:16-19.)

The word *fear* here means respect. To "fear God and give him glory" is the experience of learning to know God so well that your heart throbs with the deepest kind of ardent love and reverence. It is your highest joy and choicest privilege to explain Him to those who are still threatened by His exaltedness. You literally "give him glory" by attributing to Him accurately His wonderful character. He's been misrepresented to the human race since Eden. But "the hour of his judgment has come," and we get to be His character witnesses!

We are also given the privilege of worshiping Him. This is no "groveling in the dirt" kind of servility! Rather, like the dignified, impassioned salute one might give to a returning king, victorious in an ugly battle, we may render homage to the great God who is our Father and our friend.

Now that is about the best news I can think of!

FINANCIAL ABSURDITIES

As neither had anything to pay with he let them both off. Now, which will love him most? Luke 7:42, N.E.B.

This creditor is going to be in real trouble with his accountant. He is going to have to explain why it is that two debtors are being treated as if they didn't owe any money when, in fact, they each owe a tidy sum. They know it. The creditor knows it. And the accountant knows it. What kind of accounting fiction will he need to create to make the books balance at the bottom of the page?

It reminds me of some of the discussions we used to have in college religion classes about forgiveness. "Is it legally correct," we would ask, "to treat a man as if he had never sinned, when in fact he had? Isn't that legal fiction?" Then someone would ask, "How can we trust a God who commits legal fiction as a part of the salvation plan?"

But Jesus' question to Simon, at the conclusion of His brief parable about the two debtors, makes it clear that the Great Creditor has something more in mind than the balancing of books. Jesus asks, "Which will *love* him most?" The issue at hand is not whether the books will balance but whether the debtors will be drawn into love—whether a relationship can be restored.

The great issues in the plan of redemption center around relationships, not around bookish legalities. It is true that many aspects of God's approach to us can be illustrated by using legal metaphors—just as Jesus used a financial metaphor in the parable above. But we often fall into theological confusion and conflict when we try to force legal concerns onto what is essentially a relational problem.

Our Father wants debtors to love Him, not just to be satisfied that the books balance. His actions toward us—even through Jesus on the cross—are revelations of His truthfulness and love, that we might be won back to Him. That is what Jesus wanted from Simon that night in his home. But Simon was absorbed in the legal questions of whether Mary deserved to be accepted by Jesus. He couldn't even hear Jesus' heartbeat saying, "Simon, do you have reason to *love* Me?"

The good news for us is that we don't have to worry about God's supposed financial absurdities or legal fictions. We trust a God who has more vital things on His mind: our love for Him!

LOVING A TERRIBLE GOD

The Lord your God is in the midst of you, a great and terrible God. Deut. 7:21, R.S.V.

Remember when *bad* meant bad? And *gay* meant happy? Today, something "bad" is really fantastic, and not many individuals would ever admit to being "gay"!

We are amused at our convoluted language. A favorite quote of mine expresses it perfectly: "I know you believe you understood what you think I said, but I am not sure you realize that what you heard is not what I meant!"

How about religion? Does it ever happen that God means one thing but we assume that He means another?

Today's text says God is "terrible"! As a descriptive adjective in modern English, the word is synonymous with "awful," "frightening," and even "bad-tasting"! I have heard good, Bible-believing saints giving this word a great deal of "fire and brimstone" kind of reverence when applied to God. You get the message: You'd better watch out—or else!

If this is the meaning of *terrible,* can you ever *love* a terrible God? Theological discussions over such words will never fully settle the issues of the heart. So let us return to God's own Word, and let Him clear the air. Since we started in Deuteronomy, we'll pick up the track there:

"For the Lord your God is a God of gods and Lord of lords, the great, the mighty, and the terrible God, *who is not partial and takes no bribe"* (Deut. 10:17, R.S.V.). Here terrible conveys impartiality and honorableness.

"O Lord God of heaven, the great and terrible God *who keeps covenant and steadfast love* with those who love him and keep his commandments" (Neh. 1:5, R.S.V.). Terrible here refers to faithfulness and steadfastness.

"They forgot God, their *savior,* who had done great things in Egypt, wondrous works in the land of Ham, and terrible things by the Red Sea" (Ps. 106:21, 22, R.S.V.). Terrible is used here to describe the actions of the Deliverer.

Now if the word *terrible* is used to convey impartiality and honorableness, to refer to faithfulness and steadfastness, and to describe the actions of the Deliverer, how can we help loving Him? And our reverence for Him will be born not out of fear but of intelligent and responsive love.

IT'S HOW YOU LISTEN

Take care, then, how you listen; for the man who has will be given more, and the man who has not will forfeit even what he thinks he has. Luke 8:18, N.E.B.

"The rich get richer, and the poor get poorer." That's the way it happens in an unfair world, and only the rich think it's a good idea. Yet the verse we are contemplating today seems to put Jesus on the side of that cruel inequity. It has troubled more than one reader, for it seems to be saying that the "haves" will get more, and the "have nots" will have it taken away. If God is supporting such a scheme, we suspect He is playing favorites. Worse yet, He is blessing those who need it the least and depriving those who need it the most.

But Jesus is not dealing here with arbitrary blessings doled out at God's impulses. Rather, He is speaking of those treasures one gets by listening, by hearing the Word of God with faith. The greatest treasure that God could give to the world was the knowledge of His character, of which the world was destitute. Such treasures are available not to the privileged few, but to all who will listen.

The "man who has" obtained his treasures in the first place because he was willing to listen. As he continues to listen he will surely obtain more, for he nurtures that vital quality of teachableness. He has developed such confidence in his Teacher that he accepts whatever He has to offer. A teachable person will be right at home in heaven, for he has learned to love truth and will be eager to go on learning for the rest of eternity.

But Jesus warns against another attitude toward truth. Some have gotten into the habit of saying No to God—of silencing His gentle voice, rationalizing away His sensible counsel, and postponing His appeals. They dodge the clearest statements of reality; thus they become self-deluded. But they shall find in time that their ersatz platform cannot sustain them. In the final crunch they have nothing—no hope, no understanding, no saving relationship.

"Take care, then, how you listen." One trusted author says, "We want to become so sensitive to holy influences that the lightest whisper of Jesus will move our souls.'" With so many voices clamoring for our attention, so many noises drowning out His gentle appeal, how careful we must be how we listen—and respond!

---

* Ellen G. White, *"That I May Know Him,"* p. 361.

THE GOOD IN BAD DECISIONS

One man esteems one day as better than another, while another man esteems all days alike. Let every one be fully convinced in his own mind. Rom. 14:5, R.S.V.

No one likes to be wrong. But some people fear being wrong to the extent that it keeps them from making needed decisions. Perhaps somewhere in their lives they were made to feel that making a wrong decision was equal to having a defective character.

Are not children often told, "Good girls [boys] don't do that," as if the issue were their goodness rather than the logic behind their choice? Children treated in this manner are not encouraged to think; they are conditioned to try to please their parents and teachers. Reaching adulthood, they carry with them the idea that good people make only right decisions.

Christians are especially prone to such thinking. It is too easy for one believer to look rather askance at another believer because he made a faulty decision. Surely, if he were being "led by the Lord" he wouldn't have erred, right? You know: "By their fruits ye shall know them" (Matt. 7:20).

Our text today says, "Let every one be fully convinced in his own mind." How does one become "fully convinced in his own mind"? It is by learning through experience to discern truth. This is illustrated in a little story told of Bernard Baruch. He was asked, "To what do you attribute your success?" He replied, "To making the correct decisions." "How do you know what the correct decisions are?" "From experience." "How do you get the experience?" "By making wrong decisions."

God understands that sometimes we err as we process information— not because we are bad people but because we are learning as we go along. He would rather we keep processing, keep on making decisions, albeit bad ones, than allow ourselves to become mired in indecision. He can work with our errors; He cannot correct wrong thinking if we never own up to it. Perhaps that is why, when addressing the Laodicean church, He says, "I know your works: you are neither cold nor hot. Would that you were cold or hot!" (Rev.3:15, R.S.V.).

I am impressed by the way God handles error-ridden humanity. He gives us room to grow, to make decisions, even bad ones. He knows what He's doing. He's giving us back our sense of self-worth while we strive to know for ourselves the meaning of life.

AMAZED AT MAN

What is man that you are mindful of him, the son of man that you care for him? You made him a little lower than the angels; you crowned him with glory and honor and put everything under his feet. Heb. 2:6, 7, N.I.V., margin.

The restoration of antique automobiles has become a highly refined and exotic art form. Some collectors invest thousands of hours bringing rare and classic autos virtually back to their original condition. When the finished car is put on the auction block, the fainthearted fade back quickly as the sparkling gem commands a stunning price.

I remember my first visit to an antique car rally. In amazement I walked among hundreds of spotless specimens I had never heard of before, marveling at their shapes and curious features. A 1913 Lozier grabbed my attention for many long minutes. Wanting to express my appreciation for such a masterful piece of restoration, I blurted out to the owner, "It must have been in great shape when you found it!"

Being patient with my naiveté, he led me to the far side of the car, where he had a photograph of the car taken the day he found it. Abandoned in a field, it had weeds growing through its spokes, rust on its body, and chickens roosting in the upholstery. I was stunned.

Later I reflected on how glad I was that this man had taken the time to restore that Lozier so perfectly. How could I have known what a superb car it was made to be if I had seen only a tattered wreck with the Lozier marque on the big brass radiator? I appreciated not only the quality of the car but the skill of the restorer as well. He had looked at that pile of rust, and he knew exactly what he could make it become.

How I wish I could always look at people, seeing in them not the tarnish caused by sin but the incredible God-given potential built into them at Creation! How grateful I am that God has put on display before us one perfect Model of humanity.

Paul asked with amazement, "What is man" that God should hold him in such high regard? For when he looked at man, he didn't see him in the high position God had ordained for him (see Heb. 2:8). But he saw more than sin-damaged humans; he looked at that perfect specimen and said, "We see Jesus" (verse 9).

THE UNTHINKABLE SACRIFICE

The time came when God put Abraham to the test. "Abraham," he called, and Abraham replied, "Here I am." God said, "Take your son Isaac, your only son, whom you love, and go to the land of Moriah. There you shall offer him as a sacrifice on one of the hills which I will show you." Gen. 22:1, 2, N.E.B.

What Christian has not been thrilled by the story of Abraham? He loved God as we long to love Him; trusted Him in the face of unfathomable personal agony. With each new insight, we gain an increasingly vivid picture of a marvelous patriarch. But this incredible story is *not* primarily about Abraham!

The express purpose of Scripture is to reveal to us the character of the Father. What does the story of Abraham's journey up Mount Moriah teach us? Is it possible that we have allowed our preconceptions about God to color the message presented in this most moving saga? Have we seen Him as sovereign of the universe, playing "faith games" with hapless mankind? We empathize with Abraham; but candidly, do we find God's motivation less than delightful?

How do you feel about God asking Abraham to perform child-sacrifice—especially when He had made it very plain what He thought about the surrounding heathen nations who commonly practiced such abominations? How could God ask such a thing, even for the sake of testing Abraham's faith? Is there any other way to understand this story without portraying God as in conflict with Himself?

God wants to touch the central nerve of our fear of Him in order to bring relief and healing. Paint it any way you like, obedience is often the product of fear. "Faith" can end up as window dressing for a very unhealthy God-view. Could it be that God decided to give full body to our fears—in the person of Abraham? What if it were *your* child? Do you feel your stomach wrench as you hear this very request being made to an old man of the desert? Surely his agony was the epitome of the dread of God that the whole human race has borne since Eden.

This story reveals that *God is not like that!* God used that dramatic setting to give Abraham a precious lesson about Himseif. Abraham did not lose his son on Mount Moriah. But in the symbol of the ram caught in the thicket, God freely gave His!

LOVE IS MUTUAL

We should keep in mind the words of the Lord Jesus, who himself said, "Happiness lies more in giving than in receiving." Acts 20:35, N.E.B.

From childhood we have heard that JOY is an acronym meaning Jesus first, Others second, Yourself last. It implies that true joy is found when one seeks Jesus first, then always sets aside one's own needs in favor of the needs of another. And—generally speaking—that is true.

But consider, for example, the experience of a young man who fell in love with a young woman and devoted himself fully to meeting her needs. So convinced was he that joy could be found only in unselfishly loving her that he felt guilty even evaluating how well she met his needs. After a while the relationship seemed to become more of a duty than a delight, but he had read that it is more blessed to give than to receive, and so he persisted in the increasingly empty relationship.

Then it dawned upon him that she too needed to give! She also must feel that her life was potent, by being a valuable giver within the friendship. So he began to speak openly with her about the needs for understanding and encouragement that he brought to the friendship, and affirming her power to meet those needs. And the zest returned to their times together!

The best relationships are those that involve mutuality—where we are consciously aware that we are both giving to the other and being blessed by the other. It means that we are trusting our God-given capacities to bring joy and healing to another and that we openly avow God's plan to represent Himself to us through other humans who are in close fellowship with us.

But this concept—this lived experience—of mutuality takes on exciting dimensions when we consider that we are created in the image of God. That the desires and capacities for mutuality reflect His own heart. That He not only takes delight in giving to us, but He wants us to be delighted with the awareness that we are giving to Him through our relationship with Him!

It is still true that it is more blessed to give than to receive. But it is also true that God gives to us in order to restore in us the capacity to give back to Him—to give the delights of mutual fellowship for which He created us.

MUTUALITY AND SUCCESSFUL RELATIONSHIPS

Therefore God has highly exalted him and bestowed on him the name which is above every name, that at the name of Jesus every knee should bow . . . and every tongue confess that Jesus Christ is Lord, to the glory of God the Father. Phil. 2:9-11, R.S.V.

Excitement filled the auditorium. In a moment the new student body president would be announced. Much discussion had taken place as to who was best suited to the task. Votes had been cast. Hopes were high that the person chosen would be able to represent successfully not only the students to the faculty but also the faculty to the students.

A hush fell over the room as the principal stepped to the podium. As he made the announcement his voice was drowned out by cheering and whistling students. Faculty members exchanged pleased comments. There was no doubt about it; the young man elected had the ingredient most essential for a successful term of office: mutuality with both students and faculty.

Jesus has been chosen by the Father, on our behalf, to become our representative between heaven and earth. Today's text says that He has been exalted and given the name that is above every name. Verse 7 tells us why: Jesus emptied Himself and took the "form of a servant, being born in the likeness of men." In other words, He chose to become one of us. We can confidently put Him forward as our representative.

The wonderful thing is that we can be equally certain that He adequately represents God. He has been given His exalted position "to the glory of God the Father." This means simply that God's character—His attitudes and perspectives—are effectually carried back to us as we learn to dialogue with the Father through Christ.

The thought is held out in this passage that everyone in the universe should readily agree that Jesus is well qualified for this task. He alone is capable of standing in this position. Not only is He one with us, but He is equal with the Father (verse 6). There is simply no one else who fits this description. And let's not forget that God is the one who has sought to provide us with a sense of mutuality between heaven and earth: In accepting Christ, the Father accepts us—even as we ourselves accept God in the person of Christ.

Honestly, it makes me want to whistle and cheer! How about you?

HE CLAIMS US

He came unto his own, and his own received him not. John 1:11.

Parents are aware of a certain pattern of intense feelings that surface in their children each fall just as school is about to begin. Along with all the boundless eagerness to get back onto the schoolgrounds and see all their friends, the children often reveal tinges of apprehension. Their nervousness wears a familiar label: "Will my old friends still accept me? Will I be able to make friends with the new kids?"

Though Jesus was king of the universe, He had set all that aside to walk among men, with the same feelings and needs as they whom He had created in His own image. He too longed to be accepted by His friends, especially when He knew that He had so much to give them.

From all the usual reference points of deity, royalty, and sovereignty, Jesus could have said with proper dignity, "If these common sinners don't accept Me, that's their problem. I have every right simply to set them aside. I will call them My friends only if they are decent enough to accept Me as their friend."

But the apostle John, in what may sound like an incidental piece of historical detail, speaks volumes about the attitudes of our Saviour. "He came to his own, and his own received him not." When Jesus came looking for His people, He claimed them as His own, without reference to whether they accepted the relationship so freely offered.

For you see, He knew things that they did not know. He knew that they were His by design, creation, and redemption. Their Satan-induced delusions could not alter those facts. His attitude toward them was unconditional, because it was rooted in unchangeable facts of reality, not in flighty feelings. So He claimed them as His own and came to them.

Yet, because a relationship is two-sided, it could be only to those "who received him, who believed on his name," that He could give "power to become children of God" (John 1:12, R.S.V.). That invites us today. Our Father is coming to us even this morning, announcing with intense gladness on His face, "You are My very own; I claim you as Mine. Won't you be set free from the enemy's delusions and recognize who you really are?"

God does not wait until we become worthy of His claim. Rather its truthfulness, when grasped, has the power to change us!

FOR SHEER JOY!

**The kingdom of Heaven is like treasure lying buried in a field.
The man who found it, buried it again; and for sheer joy went and
sold everything he had, and bought that field. Matt. 13:44, N.E.B.**

Telling Bible stories to children can be fun. For one thing, children
need more word pictures because their vocabulary is limited—which, of
course, tends to make the lesson more vivid. And more simple, which is
equally important, because youngsters respond to simplicity. Unfortunately, by the time we reach maturity we seem to have "graduated" to
more complex (and often obscure) religious terminology. For a lot of
people, this takes the fun out of Bible study, and out of knowing God.

I have good news: God too enjoys storytelling! Most of the Bible is
written in story form. Jesus, who was "God with us," loved to gather a
cluster of people around Himself and tell them parables. One such
story-lesson involved a man who found buried treasure. Though the
Scripture record is but one text in length, I can easily imagine Him
describing the incident with relish. Knowing how dreary and uninviting
the priests had made spiritual things, Jesus sought to underscore how
exciting it can be to "discover" the truth about God and His ways.

By portraying this knowledge as buried treasure, Jesus gently offered
comfort to His listeners. He implied that they were not at fault for not
readily seeing how exciting and enrichening it is to know God—such
truth had been buried under mounds of ritual and falsehood. But there was
hope! Hidden in a common field, the treasure lay, waiting to be
discovered. I can just see Jesus pausing here in the narrative, smiling
slightly, waiting for them to notice His lowly garb, His sandaled and
dusty feet.

Then, not to keep His listeners in suspense, He quickly assures them
that the treasure is indeed found, but not without some price to the finder.
The man who found the treasure sold everything he had to purchase the
field in which it lay—but it was *for sheer joy* that he made such sacrifice!
And who would doubt that he *lost nothing* by doing so? What a contrast to
their feelings of being taken advantage of by the priests—and
consequently, by God!—during the rites of sacrifice in the Temple
service!

Friend, our exciting God is waiting for you to find Him! And finding
Him will bring *you* sheer joy!

ALL SHALL LIVE IN CHRIST

For as in Adam all die, so also in Christ shall all be made alive. 1 Cor. 15:22, R.S.V.

At first glance, this verse is unqualified good news. It is the assurance of the resurrection, the promise that Christ has provided life for all the condemned children of Adam. What is more, it affirms that *all* shall be made alive! According to Revelation 20:5, even the wicked shall be brought back to life at some point in the future.

But since those wicked shall be brought back to life, only then to receive the sentence of eternal death (verses 9, 10, 12-15), it could raise the question of whether such an event is necessary. Why bring a lost person, one who may have suffered terrible pain during his life and died a tragic death, back to life, only to let him live a brief but traumatic span and then cross the dark abyss again?

The graves of this planet are filled with the remains of both the righteous and sinners. In most cases the wicked have died from the same causes as have the righteous. The huge bombs of war, the crumpling of car metal, the ravages of terminal diseases, and the onward march of old age dismantle the bodies of the good and the bad alike.

Some could wonder if being on Christ's side has offered any benefit to Christians in the face of death. For they die too. So Jesus has promised to bring all mankind back to life in order that the spotlight could be focused upon the real issue: What has one done with Jesus, the Life-giver?

For it is at the time of the resurrection of the wicked that each person's ultimate choices shall be revealed. This is when all people shall get what they have really wanted. The righteous shall get eternal fellowship with the One they have loved and admired. With no lingering involvement with the great controversy, they shall be with Him forever. God shall also respect the free choices of those who have avoided and rejected Him. He will not force His life-giving presence upon them. Separation they wanted; separation they shall have. They shall die the second death. They will not die because of their sinful behaviors. Jesus' death on the cross covered those; their own resurrection is proof that ''in Christ shall all be made alive.'' But they shall die because they have rejected the Life-giver.

FALLEN SPARROWS AND THE FATHER'S HEART

Yet not a single sparrow falls to the ground without your father's knowledge. . . . Never be afraid, then—you are far more valuable than sparrows. Matt. 10:29-31, Phillips.

She sat alone, painfully thin and haunted-looking. Her dark eyes were cast downward, her shoulders drooped. It seemed hard to believe that this young woman had ever been vibrant and excited about life. Not so long ago she had been full of song and wonderful dreams. Now she was like a little sparrow whose voice had been stilled, her head bowed in submission to the harsh winds and stinging rain that pelted her frail body. She was slowly starving herself to death. She suffered from anorexia nervosa—an often fatal disease that amounts to sophisticated suicide.

A frighteningly increasing number of young women are falling prey to the ravages of this perplexing disease. Are they to be scolded into eating? Force-fed? Gravestones testify to the invalidity of such treatment. The truth is that healing must begin from within the mind. All other methods are transitory and ineffective.

God knows about sparrows—both kinds. He sees the hearts of His tired and distraught children. Whether our problem is anorexia or alcoholism or anything else, He sees us huddled against the chilling winds of this earthly life and takes pity on us. He knows that it is no use to scold us or to force us. What we need is His healing love.

And so He begins. Little by little He wins our confidence. So as not to frighten us any further, He speaks to us in a still small voice. Soothingly, He gently draws us to Himself. We discover He understands us, that He cares—that He *likes* us! Gradually we are able to let go of our death grip on whatever ''branch'' we are clinging to. He is able to free us from being trapped in the storm. He encourages us to sing again and then to soar. And the joy of His presence becomes our reason for living.

Well might we consider each other as He considers us, how He deals with us. Perhaps it would temper our anger at one another's failures. Certainly it offers us valid suggestions as to how to respond to the circumstances in our own lives and other people's lives that are beyond our control. (Force does not bring control!) Having experienced His healing love ourselves, we know that there is no better way to treat each other.

HOW NOT TO SPARE THE ROD

A father who spares the rod hates his son, but one who loves him keeps him in order. Prov. 13:24, N.E.B.

There is a lot of conventional wisdom going around about the meaning of that supposed Bible text, "Spare the rod and spoil the child." This widely held wisdom firmly states that the rod is to be used by parents as a means of inflicting pain on disobedient children. Parents tell their children what to do, and if they don't do it (as one parent told me), "You hit them, and you hit them hard."

And, of course, since this is thought to be Bible wisdom, children inwardly conclude that the Bible's Author is behind such an approach. They fear that the rod that is spoken of is not the Shepherd's rod of the twenty-third psalm, intended to guide gently through difficult places and to ward off the enemy, but a weapon to be dreaded, a way for irate authority figures to express their anger upon those who have affronted their authority.

Parents are indeed expected to teach their children to walk in the paths of blessing. And sometimes a self-willed child may need to be brought back to his senses. But all too often parents have not given priority to establishing a warm and vulnerable relationship with their children. They have not experimented with the power of healing love, and they feel that the only influence they have over their child is through their "duty" to inflict pain on him when he does not dutifully obey.

Some openly rebel against this approach, and understandably so, for it is alien to the way God made His people to learn and grow. Such a person is seeking to preserve some semblance of his personhood. His rebellion is not only against his parents but also against the religion that led his parents to act the way they did.

On the other hand, a child may meekly submit to his parents' rod-oriented mode of discipline. Since he is not rebelling, the parents assume that their method is working. But the chances are high that some twenty years later, in some destructive mid-life crisis, the apparently obedient person goes off in search of his freedom and identity, leaving behind a religion that has brought him much anxiety and guilt. Ironically, he also rejects his heavenly Father, who knows that one doesn't beat one's children into submission.

LEARNING TO TRUST IN THE LORD

Many when they see will be filled with awe and will learn to trust in the Lord. Ps. 40:3, N.E.B.

Have you ever met someone whom you didn't think you were going to like very much, and in time that person became one of your most cherished friends? Even in relationships where you start off liking each other, it takes time to establish trust and love. It takes being together in different settings and sharing thoughts and feelings. "Tried and true" friendships are not quickly formed or quickly forgotten. Yet we tend to think that accepting Christ as our Saviour brings instantaneous closeness.

I firmly believe that accepting Christ is only the very beginning. Like any new relationship, there is so much to learn, to experience together. Our reservations are seen by Him not as sins but merely as the natural "in process" emotions we carry with us through all of life. He is not offended when we feel a need to test His responses. It is His delight to act out His part in the bonding process. "Test Me! Prove Me!" He invites. "See if I'm not the best friend you've ever known!"

"But it's a sin to doubt Him!" a concerned believer cries. And so many struggling followers cringe in shame and self-reproach because they know they still have inner questions and lingering fears. Trying to muster up the needed trust, they find they are paralyzed by their own efforts. The fact is that no one can make himself trust another person—even if that person is God! Trust is a learned response, not merely an intellectual exercise.

Jesus spent three and one-half intense years with twelve men who were still full of questions even on the night of the Crucifixion. One continued to doubt even after the Resurrection—until Jesus accommodated him by allowing him to put his hand into His wounded side. The point is not that these men were so terribly sinful. Our attention is drawn to how the Master met their inability fully to believe. He was not repelled by them! He constantly worked to still their fears and give them reasons to trust Him.

To know Him is to love Him. To know Him in part is to love Him in part, to trust Him tentatively. The devotional life of the believer is not to prove his spirituality; it is to improve his ability to trust the One who is altogether trustworthy. And that takes time.

WHY YOU CAN'T KEEP
A GOOD MAN DOWN!

For though a righteous man falls seven times, he rises again, but the wicked are brought down by calamity. Prov. 24:16, N.I.V.

He fell while going into the last turn of the race. In a moment he was up again and running. Though he didn't finish first, he won the hearts of the spectators.

What gives some people the pluck to get up and keep going after misfortune strikes, while others tend to "curl up and die"? May I suggest that self-worth has a lot to do with it? No doubt, being able to keep things in perspective helps, too. In other words, having a good sense of who you are and where you are going can provide you with an inner dignity and strength with which to meet difficulty and failure.

Falling in one race, however, is different from falling in seven races in a row. Repeated or multiple troubles have the potential of totally stripping you of any reserves of strength. And those who might have cheered you on during the first fall, and maybe even the second and third, tend to grow silent if trouble persists. Like Job's friends, they begin to wonder about *you*.

Our verse today speaks of a righteous man—a man who "has it together with God"—falling seven times. Do we need to analyze his circumstances in order to appreciate the awful tragedy of one of God's own facing failure after failure? What must his fellow church members think? What must *he* think! What enables him to get up again and again and again? When all his own sense of self-worth has been dashed to pieces and his potential for personal achievement seems thwarted, what is left that causes him to get up once more?

Only our understanding of the Father and the Father's perspectives can enable us to get up again after falling "seven" times. God is not playing word games when He sees "uninterrupted victories" where we see only "failure." He counts our recovery of more value than any temporary loss of footing. Only when we refuse to be taught by an experience are we lessened by it.

Knowing that God is completely committed to restoring us to wholeness, we may confidently—under any circumstances—trust that He continues to cheer us on though everyone else has departed. He knows what we may become, regardless of how many failures we might experience in the process.

WHO CONVICTS OF SIN?

Then he showed me Joshua the high priest standing before the angel of the Lord, and Satan standing at his right hand to accuse him. Zech. 3:1, R.S.V.

He sat on the forward edge of his seat, wringing his hands until his knuckles turned white. He had failed to carry a certain responsibility that had been entrusted to him, and the other church members were aware of it. Though we talked about the best way to move forward, he always seemed to come up against a very strong emotional block. "Oh, I just keep feeling so guilty!"

Though all of us have at times felt guilty, those who are truly conscientious are particularly prone to the convicting awareness that they have failed to measure up. High personal standards and lofty spiritual ideals can expose one to constant feelings of guilt.

But it is worth noting that *both* Satan and the Holy Spirit are involved in the activity of convicting of sin. Just as Zechariah reported that Satan stood by Joshua to accuse him, so Jesus also promised that one work of the Holy Spirit would be to convict of sin (see John 16:8, 9). And because the effects are often so similar at the feeling level, many carry a Satan-loaded burden of guilt that they are certain was intended by God.

There are, however, vital clues that distinguish God's methods from those of Satan—methods that reveal His character. For example, it is Satan's desire to crush with condemnation rather than to heal. He longs to overwhelm the sinner with the awareness of his sins, asserting that he is beyond the scope of God's inclination to forgive, for then he will release his hold of faith in the Forgiver and—by that fact—be lost.

By contrast, God is intent on healing the sinner. He never, absolutely never, points out sin without at the same time uplifting the Saviour. He exalts the surpassing excellence of a better way, rather than pushing the sinner's face into the despairing failure of his own past ways.

Our Father's goal is to heal, not to crush. It is to establish a union by showing how well we can trust Him, not to destroy a union by showing how much we should fear Him. For it is in union with Him that all healing happens. The Spirit's convicting is a nudge toward wholeness; Satan's convicting is a large stone thrown at the already quivering sinner.

WHERE IS YOUR SECURITY?

Jesus Christ is always the same, yesterday, today and for ever. Heb. 13:8, Phillips.

Many people find security in living predictable lives. As such people group together, a kind of socially accepted rigidity may result, a conventionalism that defies changes. This is true among Christians as well as in other levels of society.

With all good intentions, Christians tend to seek traditional concepts of systematic theology rather than a vital, spontaneous friendship with a Person. Security often comes through behavioral conformity rather than in knowing that God is totally trustworthy (and fantastically innovative!) in His dealings with mankind. Sadly, they limit themselves as they limit their willingness to see how infinitely ready God is to interact with His erring children.

We read that "Jesus Christ is always the same, yesterday, today and for ever." Does this imply that He always uses the same methodology, always requires the same responses from His followers? If so, here is ground for the endless calls to reform that include long dresses and primitive living styles as exampled by godly men and women of the past century.

If the sameness spoken of by Paul refers to God's character, it is altogether a different matter. Well might we find security in knowing that God always is willing to forgive our stubborn ways, that He never tires of hearing our prayers. No matter how far we've strayed from His good plan for our lives, no matter how long we've absented ourselves from His presence, when we desire to find Him again, we shall discover that His attitude toward us has never changed. And, friends, *that* is security!

But what of "the old paths" we are admonished by God to ask for in Jeremiah 6:16? Does this prove that conformity to established religious patterns will bring "rest for [our] souls"? Or is this simply counsel for those who have lost their way, as had ancient Israel? There is a difference between finding your way *back* and forging ahead with God as your guide.

Even "baby" Christians should be taught that their security rests in who God is, not in how He may have chosen to act in any particular instance. To teach otherwise is to leave them vulnerable when God doesn't act in a manner that we think He should—according to how He acted in the past. How much better to trust a *Person,* rather than to try to figure out what that Person may do next.

NEAR TO THE HEART OF GOD

No one has ever seen God; but God's only Son, he who is nearest to the Father's heart, he has made him known. John 1:18, N.E.B.

There is one memory that I vividly recall from my childhood—a memory that is triggered by certain sounds. I can recall riding in the back seat of my dad's big chrome-toothed Buick, listening to the scratchy sounds of the AM car radio as he would tune in that classic broadcast, The Voice of Prophecy. Just before H.M.S. Richards would speak, their male quartet would always sing that familiar hymn, "There is a place of quiet rest, near to the heart of God, a place where sin cannot molest, near to the heart of God."

I am probably among thousands of listeners who, to this day, cannot sing that hymn in church without recalling the mellow sounds of the old King's Heralds Quartet reverently intoning the bliss of being "near to the heart of God." But may I invite us all to go beyond our reverie, to probe for the deeper meaning of that experience of being near to the heart of God.

It is, after all, a biblical phrase. Today's verse says that Jesus had the privilege of being the "nearest to the Father's heart." Though John is using a very picturesque metaphor, we can see clearly that he is speaking of something more than just physical closeness to the Father. He says that Jesus is qualified by that closeness to make the Father known to people who have never seen Him.

Being near the Father's heart, then, must have something to do with understanding the Father's character, with knowing the things that are important to God. John's Gospel is filled with the theme of Jesus' coming to this earth in order to make the Father known to us. He begins at the beginning: Jesus can tell us about the Father because He is nearest to the Father's heart.

We too are nearest to the Father's heart when we listen to what Jesus is telling us about the Father. John says that Jesus' message about the Father was more than just spoken; it "became flesh," a tangible, visible, personal presence. In beholding Jesus' life we behold "the glory . . . of the Father." In being drawn to Jesus we are being drawn to His Father, the source of eternal life. And that *is* eternal life.

FAITH FREES THE HEART

Moreover, God who knows men's inmost thoughts. . . . He had cleansed their hearts by faith. Acts 15:8, 9, Phillips.

A man had a well from which he drew all his water. Because the water was brackish, he distilled it for drinking and cooking. A neighbor dropped in one day during this process and inquired why the man did not dig a new well. The man shrugged, saying, "I've done this for years. It's OK; I'm used to it."

Sometimes we get used to a certain way of thinking. Though we know that it is not totally suitable, we tend to consider such thinking as "right" simply because it is so familiar. The practice is no different in the area of religion. Many familiar ideas about God seem to be "right"—mostly because they've been around for so long. However, we end up having to "distill" them intellectually before we can "swallow" them emotionally.

Take, for example, the ideas that surround the truth that God is our judge. Hasn't He long been pictured as stern and/or exacting? It can be an unpleasant thought, especially when tied to the concept of His omniscience. Visualizing Jesus pleading His blood on our behalf allows us to accept the judgeship of the Father, but it does not help us accept the Father Himself!

Our text today tells us that God knows our inmost thoughts. He knows better than we do how unsavory are some of our ideas about Him. He also knows that unless our opinion of Him changes, we will tend to concentrate on acts of obedience rather than in having an intimate relationship with Him. And no matter how many right things we do, misgivings about God will not have been purged from our hearts if we have not come to know Him as He really is.

Jesus said, "Anyone who gives heed to what I say and puts his trust in him who sent me has hold of eternal life" (John 5:24, N.E.B.). As we come to know God our fears and doubts about Him are replaced by the excitement of discovering how real and relevant He is, how reasonable and reliable His plan for our lives. In this way—by giving us understanding about Himself—God removes forever from our hearts any reasons we felt we had for not wanting to be His friends. And as our faith in Him grows we are set free to enter into ever-deepening fellowship with Him.

THE POWER OF POSITIVE PRIVILEGE

So you are to be perfect, as your heavenly Father is. Matt. 5:48, Goodspeed.

We were engaged in brisk conversation after the morning presentation at a camp meeting. The sermon had been on our freedoms in Jesus—freedom from guilt and from manipulation. Obviously concerned, a woman asked, "But we've still got to reveal the character of Christ, don't we?"

"No," I interrupted, "we *get* to reveal the character of Christ. There is an important difference."

She stood for a moment, pondering the subtleties: "got to" versus "get to." Heavy weight of burden and responsibility versus exhilarating sense of delightful permission and promise. "I think this is a key that will unlock many puzzles for me," she concluded.

Later she stopped me in a hallway. "Those two words have turned around the motivations of my whole Christian life. I'm seeing that Christlikeness of character is not a duty I must perform in order to find God's acceptance. Instead, it is an experience I long for, to make Him known to others, because He has already accepted and loved me."

Speaking to the eager crowd on the mountain, Jesus had told them that His Father loves His enemies; He seeks to disarm their hostilities, so His enemies will let Him get close enough to heal them with His love (Matt. 5:38-47). Then Jesus concluded, "You are to be like your Father—as perfectly merciful as He is." (Compare Luke 6:36.)

But was He saying, "You had better become just like your Father"? Or was He saying, "You are going to become just like your Father"? Remembering that all God's biddings are enablings, that nothing is to be done at His command that cannot be accomplished in His strength, it really doesn't matter which He meant.

The Goodspeed version expresses Matthew 5:48 in a delightfully ambiguous way. Depending on the emphasis, it can be either command or promise, duty or privilege. Jesus has set before us the most enticing portrait of His Father. Through His words and life, Jesus has shown us One whom we can adore and trust. Then He inspired Paul to promise, "As you behold Him, you will be changed into His very likeness" (see 2 Cor. 3:18).

Can you imagine that? We sin-blunted humans have before us the incredible privilege of becoming like Him. Since He is infinite, this growth-goal is a direction of travel, not a single destination. And we shall travel it together—eternally!

AN ENCOUNTER WITH LOVE

"Then neither do I condemn you," Jesus declared. "Go now and leave your life of sin." John 8:11, N.I.V.

She was humiliated. Dragged into the dusty street to stand in front of a Man she knew to be of utmost quality, she felt frighteningly exposed and defeated. A lifetime of heartache welled up inside her as she realized that she had been deliberately trapped and used by the very men who now spelled out her sin so explicitly. Waiting for the first crushing blows of the stones she knew would end her miserable life, she was startled when the Master stooped down and started to write on the ground with His finger.

We know the story. As the crowd slowly dispersed, one by one, leaving this obviously guilty woman alone with the Man among men, "Jesus straightened up and asked her, 'Woman, where are they? Has no one condemned you?' 'No one, sir,' she said. 'Then neither do I condemn you,' Jesus declared. 'Go now and leave your life of sin' '' (John 8:10, 11, N.I.V.).

Amazing! The guilty not condemned! Why? Before we take up theological jargon and begin to analyze the scripturally legal implications, let us stop and witness a miracle—the miracle of His healing love! Jesus was not one to delve into intricate profundities. His focus was on people. And at that moment His focus was on this poor woman who had been stripped of her self-worth. She needed to experience the genuineness of unconditional love.

She needed to know that no one on earth had the right to condemn her and that no one in heaven wanted to; that God does not use condemnation to force us to contrition, because rejection never heals. She also needed to grasp that acceptance does not condone misbehavior, though it puts an unqualified value on the individual involved. Jesus expressed these two vital realities in His brief discourse with her.

By Jesus' noncondemning posture, He allowed this emotionally scarred individual to regain a measure of dignity. And in His gentle command for her to leave her life of sin He expressed His faith in her capacity to live within the nurturing power of His acceptance of her. Sin—the word used to describe the quality of life lived apart from the reality of God—need never bind her again. She had come face-to-face with God, in the person of His Son, and He had told her plainly how He felt about her!

WHAT WAS WRONG WITH THE FRUIT?

And the Lord God commanded the man, saying, " . . . Of the tree of the knowledge of good and evil you shall not eat, for in the day that you eat of it you shall die." Gen. 2:16, 17, R.S.V.

This verse has suffered terribly at the hands of casual readers through the centuries. To many it seems little more than a Hans Christian Andersen fairy tale, complete with magic apples that cast spells. Only, in this case, an evil serpent peddles the fruit and an angry God casts the spell.

Other popular views end up with perceptions of God that are almost as distasteful. It is commonly held that God simply picked a tree at random in the garden, then told Adam and Eve not to touch it. It was merely a test of their obedience to arbitrary commands. An arbitrary command, since it has no inherent consequences for disobedience, must be upheld by the threatened wrath of the Law-giver. Thus God is one who deals in an arbitrary manner with His intelligent friends, and then threatens to kill them if they don't submit.

Isaiah tells us that Lucifer wanted to make himself like God (Isa. 14: 12-14)—as one who himself could sustain life. How absolutely vital it is that the whole universe be able to know the truth about who the Life-giver really is!

And so God identified two trees to Adam and Eve. To eat from the tree of life expressed their ongoing choice to draw life from the Life-giver. There was no magic in the fruit; God Himself was the source of eternal life. To go to Satan's tree would be a fatal mistake, not because God was angry with them, but because they would have traded the Life-giver for a fraud.

Satan wasn't just offering fruit; he was appealing for a shift of loyalties. He implied that God was not telling them the truth, that God was keeping them in line through false threats. He claimed he could take better care of them than the Father could, by helping them experience immediate growth. "Trust *me* as your life-giver," he said. Sadly, they did. Having broken their relationship with God, they rightfully should have died—and the second death at that!

But God had another plan in mind for upholding reality. On a rugged hill near Jerusalem, Jesus Himself revealed to the universe what happens when people separate from the Life-giver.

WHY DID THEY HIDE?

And they heard the sound of the Lord God walking in the garden in the cool of the day, and the man and his wife hid themselves from the presence of the Lord God among the trees of the garden. Gen. 3:8, R.S.V.

Which of the following statements would you select as more accurate?

  A. "Sinning causes us to fear God and to separate from Him."
  B. "Separation from God *is* the sin, and it is sometimes caused by needless fear of Him."

The question is far from religious nit-picking, for our basic understandings of God, sin, and salvation come into focus here. But sometimes the issues get so muddled up that, like the chicken and the egg, it's hard to find out which one came first—fear or separation. One of the most useful examples of the fear-and-separation cycle can be found in what happened in the Garden of Eden, for Adam and Eve knew neither one in their original condition.

Our first parents knew only the joy of uncluttered union with their heavenly Parent, until the day when Satan persuaded them to accept his interpretation of God's character and intentions toward them. They changed their mind about God and ceased to trust Him. Shifting their loyalties to the snake, they accepted his promise of life support and care. And that, in the clearest sense, was their sin.

Adam and Eve had turned their backs on God. Spiritually and mentally they were separated from Him. Believing as they did what Satan had told them about God, they suspected that God would be angry with them for their separation from Him, for the enemy had suggested that God is a tyrant against those who disobey Him.

So when God came walking in the garden in the cool of the day, they did what seemed to be the appropriate thing: they hid in the bushes. They followed the impulses of fear, forgetting not only God's ability to find them even in the bushes but—worse yet—forgetting that God was searching for His friends, not hunting for His enemies.

When God found them, His response to them was so eagerly redemptive as to settle for all time that we need not fear Him. For their nakedness He brought costly clothing. For their fearful apprehension He brought the promise that Another would bear the tragic consequences of their disobedience. For their confusion He brought the healing instruction of hard labor. Now, is that a God to be feared?

WHAT IS THE BLESSED HOPE?

"Awaiting our blessed hope, the appearing of the glory of our great God and Saviour Jesus Christ . . ." Titus 2:13, R.S.V.

"Maranatha! Come, Lord Jesus!" We sing it, we pray it, we anxiously await it. It is the "blessed hope" of the Christian. But what is the greatest thing about the second coming of Christ? Our deliverance from this sin-filled world? Our reunion with loved ones laid to rest? Our new immortality?

Stop a moment and reflect: "Why do I want Jesus to return?" Don't try to think of "correct answers"—be honest with yourself. And remember, no answer is a bad answer. God understands the deeper reasons why we think the way we do. Take a piece of paper and make two columns. On one side, list why you want Jesus to come soon. On the other side, list why you wish He'd take His time.

After having done this exercise, stop again and reflect: "What do I love the most about God? What about Him makes me feel the most uncomfortable?" Write these things down, too. And as you examine the two lists, you very likely will discover a definite correlation between them. Let me explain.

If one of the things about God that makes you feel uneasy is His role as judge, very probably one of the reasons you wish Jesus would not come very soon is that you do not feel ready. Or perhaps you listed something about wanting to have a chance to get married, or finish your education, or have the opportunity to enjoy the fruit of your labor. Possibly, if you were candid enough, you might have written that you felt put off by God's attitude toward material things.

Have you ever considered that God uses His judgeship to ward off the accusations of the devil? And that His desire that we not become attached to the things of this world is because He does not want us to be distracted from becoming friends with Him?

May I suggest that once our view of God is such that we downright relish everything we know about Him, our double-columned page will quickly merge into one under the joyous theme: "Maranatha! Come, Lord Jesus!" You see, the very best thing about the second coming of Christ is not the "when" or "what will happen" when He does. It is *who He is! He* is our blessed hope!

August 6

GOD WRITES THE LAST CHAPTER

We know that in all things God works for good with those who love him, those whom he has called according to his purpose. Rom. 8:28, T.E.V.

We Christians ought to join together and file a formal complaint against the insurance companies of the land. When we read their policy papers and find out that tragedies listed under ''acts of God'' include trees falling on cars, tornadoes tearing apart homes, and hailstorms ruining crops, we ought to protest. Who says that our God is to blame for these destructive mishaps!

To be quite honest, we Christians have been saying it. In our endeavors to portray God as sovereign and all-powerful, we have often put the blame at God's doorway for everything that happens on this earth. The medieval Christians took the position that God actively caused most tragedies as a form of punishment upon those who had earned His disfavor. Others have suggested that since God has the power to prevent catastrophes, if He does not do so it is the same as His causing it.

Still another noted Christian speaker advocates that if I am born with a deformed arm I should accept that God has ordained it that way and therefore rejoice. But regardless of which of these interpretations one may accept, they all have this in common: God gets the bad reputation, and Satan gets off free.

The Bible sets it before us in quite another light. Satan is the one who causes unending heartache and trauma in this world; but our God is so creative, so clever and resourceful, that—with our cooperation—He can turn any tragedy into a triumph.

One of my favorite descriptions of God is that He is The Great Recoverer. It is not His desire that I should be born with a deformed arm. But should I suffer such a mishap, He is marvelously able to turn it into an occasion for growth: for deeper dependence upon Him and clearer settling of true values. It was not God's hand that broke Joni Eareckson's neck, but it was surely His hand that guided her spirit into praise and ministry for others.

As the story of my life unfolds, with so many of its key passages having been authored independently, I rejoice in knowing that our God is always able to write the last chapter. Though I cannot rewrite past history, I can turn the future into the hands of a better Author.

MARRED IN HIS HANDS

But the pot he was shaping from the clay was marred in his hands; so the potter formed it into another pot, shaping it as seemed best to him. Jer. 18:4, N.I.V.

The classroom was filled with active minds and restless feet. The teacher seemed unconcerned about making his lesson interesting to his young students. He simply droned on and on from the textbook, entirely unaware that he had lost not only their attention but their respect for him as well. He was doing his job, he thought, in making the required information available to them. What they did with it was their problem.

In the same building, another teacher sat on the front of his desk, in active conversation with a dozen or so of his students while the rest of the class listened. Informal in his approach, he met question after question with answers that were geared to allow young minds to wrap around them, exploring and testing their content. It was exciting and rewarding for everyone, including the teacher.

In order for the second teacher to provide this vital learning opportunity for his class, he knew he had to create an atmosphere of trust and acceptance. The students lost their inhibitions when they saw that he was willing to adapt the lesson material to their ability to understand. They felt good about what was happening and consequently learned quickly. By the end of the year, not only had most of the students mastered the subject, but many felt that they had gained a lasting friend in their teacher.

Our God is like the second teacher. In a metaphor to ancient Israel, He portrayed Himself as a potter shaping clay at a wheel. When the pot he was making was marred, he did not cast it aside but simply modified his plans and continued working with it. Unlike an impersonal machine, the potter is attuned to the condition of the clay he is molding. In the same way, God is aware of what is happening in our lives, and He adjusts His dealings with us accordingly. Even if He has to adjust His approach to us, we may rest assured that we are still *in His hands* and that He will continue to work with us.

Of this we can be sure: because of the wonderful ability of the great Craftsman, the clay He is molding will turn out wonderfully! And in these ''earthen vessels'' He places the treasure of the knowledge of who He is.

WHEN I NEED HIM MOST!

If I had cherished evil thoughts, the Lord would not have heard me. Ps. 66:18, N.E.B.

Though he was making a statement, I could tell he was asking a question. And the earnest frustration on his face let me know that the young man was asking no idle question. "I don't like the idea," he said, "that God won't hear me as long as I cherish any evil thoughts. It seems to me that the only possible way I could ever overcome my evil thoughts, especially the ones I cherish, would be if I ask God for help, and He hears me! What hope is there for any of us if the Lord hears us only after we have stopped thinking all evil thoughts?"

It was one of those vital moments when one's faith is either nurtured or oppressed by one's understanding of how God deals with us sinners. And it is not an uncommon perception that we must do a whole lot of internal housekeeping before God will condescend to stoop through our shabby doorways. But is this what David had in mind when he penned today's verse?

Or is David challenging those of us who would be inclined merely to "use" prayer? Or, more accurately, to "use" God through prayer? You know, like the person who smokes several packs a day, then prays for good health. Or the one who spends three hours in front of the television tube for every ten minutes he spends with the Word, then prays with deep fervency for rich spiritual blessings. If God were to step outside the boundaries of reality and grant those requests, arbitrarily "dishing out" bountiful blessings to people who are walking outside the path of blessing, He would utterly confuse people about that very path.

We have to admit one thing about our God: He is totally committed to reality. As much as He wants us to enter into prayer with Him, He is too wise to let us come with our "want list" on our lips but with our "self-destruct" list warmly embedded in our hearts. He is not (as some people would appear to think) a softhearted Santa Claus who is easily hoodwinked into thinking that we're not naughty, but rather quite nice.

Far more important than the gifts we wish He would give us is the wisdom He wishes to give to us. More than merely being blessed, He wants us to be taught the ways of righteousness—which really is the best blessing. And all who long to be taught by Him have His ear!

"PRAYING IN THE SPIRIT"

He who searches our hearts knows the mind of the Spirit, because the Spirit intercedes for the saints in accordance with God's will. Rom. 8:27, N.I.V.

Have you ever felt something that you just couldn't put into words? Then someone came along and verbalized your sentiments exactly. It was exciting and somehow comforting. Exciting because it gave your experience tangibility, comforting because you were no longer "alone" in it.

How many times we come to God in prayer and cannot find the words to encompass our yearnings and fears! Perhaps we desperately need to make ourselves understood but aren't even sure *we* totally understand. And so we struggle in prayer, hungry for the assurance not only that God is hearing us, but that His heart and ours are vibrating in unison.

God's great heart *is* vibrating in unison with ours! He picks up our sentences and finishes them. He gives our inner groanings a vehicle of expression that is unmatched in its comprehensiveness. In every way possible He echoes our own thoughts and feelings, affirming our tentative faith in His total commitment to our personhood. He does this for us in the person of His Spirit.

In our text today we read that "the Spirit intercedes for the saints in accordance with God's will." If we see God as so totally exalted above us that He requires a go-between in order to make our prayers fit for His ears, we cannot readily enter into the bonding experience afforded to us through communion with Him. It cannot help underscoring our feelings of inadequacy if we think that our prayers have to be "laundered" or restated by the Holy Spirit before they become viable.

However, when we understand that it is God's posture to "lean forward" as it were, to catch every nuance of meaning as we talk to Him, we realize that the provision of the Spirit is for *our* sakes, not His. It is His way of helping "us in our present limitations" (Rom. 8:26, Phillips) to know that He knows what we are trying to say—because He can even provide the words! We may know that "He who searches our hearts" does so not to find fault in us but to assure us of the intensity of His desire to enter into total union with us.

"What, then, shall we say in response to this? If God is for us, who can be against us?" (verse 31, N.I.V.).

WHAT MAKES PEOPLE ACT THAT WAY?

When he came in sight of the city, he wept over it. Luke 19:41, N.E.B.

I was single-mindedly boring down the freeway, intent only on the destination I had in mind. Suddenly another driver swerved into my lane, in the very spot that I felt should have been occupied by my front fender. I was more than irate; I was fuming. By my feelings, I must have assumed he was meanly glancing into his rearview mirror, with a fiendish glint in his eyes, thinking, "I'll wait till he gets right next to me; then I'll cut suddenly into his way." Calculating. Perverse. Deliberately sinful.

It was only the next day, on the same stretch of freeway, that I failed to see a car in the blind spot between my mirrors, and I ducked suddenly into his path. His screeching tires and the lengthy blast of his horn told me exactly what he was thinking of me. But I was innocent! Careless, perhaps. But not at all the mean, deliberately perverse road animal his shaking fist and blaring horn were accusing me of being. I wanted to defend myself. To explain to him. But he had barreled on by, probably mumbling something about getting out of the range of such dangerous people.

Does it matter how we view our fellow-strugglers on this sin-blasted planet? I see a supermarket cashier being sharp with a customer. Do I assume that she got up that morning, looked herself in the mirror, and deliberately said, "I'm going to give everyone fits today"? Or do I assume that she is under extreme pressures that I know nothing about and is coping the best she can with a hard and thankless task?

Speaking of the vast majority of sinners, the garden-variety humans all around us: Are they perverse, deliberately evil people who set out every morning with the sole intent of being crassly selfish? Or are they stumbling, confused, wounded people who would like to defend their actions . . . or at least apologize for them? Our answer will determine whether we will view them with disgust or with compassion. It will dictate whether we will wish to harangue them or to educate and heal them.

How do you think Jesus viewed all those sinners in Jerusalem when, just hours before they turned against Him, He sat on a hill overlooking their city, weeping until His body swayed like a tree in a high wind?

THE PRIVILEGE OF SUFFERING

**For you have been granted the privilege not only of believing in
Christ but also of suffering for him. Phil. 1:29, N.E.B.**

Though she had the money to purchase good-quality clothes, she
wore tattered, thrift shop garments. Her house was sparsely furnished and
her table set with only the plainest of provisions, all unseasoned and
meager. She smiled only faintly and spoke in the hushed tones of
someone in the terminal ward of a hospital. More often than not, when
you called on her, you would find her seated at her table reading her
Bible.

Most of us are a little taken aback by people who impose suffering
upon themselves as a means of attaining piety. We are repelled at the
thought that that's what it takes to be "godly." About the only thing
that's worse is to believe that God Himself sometimes imposes this kind
of suffering upon people in order to "build their characters."

What was Paul talking about in today's scripture when he said that it is
our privilege to suffer for Christ? Is he talking about just bodily distress?
In his Second Letter to the Corinthians he states, "Indeed, experience
shows that the more we share in Christ's immeasurable suffering the more
we are able to give of his encouragement" (chap. 1:5, Phillips). Perhaps
the answer can be known only if we stop to consider what made Christ
suffer. We most naturally think of Calvary as the place of His agony, but
does His physical ordeal at Golgotha really epitomize the suffering He
endured as the "Man of sorrows"?

See His tears at the tomb of Lazarus as Martha expresses her sorrow
that He *could have* saved her brother from death. Hear the pain in His
voice as He addresses Peter, dripping wet from being pulled from the sea
upon which he had just walked: "Why did you doubt [Me]?"
(Matt.14:31, N.I.V.). Be shocked at the intensity of His grief as He
weeps over Jerusalem, where His rejection as the Son of God will be fully
revealed. And remember: in each of these incidents, He sorrowed not for
Himself, but for His earthly children who sustained needless woe because
they did not understand who He was, or the Father who sent Him.

It is our privilege not only to believe in Christ, but to be so healed by
our friendship with Him that we share the great passion of His heart: to
reveal the Father to hurting mankind.

DIVINE SURGERY

For the word of God is alive and active. It cuts more keenly than any two-edged sword, piercing as far as the place where life and spirit, joints and marrow, divide. It sifts the purposes and thoughts of the heart. Heb. 4:12, N.E.B.

I forgot all about the sandwich I had been eating as I listened with increasing interest to my friend's description of the surgery he had been performing. Working in the area of his specialty, he had operated on a man with a cancerous growth in his face. For hours, working through a microscope, he endeavored to remove every cancerous cell, yet not damage the nerves that control the man's eyes, mouth, and ears. I nearly shared his own relief when he told me that the procedure had been successful.

What admiration I have for the skill of a master surgeon! I admire his courage to move so close to the very springs of life to search out and remove that which would destroy life. And while no patient ever relishes that kind of surgery, he must admit that it is, after all, better than the alternative. Often the surgeon must persuade the patient to submit to this life-rescuing procedure.

Our God brings to us the skill, the courage, and the compassion of a master surgeon. He uses a scalpel that is sharp enough to divide that most intricately interwoven part of us: our motives. With selfishness intermeshed with the motives of love, and protected with layers of defensiveness, denial, and self-deception, it demands the skills of the best Surgeon to unravel.

As we expose ourselves to the penetrating, searching mind of God as revealed in His Word, the surgery begins. The stern rebuke, the harsh rejoinder we just unleashed on the children in the name of "firm discipline," becomes exposed as merely defense of parental prestige. The questionable television program viewed because "I need to relax" surfaces as thinly veiled voyeurism. The dust on the Bible's cover, gathering because "I am just so busy," is gently exposed as evidence of spiritual laziness.

How good it is to know that our Father is not standing over us at these sensitive, embarrassing moments of self-discovery, gleefully saying, "I caught you in another one!" He who instructed Paul to tell us not to keep score of wrongs (1 Cor. 13:6) is quick to set the past behind and to walk with us into the light of greater honesty, stronger wholeness, and finer unity with His wise will.

GOD'S UNSPEAKABLE JOY

To him who is able to keep you from falling and to present you before his glorious presence without fault and with great joy ... Jude 24, N.I.V.

If you want to divide a group of believers, just ask the question "Can you stop sinning?" Even the Yeses and the Nos will be divided because of all the various ideas at large on the subject. To some it depends upon whether you are talking about "known sins." To others the issue is the forensic quality of justification by faith. To those who struggle daily against inward and outward evil, the question seems laced with awful hopelessness. To Paul, it was a matter for rejoicing.

What does it mean to stop sinning? If our focus is upon behavior, we might argue endlessly. If our emphasis is upon legal metaphor, we can sterilize the framework of vital spirituality until it is inoperative. However, if we are looking at our relationship with God, Paul's attitude is most encouraging.

Since *sin* is the word used to describe the broken relationship between God and humanity, then let us rephrase the question accordingly: "Can your broken relationship with God be totally healed?" The answer is thrilling—"Absolutely!" And in case there is any doubt as to how this is to be accomplished, today's text declares that *God* is "able to keep you from falling and to present you before his glorious presence without fault and with great joy." God is able to heal our broken relationship—and keep it healed! Our friendship with Him puts us "above reproach" (N.E.B.) in His own eyes and in the eyes of the whole universe. And all of this brings Him "unspeakable joy" (Phillips)!

Does this bring tangible results to our lives this side of the kingdom? "Love is made complete among us so that we will have confidence on the day of judgment, because in this world we are like him" (1 John 4:17, N.I.V.). To know Him is to love Him, and to love Him is to be made like Him. As our confidence grows in who He is, and that He has called us His friends, we are progressively set free from self-seeking, that quality displayed in insecure and unloved individuals.

Friends, let us leave the past behind and "with hands outstretched to whatever lies ahead . . . go straight for the goal—my reward the honour of my high calling by God in Christ Jesus" (Phil. 3:14, Phillips).

HIS FINAL WORD

God, who gave to our forefathers many different glimpses of the truth in the words of the prophets, has now, at the end of the present age, given us the truth in the Son. Heb. 1:1, Phillips.

What do you do when you read a text like this one: "But Moses said, 'O Lord, please send someone else to do it.' Then the Lord's anger burned against Moses" (Ex. 4:13, 14, N.I.V.). Then turning to Matthew 5:22, you read, "But I tell you that anyone who is angry with his brother will be subject to judgment" (N.I.V.).

A candid person will have to admit that it raises several questions. Why did God have to get burning angry against Moses when all he did was plead his feelings of inadequacy? Why does Jesus later warn us against becoming angry with other people? Are Jesus and God working from a different set of rules? Does God "get by" with certain behaviors that are against the rules for us, but allowed for Him since He is in charge? And since anger is so unproductive of good anyway, why does God have to express it against His friend Moses, especially when He has already sent Aaron along to speak in his place? There must be a better solution than to see a gentle Jesus in the New Testament and a short-tempered despot in the Old.

It is a mark in God's favor that He always speaks to His people in words and through meanings and experiences that make sense to them. You couldn't call it "communication" if He didn't. Certain idioms of thought and of interpretation make good sense to one culture but seem strange and puzzling to another. Each segment of the Bible was written in the context of a people and their familiar expressions.

Moses sensed that his courage was not yet up to doing all that God was eager for him to do. He felt the chagrin of knowing that because of his weakness God had had to resort to a backup plan to get the message to Pharaoh. It was not uncommon for the Hebrew mind to speak of God's feelings in very intense terms, thus speaking of His disappointment as burning anger. But we look in vain for any evidence of angry feelings or action in the paragraphs that follow.

God spoke His final word about Himself, however, when He sent His Son to be the "flawless expression of the nature of God" (Heb. 1:3, Phillips).

THE INSUFFICIENCY OF GOOD BEHAVIOR

And Jesus looking upon him loved him, and said to him, "You lack one thing; go, sell what you have, and give to the poor, and you will have treasure in heaven; and come, follow me" (Mark 10:21, R.S.V.).

He'd been raised in the church. Before he scarcely knew how to talk, he'd been taught memory verses from the Bible. Eager to please, he was always a model student. After college he entered the business world, and because of his strict sense of honesty and good dealing, he soon accumulated wealth. He served on the church board and, on occasion, led out at the Wednesday night prayer meeting. In short, he had everything: wealth, a good reputation, and religion.

One day he saw Jesus of Nazareth with some children. He was impressed by the way He handled them, how tenderly He received them. A tremendous desire was awakened in his heart to become His disciple. As Jesus started to leave, he ran after Him and fell at His feet. "Good Teacher," he implored, "what must I do to inherit eternal life?" Jesus answered him, "Why do you call me good? No one is good but God alone" (Mark 10:17, 18, R.S.V.).

Jesus' reply was not meant to put off this young seeker. From the next few words of exchange, we may understand that Jesus was working to redefine the man's internal values. "Good" had always been associated with behavior; Jesus obviously had good behavior! So had the young man; yet he felt he was missing something. By singling out God only as "good," Jesus sought to differentiate between behavioral religion and an awakened understanding of God. To follow Christ means more than the performance of good behavior; it is friendship of the highest quality.

What was Jesus' intent in telling the young man to sell all that he had and give to the poor? Would not this encourage him to "do" even more, a religion by works? May I suggest that, quite to the contrary, getting rid of his riches would severely restrict his present ability to perform. Evidently his status as a wealthy and respected man in the community afforded him endless opportunities to practice his religion of goodness. It simply was too easy for him to "give" good behavior rather than to give of himself. Consequently, his focus was on the gift of eternal life rather than on the Giver.

Fellowship with Christ would have refocused his life. Let's let it refocus ours!

PRESCRIPTIVE OR DESCRIPTIVE

If you love me, you will keep my commandments. John 14:15, R.S.V.

Try to remember what it was like when, as a child, your parents asked you to do something you really didn't want to do. They tried to find various ways to persuade you to do it, from promising a reward to gently threatening that there might be a "laying on of hands" if you didn't comply! Perhaps they even used the familiar approach of reminding you of all the good things they had done for you, from the gifts at Christmas to the warm bed and plenty of food. Then they would ask, "Do you love us?" In a tiny, cautious voice you would answer, "Yes." Then you would hear the logical trap spring shut with a note of triumph: "If you love us, you will do what we say."

It's called being manipulated by love, and it doesn't feel very good. But what can you say without sounding like an ungrateful cad? Many Christians read John 14:15 through those same eyes. They see God as parading in front of us the infinite evidences of His generous love—life, health, salvation in Jesus Christ, and all the gifts and blessings of His kingdom. Then as we look in slack-jawed amazement at the immensity of it all, He has us right where He wants us and He tightens the noose. "For all of this," He asks, "do you love Me?" We nod dutifully. "If you love me," He concludes, "keep my commandments."

There isn't a shadow of doubt: God really *does* love us. But His love is intended to heal us, not to manipulate us. His great caring for us is intended to make us inwardly adequate, not to make us feel trapped. It enhances us; it does not obligate us. When Jesus said, "If you love me, you will keep my commandments," He was *describing* what we *will* do, rather than *prescribing* what we *must* do. It was a statement of fact: This is what people *do* when they love their Saviour.

So highly does our Father prize our freedom of choice that He does not use even His great love for us to "twist our arms" into obedience. Though we quickly see that He does not use physical force to cause us to obey, it is vital to notice that He also avoids using emotional force. For only the love-healed heart truly can obey!

THE GREAT AMONG US

Whoever wants to become great among you must be your servant. Matt. 20:26, N.I.V.

The missionaries traveled deep into the desert wasteland, encountering many interesting tribesmen. Though uncivilized, these natives had a culture that was rich with elaborate ritual and dress. Claws, feathers, and the teeth of wild animals adorned their bodies as they danced to the beat of hollowed-out log drums. As the missionaries moved closer to areas settled by white Europeans, they noticed the subtle intrusion of modern paraphernalia into tribal attire. Cast-off tin lids and other odd items were included in the decorations worn by the dancers.

We smile at the innocent ignorance of such heathen peoples. Not knowing what to do with the items they discovered while foraging near civilized communities, they simple wore them. I wonder if we as Christians sometimes haven't done similarly as we "discover" the teachings of the Master. Take, for example, His statement about greatness: "Whoever wants to become great among you must be your servant."

Some get the idea that the lowliest station in life is to be worn as a sort of badge of humility—that any kind of personal achievement is to be shunned because self-depreciation equals piety. Such ideas are gathered up and uselessly hung upon the life of the Christian. The sad part is that no good is brought to the wearer, and others are misled as well.

In the first place, humility is a quality of spirit, not an outward adornment. Someone who has a heart to serve will do so in any capacity. If the need arises for great achievement in a given field in order to accomplish the highest service, the Christian who has the spirit of humility will not defer because of some compulsion to announce inner piety.

In God's eyes, true servanthood makes for greatness, whether an individual is in a prestigious position or a lowly one—which tells us something about our "great God!" In the passage in which today's scripture is found, Jesus touched the nerve of the Israelite nation by alluding to Roman rulership. He said, "You know that the rulers of the Gentiles lord it over them [and you], and their high officials exercise authority over them. Not so with you" (verses 25, 26, N.I.V.). "Don't lead as they do!" was what He was saying, not "Don't seek to be leaders."

Rather than seeking to avoid achievement, let us seek to utilize all our abilities to attain excellence in service.

A FRUITLESS SEARCH

When that day comes, you will make your requests to him in my name, for I need make no promise to plead to the Father for you, for the Father himself loves you. John 16:26, Phillips.

I had heard it so often that I finally decided I would find its biblical basis. I had been hearing that Christ's righteousness is something like a robe that He puts over us to make us acceptable to the Father. I had heard that Jesus presents the merit of His own perfect life to the Father, and that the Father then agrees to view the sinner differently because of the substitutionary merit of the Son. In brief, I heard that Jesus changes the Father's mind and heart toward us, which is necessary in order for us to be saved.

Assuming that no biblical personality knew more about the plan of salvation than Jesus did, I decided to go to the Gospels, particularly the spoken words of Jesus, to find evidence for such a view. I searched for any place where Jesus expressed or implied that His Father's attitude toward us was changed or modified by the Son's appeal, merit, substitutionary life, or legal covering. I found none. I would encourage you to check for yourself; it just isn't there.

Instead, I filled a half dozen notebook pages full of verses in which Jesus is telling us how much the Father already loves us and pleading with *us* to change *our* opinion of the Father! And in the context of this particular quest, how grateful I was to come across the familiar text quoted above. What could be more explicit? Jesus is promising *not* to plead with the Father to change in any way toward us! The Father, He assures us, is already steadfastly loving toward us.

What is more, Jesus has just finished saying ''the time is coming to give up parables and tell you plainly about the Father'' (John 16:25, Phillips). With only hours left with His earthly friends, Jesus needed to move beyond limited insights, trimmed down to accommodate the dull understandings of the masses. He wanted to speak the most accurate, complete, and vital truths about His Father that their growing minds could grasp. He wanted them no longer to cower in fear before God, rendering the trembling obedience of a whipped slave. Rather, He wanted them to be made whole by His Father's loving acceptance.

My search, then, was far from fruitless!

YOU DO KNOW HIM!

If you really knew me, you would know my Father as well. From now on, you do know him and have seen him. John 14:7, N.I.V.

Jesus was going away. The eleven remaining disciples at the Last Supper wanted to go with Him. Their anxious questions caused the Master to utter some of the most explicit language ever recorded in Scripture concerning the Father. He was not going to another village; He was going to His Father in heaven.

The disciples simply could not grasp what He was telling them, even as He told them more about where He was going—how much room there was in His Father's house. "I will come back and take you to be with me," He told them reassuringly. "You know the way to the place where I am going" (John 14:3, 4, N.I.V.).

Their response was amazing. "Lord, we don't know where you are going, so how can we know the way?" (verse 5, N.I.V.). To say that they did not know where He was going said, in essence, that they did not know the Father. "Jesus answered, 'I am the way and the truth and the life. No one comes to the Father except through me.' " Then He told them plainly, "If you really knew me, you would know my Father as well. From now on, you do know him and have seen him" (verses 6, 7, N.I.V.). "To know Me *is* to know the Father!"

Dear reader, has your heart ever cried out to really know God, yet He seemed very remote, quite far away? Focus in upon His Son, the "express image" of the Father (Heb. 1:3), and be assured that in knowing Him you *do* know God! You need not allow your feelings of estrangement from Him to persist as did the disciples. You may trust the Saviour's pronouncement.

Read the rest of John 14; go on to chapters 15 and 16 until Jesus sighs with loving relief, "You believe at last!" (chap. 16:31, N.I.V.). "You believe that My Father has shown Himself to you in Me! You know that the Father Himself loves you! You understand that His eagerness to have you with Him is no less than Mine."

Let our hearts be comforted, which was Jesus' desire. Let us know that the Father's heart yearns for us. So much so that He sent Jesus to give us that very message. And let this knowledge set you free to engage actively in friendship with Him.

THE MORE EXCELLENT WAY

If I . . . understand all mysteries and all knowledge . . . but have not love, I am nothing. 1 Cor. 13:2, R.S.V.

I am almost embarrassed to admit it, but when I would see him coming toward me from across the campus I would quickly find a pressing appointment that would justifiably steer me in another direction. It's not that I was afraid of him; he was really quite harmless. He was simply an obnoxious know-it-all. With a keen mind, a photographic memory, and a voracious appetite for books and technical magazines, he seemed to know at least something about almost everything. And every encounter gave him an opportunity to tell you more than you really cared to know about whatever was on his mind.

For most of us common mortals, who still puzzle over the instructions for our new pocket calculator, know-it-alls are often quite intimidating. And if we feel this way about people with vast information about historical or technical matters, we are even more put off by people with all the religious answers. Perhaps this is because it exposes our own confusions in this vital area that is so close to home—which should serve as a caution to all Christians bound to share their faith (their vast knowledge of truth) to any listener.

How easy it is to feel that people who "have all knowledge" have accumulated it more that they might impress others than that they might help others. Hurting people need more to be loved than to be overwhelmed. More than having their ignorance exposed, they need their tender self-esteem sheltered by sensitive, caring arms.

Paul understood how easy it is, even for Christians, to become caught up in the self-congratulations of the knowledge they have gained—even though it is true knowledge. He cautioned Christians not to become known in the world as a group of pious know-it-alls, because Christians are going forth to reveal One who *really does* know it all! Bruised sinners, who could be so easily crushed by the Omniscient One, need first to be assured that He is loving.

James assures us that people can come to the One who really does know it all and ask Him for whatever insights they need without His "making them feel guilty" (James 1:5, Phillips). His first commitment to His people is to calm their fears, for only then can He teach them. That certainly is the more excellent way.

TRUTH OR CONSEQUENCES

The wrath of God is being revealed from heaven against all the godlessness and wickedness of men who suppress the truth by their wickedness. Rom. 1:18, N.I.V.

For a long time preachers have been "calling down" the wrath of God against sinners. The message is plain: "If you don't shape up, God is going to get you. And good!" Though they never really say it quite this way, they might as well: "Love God—or else!"

What an incentive to love! But love never happens when demanded "at gun point," as it were. And even if He puts the gun away, as long as you know He's wearing it in His holster and that it's loaded and ready to shoot, it's difficult to warm to His overtures.

What about God's wrath, anyway? It's about time we take a good look at it and see it for what it is. Will what we discover fit into our growing understanding of who God is? Or will we have to live with our old ideas of God's wrath, like it or not? After all, He *is* God! And the Bible does use words such as "wrath" and "anger" when describing the punishment of the wicked.

The clearest explanation of the wrath of God is found in chapters 1 and 2 of Romans. In our text for today we read, "The wrath of God is being revealed from heaven against all the godlessness and wickedness of men who suppress the truth by their wickedness." The first indication of what this wrath is referring to is found in verse 24: "Therefore God gave them over in the sinful desires of their hearts" (N.I.V.). Verse 26 echoes this thought, and verse 27 becomes explicit: "Men . . . received in themselves the due penalty for their perversion" (N.I.V.).

It is evident that God's wrath is His posture of allowing the consequences of sinful acts and behavior to fall upon man. In Eden He set in motion the plan of salvation whereby we have been spared, to a great degree, the effects of separation from Him. Were we to experience the actual results of this separation, we would not live to learn the awful truth of it. However, in order for us to experience reality, He allows us to encounter, even now, a measure of the consequences.

Romans 2:5-8 describes the final results of our choices. Those who have sought the Life-giver shall live. Those who have rejected Him have rejected life.

EARTHY RELIGION

If anyone gives so much as a cup of cold water to one of these little ones, because he is a disciple of mine, I tell you this: that man will assuredly not go unrewarded. Matt. 10:42, N.E.B.

Many of this world's religions divide all of life into two categories: the sacred and the secular, the religious and the common. Religious experience includes never letting the two get mixed up. Things religious have their own vocabulary, their own frame of reference.

But Christianity does not follow this pattern. There is not a sacred part of life versus a secular part of life. There are not two distinct ways of speaking and thinking, because for the Christian all of life is sacred. His relationship with Christ flavors every dimension of living, even the most mundane.

I have known more than one perplexed Christian who has wished for a deeper involvement with the things of God. These devout people have longed for greater preoccupation with spiritual themes, for more absorbing interest in heaven and the world to come. Some of them seem to have missed Jesus' surprising revelation that one's readiness for the coming kingdom is measured by some very earthy actions. In today's verse we hear Jesus describing discipleship in terms of one's readiness to give a cup of cold water to a young child.

Sometimes it is easier to think in religious terms when one is in church or enjoying a group Bible study. It is easier to affirm one's interest in heaven when other heaven-bound pilgrims are nearby to say "Amen!" We can quickly recognize certain behaviors as correctly religious—such as giving offerings to the church, singing certain songs, and attending religious meetings.

But Jesus (who urged us to be salt in the earth, not in the church) keeps challenging us to ignore that artificial line between church-life and the life of the world around us. One who has the mind of Christ—the Christ who lets His rain fall on the just and the unjust—is going to give a cup of cold water to a child because that's the kind of person he is. He is not going to do it because he can report it during the missionary emphasis period in church or because the child is a member of his church. It will be the free-flowing expression of his very character, and that's why it can be such a reliable measure of his readiness for the kingdom.

CONFIDENCE IN THE MASTER
OF THE PLAN

But he knows the way that I take; when he has tried me, I shall come forth as gold. Job 23:10, R.S.V.

Everything possible had happened to Job. He'd lost his herds, his servants, his sons, and his health. His wife did not understand him; his best friends suspected him of some secret misbehavior. Still his trust in God remained unshakable. "Though he slay me, yet will I hope in him" (Job 13:15, N.I.V.).

Though we tend to admire Job for his courage and fortitude, it was not his own inner strength that got him through his troubles. It was his understanding of and relationship with God that sustained him. In the first ten verses of chapter 23 we are given an insight into the kind of relationship that existed between God and His friend Job.

Job begins by acknowledging that he feels as though God has laid a heavy hand on him. But he does not allow those feelings to overwhelm him or to make him doubt God's purposes. And, far from making him seek distance from God, he wishes that he could be in His very presence! "I would state my case before him and set out my arguments in full; then I should learn what answer he would give and find out what he had to say. Would he exert his great power to browbeat me? No; God himself would never bring a charge against me" (verses 4-6, N.E.B.).

Job knew that God had a "master plan" for his life. And though at the moment he was completely confused as to what was happening in his life, he had confidence in the Master of the plan! He knew God to be open and fair. He also knew that it was not like God to use His power to manipulate people, that God was reasonable (verse 7). Even through his struggle against his feelings of separation from God, he never considered that God was distancing Himself from him because of some wrong he might have committed. "He knows the way that I take [He is intimately involved in what is happening to me]; and when he has tried me, I shall come forth as gold" (verse 10, R.S.V.).

In the end, after Job was restored, God told Job's three friends, "You have not spoken of me what is right, as my servant Job has" (chap. 42:7, R.S.V.). God knew He could trust Job because they were friends.

JESUS CHERISHES CHILDREN

Never despise one of these little ones; I tell you, they have their guardian angels in heaven, who look continually on the face of my heavenly Father. Matt. 18:10, N.E.B.

Imagine that a local business executive and his wife are coming to your home for dinner. They ring the doorbell and, without looking up from the stove, you shout, "Wipe your feet as you enter; I don't want any mud on my carpet. And shut the door! You weren't born in a barn, you know." Later, as they eat around the table, you snarl at them, "Chew with your mouth closed. And remember, if you don't eat all your vegetables, you don't get any dessert."

The scenario is ridiculous, at first glance, because we sense that it simply wouldn't be appropriate to treat a dignified adult in that manner. But an equally heavy wave of embarrassment should hit us that we find it so easy to speak to our children in this way. Sensing that it is wrong to hurt the feelings of adults by speaking in belittling ways, we wonder why we so readily try to control our children's behavior through this kind of despising harangue.

Children apparently suffered these kinds of indignities in the time of Christ also. Even Jesus' disciples had carelessly picked up the habit of treating children as half way between humans and animals. They were convinced that children were not worthy of the Master's attention and that they were doing Him a favor by keeping these not-yet-persons on the outer fringes of Jesus' admirers.

But Jesus knew what was happening in those young minds—that they were forming their most fundamental pictures of themselves. He wanted to protect that precious self-image within them, knowing that they would need it throughout their lives.

Yet there was another vital concern in Jesus' mind. He knew that in those tender years the children were building their basic understanding of their heavenly Father—an understanding that would be written deep in their minds and not easily changed by later verbal instructions. Children form their understanding of God far more through the relationships they experience with their parents than through the concepts spoken to them by those parents.

If parents despise or belittle the children, especially when in the process of disciplining, those children will grow up believing that God treats them in the same way. Who would love and trust such a God!

HAVING HIS NAME ON OUR FOREHEADS

**They shall see his face, and his name shall be on their foreheads.
Rev. 22:4, R.S.V.**

The hope of the Christian is the second coming of Christ. It will be a time of rejoicing, for all the sorrows of this life will come to an end. We will never again be sick, or die, or be separated from our loved ones. We won't get weary, or confused, or have our houses repossessed. And our souls will no longer be in jeopardy—that is, we won't have to worry anymore about whether or not we will be saved.

Friends, if we think the matter of being saved is risky business, we have a problem that the Second Coming is not going to solve. If, in our thinking, being sin-free is in the same category as being sick-free and mortgage-free, our understanding of the sin problem needs updating. Being sin-free is not ensured by the fact that there is nothing around left to tempt us; it is the condition of the heart that no longer retains any doubts as to God's character.

Our text today describes the redeemed: "They shall see his face, and his name shall be on their foreheads." What does "his name shall be on their foreheads" mean? May I suggest that God shall be the center of our thoughts? And this begins now, this side of the kingdom. Our focus will shift from thoughts of "getting saved" to God Himself. And since God *is* life, we cannot help but live when we accept the Life-giver. Our present mortality is no indication that eternal life has not begun for us. That vital connection that makes us immune from the second death (the first death is only a sleep) has already been established.

The second coming of Christ is an event that makes visible the already factual union of God and His people. In heaven we will no longer be sick because we will have been removed from this ecologically imbalanced planet. We will be mortgage-free because mortgages will have ceased to exist. But we will be sin-free because the great controversy over the truth of who God is will have already ended in our hearts.

It will be wonderful to see God face-to-face. But we may "see" Him even now through His Written Word. We may now be totally sure of who He is, and our lives are thus forever secure in Him.

HIDING WHAT WE REALLY ARE

Alas for you, lawyers and Pharisees, hypocrites! You clean the outside of cup and dish, which you have filled inside by robbery and self-indulgence! Blind Pharisee! Clean the inside of the cup first; then the outside will be clean also. Matt. 23:25, 26, N.E.B.

I once bought a large hydraulic jack at a yard sale, and I was excited. For only $15 I brought home a shiny, hefty-looking piece of equipment that the pleasant lady behind the table had assured me was almost new. As I tried it out under our car, I bragged about my clever purchase to my wife. My face became red with anger (and embarrassment) as the jack oozed hydraulic fluid all over the floor and the car sank slowly down.

Jesus is absolutely committed to reality. He wants everything in His kingdom actually to *be* on the inside what it claims to be on the outside. Nothing short of this would allow us to trust each other throughout eternity. No wonder He spoke so severely to those religious leaders who were practiced veterans of pretense. Claiming to speak on behalf of God, the Pharisees were giving the people reason to believe that God Himself would be content with an outward show of righteousness, overlooking the reality of the inner condition. But Jesus was telling all who would hear that His Father, too, was committed to reality.

This raises an interesting question. If Jesus decries the idea of a person being clean only by outward appearance while in reality being still attached to sin, then what is the difference between an outwardly scrubbed cup and the "robe of Christ's righteousness," as it has often been understood? Rather than hiding our real condition from the eyes of man (as taught by the clean cup metaphor), the robe of Christ's righteousness is presumed to hide our real condition from the eyes of God. This idea suggests we can "hide" under the substitutionary merit of Christ's perfect righteousness and the Father will accept us to be what in reality we are not.

But the robe of Christ's righteousness is never intended to be a falsification of reality. Christ does not provide it either to fool or to change the Father. The robe is Christ's potent statement of the Father's love and acceptance for the sinner, which—when claimed and worn with pride—will produce actual cleanness within the sinner. And God need make no provision to hide sins that He is confident He can heal.

SALVATION BY RELATIONSHIP

For as the Father has life-giving power in himself, so has the Son, by the Father's gift. John 5:26, N.E.B.

Can a light bulb give off light without having a relationship with the dynamo? Can a baby calf live without having a relationship with its mother? Can a plant grow without having a relationship with the soil? Can a God-created human live without being in relationship with Him who has life-giving power within Himself?

The answer to the first three questions above seems so very obvious to all thoughtful people. In each case, if the relationship is broken, the negative results very quickly become evident. But what complicated challenges God faces in trying to tell us that the pattern holds true for the fourth question as well! He did, after all, give us the power to choose to break that relationship. Yet if, when we break from Him, we were to experience the immediate consequences of the choice, we would be in no condition ever to change our minds. On the other hand, when God—in an act of mercy—holds off those consequences, we fall for Satan's deceptions and think that we really can live apart from God.

There is nothing that Satan will seek to do with greater diligence than to get us to ignore that life-giving relationship with God. He will try to distract us with the enticements of the senses or with our handmade endeavors to build our own wall of security against the trouble to come. Or he will coax us to believe that a heavy involvement with religious busy-ness is a good substitute for involvement with the person of God.

But here is a very subtle way that Satan can get us to neglect the vital relationship with God that we call faith. He can entice us to think that faith is simply our acknowledgment of a legal transaction outside of ourselves in which Jesus makes some helpful arrangements with the Father so that we can be forgiven, and no personal connection with God is necessary. This view sometimes sneaks around under the heading of "righteousness by faith," but it strips all the essential meaning out of the word *faith*.

Jesus Himself, while a man on earth, lived only by depending upon His Father for life. This was *His* faith-connection, *His* saving relationship. And the remnant are described as having Jesus' kind of faith—that same vital relationship with God.

WHY THE DEMONS TREMBLE

So you believe that there is one God? That's fine. So do all the devils in hell, and shudder in terror! James 2:19, Phillips.

Have you ever wondered about the theology of demons? Have you puzzled about what they know about God and how it affects them? Have you wondered why they know so much about God, yet still don't repent? Today's verse gives us one of those rare opportunities to examine the theology of the whole demonic host.

James makes it clear that the demons know God exists and that He is one God—not a scattered castleful of scrapping deities. But their response to what they know is that they tremble in fear. We might say, "Well indeed they *should* be trembling, with their guilty consciences and all. They've got it coming." Yet we might wonder why such terrible fear does not lead them to repentance.

But we must recall that they got their instructions about the Father from the "father of lies," Satan himself, not from God. And the old snake wasn't about to tell them the truth. Instead he told them that the thing that's wrong with sinning is not that it will hurt anyone but that it will make the Father really angry. Once one has rebelled, Satan told them, God is keen on vengeance. There is no hope of restoration, only a fearful anticipation of retaliation and wrath.

The fallen angels clung to this understanding, in spite of all that God could do to tell them otherwise. Rejecting the clearest portrayals of truth, they damaged beyond repair their ability to apprehend further truth. And they fell under the unending burden of Satan's deceptions about God. Unable to apprehend the gracious truth that alone can lead to repentance, they remain forever in the bondage of fear.

For us as well, it is clearly not enough simply to believe that God exists. Our entire spiritual life is flavored by who we believe this God to be who does indeed exist. And if our religious life is haunted with dread of judgment to come, we are either turning our backs on God or we are burdened with Satan's deceptions about who God is and how He relates to us.

Unlike Satan and his self-deceived demonic followers, we may still walk from darkness into His marvelous light—the light of truth about Himself that He longs for us to hear: that He wishes to embrace us, not to terrify us!

THE INVISIBLE JOB

When he comes who is the Spirit of truth, he will guide you into all the truth. . . . He will glorify me. John 16:13, 14, N.E.B.

During my years as an academy student my job was to operate the campus public-address systems. My boss was a very wise person. He often told me that I was doing my job best when no one knew I was there at the controls. "If the volume is turned so low that the listeners are straining to hear, they will say, 'Why doesn't that guy turn it up!' If it is too high and beginning to feed back, they will say, 'What's the matter with that kid?' But if it is just right, they will be so engrossed with the speaker they won't even know that you are there. And that's what we want."

The Holy Spirit's deepest desire is that we see Jesus. He does not wish for the attention to stop short of the Goal and to focus upon the medium. He knows that His work is to counteract that of Satan, who is busy telling lies about Jesus. In contrast, He longs for the confused children of this planet to know the truth about Him whom to know is life eternal.

One person asked, "Why do we know so much about Jesus and so little about the Holy Spirit?" I suspect that the Holy Spirit would say, "That is just the way I want it." For it is not intricate knowledge about the nature of the Trinity that brings us salvation; it is the character of God as revealed by all members of the Godhead that leads us to trust.

Christians long to be filled with the Holy Spirit, as Jesus promised we could (Acts 1:5-8). Spirit-filled Christians, as with the Spirit Himself, will be fulfilling their tasks most effectively when they draw the least attention to themselves and the most attention to Jesus Christ. The gift of Spirit-filling is not for private religious entertainment. It is not a form of sanctified ecstasy. It is not a cause for boasting about new levels of religious achievement.

John the Baptist revealed the high-water mark of his Spirit-filled life when he said, "He must increase, but I must decrease" (John 3:30). This should not surprise us, since this is a perfect expression of the attitude of the Spirit Himself. The infilling of the Spirit is the infilling of the life of Christ, that He might be revealed to others.

AN INVITATION FROM OUR FATHER

"Come now, let us reason together, says the Lord." Isa. 1:18, R.S.V.

We all have heard the old adage "Do as I say and not as I do!" You know how it goes. Mom yells at the kids, "Pick up your room! I won't have you turn my house into a pigsty!" Take a peek into her room, however, and you'll see an almost unbelievable mess. "Don't be late for supper!" admonishes Dad, who turns up an hour late himself.

Most of us are conditioned from our youth to expect a certain amount of duplicity from our parents. We know they mean well, but reality lies somewhere else. The problem is that we tend to transfer such thinking to our relationship with our heavenly Parent. We are told, "Always be prepared to give an answer to everyone who asks you to give the reason for the hope that you have" (1 Peter 3:15, N.I.V.). But we suspect that God doesn't have to have a reason for what He does. After all, He *is* God!

Here's good news: God lives by the same rules that He asks us to. The law that He desires to write in our hearts also describes His character! He asks us to live accountably and reasonably even as He Himself does. Only this wayward planet is out of step with the rest of the universe. Only sin-darkened hearts perceive God as arbitrary and power-wielding. And so, in keeping with His nature, the Sovereign God invites us: "Come now, let us reason together."

Our heavenly Parent doesn't yell at us, "Clean up your life!" He says, "Let Me show you the best way to live!" And His admonitions are ever coupled with His promise to empower. "Do as I *do!*" He encourages us, "I'll help you!" In the process we begin to know Him. Gradually we may become even more excited about His friendship than we are about all the wonderful things we are learning. No longer do we have to see His counsel as arbitrary requirements. We may gladly receive it as the best information available—and as a chance to become better acquainted with our magnificent God!

I'm glad that God has surrounded us with His loving acceptance so that we may move forward unhindered by the fear of failure. *Failure* is just not a word in the vocabulary between friends. When things go wrong, friends look for answers as they keep reasoning things out—together.

SEEING WONDERFUL THINGS IN GOD'S LAW

God spoke all these words: "I am the Lord your God, who brought you out of Egypt, out of the land of slavery. You shall have no other gods before me." Ex. 20:1-3, N.I.V.

Four thousand years ago on Mount Sinai God gave to mankind a verbalized edition of His eternal law, the Ten Commandments. Not only was it the expression of His immutable will, but it was a revelation of His divine character. And it holds His promise of restoration and redemption for all who will receive it as such.

Yet for millenniums men have trembled at the thought of God and have seen the Ten Commandments as negative warnings from an angry Deity. Thus the law has been approached as a grave duty imposed upon humanity rather than understood as a positive message of deliverance and restoration from a loving Creator. However, it is our privilege to say with David, "I will never forget your precepts, for by them you have renewed my life" (Ps. 119:93, N.I.V.).

Let's take a fresh look at these familiar precepts, with the awareness that in them is revealed the heart of the infinite God and His promise of fulfillment for His people. We may pray as did David, "Open my eyes that I may see wonderful things in your law. I am a stranger on earth; do not hide your commands from me" (verses 18, 19, N.I.V.).

The best place to begin is just before the Sinai declarations, when God expressed His desire for a relationship with His people. He said, "I carried you [out of Egypt] on eagles' wings and brought you to myself" (Ex. 19:4, N.I.V.). It is in this context that we may best understand God as He "spoke all these words: 'I am the Lord your God, who brought you out of Egypt, out of the land of slavery. You shall have no other gods before me.' "

God was reintroducing Himself to His people, not simply "yelling" at them from heaven. He declared that He was so deeply interested in their lives that He became actively involved in their deliverance from slavery. He felt absolutely sure that if they allowed Him to guide them He would lead them so well that they would no longer feel a need to seek guidance from any other source, i.e., "gods."

No wonder David asserted, "Great peace have they who love your law, and nothing can make them stumble" (Ps. 119:165, N.I.V.).

OUR PROTECTIVE FATHER

You shall not make for yourself an idol in the form of anything in heaven above or on the earth beneath or in the waters below. You shall not bow down to them or worship them; for I, the Lord your God, am a jealous God, punishing the children for the sin of the fathers to the third and fourth generation of those who hate me, but showing love to thousands who love me and keep my commandments. Ex. 20:4-6, N.I.V.

"I'm jealous!" How many times have we felt such sentiments? The neighbors get a new car. Our best friend goes to Hawaii. A coworker gets a promotion. Our insides tighten and a hotness goes through our system like a slow-spreading fire. Indignation sets in: "I deserved that!"

Is jealousy ever good? Or is it always an expression of self-absorption and competitiveness? What about the possessiveness between a husband and wife? Is it "right" for a wife to be jealous when her husband flirts with another woman? Perhaps we need to define what we are talking about when we use the word *jealousy*. Roget's *Thesaurus* couples the term with such expressions as green-eyed monster, distrust, resentment, and sour grapes. Certainly, none of the above words carry any positive aspects with them, especially when talking about relationships. Does that mean, however, that a spouse should feel nothing when his companion encourages the attentions of another man?

Love is not indulgent, neither is it blind. Genuine love seeks to protect and nurture—to guard the loved one from experiences that are destructive and/or diminishing. Could it be that a husband's jealousy might be an expression of such protectiveness? Rather than evidence that he is trying to "keep her to himself," his jealousy could portray his deep concern that his wife not be exposed to hurtful influences—influences that, in the end, might rob him altogether of the desired privilege of nurturing and providing for her.

Certainly that is what is meant when God calls Himself "a jealous God" in the second commandment. The punishment spoken of—"to the third and fourth generation"—is a statement of the long-ranging effects incurred by families who do not choose to live under God's nurturing watchcare. In contrast, those who accept and love God emulate Him in their relationships with family members and friends. In this way His love is shown a thousandfold.

And their lives reflect the protective love of our caring Father.

TRADE LAWS AND ETERNAL LIFE

You shall not misuse the name of the Lord your God, for the Lord will not hold anyone guiltless who misuses his name. Ex. 20:7, N.I.V.

The United States has trade laws to protect the consumer from the fraudulent use of brand names on merchandise that is not in truth manufactured by the companies that own the names. In this way both unsuspecting buyers and manufacturers can seek redress if poor quality merchandise is spuriously marketed as ''the real thing.'' Peddlers of such bogus products are often fined heavily and ordered to make restitution to the offended parties.

If you've ever been on the receiving end of this kind of dealing, you know how annoying and sometimes damaging the results can be. The car part that gave out halfway to Iowa; the epoxy glue that let go just as you lifted a mended hot-drink mug to your mouth. But what if the ''product'' is God? What if the ''truth'' accepted doesn't get you all the way to heaven? What if your ''mended life'' gives out on you, scalding you with feelings of hopelessness and despair?

When we ''trade'' in religion, our fair-minded God has indicated that we need to be scrupulously careful about what we present as ''the real thing.'' So much is at stake! Our view of God ultimately decides our eternal destiny! If God's name is attached to concepts that leave us inadequately prepared to meet the rigors of this life, we will come to believe that *He* is inadequate! If His name is used as authority for emotional abuse, we will learn to hate *Him!* If in His name we are plundered of our dignity and made to submit to mindless humiliation, we will never rise to the heights of godly attainment afforded us by our excitingly visionary Maker.

We can trust God. He guarantees that His ways will bring us happiness, and we may trust that the guidelines that bear His name will ultimately do just that. However, when offered such ''truth,'' we are encouraged by God Himself to look for His ''brand name'' before accepting it. ''To the law and to the testimony! If they do not speak according to this word, they have no light of dawn'' (Isa. 8:20, N.I.V.).

The third commandment underscores that God cares a great deal about the integrity of our thinking. He desires to lead us away from the slave mentality of Egypt and into reasoning like the sons and daughters of God that we were destined to be.

FRIENDSHIP DAY IN THE UNIVERSE

Remember the Sabbath day by keeping it holy. Six days you shall labor and do all your work, but the seventh day is a Sabbath to the Lord your God. On it you shall not do any work, neither you, nor your son or daughter, nor your manservant or maidservant, nor your animals, nor the alien within your gates. For in six days the Lord made the heavens and the earth, the sea, and all that is in them, but he rested on the seventh day. Therefore the Lord blessed the Sabbath day and made it holy. Ex. 20:8-11, N.I.V.

You're sitting in your favorite chair in the front room. The phone rings. As the voice on the other end begins you sit bolt upright in your seat. "Who?" you ask.

"This is the president of the United States! I would like very much for us to get together!" Flabbergasted, you reply, "Uh, that would be great! Uh . . ." Your mind races. A trip to Washington! It'll be an experience of a lifetime! Something you'll tell your grandchildren! But what's that he's saying? Once a week! "You see, I'd like for us to become friends! That's why I think we should spend at least a whole day together each week. I'll fly out each Friday evening . . ."

Hard to imagine? I mean, why in the world would the president want to spend time with just an everyday person? Let alone a whole day out of each week! And yet that is exactly what the God of the universe has done! He has set apart—made holy—the seventh day of each week and invited us to spend the day with Him! And He gives the reason why He's interested in us: He's our Creator!

God did not create mankind so that He could be some sort of divine zookeeper! He made us in His image so that He might share His life with us. He gave us minds that can grow and dream and participate in the excitement of this wonderful universe. He shared with us a portion of His uniqueness and individuality so that our inventiveness would enhance life and make His own heart glad and refreshed. His desire is that we should find friendship with Him so delightful that we begin to soar, and that our capacity to communicate with Him might continue to develop until we can enter into such provocative interchange with Him that He Himself is stimulated. And it all begins with Sabbath communion.

THE QUESTION OF AUTHORITY

Honor your father and your mother, so that you may live long in the land the Lord your God is giving you. Ex. 20:12, N.I.V.

So much of what we think about God stems from what we think about our parents—how they disciplined us, their feelings about authority, and our responses to their methods. All this adds up to how well (or how poorly) we relate to our heavenly Father. Conversely, how we relate to God inevitably decides how we relate to family members and, ultimately, society in general.

In giving the Ten Commandments, God hoped to bring healing to a nation that had all but lost the meaning of the family unit. The authority figures in their lives had been Egyptians. Little dignity had been allowed the Hebrew people, and children were heavily influenced by the way their parents had been treated. As their parents had been regarded, they regarded them; and no doubt there were resulting power struggles in the home. God had to reestablish correct relationships within the family circle. By evoking reverence for parents, God superseded the example of the Egyptian taskmasters.

Despite the wordage of the fifth commandment, however, God was not exclusively addressing children. As parents taught their offspring the principles of the Decalogue, they were alerted to the tremendous responsibility entrusted to them. The attitudes their children gained under their tutelage would depend largely upon them. Implied in the spirit of this commandment is the thought that parents should conduct themselves in a manner worthy of the respect of their children.

The central issue in the great controversy between God and Satan is the character of God—most particularly His authority. Satan has accused God of being arbitrary in His dealings with His created beings. He has claimed that God wants to control everyone just for sheer pleasure, that His demand for our worship of Him is to satisfy His need to show off His power. In establishing the family unit on earth, it was God's plan to display a working model of His true authority.

With hearts full of selfless love, parents were to nurture and wisely guide their children. In turn, children would learn to appreciate their parents' values—because what they had been taught was sensible and reliable. They would see that their parents had only their best interests in mind, that whatever authority was exercised was to preserve quality of life, never to satisfy parental power needs.

And so it is with God.

IT'S WORTH IT TO CARE!

You shall not murder. You shall not commit adultery. You shall not steal. Ex. 20:13-15, N.I.V.

Life is cheap on Planet Earth. We see it snuffed out night after night on television—either on the news or on the latest crime drama. Pictures of dead bodies are commonly displayed in every weekly news magazine. And because it is so common, we hardly flinch at the gore, the inhumanness, the waste of lives that is epidemic. And people sometimes wonder, Does God care?

Life is cheap, all right. Even when it isn't snuffed out. The value of our individuality is constantly diminished with the bombardment of profane sensuality through advertisements, the "top forty" hit songs, and countless other avenues to our senses. We are reduced to bodies—never mind our conscience or even our consciousness. And again people wonder, What is it all *for?*

But life is expensive, too—outrageously so! Even the rich are hurting. And the little guy? Well, he goes to bed at night with knots in his stomach, wondering where the ends even *are,* let alone if they'll ever meet. It's no wonder that theft is second nature to multitudes of people. It's more than taking things; it creeps over into taking positions, and reputations, and beating someone to the checkout stand at the supermarket. And we all wonder, at times, whether or not *we* care anymore.

Yes, God cares! He beholds our plight and reaches right down to our tiredness and lifts up our sense of personal worth. Life is of utmost value! It is more than the process of blood surging through arteries and veins. Who we are *in* these bodies of ours matters. Our heartaches are not merely second-class pulp novels like those that overflow bookstores, grocery stores, and airport terminals. We are real, and reality is where God lives. And when we understand and embrace Him, we embrace reality. Then people count! Their lives, in every dimension, matter. And we know that we matter too—and we can stop wondering.

That's what it means to be brought out of slavery, the kind of slavery that demotes life until it is worth less than the effort to keep it functioning. It is freedom to interface with the greatest reality mankind can know: God is our Father, and He chooses us to be His friends! We can know Him, and in knowing Him we will see ourselves as He sees us. And we will love one another as He has loved us.

THE WITNESS OF TRUE FRIENDSHIP

You shall not give false testimony against your neighbor. Ex. 20:16, N.I.V.

You get a helpless feeling when someone who you thought was your friend deliberately says something about you that is not true. People believe your friends more than your enemies. They know your enemies are out to get you. But your friends . . .

Neighbors know you too. They live near you. They know what you're up to—whether or not you yell at the kids, or return borrowed tools, or throw wild parties. So when a neighbor spreads falsehood, people tend to accept it as gospel truth.

God understands; He's experiencing it, too! That type of activity was what Lucifer did in heaven. He was the highest created being; stood next to God's throne; knew what God was up to. The worst of it was that Lucifer was also one of God's best friends. Of all the angels in heaven, Lucifer was capable of the highest communion with the Father. And because of this, his songs had the most melody; his bearing was the brightest. To him God was the most vulnerable. Lucifer took advantage of God's friendship to promote himself among the angelic family.

Through man God would demonstrate that Lucifer was wrong. He would allow man to enter into close union with Himself—and let man tell the truth about Him. But man too believed Lucifer (now Satan). But God really loves the human race and knows that we have been deceived. So He's going ahead with His plan. He's allowing us the privilege of knowing who He really is—if we choose to know. And in understanding we will see how horrible it is to give false testimony against a neighbor. We'll see what it has done to the Father and to the universe.

Like God, we'll feel no need to build ourselves up at someone else's expense. No. We'll do just the opposite. We'll give of ourselves to build up our friends and our neighbors—all those who need our love. And that leaves no one out! When we are falsely accused we will not retaliate, even as God has not retaliated against Satan. Our energies will be focused upon those who need our caring.

In giving ourselves, we will witness to our likeness to the Giver of life. In Him there is no fault at all.

WANTING IN ORDER TO GIVE

You shall not covet your neighbor's house. You shall not covet your neighbor's wife, or his manservant or maidservant, his ox or donkey, or anything that belongs to your neighbor. Ex. 20:17, N.I.V.

Why do people covet? What is coveting, anyway? Is it wrong to see your neighbor's house and say to yourself, "Someday, I'm going to build a house just like that!"? Are we not supposed to be challenged by desires for self-improvement? Perhaps it would be worth our while to examine some of the basic qualities of self-motivation in light of the high calling we have as sons and daughters of God.

First of all, we would all agree it is obviously wrong to want something that belongs specifically to another person. The reasons are simple: it means that you desire to gain at their expense, that your interests are purely selfish and, consequently, hurtful. And that is at the crux of the tenth commandment. It answers a lot of questions about God, too. He does not simply "want" from us—service, time, our income—just to satisfy an ego-centered divinity.

There is a place, however, for being stimulated toward the kind of self-improvement that involves the motivation to seek material things. The things sought are seen not as an end in themselves, but as a means of achieving the greater goal of service. A man might dream of having a house someday just like his neighbor's, not because it would bring him social prestige but because his neighbor's house fits into the man's mental picture of the kind of home that would maximize his ministry to others: a large living room with a fireplace—a good gathering place for groups of people to feel the warmth of fellowship, as well as the warmth of a blazing fire; enough tucked-away places where furniture could be arranged to encourage small-group intimacy within the framework of the larger whole—so as to provide settings where discussion and individual growth could take place.

Once again God's promise of fulfillment for us given in the Decalogue is that He will so resolve our feelings of inadequacy and lack of self-worth that we will no longer be driven to endless grasping after things that cannot bring us peace. "You will not covet—because your hearts will be content in all that I am and all that our friendship brings."

We will still want, but we will want in order to give.

GREAT IMPROVEMENTS

And this is the will of the One who sent me, that everyone who sees the Son and trusts him should have eternal life, and I will raise him up when the last day comes. John 6:40, Phillips.

My young daughter was trying to hold a conversation with her almost-as-young cousin in the back seat of the car. Cousin Debbie inquired, "How old are you?" "I'm fine," Julie replied; "How are you?" "I'm 9 too," Debbie responded. As we adults listened from the front seat we realized that each had such a clear mind-set about the purpose of the conversation that they never would know that they hadn't communicated with each other.

This is exactly what was happening with the Pharisees in their conversation with Jesus as reported in John 6. Their rigid mind-set was keeping them from comprehending that they were asking the wrong question, thus failing to grasp Jesus' utterly unique answer. They asked, "What must we do, to be doing the works of God?" (verse 28, R.S.V.). They were expecting a specific behavior assignment, some new action to perform. "This is the work of God, that you believe in him whom he has sent" (verse 29, R.S.V.), Jesus replied, getting right to the heart of the matter. Without a new relationship with the Master, what good is a new behavior to perform?

But their thinking had been shaped by a performance-oriented religion for so long that they couldn't even comprehend a relationship-oriented religion. They immediately replied with a new question about Jesus' own performance that they might decide whether to respect His answers. The larger issue at stake, however, was their understanding of the Father and the kind of religious experience He wants for His children.

The Pharisees were certain that God desires the kind of good behavior that will please Him, that will make Him impressed with them. Looking at it from a strictly human point of view, they thought that God loves only the lovely, so they set out to be lovely. But Jesus knew that His Father was not impressed with self-contrived goodness—nor put off by its absence. Jesus keenly wanted His hearers to grasp the concept that any genuine improvement in the human condition happens only when we are in happy, personal union with our Maker. Indeed, "everyone who looks upon the Son and puts his faith in him shall possess eternal life" (verse 40, N.E.B.). That's how great the improvements are!

GOING ON FROM STRENGTH TO STRENGTH

Blessed are those whose strength is in you. Ps. 84:5, N.I.V.

Vitamin pills, protein drinks, aerobics—America is on a fad of getting fit. Posters displaying muscular bodies abound; "no pain, no gain," viewers are advised. But bodies grow old regardless of what people do, and disease can rob the most enthusiastic person of his health.

There is one Source of strength that will never fail! "Blessed are those whose strength is in you, who have set their hearts on pilgrimage. As they pass through the Valley of Baca, they make it a place of springs; the autumn rains also cover it with pools. They go from strength to strength till each appears before God in Zion" (Ps. 84:5-7, N.I.V.).

Our only lasting happiness comes when we know the Father. Our strength is in that knowledge; we know we are only pilgrims here on this weary planet. And each day that we must pass through the bone-dry desert of misconceptions about God's character that prevail in our world, we may make places where springs of living water offer hope to the tired and dying. The autumn rains, the pouring out of the Spirit of God at the harvesttime of earth's history, will pool together as those who delight in Him draw others into like fellowship. So we go from strength to strength until we gain our heart's desire: to be with the Father forevermore.

It is possible, because "we have this treasure" of the knowledge of God "in jars of clay to show that this all-surpassing power is from God and not from us. We are hard pressed on every side, but not crushed; perplexed, but not in despair; persecuted, but not abandoned; struck down, but not destroyed" (2 Cor. 4:7-9, N.I.V.). Our strength is our unshakable consciousness of who God is; our impregnable friendship with Him causes us always to hope. No future with Him could ever be dim!

So we cry with joy unspeakable, "Who shall separate us from the love of Christ? Shall trouble or hardship or persecution or famine or nakedness or danger or sword? . . . No, in all these things we are more than conquerors through him who loved us . . . [Nothing] will be able to separate us from the love of God that is in Christ Jesus our Lord" (Rom. 8:35-39, N.I.V.).

Inseparable! Our friendship with God is going to last! It makes you feel like living forever! And so we shall.

FOR HIGHER REASONS

God must prove true, though every man be false; as the Scripture says, "That you may be shown to be upright in what you say, and win your case when you go into court." Rom. 3:4, Goodspeed.

A skilled attorney is preparing to plead a case on behalf of a defendant. He builds his case with great care, covering every possible area that the prosecution might try to use against his client. He anticipates every legal intricacy, every aspect of witness credibility, that could be brought up in court. He knows his opponent is a clever prosecutor, and he wants no surprises.

At last his client says, "That's enough! You've built a solid case for me; I'm sure the judge will rule in my favor." But his attorney knows that the best way to win the case is by careful attention to detail. Furthermore, he knows that this is a precedent-setting case. It will have impact on perhaps thousands of others. And so he continues with great thoroughness.

How narrow we often have been to assume that the issues in the heavenly judgment center only around ourselves. We have often forgotten that more is at stake in the divine proceedings than our own salvation. What is necessary to end the great controversy is far greater than what might be necessary for securing just my own salvation (though in the end they cannot be separated). The universe-wide problem of sin is rooted in Satan's accusations about the character of God; his challenges must be answered in such a way that—billions of years later—brilliant people will never challenge the verdict.

God's people share Paul's conviction that when the verdict comes in from the heavenly courtroom, God will be shown to have always spoken the truth. With great eagerness His people long for this to happen, for not only are they jealous for His reputation, but they also wish for the tragedy and pain to be over throughout the universe. This becomes such a driving motivation in their lives that it leads them to reflect His beauties to others, that they might choose Him.

Of this we can be sure: If God will be vindicated in every one of His actions and decisions, then His decision that I am in a saving relationship with Him will never be successfully challenged throughout eternity!

DOES FAITH TWIST GOD'S ARM?

Then Jesus answered her, "O woman, great is your faith! Be it done for you as you desire." And her daughter was healed instantly. Matt. 15:28, R.S.V.

There is hardly a parent whose child was seriously ill, who didn't feel, with this ancient Canaanite woman, an intense desire for divine healing. She has, in fact, been lauded as a model of faith in that she persisted in asking for Jesus to heal her daughter even after He apparently put her off. But what mother, with the very life of her child hanging by a slender thread, would have given up quickly?

Unfortunately, this encounter between Jesus and a tenacious mother has sometimes been interpreted as the way in which one's faith is used to extract favors from God. Some assume from this story that Jesus was perhaps reluctant to perform the requested miracle and that the woman's faith somehow coaxed Jesus to do it for her. This seems to confirm the misconception held by too many that if one asks for a specific miracle and it is not granted, this is because one did not have sufficient faith to "twist God's arm" and obtain the blessing. This has led to a great deal of needless self-depreciation and distress in the presence of God.

Actually, the actions of Jesus in this situation reveal some precious qualities about our God. Rather than being imposed upon by the Canaanite woman, He had actually traveled a great distance out of His way just to be available to meet her need. His apparent indifference to her need drew His prejudiced and indifferent disciples into understanding the hurt such attitudes can inflict. By healing her daughter, Jesus rebuked the insular narrowness of the Jews.

Jesus' love for this unnamed woman's daughter was matched by His eagerness to let this woman reveal a priceless quality of faith. She had heard about Jesus' ministry and teachings, and she responded by placing her full confidence in Him. This confidence led her to Him with her request, but her confidence was not based on His response to that request. She adored Jesus because of who He was, not because of what He would or would not do for her. As with Job, her trust in God was based on something larger than her personal circumstances. For faith is not the Christian's "inside track" to obtain special favors from God. It is trusting God for God's sake alone!

WHO SHUTS THE LAST DOOR?

Let the evildoer still do evil, and the filthy still be filthy, and the righteous still do right, and the holy still be holy. Rev. 22:11, R.S.V.

For more than six thousand years God has done everything His creative mind and loving heart could do to get evildoers to stop doing evil, and the filthy to become pure. Then with equal energy He has worked with the righteous to help them remain in that vital relationship with Himself.

How strange it is, then, to hear Him speak the utterly final words in today's text. He declares that a solid wall exists between the evil and the holy, and that it shall not be crossed from either direction. Does this mean that God Himself has slammed the door on repentance or turned His back on free choice? Or has He run out of patience with the increasing wickedness of a sin-sick planet?

God spoke of a time when the people of this planet will have sorted themselves into two groups: "For behold, darkness shall cover the earth, and thick darkness the peoples; but the Lord will arise upon you, and his glory will be seen upon you" (Isa. 60:2, R.S.V.). In Bible symbolism, "light" represents truth about God and "darkness" stands for error or deception about Him. Into a world that presently lives in various shades of gray, God will send increasing beams of intense, winsome truth about Himself. And people must respond.

Those who choose to be enlightened by that truth will be marvelously changed by it! Their spiritual capacities will be enhanced, their characters more and more transformed into the likeness of the One they love to behold. They will become so resolutely settled in their unshakable loyalty to God that no deception of the enemy could turn them away. They *will not* change their minds.

Something equally powerful happens to the minds of those who turn their backs on truth. According to Paul (see Rom. 1:18-23), they become futile in their thinking and their minds become darkened. Claiming to be wise, they become utter fools until they destroy the very capacity to receive light from heaven. As a result, they *cannot* change their minds. At that time God will announce that the time for choosing is over, not because He has arbitrarily shut it down but because everyone will have made final choices. No one will be changing his mind! The righteous will not; the wicked cannot.

NO HANDLES OUT

When he was abused he did not retort with abuse, when he suffered he uttered no threats, but committed his cause to the One who judges justly. 1 Peter 2:23, N.E.B.

Some psychologists speak of us as having "handles" sticking out—those vulnerable, sensitive areas of our lives by which other people can influence us or even control us. Like the handles sticking out from a pot on a stove that people can bump or grab, our feelings and actions often are controlled by people touching these sensitive areas.

For example, I am feeling unsure about my slightly chunky appearance, yet it means a great deal to me that others view me as attractive. An admired friend makes one small, negative comment about people who are overweight, and it sends me straight into an unhealthy crash diet. Or one of my colleagues on the job stifles a yawn while I am expressing an opinion and I become darkly discouraged, even unwilling to talk, nursing my bruised sense of self-worth.

While He walked among insensitive men, Jesus was a perfect example of one who had no "handles" out. There was no way in which the abuses, the attacks, or even the unintentional snubs of petty people could cause Him to lose His composure. His stability did not result from other people always treating Him properly, but from knowing that He was loved by His Father.

Jesus, "knowing that the Father had given all things into his hands, and that he had come from God and was going to God" (John 13:3, R.S.V.), was able to minister to the needs of His disciples. What a challenging insight! The one who most securely knows that he is a child of God really is the most adequate, the most secure, person. He does not need to boast, to create status positions for himself, or to defend himself against someone else's false views of him. He knows who he is and can now help others discover how valuable they are too!

The means by which Jesus cures our offensive attitudes and actions are not religious mysteries. He knows that we do most of the stupid things we do because we are frantically trying to prove to others and to ourselves how valuable, how worthwhile, we really are. With nail-scarred hands extended, with embracing arms, He comes to us announcing warmly that we are His children, purchased at a great price. What healing love this is!

LEARNING TO LOVE REALITY

If it is hard for the righteous to be saved, what will become of the ungodly and the sinner? 1 Peter 4:18, N.I.V.

You know them. They live their lives in mortal fear that they will do something to merit God denying them eternal life. They continually measure the hems of their garments and spend hours reading labels in the supermarket. Their libraries are full of books that admonish, their cupboards reflect a careful sterility, and their sleep is like that of one on death row who has been granted only a tentative reprieve. Yet they say that God loves them.

Perhaps they have read today's text and shuddered. But, friends, Paul is *not* saying that it is hard to be saved! He is addressing the attitude of believers who *act* as though it is. In verse 12 he begins, "Dear friends, do not be surprised at the painful trial you are suffering, as though something strange were happening to you" (N.I.V.). It is not strange that we who are in this world should experience hurt—Jesus Himself did. This world is a hurtful place because it has rejected the One who is the source of all goodness and love. That is reality. If we do not accept this reality, feeling that our connection with God should somehow prevent any further hurt done to us, we will never experience being "overjoyed when [God's] glory is revealed" (verse 13, N.I.V.). The revelation of who God is, is inextricably connected to that very reality—and if believers have a hard time experiencing joy over God, "what will become of the ungodly and the sinner?"

Paul's advice is that we should "commit [ourselves] to [our] faithful Creator and continue to do good" (verse 19, N.I.V.). We need not be dismayed by the trials of this life and the hurt that inevitably follows. We may learn to love even painful reality because of the larger reality of who God is. In seeing His commitment to salvaging every fragment of our hopes in hopeless situations (without compromising the personhood of any individual), we experience comfort. In realizing that we are exposed to grief, not because of some inadequacy on our part (or God's!) but because of God's reluctance to manipulate circumstances, we find peace in knowing that He will never manipulate us.

Let us make a firm commitment not to let our relationship with the Father look so unpleasant and tenuous that we turn away those who do not yet know Him.

MAKING A NATION GREAT

And what other nation is so great as to have such righteous decrees and laws as this body of laws I am setting before you today? Deut. 4:8, N.I.V.

We often hear news reports of "bloodless coups d'état," in which some country's government has been overthrown by key people within its own ruling class. These self-asserted leaders, who sometimes turn out to be national heroes to succeeding generations, usually claim their right to take over the government because the previous leaders were mismanaging the country. They claim to offer a better form of government.

That is precisely the charge that Lucifer brought against God when the rebellion began in heaven! Though Lucifer's coup attempt was not successful, God did not count Himself to be victorious simply because He had removed Lucifer and his followers from the seat of government. Questions had been raised that would linger in the minds of all of those who lived within God's realm. Since God relishes free, thoughtful loyalties, won without force or coercion, He had but one option. He had to demonstrate the actual superiority of His government so that His people might make informed choices to live with Him.

We earthbound children of the King are also invited to cast our own votes—indeed our destinies—in this great conflict. But we who live such short lives, who operate with such a miniature reference point, who barely comprehend what we see (much less the unseen), and whose thought processes so readily get lost somewhere between "cause" and "effect"—how shall we see the government of God in operation, that we might properly cast our votes of loyalty?

Our Father, who has always specialized in parables, has given us an acted parable, a lived demonstration tailored for our level of understanding, of the government of God. He has given us principles for human government that, when put into practice, give us glimpses of His goodness. Admittedly adapted for sinful people, these principles still demonstrate God's respect for each one's personhood, dignity, and freedom. They exalt the power of love and cooperation, and offer provision for restoring the errant. Revealed most extensively through Moses and richly amplified by Jesus Christ, these principles for human government are clearly the best that this sin-burdened planet could ever know.

God's desire for Israel, and for all who find His government to be wise and gracious, is that all nations should come to know the greatness of a God who governs so wonderfully.

IT DOES HAVE TO MAKE SENSE!

Grain must be ground to make bread; so one does not go on threshing it forever. Isa. 28:28, N.I.V.

"Just do it!" Tired of explaining everything to her 5-year-old, Mother had finally resorted to simply commanding. "But it doesn't make sense!" lamented the young lad. "I don't care! Just *do* it!" answered his mother with a great deal of exasperation. "It doesn't have to make sense!"

Ten years later it was Mother, referring to her son's wasted condition from drug use, who lamented, "But son, it just doesn't make sense!" Turning to go out the door, he paused only long enough to mumble, "It doesn't have to make sense!"

Sometimes God asks things of people that seem to make no sense. Some people reason that since God is an authority figure it doesn't have to make sense. However, if you believe this, you have some exciting things to learn about Him! God's actions are full of integrity, and they make the very best sense! The times we have difficulty finding meaning in our circumstances may be when our reference point is too narrow. Often we have a mind-set that overrides our ability to analyze and appreciate the larger picture—the reality that encompasses more than just our personal areas of concern.

Our text today reminds us to consider the larger picture. "Grain must be ground to make bread; so one does not go on threshing it forever. Though he drives the wheels of his threshing cart over it, his horses do not grind it. All this also comes from the Lord Almighty, wonderful in counsel and magnificent in wisdom" (Isa. 28:28, 29, N.I.V.). If we were to focus solely upon the grain with no thought of the sweet-smelling bread that would eventually result, we might wonder at the whole process. Why crush wheat? In what manner should it be crushed? And, with no understood objective, timing becomes distorted: What is too long and what is long enough?

Our loving Father's wisdom *is* magnificent! We may trust that He is able to handle all the intricate details of "the larger picture" without diminishing a single individual or minimizing anyone's specific needs. We may know that His actions, or apparent lack of them, are precisely chosen and perfectly accurate in every circumstance. Whether He allows us to experience painful consequences or moves to alleviate our distress, we may know with perfect confidence that God has chosen the most sensible option.

JOY TO THE WORLD

You have given more joy to my heart than others ever knew, for all their corn and wine. Ps. 4:7, Jerusalem.

"You just can't make a case against liquor from the Bible!" Her telephone voice carried urgency and conviction, suggesting important personal reasons why she had to hold that point of view about alcoholic beverages. Rather than trying to defend the Scriptures, I asked her why she felt it was so important to defend liquor, especially since I knew she had been raised a nondrinker. "What do you seek to accomplish by it?" I asked.

"I feel better able to handle stress, to mingle with people, and to enjoy myself," she explained. "It just gives me a good feeling after I've had a little wine." We spoke for a while about the difference between the actual, real world and a chemically altered perception of the world. I expressed my conviction that Jesus gives us strength and perspective to face life as it is, rather than "granting us permission" to pretend to escape from the demands of life through a chemical numbing of the brain.

But I could tell she was more than just philosophical about the matter. She was frightened. She was terrified about facing life's demands without the comforting illusions of adequacy that the bottle promised. At the root of it all, she simply doubted that God could enrich her life with a quality of joy and confidence that was superior to her chemical buzz. It was a crisis of faith, a concrete battle with the object of her trust. But she thought she had already heard all the "religious answers." She was one of the most talented, promising, and attractive of my schoolmates, and I was grieved to hear, several years later, that she had committed suicide.

Could it be that many people are drawn to the illusory joys of an increasingly drugged world because they have never tasted (as had David) of the kind of joy that God imparts? Worse yet, could it be that many Christians don't know that God intends that they should know such joy? When the angels sang, "Joy to the world," they meant it! They were announcing that we should even now know the joy of being intensely loved, freely forgiven, personally guided, and richly enabled by our Father. He pervades our problematic world with such hope and meaning that each succeeding conflict with the forces of darkness brings us new springs of joy.

THE GOOD NEWS IN GOOD MANNERS
Love has good manners. I Cor. 13:5, Phillips.

He had all the right answers. He knew where the texts were in his Bible and understood a great deal about the original manuscripts. Well-read in Christian literature, well-versed in current events, he was regarded as a theologian, though he held no degree. Yet he was offensive in his manner of speaking to people. He seemed more interested in being right than in being careful.

A Christian, she dressed properly enough. Her skirts were an acceptable length, and her necklines were modest. She didn't attend unseemly gatherings, and she taught her children to memorize scriptures. Yet her conversation was sometimes less than appropriate, her manners slightly coarse. She prided herself in the fact that her worldly neighbors counted her as "one of the gang," but she did not seem to realize that her compatibility came at the expense of deeper, inner virtues.

Paul states that "love has good manners." How important are good manners in sharing the good news about our Father? Is He not judged by the deportment of His followers? God is love, and God has good manners. When those who profess to follow Him display rudeness of any sort, or lack of finesse, they cannot help but stain God's character—no matter how properly they are attired or how many scriptures they are able to quote. Lack of dignity reveals a lack of caring respect for others. It's like serving the truth of God on the tip of a poisoned arrow.

Having good manners means far more than knowing which fork to use for your salad. It is the whole presentation of a person in every setting and at all times. And mannerliness does not end when one is out of the sight of others. Though a quality of inner dignity and outward composure that finds its best expression in deferring to other people, it also operates in total privacy. When a person has a sense of personal worth, it is reflected in even the minutia of life.

God is like this. Go to the desert and see how perfectly formed are His tiny living things. Who sees them? Go to the sea and witness the extravagant detail of microscopic marine life. Why does it matter? Then go to your prayer closet and discover how careful He has been with every detail of your life. Even when it didn't matter to you!

Friends, we can trust our lives to the Father!

ENOUGH!

So you should rather turn to forgive and comfort him, or he may be overwhelmed by excessive sorrow. 2 Cor. 2:7, R.S.V.

In Paul's tender pastoral letters to his friends in Corinth, we can see him "walk with them" through several stages of spiritual growth—stages that we can recognize by experience. As with many new believers recently come from a very depraved world, they had lost some of their sensitivity to the hurtfulness of sin. They were willing to tolerate something as destructive as incest within the body of Christ, incapacitated with uncertainty about how to deal with their friends in trouble.

When Paul appealed to them to deal decisively with evil in their midst, they were most eager to show themselves obedient to his leadership. They dealt so harshly with the offender that Paul needed to write again, reminding them that restoration of the sinner is the ultimate goal.

But most of us would admit that this is the more difficult transition. It is often easier to become indignant with sinners, particularly when we perceive their sins to be especially offensive, than it is to love them back into our fellowship. When we see them tentatively approaching the church doors, embarrassment on their faces and hesitant confusion in their steps, how easy it is to ignore them—sometimes with an obvious deliberateness. We often justify our coolness by asserting that we do not wish to be thought of as condoning their sins. More likely, we reveal our inadequacy in knowing how to love them dynamically, creatively, into wholeness.

Involved here is something very central to our witness about the character of God. Where do so many people get the idea that God frowns at sinners, holding them off at arm's length until their reputation (by some self-wrought means) gets cleaned up? Have they been watching us Christians? Is this where so many people miss the central truth that we become whole only by being embraced by the Father?

Disfellowshipping a believer for obvious sin has the dual purpose of seeking to gain his serious attention and of announcing that the body of Christ does not embrace such behavior. But how quickly the church must then act to clarify that God does not use rejection as leverage for character change! It is our God who inspired Paul to plead with the Corinthians, "It is enough! Now restore him." Because that's exactly what God would do. Let's embrace them in His name!

NOW AND FOREVER

See! The home of God is with men, and he will live among them. They shall be his people, and God himself shall be with them. Rev. 21:3, Phillips.

Picture this: A lovely wedding has taken place. Candles were lit, vows taken, matrimonial cake shared. The bride, wreathed in smiles, waves as she rushes away to enjoy her long-awaited honeymoon—apart from the groom! Smiling indulgently, he sees his bride off, glad for her happiness. Having made her secure in his love and financial support, he is content for her to spend the rest of her life free from worry, though they will actually see little of one another.

Absurd? Of course. But let's stop and think a minute. In the metaphor of marriage with the Lamb, Christians anticipate more than an occasional encounter with God—though, in fact, some might be far more comfortable if He would be content to "see them off" to roam happily among the galaxies forevermore. Heaven is a wonderful idea if only they didn't have to meet up with God very often—once a week in a worship service, perhaps.

Our text today says that God is going to make His home with us! In other words, after the honeymoon (the millennium?) we are going to live together! And not at opposite ends of the universe, either! Those who find their times of communion with the Father to be their greatest joy on earth experience great agony in being separated from Him. A bride and groom do not wait eagerly for their wedding day so that they may continue to live apart! If they did, it would make no sense for them to consider marriage.

How, then, can it be so for some Christians? Simply enough, they understood that the only way to live forever is through "marriage" to God. Thus, it is considered a "marriage of convenience" in the hearts of many believers, rather than a celebration of the union of hearts. The astounding part of this is that they secretly think that God feels the same way—that He has to take us because of the death of Christ.

In choosing the marriage metaphor, God wanted to portray Himself as eager to live with us! "You'll be mine at last!" He exclaims from heaven. But only when our hearts burn with the same desire will He commence the wedding. Then He will wipe away the tears caused by separation from Him. And we shall be one.

UNIQUENESS WITH A PURPOSE

John was dressed in a rough coat of camel's hair, with a leather belt round his waist, and he fed on locusts and wild honey. Mark 1:6, N.E.B.

Scholars have argued for many centuries and through volumes of research whether the locusts that comprised a part of John's diet were the beans of the carob tree or whether they were indeed a small crunchy insect. In any case, his manner of dress and his peculiar dietary pattern were worthy of note by both Matthew and Mark. No doubt these interesting features also drew the attention of the populace, for they came out in vast numbers to hear what he had to say.

But when they walked away after listening to him, their memories were not full of visions of a strange man with unique dress. They were full of excited expectancy for the coming Messiah, whom John had described in appealing terms. Jesus Himself bore testimony that no greater than John had walked among men. Yet He said this, not about John's personal traits, but about that spirit in him that cried, "He must increase, but I must decrease" (John 3:30).

Virtually every Christian denomination or persuasion has at least one unique feature that marks it as distinctive from the others. That unique feature—which may relate to a doctrine, to the manner of worship, or to the individual member's lifestyle—came into being out of conscientious conviction. As such, it is not to be despised by others who may not appreciate it. However, it would be well for every Christian continually to ask, "How does this special aspect of my life help to present a more attractive picture of Jesus Christ?"

For example, some Christians have—as did John—some dietary preferences and convictions that set them apart from the masses. They choose to eat some special foods and avoid others. Too often, entire denominations become known for what they won't eat! But if those dietary convictions become in themselves the focus of attention, and others do not see in them something sensible about God, they are more than a wasted uniqueness; they are a stumbling block.

Our Father does not hand down strange menus to us, simply to test our submission or to make us peculiar for peculiarity's own sake. As a loving God, committed to our happiness, He offers us what He knows will lead to optimum health. When we express our uniqueness in this way, we let Jesus increase.

AFTER ALL THIS!

After all this, O Lord, will you hold yourself back? Will you keep silent and punish us beyond measure? Isa. 64:12, N.I.V.

No matter how bad they behave, they are still your children. They may trample your gardens, insult your reputation, and thanklessly eat all the food in your refrigerator, but you still love them. And in loving them you allow them to experience the consequences of their actions. When they trample your gardens, there are no roses for their vases. When they insult your reputation, they cannot use your name to their gain.

The Israelites were wayward children. Because God loved them, He allowed them to reap the consequences of their actions. Their sacred cities had become a desert, their holy Temple had been burned with fire. All that they treasured lay in ruins (Isa. 64:10, 11). Yet God was their Father (verse 8)! And so they cried, ''After all this, O Lord, will you hold yourself back? Will you keep silent and punish us beyond measure?''

The punishment spoken of here may be understood in terms of cause and effect. The question was really ''Will You let us bear the effects of our actions beyond the point of profitableness?'' Though many in Israel still defied God, others had been educated by their mistakes. To these, reassurance was given in verse 8 of chapter 65. ''This is what the Lord says: 'As when juice is still found in a cluster of grapes and men say, ''Don't destroy it, there is yet some good in it,'' so will I do in behalf of my servants; I will not destroy them all.' ''

Parental love longs to uplift and restore. But wise parents know that unless their children come to accept accountability for their actions, any intervention on their behalf would be counterproductive. Once learning occurs, however, it is unnatural for loving parents to want their children to experience prolonged suffering. When the principle of accountability is internalized, personal growth can be achieved. As far as possible, hindrances should be removed so that positive affirmation of such newly acquired attitudes can issue.

God has never held Himself back from those who seek Him. Throughout earth's history He has acted the part of a loving father, eager to uplift and sustain His children. Even when it becomes necessary to allow us to experience the consequences of sin, His attitude toward us is unchanging.

Then let us learn quickly!

WHEN NOT TO BELIEVE JESUS

If I am not acting as my Father would, do not believe me. John 10:37, N.E.B.

Imagine the setting: Jesus is speaking to a very religious people, but He keeps saying things that seem to contradict much of their religious practice and beliefs. They don't know how to evaluate what He tells them. For example, they have believed that they must not do anything on the Sabbath that could even be thought of as work—not even healing sick people. They hold this conviction because they do not wish to displease God, who is the authority behind the Sabbath command.

But Jesus, who also claims to hold God and His law in very high regard, seems almost deliberately to flaunt His freedom from these traditional Sabbath constraints. He goes out of His way to heal people on the Sabbath, even asking one to carry his bedroll across town as joyous evidence of his healing. How does the common person process these conflicts? The religious leaders say Jesus is wrong. Tradition says He is wrong. Those who interpret the fine points of Scripture say He is wrong. Most other authoritative religious documents pronounce Him to be wrong. Yet something powerful that cannot be ignored is happening through Him. What is the reference point for deciding?

Jesus offers a single criterion, a universal reference point, that is equally powerful in our own time. He says simply, "What would My Father do?" Measure every teaching, every behavior, every attitude, by the values and attitudes of the Father. Is this the kind of thing the Father would do? Does He love people enough to heal them on the day He designed to spend with them?

Of course, in order for a person to use this as the final guide for his life, he must know to some degree who the Father is. He must know the difference between God as portrayed in Scripture, and the "God" often portrayed by religious leaders, and "folklore theology" drifting around among church people. Jesus knew about this problem. He knew that many of the very people He was talking to didn't understand their Father. But in challenging them to weigh His teaching against the character of God, He was pulling their attention to where it belonged in the first place. And we today need to become skilled in weighing all that we are by our growing understanding of the character of the Father. He is Himself the truth.

SPEAK TO ME!

Be happy in your faith at all times. Never stop praying. 1 Thess. 5:16, 17, Phillips.

I was telephoning the academy boys' dorm. On the second ring, a young man answered. "Speak to me!" he said passionately. Though I had to laugh, the incident made me think.

For several months now we have been looking at Scripture pictures of the Father. We have found Him to be fair, loving, reasonable, and relevant. He is also intensely interesting and thoroughly personable. We've learned that He calls us His friends and wants us to live with Him forever. Has this knowledge led us into communion with Him?

God calls passionately, "Speak to Me!" promising to hear and answer us. Yet we draw back, hindered by prayer habits that do not promote confidence that we are holding fresh, two-way conversation with the great God of the universe.

Our text today encourages us never to stop praying. However, this cannot happen without our first being delighted with our relationship with the Father. You are never delighted in someone you fear. You never easily enter into conversation with someone who is critical of everything you do, who probably doesn't even like you very much and has the power to make you crawl or to set you up as a king. With these leftover Satan-induced perceptions boiling in your heart, speaking to God can never be pleasant, let alone ongoing. Especially when you think you have to pray, or lose eternal life if you don't!

Unavoidably, prayer of this nature is not spontaneous or enjoyable. Using "acceptable" wordage, you kneel, keep your eyes closed, and never forget to end "in Jesus' name." Having learned these standard prayer habits, deviating from them seems terrifying—until you realize how unflavorful it is to God too. Then you start thinking about change.

May I suggest that there are no particularly "acceptable" words that make prayer viable? Just *talk* to God—while driving in your car, reading a book or anything else that makes your mind active. Ask Him questions and expect interested answers. He *will* discourse with you! Maybe right then, by sparking thoughts in your mind. Maybe not until you are singing out of the hymnal and a particular phrase jumps out at you. Often it is in the course of your daily devotional reading. As specific as you are, He will be. And once you discover this wonderful process of friendship with the Almighty, you'll never want to stop!

UNDERSTANDABLY SELFISH

His purpose in dying for all was that men, while still in life, should cease to live for themselves, and should live for him who for their sake died and was raised to life. 2 Cor. 5:15, N.E.B.

Imagine that you have not had anything to drink for more than a day. A hot day, at that. Your mouth feels like it is full of cotton. How would you feel if I were to say to you, "You ought to be ashamed of yourself for being so thirsty"?

Or what if you had been cut off from all of your close friends for some length of time, isolated from all companionship of the heart and meaningful conversation, and I were to say to you, "You really shouldn't be so lonesome; that's very immature"?

You would wonder about my putting a negative judgment on what seems such an understandable feeling of need or desire. In the same vein, sense yourself as being cut off from the great Lover of your soul, distant from the One who created you for the high purpose of enjoying fellowship with Himself. Feel the consequences of being alienated from Him who is the very center of your being, the focus of your living, the source of life itself. How would this affect you? Would it leave you groping in fearful confusion, wondering about your whole reason for living, and the possibility of a future?

What if I were again to accost you: "You really shouldn't be so selfish, so preoccupied with yourself and your problems. You ought to be completely unselfish"?

We need to recognize that what we often think of as selfishness is not the result of a deliberate, perverse choice. Rather, it is the inevitable result of being out of relationship with our Father. Conversely, the problem cannot be solved by a simple choice to become unselfish. If it is caused by being alienated, it can be cured only by being reconciled.

Sometimes we feel guilty for coming to Christ out of selfish motives. But the facts are that we have no choice, because that's exactly how sin has damaged us. We are guilty and long to be forgiven. We are lonesome and long to be loved. We are confused and need to be guided. We are hurting and need to be healed. Jesus' promise is that He can meet every last one of those needs so fully that we need live no longer for ourselves, but for Him.

LIFELONG WATCHCARE

The Lord your God has blessed you in all the work of your hands. He has watched over your journey through this vast desert. These forty years the Lord your God has been with you, and you have not lacked anything. Deut. 2:7, N.I.V.

They had gone into the wilderness forty years ago. The Promised Land seemed a lifetime away. For many it was. Children had grown up and had children of their own. They traveled continually over dusty and barren terrain, yet daily tasks of living had to be performed. Despite the apparent futility of it all, they had kept busy tending flocks.

There had been a lot of complaining, a lot of despair. To the majority it seemed as if God were just biding His time before He disposed of them. In the meantime, He demanded their worship. Many of these people died, but their distorted picture of God lived on. Now it was again time to enter Canaan. Surely the memory of what had happened before was on their minds. So God did what He always does. He tried to calm their fears by telling them the truth about His attitude toward them.

What He said should have convinced them that He never had intended to dispose of them. He had given them tasks that would enable them to experience success, which they considered "blessings." Though they did not perceive it, He had done this to rebuild their damaged self-image. He told them that He'd been with them every step of the way and that they had lacked nothing. In essence, He told them that they mattered very much to Him and that they could trust Him to take excellent care of them.

Are you experiencing a wilderness journey? Does heaven seem more than a lifetime away? Does it sometimes appear futile to go on? Then today's text is especially for you! Though you may not feel it, you matter very much to your heavenly Father. He knows and marks each of your steps; you shall lack nothing that is essential to your well-being. There will always be tasks at hand at which you can succeed. God wants you to know that He sees in you great potential. If you allow Him to, He will so heal your life that you will never again know poverty of spirit.

To know God is to know lifelong watchcare, in a desert wilderness or upon entering Canaan.

BEING ASHAMED OF JESUS

If anyone is ashamed of me and my words in this unfaithful and sinful generation, the Son of Man will be ashamed of him when he comes in the Father's glory with the holy angels around him. Mark 8:38, Phillips.

I will never forget the burning tears that flowed down my red cheeks as my teacher spoke to me. As an impulsive fifth grader I had shoved or otherwise annoyed a classmate, who had yelled at me in retaliation. My teacher probably didn't know that I practically worshiped her. So when she spoke words of discipline she never sensed how deeply they cut. ''I am so ashamed of you,'' she said.

Some of those same feelings want to resurface when I read that, under certain circumstances, Jesus would be ashamed of me. It seems somehow out of character for Him to employ such a crushing approach in an attempt to draw me upward. If He would die for me while I am still a sinner; if He would offer me the robe, ring, and sandals of sonship while I still smelled of the pig farm, then why would He ever turn toward me and say ''I am ashamed of you''?

The feelings of being ashamed often arise when two value systems are in conflict. For example, I have declared myself to be a Christian. But in my heart I am not really sold on Jesus, not fully persuaded of His lifestyle. Among my more worldly friends I will be ashamed to act as a Christian. Among my Christian friends I will be ashamed of my worldly leanings.

Shame vanishes when I am *proud* of Jesus. There is no occasion for it when all my actions are in perfect harmony with my spiritual values and when I am comfortable in His presence with my present actions. And since Jesus is also a thinking, valuing Person, this flows both ways. For Jesus to be ''ashamed'' of me is to acknowledge that we are out of phase with each other—that we are not at peace in each other's presence.

When Jesus comes in the clouds of glory to take people home to live with Him forever, He who always tells the truth must take a position about who is really ready to live at peace with Him. He who felt no personal embarrassment at eating dinner with prostitutes does not have His personal identity at stake. Rather, He has the happiness of the eternally redeemed at stake.

WHEN YOU FEEL ALARMED

In my alarm I said, "I am cut off from your sight!" Yet you heard my cry for mercy when I called to you for help. Ps. 31:22, N.I.V.

Little Suzy had wandered away from Mommy's side at the large department store! Suddenly noticing that Mommy was nowhere in sight, she began running down one aisle after another crying, "Mommy! Mommy, where are you?" Hearing her little daughter in distress, Mother began calling back to her. Full of alarm, Suzy pleaded, "Find me!"—which Mommy did in short order. Soothingly, Mother inquired, "Why were you so afraid?" "You couldn't *see* me!" answered Suzy.

Young children often feel safe as long as we can see them. Their dependency is touching; they believe we will keep them from all harm. If we can't see them, however, they fear we might miss the danger that threatens them. Maybe that's part of the reason some like a light left on in the bedroom at night.

There is a little of the child left in all of us. Becoming a Christian does not instantly remove these latent feelings of vulnerability. We sometimes feel a need for God to reassure us that He's looking. Appreciating our feelings, God comforts us through His Word with texts such as "The eyes of the Lord are on those who fear him, on those whose hope is in his unfailing love" (Ps. 33:18, N.I.V.) and "For the eyes of the Lord range throughout the earth to strengthen those whose hearts are fully committed to him" (2 Chron. 16:9, N.I.V.).

Yet occasionally times come in our experience that are as dark as a moonless night. We become alarmed and, in our despair, wonder if we have done something to make Him turn away. "God has forsaken me!" we cry. We begin to expend all our energies trying to figure out what we did and how to get God to turn back to us. But it is a misconception to think that when we do wrong God quits watching out for us. That's what Job's friends believed. And God plainly said they were wrong (Job 42:7)!

Whatever the reasons for our becoming alarmed—whether we've really done something wrong or just feel that we are "cut off from [God's] sight"—we may trust that God will always hear our cry when we call to Him. As with Suzy's mother, anger is never the issue. He will "find" us and take us into His arms of love.

WHO NEEDS THE LAW?

We also know that law is made not for good men but for lawbreakers and rebels, the ungodly and sinful, the unholy and irreligious. 1 Tim. 1:9, N.I.V.

Do you think you might ever walk into an elementary school classroom and find a large poster in front of the children that reads, "It is a law that you must like ice cream"? Who needs a prominent law to tell someone to do something that already is the natural longing of one's heart?

By the same token, can you imagine large posters attached to the walls of the New Jerusalem warning the inhabitants that stealing gold from each other's mansions is strictly forbidden? Paul's letter to Timothy stirs our minds to remember that in our original condition (as well as in our restored condition) God didn't need to tell His people what to do or how to behave. It was written on our hearts.

But when human hearts went astray from their Lord, and thus from His wise will, it became necessary for Him to warn us, to guide us, even to command us, to live in certain responsible and healthful ways—to protect ourselves and others from pain and destruction. It was no longer natural for our hearts to do the loving and wise thing. Paul clearly identifies just who it is that needs the law: It is people who wouldn't otherwise live by its principles. Not that the law can change one's inner values, but it can point out the need for a Christ-wrought inner change.

Many Christians have believed that the law serves only to pass condemnation on us, and that once Jesus has given us a legal covering of "declared righteousness," the need for the law vanishes. But in reality the law changes its posture, its means of working. It moves from external to internal, from a statement of what one *must* do to a description of what a loving person *will* do when bonded to Jesus through faith. As Paul says: "Are we then undermining the Law by this insistence on faith? Not a bit of it! We put the Law in its proper place" (Rom. 3:31, Phillips).

That proper place, of course, is written in the heart. For the law is an expression of God's character, a restatement of His values. Those who adoringly behold Him will become like Him—in their hearts.

WHAT IS YOUR RESPONSIBILITY?

Be ready at any time to give a quiet and reverent answer to any man who wants a reason for the hope that you have within you. 1 Peter 3:15, Phillips.

Responsibility. The word itself brings a sense of weight to most people, perhaps because of the way it is usually used. "It's your responsibility!" comes the directive—to clean up the garage, to walk the dog, to mow the lawn. "Who's responsible for this?" someone asks tersely. You get sweaty palms, hoping it's not you.

I like words. Many people tend to run through conversation like someone running to catch a bus. Their main object is to "get there," not to notice, as it were, the little flowers peeking through the grass. Take our word, *responsibility*. It legitimately could be spelled response-ability, suggesting the ability to respond properly. Viewed in this light, it suddenly seems like a very desirable quality to possess. I think that is exactly what God has in mind for each of us.

Our Father intends for us to become wonderfully able to respond to every individual with whom we come in contact. Not in order that the record books in heaven will be filled with good marks, but so that the people in our lives can be surrounded continuously by the same healing love that has made us whole.

With this in mind, let's take a fresh look at today's text. We are told, "Be ready at any time to give a quiet and reverent answer to any man who wants a reason for the hope that you have within you." If you have felt uneasy and trapped by these words, if you have felt inadequate and condemned because you don't think you have enough "proof texts" in your mind to meet the requirements of such an encounter, take heart! Your Father's biddings are His enablings. Built right into this scripture is the key to how it is to be accomplished.

Only when our hearts are filled with hope do we have anything to say to anyone. The hope we have is in God—more specifically, in who He is and in the friendship we share with Him. Having such hope gives us not only confidence but the ability and the desire to respond when we are asked about it, because it gives us an opportunity to share the most wonderful experience of our lives: knowing and loving our loving Father!

RESPECTING OUR ENEMIES

But I would remind you that even the archangel Michael when he was contending with the devil in the dispute over the body of Moses did not dare to condemn him with mockery. He simply said, the Lord rebuke you! Jude 9, Phillips.

It would be hard to imagine a stranger match. The liberal Democratic senator Ted Kennedy was speaking in the church of the conservative Republican minister Jerry Falwell. One could have expected fighting words from both directions. Instead, Senator Kennedy said, "When speaking of people who disagree with us, we must still count them as men of integrity."

This sentiment recognizes that our common humanity extends beyond our political persuasions. It means that when we look at another person we do not immediately recognize a foreigner, a smoker, a criminal, a homosexual, or even an enemy. It means that our very first impression is of a fellow human being struggling against the weights of heredity and circumstance just as we are. We see one who both longs for and deserves to be treated as a person of integrity.

Few drives of the human heart are more raging than that of proving ourselves right. We quickly bruise the feelings and images of others in our rush to stand on the top of the heap, fearing nothing more than that others should find us wrong. But when we stand on the tops of our little self-made mountains, we are stunned to recognize that all the people we've injured on the way up really don't care if we're right!

People who disagree with us are seen as threatening; rather than reexamine our own positions or simply state our position in contrast to another, we find a need to view our opponents as enemies. Rather than face our insecurities, we act as though another has chosen to be stubborn, deceived, or fraudulent.

I know of no person who has set out to be a failure. I do know a lot of people who are hurting, and I wonder why I have so often hurt them further in the name of righteousness. There is still a major gap between the way we so often treat our enemies and the way God treats His. One difference, of course, is that God doesn't need to trounce His opponents in order to prove that He is right. In fact, were He to do so, that very spirit of retaliation and vengeance would be evidence of His weakness, His error. It would prove Him wrong.

But God has great confidence in the winsome power of truth. Given the right setting, truth will shine. But disrespect toward another will always cloud that setting, making it harder for people to discern truth.

THE END OF ALL HURT

They shall not hurt or destroy in all my holy mountain, says the Lord. Isa. 65:25, N.E.B.

Christians look forward to the new earth for a number of reasons. For one thing, all that hurts us will be no more. Even the animals will no longer experience discord. "The wolf and the lamb shall feed together and the lion shall eat straw like cattle" (Isa. 65:25, N.E.B.). The second half of this text (referring not just to animals, but to all the inhabitants) reads, "They shall not hurt or destroy in all my holy mountain, says the Lord."

What brings this state of harmony into existence? Will the second coming of Christ radically alter the character qualities of those He comes to redeem? Or will those who are to inhabit the new earth already have reached the place where they no longer are hurtful to one another? Let's take a look at Hebrews 8:10, 11: "For the covenant I will make with the house of Israel after those days, says the Lord, is this: I will set my laws in their understanding and write them on their hearts; and I will be their God, and they shall be my people. And they shall not teach one another, saying to brother and fellow-citizen, 'Know the Lord!' For all of them, high and low, shall know me" (N.E.B.).

It is our privilege to begin to know God *now*. As we come to know Him as our best Friend we shall see that His law is the transcript of His character. His ways shall become a very part of us, because we are so enthralled with the quality of life that is in Him. We shall no longer feel the need to take care of ourselves—the root cause of our hurting others—because we shall no longer experience any emotional deficits. Who He is shall so satisfy our hearts, so excite our intelligence, so motivate our actions, that we shall have no more misgivings about Him or about ourselves.

Freed from self-concerns, we shall be able to focus fully upon others. We'll listen to what they have to say without interrupting to make sure what *we* think is understood. We'll make sure they feel adequate without ourselves needing to grasp for our self-assurance. All this is ours to know and become—before there is a new earth. It is, as Jesus said, "because the kingdom of God is within you" (Luke 17:21, N.I.V.).

WHAT KIND OF POWER?

For I am not ashamed of the Gospel. It is the saving power of God for everyone who has faith. Rom. 1:16, N.E.B.

I could hear him coming even before his car rounded the corner into my driveway. It was the muffled, throaty roar of a highly tuned engine, impatient with slow travel. But the sleek, brilliant red car was enough to make any man's blood pressure rise. It was a flawless De Tomaso Pantera Stage 3, one of the most exotic performance cars on the road today. When he handed me the keys and said, "Take it for a spin," my knees went weak.

I topped sixty miles per hour before I shifted out of second gear. It had the kind of power you feel shoving against your lower back. In my timidness I slacked my speed quickly, but he assured me I had come nowhere near sampling its upper limits. And all that power was available simply by pressing down the toes of my right foot!

Many times we Christians long for a power in our daily living that is just as tangible, just as muscular, and just as quickly available as that huge V-8 engine. We wish for a divinely magical shove in the lower back that would keep us away from a second helping of dessert. We'd like a strong "hand" placed firmly over our mouths when we are angry or over our eyes when we are lustful. We ache for something that would kick us out of our chairs to shut off the TV. And then we sometimes fault God for not providing just that kind of power when we needed it.

But salvation, at all its levels, is not a product of physical power. It is not a sanctified shove toward righteousness. It does not "make" us do something we don't want to do or have desires that we have not consciously chosen to relish and nurture. God works through the power of truth that appeals to the intellect and the loyalties. We are on Christ's side because we have seen the beauty of who He is, and we have chosen Him as Lord. We embrace His lifestyle because we have found it to be sensibly appealing. We love His Word because it appeals to the highest levels of our beings. We open our hearts to His Spirit because, as a gentleman, He respects our freedom. There is nothing of coercion in the kingdom of Christ, not even toward the right!

THE WHOLE DUTY OF MAN

Now all has been heard; here is the conclusion of the matter: Fear God and keep his commandments, for this is the whole duty of man. Eccl. 12:13, N.I.V.

You have been hired to be the executive director of a newly formed company. You know you are going to be paid a terrific salary, that your employee benefits are very adequate, and that your office is comfortably and stylishly furnished. What else could you possibly need to know? Your duties, of course!

We have been called to work for the Master. We know that our reward is eternal life and that all the resources of heaven are at hand to help us. What else do we need to know? What duties are required of us? Today's text makes it very plain: "Fear God and keep his commandments, for this is the whole duty of man."

It reminds me of another scripture found in Revelation 14:6, 7: "Then I saw another angel flying in midair, and he had the eternal gospel to proclaim to those who live on the earth—to every nation, tribe, language and people. He said in a loud voice, 'Fear God and give him glory, because the hour of his judgment has come. Worship him who made the heavens, the earth, the sea and the springs of water' " (N.I.V.). Verse 12 describes those who accept this message as "those who keep the commandments of God and the faith of Jesus" (R.S.V.). It appears that the whole duty of man involves nothing less than appropriating the eternal gospel to our lives.

Jesus was asked, "What must we do to do the works God requires?" He answered, "The work of God is this: to believe in the one he has sent" (John 6:28, 29, N.I.V.). And so it all begins to fit together. To fear God is to respect and reverence Him—to believe Him! But that cannot happen unless you know Him. The way to begin to know Him is to learn His ways and to follow His guidelines. And these guidelines were amplified in the person and life of His Son. By looking to Jesus, you will see how reasonable and trustworthy God the Father is. You will be able to speak to others accurately about who He is, which glorifies Him.

In a nutshell, our duty is to come to know and enjoy our wonderful Father! Now, isn't that good news?

WAS JESUS LIKE ME?

It was imperative that he should be made like his brothers in every respect, if he were to become a High Priest both compassionate and faithful in the things of God, and at the same time able to make atonement for the sins of the people. Heb. 2:17, Phillips.

You are asked if you believe that Jesus is really like us. That is, did He have the fallen nature of all humanity, that of Adam after the Fall? Or was Jesus protected from these effects of sin? Was He, as the second Adam, like Adam was before the Fall?

Now, before you vote, you should consider the following. If you say that Jesus was like Adam was after the Fall, that He really did identify with humanity, then you are faced with a problem. Doesn't having a sinful nature imply that He found sin to be appealing (though we all agree that He didn't give in to those urges)? And it means for us that the best victory we can hope for in this life is an ongoing struggle against sinful desires.

But if you vote for Jesus being like Adam was before the Fall, you haven't escaped all the problems, either. It suggests that, though He was the spotless Lamb, He really isn't that relevant to us in our struggles against sin. He wasn't burdened with this inherited anchor of a sinful nature as we are. To be holy in His character, then, was vastly easier for Him. The best we can hope for is to be covered with God's declaration of legal righteousness.

There is, however, a third option. As we have affirmed many times, the problem of sin isn't located in physiology or inheritance. It has to do with one's relationship to God! Jesus maintained that same loyal, unbroken relationship with His Father that Adam had before the Fall. As regards the real sin problem, Jesus was like Adam was before the Fall—perfect and sinless.

At the same time, we can acknowledge that His physical and emotional being bore greater consequences from the sinful choices of others than did Adam's. Thus He could indeed be made like His brethren in every way, yet without sin (Heb. 4:15), because He never broke the relationship!

The hope for each one of us is that, while still burdened with a sin-damaged humanity, we can have the same faith relationship with the Father that Jesus had.

ONWARD, CHRISTIAN SOLDIERS!

Our battle is to break down every deceptive argument and every imposing defence that men erect against the true knowledge of God. We fight to capture every thought until it acknowledges the authority of Christ. 2 Cor. 10:5, Phillips.

I cringe whenever I hear the newscasters from Belfast or Beirut identifying the various warring factions as ''Christians,'' ''Protestants,'' and ''Catholics.'' I wonder if the average listener simply assumes that Christians are in favor of killing fellow human beings as a means of settling differences. Through the ages, however, Christians often have used military means for advancing supposedly spiritual causes. It's not surprising that people would not be jarred to hear ''The Christian militia today set off a car bomb, killing twenty-five civilians in a Beirut suburb.''

Much of the imagery we use in our hymns and in our sermons, however, is based on military metaphors. We have sung for decades ''Onward, Christian soldiers! Marching as to war.'' While it is definitely true that we are in a battle against principalities and powers, against spiritual wickedness in high places, it is just as true that the weapons of our warfare have nothing to do with compulsion. And the victories gained never leave a reluctantly conquered foe. As Paul said, ''Each one must do as he has made up his mind, not reluctantly or under compulsion'' (2 Cor. 9:7, R.S.V.).

Paul is one who had learned the awesome, life-changing power of truth—truth that brings one the knowledge of God as He really is. He used this weapon throughout his ministry and was constantly gratified by its power to bring about the desired changes in people's lives. We never would have heard Paul simply commanding people to submit to his authority or to bow to his position of power over them.

Christians who resort to any form of force or coercion when seeking changes in their fellow humans simply have not tasted the immense power available to them through the presentation of truth. Parents who seek simply to control their children, or husbands who demand unthinking submission of their wives are revealing how little they know about God's methods for accomplishing change in another's life. They must reflect God's goal of having a people in whose hearts the principles of His law have been written.

When Jesus leads His redeemed through the gates of the New Jerusalem there will be no chains, no forced smiles. They will be gladly, freely, following the Master whom they know and love.

GREAT IS THY FAITHFULNESS

The steadfast love of the Lord never ceases, his mercies never come to an end; they are new every morning; great is thy faithfulness. Lam. 3:22, 23, R.S.V.

A husband and wife whose marriage had gone through some turbulent years were commenting on what had helped to hold them together. "We were never both down at the same time," he said. "When she was discouraged, I was optimistic; when I was troubled, she was steady. I'm afraid of what would have happened had we both been alienated at the same time."

A relationship as close as marriage, needing much energy and creativity to keep it vital, will quickly sour if both parties lose their commitment at the same time. In Jeremiah's bitter-sweet meditation, Lamentations, he freely admits that his people have wandered from their commitment to their Lord. They have been unfaithful, restless, even rebellious. Were their relationship with God to have been totally dependent upon *their* commitment, it surely would have died.

Knowing as he did that Israel's faith relationship with her Maker was absolutely necessary to her very existence, as well as to her people's eternal life, Jeremiah had cause to rejoice over God's faithfulness. How glad he was that they were not both down at the same time. In fact, Jeremiah was celebrating the good news that God never is down on His people, ready to annul the relationship for nonperformance. Every morning presents a new discovery of His mercies. He is the faithful one, regardless of our lack of loyalty.

Oh, how encouragingly this should speak to our hearts. We who often treat our friendship with God with studied neglect, who catch ourselves after the fact having ignored Him for lesser attractions, and who are more aware of having hurt Him than of having brought Him delight—how glad we should be that He is the faithful one!

Some have been concerned that a God who never says "I quit!" when His people keep walking away might lead them to be indulgent and presumptuous—to keep on sinning and wandering, always counting on God to "be there" when they get back. But God wants them to see that it is the wandering itself, not His possible rejection of them, that is so damaging. Disloyalty to God and His ways has its own built-in hurts; God doesn't need to add to them by His being unfaithful to us. Indeed, His faithfulness is intended to heal that hurting!

LOOKING BEYOND THE "GOODIES"

Though the fig tree do not blossom, nor fruit be on the vines, the produce of the olive fail and the fields yield no food, the flock be cut off from the fold and there be no herd in the stalls, yet I will rejoice in the Lord, I will joy in the God of my salvation. Hab. 3:17, 18, R.S.V.

A number of popular media preachers today are offering a quickly accepted brand of religion. They are boldly asserting that God's plan for every one of His children is that he be wealthy. Not just comfortable, but outright rich! Those who are not rich, they suggest, must not be following the formula earnestly enough. Prosperity, to them, is not only a sign of God's favor; it becomes reason enough in itself to serve God.

Though this kind of blatant materialism seems crass in its most overdrawn form, we have to admit to finding it in lesser forms on other occasions. A hailstorm flattens our crops, and we say, "Lord! Why me? What have I done to deserve this?" A loved one dies an untimely death, and we protest, "But, Lord, he was a good man!" We so readily see God as a wealthy dispenser of material and physical blessings to all who serve Him. And when we serve Him, yet are not blessed, we feel cheated.

Habakkuk protested directly to God, complaining that Israel hadn't been all that bad as to deserve the Chaldean invasion that God had foretold. Even as a prophet, he still wasn't immune from the reward-punishment scheme so commonly held by his people. To him, something was wrong with God's plan not to bless the nation. So he complained. (See chapter 1.)

The Lord's answer to Him was surprising. He did not say that a righteous person lives by, or even for, His blessings. Rather, "the righteous shall live by his faith" (Hab. 2:4, R.S.V.). The truly righteous person is one who is attached to Him, not to the blessings He can bestow. He trusts God because of who He is, not because of the way God hands out that which man would call blessings.

When Habakkuk saw this larger picture, one that looks beyond the "goodies" we humans crave for our security, his own faith grew. His closing testimony was that, regardless of what happened to his personal "creature comforts," his confidence in God would remain firm. He would rejoice, not in the Lord's blessings, but "in the *Lord*" (chap. 3:18).

PROCLAIMING LIBERTY

The Spirit of the Lord is upon me, because he has anointed me. . . . He has sent me to set at liberty those who are oppressed. Luke 4:18, R.S.V.

The first time I read this verse, I had just completed reading a history of the American Civil War—the war to end slavery in the United States. It was thrilling to recall that so many people had given their lives, at least in some degree, to set others free. It was easy, then, to connect the spirit of this verse with the acts of Christians to end physical slavery. And thus I read it for many years.

Not until recently did I begin to discover how many different types of oppression the enemy has invented with which to crush the human race. By design as well as by neglect, we have become skilled at foisting economic, racial, sexual, and religious oppression upon those too weak to fight back. Perhaps more often we have practiced emotional oppression upon each other, even within the family and the church.

When we discover that it is the character of our Saviour to "set at liberty those who are oppressed," we are challenged to do more than say, "I'm glad they don't practice slavery here anymore." Those who would represent Him aright must become alert to every occasion when the personhood of another is being stifled. And they must hurt with him, even as Jesus does.

Walk onto a playground and listen to the children as they play. Notice how often they lash out with cutting "put downs" of their peers. Observe how parents speak to their children when they are upset, and ponder what it is doing to the self-esteem of those young human beings. Remember the conversations in a college dormitory and recall how easy it was to cut down those not present to defend their uniqueness.

When we sense how readily we dismiss these oppressive acts as simply normal human life, we wonder if the liberating work of Christ should not begin by setting our own hearts free from the spirit of pettiness and calloused indifference. How we need to pray for divine sensitivity to any word that cuts or belittles another! Rather than being so often caught up in major doctrinal issues, we need to sense that Jesus will more potently be revealed to others by subtle personal interplay. To fail to be sensitive to words or attitudes that oppress others is to misrepresent Him who came to liberate the oppressed.

LOOKING FOR TROUBLE!

"For the eyes of the Lord range throughout the earth to strengthen those whose hearts are fully committed to him." 2 Chron. 16:9, N.I.V.

He was out on the streets at night looking for trouble. At the least provocation he started a fight. Even his friends were wary of him, not knowing what might set him off. They constantly tried to appease him by praising him and telling him how much they liked him. In reality, they were terrified of him and would have avoided him if they hadn't needed his protection against other bullies.

As you read the above description, did you find even a faint similarity to your walk with God? Do you see Him, as it were, walking the streets both day and night, looking for trouble? And when He finds it, do you see Him chastising and belittling those involved into a fearful submission? Do you praise God, hoping to appease Him? Do you really like God?—or do you fear Him and wish you could avoid Him? If only you didn't need His protection from Satan!

Let's talk about it! Yes, God is out "looking for trouble"! But His reasons are far different than we might have previously thought. Our text for today says, "For the eyes of the Lord range throughout the earth to strengthen those whose hearts are fully committed to him." His purpose is to heal, to strengthen and uplift, even when the trouble He finds is *in* you more than in the circumstances around you. Being fully committed to God does not mean that we no longer are prone to inner trouble. It means that we are totally committed to finding answers to all the inner conflicts we face as damaged human beings. And we know that He *is* the answer!

We need never be fearful of having trouble in our outward lives or in our very souls. To have really serious questions about church doctrines does not have to mean that we are ready to throw away our commitment to God. To discover an awful weakness in ourselves does not have to equal a lack of dedication to Christ. We do not need to experience a hot feeling in the pit of our stomachs as we realize that God sees the truth about us. We can know that He's ready to strengthen us—to deal directly with the issues at hand so that we can get on with life. That's just how He is!

WHAT IS THE ALTERNATIVE?

But if serving the Lord seems undesirable to you, then choose for yourselves this day whom you will serve, whether the gods your forefathers served beyond the River, or the gods of the Amorites, in whose land you are living. But as for me and my household, we will serve the Lord. Joshua 24:15, N.I.V.

Often, when faced with hard decisions, it is useful simply to ask, "What is the alternative?" Your young son doesn't want to wash the dishes; the alternative is that he either eats off dirty dishes at the next meal or he hands the chore off to someone else. Faced with those unappealing options, he just may wash them. You don't feel like paying your income taxes—until you face the alternative. It can be very sobering.

Many end up turning their backs on God almost by default; they just don't look straight at the options. Joshua was using a very pointed technique when he asked the people to consider seriously whether they had a better alternative than to serve the Lord.

When we are asked to make a public choice, it is assumed that we can defend the choice with good reasons. In favor of his choice, Joshua had just reviewed his evidence: "You know in your hearts and souls, all of you, that not one thing has failed of all the good things which the Lord your God promised concerning you; all have come to pass for you, not one of them has failed" (Joshua 23:14, R.S.V.). In the face of such evidence, one would have to be utterly foolish to turn away from such a God.

The people of Israel had the same evidence that Joshua had. Yet, while Joshua was confident, they were hesitating. We may not have to search beyond our own hearts to find the reason why. While the Egyptian or Amorite deities had not taken better care of them than God had, to be honest, these pagan gods did promise a bit more immediate fun and sensual indulgence, both in their worship and in their daily practices. And that, for many, tended to tilt the final vote.

It is hard for people who want to regard themselves as thoughtful to stand up and say, "I am trading long-range joy and eternal life for present pleasure trinkets." It is just too crassly stupid. That's why so many decisions against God have to be hidden behind drugged stupors, intemperate hours, or practiced illogic.

A LAW OF THE MIND

Their idols are silver and gold, made by the hands of men. They have mouths, but cannot speak, eyes, but they cannot see. . . . Those who make them will be like them. Ps. 115:4-8, N.I.V.

Recent government-sponsored research is tending to verify that the more than eighteen thousand hours of television viewing that the average youth does before he graduates from high school really is having an impact upon his value system. Particularly, certain temperament types who behold a heavy fare of tele-violence are less shocked to see it in real life and are more prone to enter into it themselves.

This research confirms a principle expressed in a positive manner some nineteen hundred years ago by the apostle Paul. By beholding Christ, he said, we become transformed into His likeness. (See 2 Cor. 3:18.) That is, the mind gradually embraces the values, attitudes, even the expressions, of that which one chooses to behold. It becomes like that which one is accustomed to love or reverence. This powerful law of the mind can readily be used to advantage by those who long to be like Jesus. It is the strongest argument in favor of regular time spent in private devotions, in meditation upon the life and teachings of Jesus.

But it is a law of the mind that still works with equal force when one shifts attention away from Christ and toward the idols of this world. David spoke of the mindless, unresponsive, inert qualities of idols his people were worshiping; then he warned them with certainty that they would soon become just like those idols. They would become incapable of responding to important moral-choice situations with decisiveness and direction. They would, though alive, become ineffective in living.

Satan is no fool. He understands this principle and uses it constantly to his advantage. He dresses up the value system of his kingdom in the most dramatic, attention-grabbing, emotion-jolting form that our high-powered media can transmit. He makes it continuously available, even while we are out walking. He portrays it as socially appealing, ''fun to do with our friends.'' Then he builds a whole subculture around the worship of the media heroes that—like a black hole—draws everything into it.

Since our every waking moment is spent in some type of beholding, and thus in becoming, how carefully we must choose. The kind of persons we become will determine not only our effectiveness here but our eternal destiny as well.

October 13

READINESS TO LEARN

And if they are ashamed of all they have done, make known to them the design of the temple. . . . Write these down . . . so that they may be faithful to its design and follow all its regulations. Eze. 43:10, 11, N.I.V.

Geometry teachers, I believe, have just about the hardest job in the whole teaching profession. Their task is to present a textbook full of excellent answers to young people who simply don't appreciate the questions. And the more complex the answer, the more convinced the ninth-graders are that there just isn't a question around that requires such an answer.

But teachers have come to know that true education is not the forcing of knowledge upon an unready mind. They spend a good deal of time helping a student recognize his need for certain information; then they present it to him.

Our heavenly Father, the Master Teacher, has packed enough answers into His sanctuary to save the whole human race. It portrays the cross of Christ, the ministry of the Holy Spirit, the good news of final judgment, and the path to personal salvation and to holiness of life, just to name a few. It is a marvelous teaching device, a life-size object lesson, an acted parable of the redemption plan.

But as with the geometry class, few people care about the answers because they haven't yet discovered the questions. The plan of salvation is exciting to only those who know that they are lost. The way in which the sanctuary reveals how God will end the cosmic conflict is thrilling to only those who know that the sin problem is that big.

God instructed Ezekiel to explain the whole plan of salvation as revealed in the sanctuary to only those who had first come face-to-face with their own desperately sinful condition. Only then would they appreciate the answers. It should not surprise us, then, to find God working to show us our true condition, even though that is a painful thing for us to discover. The embarrassment of our broken promises, the shame of our unholy acts, the alienation of our deceptive ways, can be the very readiness we urgently need in order to appreciate God's totally adequate answers.

Satan is also interested in showing us the corruption of our hearts. But his goal is to crush us, not to enlighten us. He hates the sanctuary, and he has always tried to destroy it (see Dan. 8:11, 12) because of the powerful truths it reveals to ashamed sinners.

MUTUAL PRIDE

This third I will bring into the fire; I will refine them like silver and test them like gold. They will call on my name and I will answer them; I will say, "They are my people," and they will say, "The Lord is our God." Zech. 13:9, N.I.V.

Many Christians have puzzled over God's plan to allow His sealed remnant to go through a period of serious trial before He rescues them from this dying planet. (See Dan. 12:1, 2; Rev. 7:13, 14.) But ask a man who is buying gold ingots if he is glad that the refiners have purified the gold until it can be certified 99.999 percent pure. For God is about to bring home a people that He can "certify" as safe to save, totally cleansed from any lingering attachments to Satan's deceptions and values.

The Bible often uses the imagery of "a third" to describe God's remnant—that minority who remain loyal to His purposes. When Zechariah portrays that time when God will purify His own, there is a note of special pride in the passage. God puts into the purifying fires only those whom He knows can handle the heat. When He permits them to experience great trial, it is actually a statement of confidence in His people. It's as though God is calling all His friends from around the universe to look over the balconies of heaven and to watch how His people respond when every earthly means of support has been stripped away.

But there is a two-way message in this verse. God is saying, "Look at them! Don't you agree that we can be proud of them? If they remain loyal under these most trying circumstances, can't we trust them throughout eternity? I'll claim them; they are *My* people!" At the same time, God's people—though surrounded with every manner of threatening circumstances—are looking above it all. They are looking up and saying, "The Lord, He is *our* God. We are done with every lesser object of trust, every inducement to doubt, every trace of rebellion."

What could be finer! Mutual trust, mutual pride, mutual adoration. This is a relationship that will last. For all who wish to prepare themselves for the trials of the last days, this is the key: Become so deeply acquainted even now with your Father that in every trial you can look to Him with utter confidence. After all, that's exactly how He wants to look at you!

GOD'S "PLAN A"

Loyalty is my desire, not sacrifice, not whole-offerings but the knowledge of God. Hosea 6:6, N.E.B.

One feature of modern high-level management training is teaching executives to have backup plans. While planning and hoping for success in every new product line, every sales or service campaign, it is still wise to have contingency plans. If the first goals are not reached, the whole plan should not be scrubbed. The wise manager has a plan for redeeming as much as he can from the efforts invested. He knows that "Plan B" may not be as ideal as "Plan A," but it's far better than having no plan at all.

God is a wise manager. Creating this new and unique order of beings on this planet was quite an adventure. His "Plan A" was that we should enjoy unbroken, ever-growing friendship with Him, for our mutual joy. But giving us as He did that unpredictable capacity of free choice, from the foundations of eternity, He designed a "Plan B." Should His people ever break the life-sustaining relationship with Him, He designed that He Himself (in the person of the Son) should bear the ugly death of separation.

It was not long before our first parents and all their children were very much in need of "Plan B." As a four-thousand-year pledge that He Himself would die in our place, Jesus provided the symbol of the sacrificial lamb. Every sinner, convinced of his destiny of eternal death, could bring a lamb to the altar as an expression of his hope in the Lamb of God as an atonement for his sins.

It was also not very long before God's people began to prefer "Plan B" to "Plan A." There seemed to be something so very convenient about it. They could continue to live with some degree of carelessness, sometimes even committing overt sin. But the solution (they thought) was simple: Let the lamb bear the problem. Furthermore, bringing lambs to the Temple seemed easier than intimate fellowship with their God. They came to think of "Plan B" as God's ideal.

Hosea's plea did not diminish the sacrificial lamb. Indeed, who could live without it? But he reminded them (and us) that God's "Plan A" is not that we should settle into an endless cycle of sinning and repenting, sinning and repenting. Our highest calling is to enter even now into unchanging loyalty to Him. For that, precisely, is God's "Plan A."

TO BRING US HOPE!

But now in Christ Jesus you who once were far away have been brought near through the blood of Christ. Eph. 2:13, N.I.V.

His family was in East Berlin. Though he had managed to escape several years earlier, he had not been successful in his attempts to get his wife and children out. Each year his hopes diminished until, at last, he found himself with no hope left. And so he lived, lonely and despondent, in New York City for the rest of his life.

A great many people in this world live out their lives in a state of hopelessness. Things just never seem to turn out; plans are aborted, children turn against parents, the stock market fails. Without the knowledge of God, they have nothing to look forward to either in this life or in the life to come.

God's heart goes out to such people! In Ephesians 2:12, 13, we read, "Remember that at that time you were separate from Christ, excluded from citizenship in Israel and foreigners to the covenants of the promise, without hope and without God in the world. But now in Christ Jesus you who once were far away have been brought near through the blood of Christ" (N.I.V.). Let's examine this text carefully, so as not to miss the beauty of what Paul is saying.

To know God generates hope. You begin to realize that when God made covenant promises to Israel, it was a means of giving Himself to them. The tabernacle service was initiated so that God could "dwell among" men. The coming Messiah was referred to as Immanuel, which meant "God with us." And Christ's death demonstrated the extent to which God would go to secure us forever as His friends. This knowledge is meant to cause our hearts to raise up within us! There is more to life than heartache and shattered dreams. There is God with us.

He has drawn us near to Himself in the person of His Son. He walked lonely roads, bedded down among men who struggled with poverty, spoke to outcasts. He deliberately chose to have no home of His own, for He was making His home with us. The very last words that came from the Saviour's lips were " 'Remember, I am with you always, even to the end of the world' " (Matt. 28:20, Phillips).

"May the God of hope fill you with all joy and peace as you trust in him" (Rom. 15:13, N.I.V.).

DOES GOD CRY?

**"Where have you put him?" he asked. "Lord, come and see,"
they replied, and at this Jesus himself wept. John 11:34, 35, Phillips.**

On those few occasions when artists have attempted a portrait of God the Father, they seem to have been struck with those sterner qualities of justice and power that describe the Almighty. And we who, as children, formed our first impressions of God from the pictures in our books, had trouble feeling close to Him in our tender moments. We didn't see Him as tender. We were comforted that at least Jesus had that capacity.

I, for one, am glad that when Jesus said He had come to show us the Father, He had clearer perceptions of His Father than most current artists. And I watch carefully the subtleties of Jesus' manner and style, grasping every shade and shape to add to my refining understanding of God. I have come to believe that had Jesus remained in heaven and had the Father come to earth to live and to die among men, the New Testament history we have would not be changed one bit.

And so I was warmed to read that when His close friend Lazarus died and Jesus was mingling among sorrowing people, His tears flowed with theirs. I am somehow both comforted and touched to realize that, should I be lost, my Father would weep for me. A Spirit-placed tug in my heart goes beyond mere lists of qualities about God that my intellect can appreciate. I am living in the presence of a whole Person, with sensitivities of the heart that answer to those which He Himself placed in my own heart. If He can weep with sadness, then can His eyes not also brim over with joy when His children come home?

We are not talking about a weak, sentimental God—the kind some lightweight gospel music tries to glorify, who fawns over His children with maudlin gushiness. Rather He combines great strength with true kindness. He shows me that I can be a manly Christian, yet still feel the full range of proper human emotion. He presents a Christianity that affirms fully developed personalities, completely alive to others, able to "rejoice with those who rejoice, [and] weep with those who weep" (Rom. 12:15, R.S.V.). Though, in the new earth He will wipe away the tears of sadness, I suspect we shall more than once weep together for sheer joy.

THE CENTER OF THE UNIVERSE

Behold, the dwelling of God is with men. Rev. 21:3, R.S.V.

"Imagine that the thickness of this page represents the distance from earth to sun (93 million miles, or about eight light-minutes). Then the distance to the nearest star (4⅓ light-years) is a 71-foot-high sheaf of paper. And the diameter of our own galaxy (100,000 light-years) is a 310-mile stack, while the edge of the known universe is not reached until the pile of paper is 31 million miles high—a third of the way to the sun!"—*National Geographic,* May, 1974, p. 592.

Our eyes can read these words; our lips may even repeat them to someone else. But when it comes to fully comprehending such enormous distances, such vast measurements of matter and emptiness, our minds go numb. It is so far beyond us as to make us feel almost silly, standing on this microscopically small planet, looking outward to a virtually endless universe.

Yet one truth jumps out beyond even these stunning measurements of space. And that is that the God who created it all has taken an almost consuming interest in this planet. What is more, this preoccupation with earthlings is not warranted because of any thrilling virtue on our part. Indeed, it appears that it is our very foolishness, our self-chosen helplessness, that has drawn out His attention the most. To ask "Why?" is to phrase in one word a question that will take an eternity to answer, for such is the measurement of the love that motivates it.

But that is not all. This is no temporary interest in this planet, to be "set back into perspective" once all our problems have been solved. God's attention will not simply pass on to more pressing and worthy matters once redemption has been accomplished for mankind. The promise of Scripture, as recorded in today's text, is that God is going to relocate headquarters! *He* is going to move in with *us!* The dwelling of God shall be with men.

But the amazement still doesn't stop, for there is every indication that this anticipated move on God's part is something that will bring Him great personal delight. In it is not one hint of condescension, not a trace of reluctantly fulfilled duty. When Jesus became a man, that was a down payment, an acted pledge, of God's joyful intention to spend eternity with this human race. Don't you just love our Father!

WHAT MAKES JESUS SORROWFUL?

Anguish and dismay came over him, and he said to them, "My heart is ready to break with grief." Matt. 26:37, 38, N.E.B.

We urgently need to see, with spiritual eyesight, just what was bringing such great anguish upon our Lord during the final hours of His life. For it will unfold to us some exceedingly rich understandings of the meaning of the cross.

Certainly He was dismayed by the betrayal of His friends; as a feeling, social being, He felt the loss of their presence. Yet many people through the ages have been abandoned by their friends at crucial moments; but this seldom has led to near-fatal anguish. Obviously He was not looking forward to the pain and suffering of the cross. No feeling person would. Yet many condemned prisoners have faced their final moments with stoic bravery. There must have been something deeper.

It was there in the garden, just before His capture, that Jesus began to bear the sins of the world. There, in the crucible of the experienced anguish itself, Jesus had to make the decision to continue with the plan of redemption. The events that followed—the mockery of a trial, the humiliation, the painful death—were but the carrying out of the decision that He made in Gethsemane.

But in what specific way was Jesus bearing our sins that dark night? What was the cause of such anguish that, had the angel not strengthened Him, would have snuffed out His life even before the cross? The evidence is this: Jesus began during this hour to experience what all unredeemed sinners will experience—the breaking up of His relationship with the Father. For this, precisely, is the consequence of sin. This is what Jesus has experienced in our place. This is how He was the sin-bearer for all mankind.

In a very real sense, it was far more dreadful for Jesus to experience separation from His Father than for any other human, because Jesus always had enjoyed a richly close fellowship with Him. We, by contrast, usually experience such a sparse and threadbare relationship with Him that we hardly feel the difference when it dies completely.

What a wonderful statement of spiritual maturity it would be if we had such a close relationship with God that any distance, any hint of separation, would bring us immediate anguish. Of all the things that could cause us sorrow, what could be more beneficial?

EAGER FOR JUDGMENT

I will bear the indignation of the Lord because I have sinned against him, until he pleads my cause and executes judgment for me. He will bring me forth to the light; I shall behold his deliverance. Micah 7:9, R.S.V.

The young man was pacing the floor in front of the principal's office. His palms were sweaty, his eyes cast downward. He knew he was guilty, and the principal was about to deal with him. Fearfully he entered the room. But perhaps in contrast to many such familiar scenes, when an hour had passed and the door opened again, student and principal stepped out with arms around each other. Both were smiling. Yes, the student had lost some of his privileges. But more than that, the principal had helped him overcome the weakness that had gotten him into trouble in the first place. And they were friends.

The prophet Micah viewed God in much the same light. He knew that he had sinned and that his sin was against God rather than against some abstract legal code. What gave him the courage to be honest about his sins, however, was his confidence in how God would deal with him. Though he knew that there would be consequences (since God deals in a world of moral realities), he knew also that God would deal redemptively with him.

Micah actually looked forward to the time when God would plead his cause, executing judgment *for* him. He knew that in the final reckoning God would be on his side, working in his favor. Judgment is that time when all the universe sees things as they really are; if Micah's loyalties really were with his God, then why should he fear? He had declared his position: "But as for me, I will look to the Lord, I will wait for the God of my salvation; my God will hear me" (Micah 7:7, R.S.V.).

Too often the judgment has been presented as an awesome event, to be dreaded by all who fear the Judge. It is assumed that His intent is to screen out as many applicants for the kingdom as He possibly can, using a strict measurement of behavior as the criterion. On that basis, who can stand?

But God is interested in one central issue in the judgment: on whose side have our loyalties been placed? If we are *for* Him (as evidenced by our lives), then He has every right to be *for* us. We fully trust our Deliverer.

WHAT MADE GIDEON GREAT?

And the angel of the Lord appeared to him and said to him, "The Lord is with you, you mighty man of valor." Judges 6:12, R.S.V.

Far be it from me to disagree with an angel, but I'll have to make an honest confession. Even though the angel labeled Gideon as a mighty man of valor, I've sometimes suspected him of being rather weak in the faith. After all, what would you do if an angel were to come to you for a personal conversation, make your meal suddenly catch fire while it sat on a rock, then disappear miraculously from sight? Would you question the message he brought to you? On top of that, would you insist on a wet fleece on the dry ground, and then a dry fleece on the wet ground, before you believed God meant what He said?

Missing the possibility that Gideon may have simply been fearful of presumption, I've thought, *I would have said, Yes, sir! to the angel's first instructions.* Admittedly, Gideon was being asked to go on a rather dangerous mission, one that could endanger other lives as well.

Perhaps it could be said that, given the general spiritual poverty of the nation at the time, Gideon—with all his cautious faith—was the very best whom God could find. It should be noted also that Gideon did, after all, get the job done. And it is comforting to know that God can do heroic things even with people as careful as Gideon.

Which brings us to a key insight that goes far beyond the book of Judges: God is the only real hero in the Bible. The outstanding personality in this well-known story isn't Gideon, but a patient God who was able to enable Gideon to do mighty deeds of valor. The hero is a compassionate Father who understood Gideon's fears and humble self-opinion, and who—rather than chastising him for his seeking of reassurance—went ahead and gave him both a wet fleece and a dry fleece.

In the end, of course, I revise my opinion of Gideon, for he himself grasped this larger picture. He knew who the true Hero was. And when the people came rushing to him, begging him to become their leader, his response was firm: "I will not rule over you, and my son will not rule over you; the Lord will rule over you" (Judges 8:23, R.S.V.). That attitude is, in the end, what made Gideon a mighty man of valor.

TOO GOOD TO BE TRUE

"I knew that you are a gracious and compassionate God, slow to anger and abounding in love, a God who relents from sending calamity." Jonah 4:2, N.I.V.

Most children who attend Sunday school hear about Jonah. Most of the time, it's the whale that gets top billing. Adults wonder if such a thing could really happen. Maybe that's where the expression "It sounds a little fishy!" originated. At any rate it's a story about a man who thought God was too good to be true.

Very little is known about Jonah. Perhaps the most qualifying statement about him is found near the end of the book that bears his name. After all the hassle of sending Jonah to a Gentile city to foretell its impending destruction at the hand of God, God had not destroyed Nineveh. Jonah is pouting. "I knew it all along!" he told God. "That's why I didn't want to go there in the first place! I knew You were too loving to go through with destroying them. I'm so embarrassed; I wish I were dead!" (See Jonah 4:1-3.)

Jonah knew God! He knew that God was slow to anger and ready to forgive. Then why had he worked up such a head of steam because God had indeed forgiven that repenting, heathen city? We can readily see that his pride got in the way, but let's examine the situation more closely. The truth may hit much closer to home than we first imagined.

Jonah was a member of a family whose name meant "true." Jonah True was proud of his lineage, secure in his religion. No doubt he was a model Israelite in his time. A separatist at heart, he looked upon the surrounding Gentiles with disdain. He would have preferred that God simply rid the world of these heathen, but he had evidently come to know that God did not feel the same way.

Sadly, Jonah had not allowed his knowledge of God's character to draw him into friendship with the Almighty. He had not been changed by interaction with Divinity. "Right," to his mind, was defined by statute and law, not by the deeper demands of unconditional love. And so, for Jonah True, it was more important that what he said turn out to be right than it was for repenting sinners to find forgiveness.

I am glad that God is too good to be like Jonah True, aren't you?

GOD'S MAN IN A SECULAR WORLD

I am told that the spirit of God Most Holy lives in you, and that you are known for your perception, intelligence and marvellous wisdom. Dan. 5:14, Jerusalem.

When we think of people who "work for the Lord," we often think first of clergymen or others on the payroll of a church or religious organization. We seldom think of one who punches in on a factory time clock. We may be even less likely to think of a high government official, especially in a monarchical government.

Fortunately, our creative God does not draw the same arbitrary lines between the sacred and the secular that we often draw. He wants His principles and compassion to flow through every aspect of human endeavor, and He wants His people to be the channels.

We see in Daniel a prime example of God's desires to infiltrate the world outside of the church with His touch. Though we often call him "the prophet Daniel," he was known in his own time primarily as a highly esteemed statesman. And even though God worked a few miracle elements into his rapid rise to power, he held onto his high rank through three successive monarchs because of the quality of the person he had become through his relationship with God.

It is true that Daniel spent much time in prayer. But it is also true that he took the power and perspective of prayer with him into his secular assignments. He influenced the course of an empire because he saw such influence as a natural expression of his spiritual life. Among what we would call secular dignitaries, he revealed God even when he was not talking about God or about overtly religious matters.

Many people who may never see themselves as setting a foot inside a church door are intellectually hungry for better answers, emotionally starving for authentic relationships, and genuinely committed to improving the lot of humanity. If we Christians really believe that we have the best answers around, we should confidently carry those answers out of the church door and into the open marketplace, where they can be appreciated for their practical merit by honest people. The same concepts of honesty, fairness, compassion, and respect for human dignity that make a church such a warmly healing environment would be eagerly appreciated by an office staff as well.

God wants Daniel-like friends who, like yeast in the dough, can influence the whole world!

LASTING JOY

The seed sown on rock stands for those who receive the word with joy when they hear it, but have no root; they are believers for a while, but in the time of testing they desert. Luke 8:13, N.E.B.

Today's passage, in which Jesus is explaining a part of the parable of the sower, describes people somewhat like the little girl who was looking forward to going to a birthday party because she had a suspicion it was going to be a surprise party for herself. She discovered when she got there that it was indeed a surprise party. But it was for someone else. Her joy quickly vanished, and sulkingly she left early.

Hearing the word of Christ certainly is a joyful experience! And at first hearing it does appear to be good news —just about *me!* I am loved. I am forgiven, accepted by God as though I never had sinned. I have a beautiful mansion waiting just for me in a place I certainly will enjoy. I can have my prayers answered, my problems solved, my illnesses cured. No wonder I could enthusiastically embrace such a message!

But something about this type of gospel (as Jesus said) is without root. Though it brings immediate joy, it has no staying power because ultimately the "good news" is not about me. It is about God. The religious experience that is rooted in who He is, has the depth nourishment to keep on growing, the motivations to become more like Him.

Unlike the little girl at the birthday party, however, there is no reason to slink into the darkness, because the celebration of the good news about our God brings showers of good news upon ourselves. When I find Him to be, by His very nature, the Forgiver, guess who gets to be forgiven! When I settle in sure confidence that He is tender and wise, my own life is warmed and guided. But my confidence is rooted in something much greater than my own experiences.

The parable of the sower emphasizes the privilege of the new Christian to move beyond the seedling stage into maturity. The joy of the early believer is not in itself adequate basis for lasting loyalty. Unless we move on to a truly God-centered experience, we are vulnerable to discouragement when the rush of early joy turns placid. Nothing in this universe, however, is more lastingly joyous than to be rooted in Christ Jesus!

THE THRILL OF BELONGING

The Spirit you have received is not a spirit of slavery leading you back into a life of fear, but a Spirit that makes us sons, enabling us to cry "Abba! Father!" Rom. 8:15, N.E.B.

Many of us recall from the earlier decades of this century the sweet stories that were popular both in the fiction and the nonfiction markets. A familiar theme was the story of the charming little orphan girl, raised in a barren orphanage by a severe matron, who was discovered by a loving (and usually wealthy) family. The family would, of course, surmount all obstacles, adopt her, and take her home to live happily ever after.

Perhaps many readers tearfully enjoy this genre of literature because it answers to a deep longing in our hearts to be "claimed" by a loving, satisfying person. We fear nothing more than that we shall be passed by when the human race chooses its friends. To be "orphaned" can mean so much more than to be without living biological parents. Our neighborhoods are filled with emotional orphans—the neglected, the unclaimed, the inconsequential residue of a busy society.

Those with spiritual eyesight will quickly recognize that there is no more traumatic condition than to be without a spiritual Father. The vast ugliness of the whole human condition reveals that being spiritual orphans is far more than just an emotional cloud. It is an actual cause of real woe and destruction.

So Paul says that when the Spirit goes to work He gets right down inside the deepest part of our minds and prompts us to turn toward God and to speak to Him as we now see Him. And we call Him "Daddy!"—probably the best modern idiom for that ancient Aramaic word *abba*. It is a specially chosen word, conveying the confidence of a warm, secure sense of belonging. It is the word Jesus used when talking to His Father during prayer. (See Mark 14:36.)

When God solves the sin problem in our lives, He gets to the root of the matter. He *claims* us; He adopts us; He sends His Spirit to tell us "that we are children of God, and if children, then heirs, heirs of God and fellow heirs with Christ" (Rom. 8:16, 17, R.S.V.).

And this, good friends, is not a piece of literary fiction!

MOVED BY THE SPECTACULAR

One of its heads seemed to have a mortal wound, but its mortal wound was healed, and the whole world followed the beast with wonder. Rev. 13:3, R.S.V.

If you have found yourself subjected to prime-time television lately, you may have noticed a curious trend. It seems that virtually all of the thud and blunder thriller programs must have at least one high-speed car hurtling through the air, then crashing in explosive flames—all viewed in slow motion, of course. The producers apparently believe that the viewers simply won't tune them in again if their pulse doesn't race at least once during the show. Having been jaded through the years by lesser dramatic sequences, it takes much larger doses of the spectacular to move the modern viewer past a yawn.

A similar trend is happening in the world of religion. In recent years there has been an increasing number of practitioners of stunning Christianity. "Faith healings," flamboyant preachers, dramatic dreams, and various forms of the miraculous have drawn many adherents. In too many cases that which "wows" the senses has had far more impact than that which wins the reason. A God who does things decently and in order has been discredited by people who claim to be His followers.

John the revelator has foretold a time in the final throes of earth's history when Satan will stage a great false religious revival. Virtually the whole earth will be moved to worship an entity called the beast (Rev. 13:1-8). But the people are not moved by adoration of its fine qualities of character. Many will simply say, "Who can fight against it?" (verse 4, R.S.V.).

Rather than for me to name any current religious organization as "the beast," let the reader simply take note: Any organization that is so slender on truth that it must make its case by the help of political power, by constant appeal to the miraculous, and by intimidation of nonadherents is alien to the methods of Jesus Christ. But let the reader also take note that the decision will not be a simple one! It will be particularly trying, even overwhelming, for those who have allowed their mental faculties to become oriented to the spectacular rather than to the unadorned word of God.

Respecting the thoughtful dignity of His intelligent friends, Jesus longs for people to worship Him "in spirit and in truth" (John 4:24), not in adrenalin and in amazement. After all, we don't worship a beast!

THE SURPASSING WORTH

Indeed I count everything as loss because of the surpassing worth of knowing Christ Jesus my Lord. For his sake I have suffered the loss of all things, and count them as refuse, in order that I may gain Christ. Phil. 3:8, R.S.V.

Christian history is filled with moving chronicles of people who have given up almost everything in order to become Christians. Members of royalty have given up their rights to the throne; the wealthy have given up their palaces; children have been disowned by their parents; and for more than nineteen hundred years, many have given up life itself.

When Paul speaks of having "suffered the loss of all things" in exchange for the surpassing worth of knowing Christ Jesus, we readily start a mental listing of what he might have given up. His privileges as a Pharisee? Perhaps a family inheritance? Some speculate he even forfeited his marriage, since his wife may not have followed him into Christianity.

We may be surprised to learn, however, that in the context of today's passage, this isn't the type of "giving up" that Paul is speaking about. He was willing to cast aside as worthless garbage, not only money and prestige but all the hoped-for gain that his former style of religious experience had promised him. As a sinner before God, he was laying aside as worthless every prop, every merit, every trusted spiritual advantage that all of his well-honed religious zeal had supposed to give him. For years he had learned to trust these well-done works. To step away from dependence upon them would be far more traumatic than a child's first bicycle ride without his training wheels.

But Paul had found something of surpassing worth: that the essential genius of Christianity does not center in man's performance, but in union with a Person. And he discovered that the whole premise of religion being man's endeavors to impress or appease God, that God might change toward man, must be thrown on the dung-heap. In knowing Jesus Christ, he learned that God Himself is already utterly devoted to man, that religion is Jesus' endeavor to get man to change toward God! This relationship of loving trust with one's Creator—which Paul calls "faith"—is *itself* man's rightful condition. This *is* "righteousness by faith," infinitely preferred to the supposed righteousness of man's works done to try to establish that relationship.

No wonder Paul could say, "Rejoice in the Lord always; again I will say, Rejoice" (Phil. 4:4, R.S.V.).

THE SIN OF NONINVOLVEMENT

On the day that you stood aloof, on the day that strangers carried off his wealth, and foreigners entered his gates and cast lots for Jerusalem, you were like one of them. Obadiah 11, R.S.V.

I was shocked as I read the newspaper account of a woman who was stabbed to death while at least twenty onlookers refused to become involved. The article speculated as to why anyone would just stand by and watch someone being murdered. Having interviewed several of those present, the writer concluded that fear was not the main factor for their noninvolvement. Most were simply indifferent.

Even more surprising is the fact that such noninvolvement is so common in today's society. ''It's none of my business!'' has become a maxim for people wishing to escape any accountability for their fellowman. They walk away free because it was not their hands that spilled blood. Free, but not innocent. This is the essence of Obadiah's prophecy.

Only twenty-one verses long, Obadiah foretells the downfall of the Edomites, the descendants of Esau. A closer look at the passage reveals a picture of our consistent Father who tells the truth about the results of our actions. In verse 15 He predicted, ''As you have done, it will be done to you; your deeds will return upon your own head'' (N.I.V.).

The sin of the Edomites was that they ''stood aloof'' while their kinsmen, Israel, fell into the hands of foreign enemies. In God's opinion, it was the same as if they themselves had accomplished it. ''You were like one of them,'' He declared. By their noninvolvement, they, in fact, were acting as allies to their heathen neighbors. And, because of the nature of these neighbors, it was only a matter of time before they, too, would be attacked. ''All your allies will force you to the border; your friends will deceive and overpower you; those who eat your bread will set a trap for you, but you will not detect it'' (verse 7, N.I.V.).

God was simply telling them the truth. They were bringing all this upon themselves. Because He would not intervene on their behalf, even as they had not intervened on behalf of the house of Jacob, He spoke in terms of accepting the accountability for all that would happen to them. It must not be forgotten, however, that God would be acting the part of a gentleman. He would not intervene because they wanted no part of Him.

THE HARD PICTURES

The Lord is a jealous God and avenging, the Lord is avenging and wrathful; the Lord takes vengeance on his adversaries and keeps wrath for his enemies. Nahum 1:2, R.S.V.

When you get your snapshots back from the processors and begin thumbing through them, you probably look for one thing. You want to make sure that all the portraits of your family and friends are reasonably flattering. If you are like most people, you won't mount any color prints in the family album that show people with frowns, closed eyes, or unflattering profiles. You don't want your grandchildren remembering you as a dour-faced specimen.

It can never be said that when God gave us His personal portrait album within the covers of the Bible He had edited out all the difficult and potentially unflattering pictures. We have the unabridged edition, not just those portraits of a sweetly gentle "grandfather in the sky." It is inevitable that in selecting 365 Biblical sketches of our Father we should come across some hard pictures, such as the overtly severe passage quoted above.

The question, though, is whether this portrait can be reconciled with all those passages that show God as seeking to win and heal His enemies. Or can the readers go through the divine photo album, choosing to look only at the more flattering portraits? (How many of you will want to memorize today's text to quote to your friends?) What do we do with these hard pictures of a loving God?

Having been a schoolteacher, I can recall occasions when I needed to portray myself to undisciplined students as very severe. In order to bring order out of chaos, they needed to know that I had painful recourse in mind should they not behave themselves. But that is not how I wished to be remembered by my students. And so once they were sitting still enough to listen, I was quick to show them that I prized friendly interaction, gentle words, and an atmosphere of freedom and love. In their immaturity, however, they would have taken advantage of that approach had it been the only one they had seen.

Throughout the Old Testament, God often was trying to bring some order into the lives of people who had respect for only those who would inflict pain on the disobedient. In His love for them God risked portraying Himself in that light in order that the people might take Him seriously and come to appreciate His true qualities of gracious love.

BEING PUT RIGHT WITH GOD

We, too, have believed in Christ Jesus in order to be put right with God through our faith in Christ, and not by doing what the Law requires. For no one is put right with God by doing what the Law requires. Gal. 2:16, T.E.V.

Ever since the Reformation, scholars have been debating the exact meaning of a New Testament word that is translated in its various forms both as "righteousness" and as "justification." They all agree that it has something to do with the center of the plan of salvation, but they fall into two general camps as to how that is done.

Broadly speaking, the Lutherans have taken the position that justification is *declared* righteousness—that it is God's act of imputing, or crediting, the perfect righteousness of Christ to the record of the sinner, so that God views the repentant sinner as if he were righteous, even though he may still do sinful acts. They speak of it as "an alien righteousness" from the sinner's point of view; it does not arise from within him, lest he have grounds either for boasting or for endless despairing.

By contrast, the Catholic tradition has seen the word as implying a *caused* righteousness—that God works in the sinner's life, causing his behavior to become good enough to warrant it being regarded as righteous by God. (This righteousness, however, is not adequate in itself for one's salvation, and additional sources of merit must be added for that purpose.) But the idea of completely substitutionary righteousness would be regarded as "legal fiction" by many Catholics.

Both traditions, however, do share some common ground. Both of them apparently accept the assumption that God is the kind of person who needs to have merit presented to Him before He will decide to bless the sinner with eternal life. The Lutherans suggest that this merit is found only in Christ; the Catholics say it comes from Christ's work in the believer. But in either case God must be appeased or satisfied with a certain amount of merit.

But what if merit simply isn't the issue? What if we see the sin problem not as a shortage of merit but as a shattered relationship? To solve the problem, then, is to bring us back into a right relationship with God. As we read in today's text, the *Today's English Version* has chosen to translate the word in question as "put right with God." Beyond juggling of merits, it focuses on the real issue: our personal union with the Father!

EASY ANSWERS

Absalom said moreover, "Oh that I were judge in the land! Then every man with a suit or cause might come to me, and I would give him justice." 2 Sam. 15:4, R.S.V.

Seasoned administrators have become painfully aware of a certain kind of employee that seems to be sprinkled through most organizations in just enough quantities to keep the administrators humble. These certain employees are very popular with the rest of the staff because they always have a more favorable suggestion about how things should be done than the sometimes austere policies of the administration. They are skilled at second-guessing every high-level decision, clearly presenting their own ideas as better, and easier to live with, than those that come from the top.

Absalom used the same method while sitting at the front gate of his father's palace. He "stole the hearts of the men of Israel" (2 Sam. 15:6, R.S.V.). Those who do not bear final accountability for the management of a business or a nation, who do not see all the factors that have to be taken into account when making a tough decision, can always suggest an easier, less painful way of solving a problem. And people who are far from the desk where "the buck stops" quickly fall prey to these easy answers.

It is possible that administrators could have a special empathy with God as He faces some of the perplexities in solving the problems of the great controversy. Imagine Satan standing, as it were, on the front steps of Planet Earth, offering a sympathetic ear to all who come with a cause. "You're right!" he would say. "If I had been in charge, I wouldn't have been so hard on Achan and his kids. I could have found an easier way to clean things up a bit without sending the Flood. I could have stopped Hitler before the Holocaust. I wouldn't be quite so strict as those Ten Commandments. I'd be a lot more generous with the entrance list for heaven."

He could steal the hearts of all who are looking for easy answers, for Satan is running a popularity contest, while God is seeking to teach the truth to stubborn rebels. Satan can promise us anything, regardless of whether he can ever deliver, while God is cautious lest we become presumptuous of His goodness. Satan offered easy answers and quick solutions to Adam and Eve, and he "stole their hearts" from God. You'd think that we would have learned by now.

NOT JUST SENTIMENTALITIES

If you never overlooked our sins, Yahweh, Lord, could anyone survive? But you do forgive us: and for that we revere you. Ps. 130:3, 4, Jerusalem.

What would you think of a nurse who said, "I'm going to take your blood pressure," then endeavored to do it by placing a thermometer under your tongue? Would you trust a mechanic who checked the points on your engine by reading the oil pressure gauge? Even though these are all vital measurements, it can be dangerous to confuse them one for another.

What if someone were to ask you, "Have you been forgiven?" What would you measure as a means of determining your answer? Could that, perhaps, depend on what you feel to be the problem that forgiveness is solving?

In checking their forgiveness, many would first measure to see whether they have any remaining feelings of guiltiness. They would recall feelings of shame and unworthiness in the presence of a holy God. They would recall a sense of rejection, of being unloved, and of bruised self-worth. Then they would check to see whether all these feelings were gone. If any such feelings ever surfaced, they would conclude that God had not forgiven them.

But may I suggest that the very fact that you are alive is more than just evidence, it is proof, that you are forgiven. Guilt and forgiveness are more than just feelings. They are more than sentimentalities. Even though separation from God will always bring bad feelings, they are not the sum total of the guilt problem. Separation from God brings death; every living person must acknowledge that he is living in grace. He is living because God has held off that second-death consequence.

To be unforgiven, then, is not to be having bad feelings. To be unforgiven is to be *dead!* If the Lord had dealt with each of us as He rightly could have, who could survive? But He has instead offered forgiveness to all mankind. Because Jesus has borne that death-consequence in our place, we all live! This, of course, does not mean that all mankind shall be saved, for not all mankind has come to trust the Forgiver. Those who are ultimately lost will give evidence of their stubborn rejection of Him.

Every heartbeat, every breath, is a reminder that our Father "does not deal with us according to our sins" (Ps. 103:10, R.S.V.). What better reason could we find to revere Him?

311

A SIGN OF BELONGING

Moreover I gave them my sabbaths, as a sign between me and them, that they might know that I the Lord sanctify them. Eze. 20:12, R.S.V.

People from many cultures have found it helpful to come up with some kind of "shorthand" to define how one ought to relate to new acquaintances of the opposite sex. A man wants to know, for example, if a woman is available for further friendship or whether she already belongs to someone else. Most Western societies have adopted the wedding ring for this purpose. While as a symbol it has often been abused, both for giving counterfeit messages and as an excuse for lavish display, at least it can be a quick way of saying "I belong to someone!"

Since "belonging to God" is the essence of true spirituality, God wanted to give His people a meaningful symbol by which they could tell the world, "We belong to our Lord!" Even more than just a symbol of belonging, God wanted that experience actually to deepen the value of belonging. And so God repeatedly gave to His people the very thing He had given them in the garden: He gave them time—sacred time, set aside from all lesser distractions, just to enjoy fellowship with their heavenly Father.

I know of several husbands who regularly take their wives on "dates," special times alone, even after they have been married for many years. When they turn down other invitations because they say, "I have a date with my wife!" their friends know that they have a very rich relationship going between them.

That is precisely what God had in mind with the Sabbath. He wanted His people to be known worldwide as being unavailable for other appointments on the Sabbath because they were so joyously engrossed with the One to whom they belonged. Sadly, He had to report that "my sabbaths they greatly profaned" (Eze. 20:13, R.S.V.). They gave counterfeit messages with the Sabbath, flaunting it as a sign of belonging, while their hearts were far away from Him. Or they became absorbed in the ritual itself to the exclusion of the relationship.

In the final showdown of history, those who remain loyal to God will have discovered the joys and meaningful symbolism of this sign of belonging. They will be living out God's desire to "hallow my sabbaths that they may be a sign between me and you, that you may know that I am the Lord your God" (verse 20).

THE KISS OF LIFE

Mercy and truth are met together; righteousness and peace have kissed each other. Ps. 85:10.

Some people think that in order to show mercy you have to ignore truth. "We'll just pretend it never happened!" Forgiveness becomes a mind game: when you say you're sorry, it cancels out what really happened. You no longer have to deal with the facts; you just "pick up and go on." The problem is that the unhappy incident is likely to recur, because pretending does not change people.

Can you show mercy and still embrace truth? Our text today declares that God has done just that in the plan of salvation. He has shown great mercy to our fallen world in giving us His Son. And in the giving He also proclaims the unbiased truth about the sin problem. When, in Christ, He covered our sins, He was not pretending that we were never really separated from Him. He showed us what happens to people who choose to turn away from God, their life source. However, He mercifully enacted it out upon Himself so that we could live to benefit from the lesson.

In God's Son, "righteousness and peace have kissed each other"—the very kiss of life! For we see that God is at peace with the human race and that we have been brought back into right relationship with Him in the person of Christ. But it is no mind game; it is genuine and attainable. In Christ we see how the Father and mankind may relate to each other. We see how easily the Son of man entered into discourse with the Almighty, and how very good and satisfying Their friendship was! It was not as one god to another, it was you and I and the Sovereign of the universe!

God can and does deal with the reality of our separation from Him. The very reason He desires us to confess our sins is that we might come face-to-face with reality. When we have done so, He quickly assures us that He still loves and accepts us. He then counsels us, guiding us into new social patterns and better ways of living. Our broken relationship with Him is healed, and we are ourselves at peace with God and with one another.

As Psalm 85:11 says, "Truth shall spring out of the earth;"—we shall know God and understand ourselves—"and righteousness shall look down from heaven," for God shall be pleased with us.

WILL JESUS COME SOON?

As they heard these things, he proceeded to tell a parable, because . . . they supposed that the kingdom of God was to appear immediately. Luke 19:11, R.S.V.

You can read it on bright-red bumper stickers, "Jesus Is Coming Again!" You can hear it in many sermons, "Jesus is coming soon." You can read it in many Bible passages, "I will come again." You can even read it spray-painted on brick walls, "Are you ready for Jesus to come?"

Though millions of Christians share the blessed hope in the soon return of Jesus Christ, some of us have deceased grandparents, and even great-grandparents, who were absolutely convinced that Jesus would come in their lifetime. The word *soon* takes on very vague meanings when some denomination has been saying for more than 140 years that He will come soon. It was evidently a cause for concern for Jesus Himself when some people in His own day believed that He was going to return sooner than He knew He could. So He told them a well-crafted parable, specifically designed to stir them to deeper thought about His coming.

The parable, curiously enough, has virtually nothing to do with the time of His return. But it has everything to do with what they should do with their time until He does return. It has even more to do with who He is that is returning. You remember; it's the parable of the servants who are each given a sum of money and told to use it responsibly. Those who did so were highly esteemed by the Master. The one who hid his money complained that he was afraid of the Master for being "a severe man" (Luke 19:21, R.S.V.).

The point of Jesus' parable is that He wants us to get our eyes off the calendar and onto the Person. The good news is not that Jesus is coming *soon,* but that *Jesus* is coming soon. If He is "a severe man," even a million years is too soon! He wants a people who are delighted with the One who is coming, that they might be motivated to use the valuable treasure of truth to great advantage. Rather than a panic-stricken cry, "Jesus is coming soon, therefore get ready!" our privilege is to say, *"Be* ready so that He *can* come soon. Be ready to tell the truth about Him with gladness so that the world can make informed choices about Him."

WHAT MAKES PARENTS REJOICE

I was overjoyed to find some of your children living the life of truth, as the Father himself instructed us. 2 John 4, Phillips.

Only another parent could ever appreciate the thrill that parents know when their children grow up embracing the wise and loving values they have sought to instill in them. There are many deceptive side trips, many Satan-designed inducements, to hurt these precious lives that are an extension of our own. To see them pass through the formative years into settled Christian adulthood brings a deep satisfaction to parents that perhaps nothing could equal.

It is interesting to notice, however, the words that John chose to use when he spoke of these early believers whose youth, or new converts, made the right choices. He didn't say that they had chosen to obey the rules, or to join the right church, or to submit to their parents' authority. He didn't commend them for being nice people, or for wearing the right clothes. Rather, John rejoiced that they were "following the truth" (R.S.V.), or "living by the truth" (N.E.B.). His focus is upon truth, not upon any lesser reference point.

The apostle John, more than the other Gospel writers, built the story of Jesus around the conflict between truth and error. He often used the metaphor of light and darkness, and thus was fond of calling Jesus the Light of the world. John knew that the crux of the great controversy is a battle for the loyalty of men's minds and that God's ultimate weapon is truth—truth about Himself.

Children who merely conform to their parents' wishes for fear of offending them bring their parents no lasting consolation. Children who join "the right church," perhaps because all their friends have joined the same fellowship, are also on shaky ground. Enduring confidence in the spiritual life of our children, however, will come when we see that they are excitedly aware of the beauties of Jesus and, with intelligent reflection, have chosen to live as He lives.

My teenage daughter told me recently, "I am listening carefully to what my teachers are saying about who God is; and I'd be willing to speak out if I question what I hear, because I don't want my classmates to get a wrong picture of Him!" I had a sudden thrill very much akin to the one John expressed in today's text. There isn't a more reliable and rewarding guiding star for one's life.

LIMPING WITH TWO OPINIONS

Elijah came near to all the people, and said, "How long will you go limping with two different opinions? If the Lord is God, follow him; but if Baal, then follow him." And the people did not answer him a word. 1 Kings 18:21, R.S.V.

Even though our teachers had told us not to play "crack the whip" while skating in the old gymnasium, the game was popular to try when the teachers were not looking. The large pillars that broke up the floor area— part of the reason for our teachers' warnings—just served to make the game more challenging. But I'll never forget watching one young man as he snapped at blurring speed from the end of the whip, to find himself heading straight for a pillar. For a split second he thought he would steer to the left. Then he changed his mind and tried to pass it on the right. From all appearances, however, his final decision was to go on both sides at once. He limped very painfully off the skating floor.

A young girl was portraying among her friends the image of a worldly-wise, liberated former Christian. Yet she was careful to live in her parents' presence as a sweetly docile model of innocence. It was a painful day for her when her friends came for a visit and, within her parents' hearing, began discussing the recent wild time they had shared with her.

Trying to try to hold two conflicting opinions at the same time is painful, even downright crippling. Living with one foot planted firmly in the value systems of the world and the other foot dangling within the supposed shelter of the church door is wrenching to one's integrity, as well as to one's reputation. This will always produce dysfunctional people, silly parodies of the strong, purposeful men and women God is capable of producing.

It is no wonder, then, that when Elijah pointed out to his people how foolish they looked limping along with one foot on either side of the fence, they had nothing to say. There is no defense for self-inflicted pain, no sensible explanation for mental and spiritual duplicity. There is something very inspiring about Elijah's straightforward manner of dealing. He sets before the people the two clear alternatives: God or Baal. Getting off the fence, even on the wrong side, makes more sense than the painful, integrity-shattering fantasy that one can walk both sides at the same time!

READY FOR THE UNREADY

I was ready to be sought by those who did not ask for me; I was ready to be found by those who did not seek me. I said, "Here am I, here am I," to a nation that did not call on my name. Isa. 65:1, R.S.V.

If you have taken a water safety instructor's course, you have learned that drowning people cannot always be trusted. In the desperation of what they fear will be their final moments they will sometimes attack their rescuers, shoving them underwater in their own frantic attempts to stay on top. The experienced lifeguard is careful to approach the victim in such a way as to avoid being endangered himself. He attempts the rescue in spite of apparent resistance.

Being lost can lead people to do some rather ludicrous things. In retrospect, how foolish it is for doomed sinners to ignore, even despise, the only One who can rescue them. But in the frantic thrashing of sinners about to drown in the guilt, pain, and confusion of their folly, level-headed judgment seldom rises to the top. We ignore Spirit-led friends, shut out of our memory the sweet recall of our former dedication, and avoid any spiritual meetings that might let Jesus tug at our hearts.

But a choice insight into the character of our God is that He does not take us seriously at such times. Like a lifeguard, He continues to offer His strong hand, saying, "Here I am!" For He is wise enough to understand what rebellious people do when they come face-to-face with their folly. He knows that we dodge and squirm and flee until, exhausted, we fall at His feet.

Because of His vantage point of both wisdom and compassion, He can say, "I spread out my hands all the day to a rebellious people, who walk in a way that is not good, following their own devices" (Isa. 65:2, R.S.V.). He is not put off by our resistance nor offended by our rebellion.

Some might fear that such infinite patience and persistence on God's part would lead to presumption on our part. We might come to indulge His goodness and walk our ways, always counting on His rescuing hand. Yet the goodness of God, not the dread that He might walk away from us, is what leads to repentance and to lasting trust.

GOOD BUT DEADLY COMMANDS

For the written law condemns to death, but the Spirit gives life. 2 Cor. 3:6, N.E.B.

A popular bumper sticker on cars around Yosemite Valley says in bold letters, ''Go Climb a Rock.'' The fine print at the bottom identifies it as the sentiments of a well-known rock-climbing club. I saw it one day as I drove to the base of El Capitan, that overwhelming rock monolith that rises abruptly several thousand feet from the valley's floor. I stood there looking up at the sheer cliffs, not even needing to wonder what would happen if I were to try to ''go climb a rock.'' A few hardy spirits, with special training and exotic equipment, attempt to scale its face every year. Most of them make it.

But what if the command, instead of the cute jargon of rock climbers, were the explicit imperative of God Himself? What if it read, ''Go Love Your Neighbor''? How would you feel as you stood contemplating a rather obnoxious neighbor, hearing the command to love him ringing in your ears? Worse yet, what if you looked for the special ''equipment'' of finding delight in the fulfilling of the command and found none?

Just as most of us flatlanders wouldn't have thought about climbing El Capitan until we saw the bumper sticker, so most of us who blindly ignore our neighbors aren't aware of how unloving we are until we hear the command ''Love them!'' Merely to look at the command is to know the keenest sense of failure and of condemnation. No wonder, then, that Paul could say that the written law condemns to death. To hear a command and not have the inner resources to fulfill it is to hear a pronouncement of failure and of death.

But the Spirit, Paul proclaims, gives life. That is, when the Spirit sheds God's love abroad in our hearts, we begin to find unsurpassed delight in actually doing what previously was an absurd impossibility. We behold our neighbor from a surprisingly new perspective, finding the ''old crank'' to be a valuable person with understandable, even crying, needs.

The experience described by Paul in Romans 7 is the ''written letter'' variety. One is aware of what the law demands and convicted that it is right. But outside of a relationship with Jesus Christ, one has no inner resources to respond. The Romans 8 experience, however, is the glad rejoicing of one whose focus has shifted away from the letter of the law to the adequacies of Christ.

REJECTED BY A FORGIVING GOD

But you are a forgiving God, gracious and compassionate, slow to anger and abounding in love. Therefore you did not desert them, even when they cast for themselves an image of a calf. Neh. 9:17, 18, N.I.V.

We often hear the phrase "Whatever works!" If what you are doing doesn't work, try something else. Is this God' approach? For six thousand years He has patiently worked through forgiveness to bring the reign of sin to an end. He has been patient and forgiving. Maybe He ought to switch to wrath.

Consider ancient Israel. God rescued them from Egypt. He kept them from being hungry or thirsty. Their experience with Him was in some ways far more tangible than any other community of believers has experienced since. Yet they murmured, complained, and doubted everything about Him they possibly could. They accused Him of contemplating their murder; they said they were better off as slaves than they were as free men under His guidance. At the borders of Canaan they wanted to choose another leader who would take them back to Egypt! Yet He consistently forgave them.

Recounting Israel's flagrantly disloyal attitudes, Nehemiah said, "They refused to listen and failed to remember the miracles [God] performed among them. They became stiff-necked and in their rebellion appointed a leader in order to return to their slavery" (Neh. 9:17, N.I.V.). But God still did not desert them. "For forty years [He] sustained them in the desert; they lacked nothing, their clothes did not wear out nor did their feet become swollen" (verse 21, N.I.V.).

For another fifteen hundred years He pleaded with them to accept His will for their lives. Yet history reveals that God had no lasting success in bringing them to their senses. In the end He finally did reject Israel as the nation through which He would reveal Himself to the world, though individually anyone still may accept Him as his Redeemer.

Did God switch to rejection because acceptance and forgiveness didn't work? May I suggest that God has never ceased being "a forgiving God" to Israel. He did, however, finally set them free from their calling as His chosen people—a privilege most of them considered an unpleasant burden. His rejection of them was only in acknowledgment of their final rejection of Him in the person of His Son—His Son, whose dying words were of forgiveness.

It is our privilege to accept the calling that Israel thought burdensome. We may be His people; we may reveal Him to the world.

WALKING OUT ON THE DOCTOR

They were not faithful to the covenant I made with them, and so I paid no attention to them. Heb. 8:9, T.E.V.

A very ill patient went to an outstanding specialist for treatment. Following a careful examination, the doctor prescribed a complex but promising course of treatment. There was every indication that in a reasonably short time the patient would have been entirely well.

But part way through the therapy the patient simply quit coming to the doctor, in spite of the doctor's urgings. His condition worsened and in time he died. His doctor noted in his files that since the patient had terminated the healing relationship by his own choice, the doctor could not be held accountable for his demise.

The Bible writers often used the term *covenant* for what we might call the healing relationship between God and man. It is prescribed by God as a powerful remedy for the ills that are caused by alienation from God. As the Great Physician, He would never prescribe a faulty remedy. Thus when the Bible writers (note especially Hebrews 8) speak of the "old covenant," they are not speaking of a remedy that is inherently faulty or inadequate. For it is nothing more than an expression of God's eternal covenant—His promise to take care of His people if they will let Him.

But the problem was that the patients walked out on the Doctor. They removed themselves from the healing relationship, from their close involvement with the only One who could cure them. And the Doctor noted (as we read in today's verse) that—being an ethical gentleman—He would not force a cure on them. Respecting their freedom, He let them walk away, even to their own death.

The new covenant, then, is not a new means of salvation. It is a renewed plea from God to come back into that life-giving union with Him that has always been His prescribed remedy. Somewhat in contrast to the heavily legal relationship between a physician and a patient, with all the concerns about malpractice and insurance coverage, the "covenant" relationship with God is a warmly personal involvement. It is so life-changing that as we remain in it our very thoughts and desires come to reflect His own (see Heb. 8:10, 11). Who in his right mind would ever want to walk away from that relationship when the cure is not only so sure but so delightful?

A CURIOUS WAY TO WIELD A SWORD

In his right hand he held seven stars, from his mouth issued a sharp two-edged sword, and his face was like the sun shining in full strength. Rev. 1:16, R.S.V.

Who ever heard of a great warrior holding his sword in his mouth? If one is going to smite his enemies properly with such a razor-sharp weapon, he holds it in his strong and agile hand. That's how all sword fighters do it.

But the apostle John doesn't miss any details when he records what he saw in vision there on the Isle of Patmos. The weapon wielded by our victorious Lord is most assuredly seen as issuing from His mouth, because it is the sword of truth. Our God vanquishes the enemy with well-established truth, not with superior force.

I can recall artists' conceptions, probably inspired by evangelists' descriptions, of the battle of Armageddon—that great final showdown between Christ and Satan. They vividly portrayed military tanks, rockets, and large guns. Today's technology would have suggested laser beams and well-placed nuclear warheads. But in either case the nature of the battle was seen as essentially force against force, with the winner having the best weapons and shrewdest strategies.

There are a number of religious persuasions today that are expecting a time of great trouble ahead, and their adherents are preparing for it much as many Americans in the late 1950s prepared for nuclear fallout. They are stashing food supplies, water, guns, and gold or silver for bartering. Some are preparing remote places in which to hide from the weapons that will stalk the land.

Though we can hardly expect an era of peace and tranquility ahead, such end-time scenarios detract us from the real preparation we must be making. That is the preparation of one's mind to discern truth from error. For Satan never has posed a military threat to the government of this universe. He is "the deceiver of the whole world" (Rev. 12:9, R.S.V.), who speaks words "against the most High" (Dan. 7:25) and whose reign of terror shall end only when " 'knowledge shall increase' " (chap. 12:4, R.S.V.).

How fitting it is that in the great prophecies of Daniel 7 and 8 the final showdown that at last delivers the eternal kingdom to Christ and His saints happens in a courtroom rather than on a battlefield. A courtroom is where issues are weighed, where swords of words, not of steel, are used to expose error.

IS GOD UNGRATEFUL?

Is he grateful to the servant for carrying out his orders? So with you: when you have carried out all your orders, you should say, "We are servants and deserve no credit; we have only done our duty" Luke 17:9, N.E.B.

More than once I have winced as I have read Jesus' statement as recorded in today's text. Perhaps you too have felt that it portrayed a heartless and ungrateful God. In the parable, the master makes his slave work hard all day, gives him not a word of thanks when he comes home sweaty and dusty, and—even worse—won't let him eat until he has fixed supper for the master, put on an apron, and served him. On top of it all, he then expects the fellow to say, "I'm just an unworthy good-for-nothing servant; I just do what I am told."

All of Jesus' parables are expected to tell us something about the Father. I suspect that if we had a videotape of Jesus telling this parable we would have seen a twinkle in His eye as He unfolded this parody of the master/servant relationship. By the tone of His voice we could have readily caught a touch of sarcasm, because Jesus was trying to expose the nonsense of people doing life's ordinary tasks for the sake of getting rewards from others.

The point is that God has unfolded to us patterns for living that have value in and of themselves. We live healthfully, for example, because it is wise to do so, not so that we can run to God with upturned palms expecting Him to give us some cherished treasure as a reward. While a child may regularly brush his teeth in order for Mother to say, "You're a good boy; I'll give you a new toy," it would be sadly immature for a grown man to expect trinkets from his dentist after every good checkup.

In the parable, Jesus described the ideal servants as ones who were at peace with the reason why they had done their daily activities. They were not seeking merit or reward, or trying by their works to curry special favors from their master.

No, our Father is not an ungrateful, authoritarian overlord. But neither does He use His gratitude to get us to do things that our own good judgment should commend to us, lest we become fearful that we may not have worked hard enough to deserve supper!

WE NEED EACH OTHER

Therefore confess your sins to one another, and pray for one another, and then you will be healed. James 5:16, N.E.B.

"Don't you think it is possible," he asked, "for us not to be influenced by how other people act toward us? Do we always have to be hurt by their rejection?" A bright student in my Marriage and the Family class, he was perplexed by our discussion of the way in which we humans influence each other. He wondered if we shouldn't, as Christians, be above all that.

But the discussion that followed wasn't unanimous. The class agreed that, though we are often hurt by each other's smallness, we also find God's love made tangible through the touch of another human being. Also, to be open to another's love is to be vulnerable to that person's potential to hurt us.

Ever since Adam and Eve first donned the fig leaves in the garden, we humans have been busy bluffing each other about how wonderfully adequate and whole we are, while hoping that no one will discover how much guilt and how many naked fears lie just below the surface. We are afraid that if we honestly admit that we are having real trouble maintaining our devotional life our friends will have doubts about our integrity. As parents, we don't want to talk about our stress points lest our image as "the adequate father or mother" be tarnished.

We all know the tendency of the human mind, once it has started on the path of hiding the truth, to hide our needs even from our own selves. But a problem that doesn't get acknowledged will not be healed. James certainly understood this when he urged the early believers to form the habit of freely admitting their failings to one another. He wanted that young expression of the body of Christ to become practiced in open honesty and trust.

James was not, however, advocating some kind of "let's bare all" encounter sessions. He urged that whatever failings we might admit to one another be made an immediate subject of prayer. He anticipated that the combination of honesty and supplication would lead promptly to spiritual, emotional, and physical healing. The church, then, could conduct thrilling experiments in the kinds of healing candor and caring that our heavenly Father longs to share with us. By nurturing each other to strength rather than condemning each other's weakness, we reflect God's character. We need each other to reveal God's love in a tangible way.

A MAGNETIC PERSON

And I shall draw all men to myself, when I am lifted up from the earth. John 12:32, N.E.B.

Shepherds in the Bible lands do things differently from their Western counterparts. When Jesus called Himself "the good shepherd," His hearers had in mind one who walks ahead of his sheep, calling them by name. Eastern shepherds develop close bonds with their sheep, such that each sheep recognizes the shepherd's voice and responds to his call. The Western shepherd, by contrast, drives his sheep from behind, often using dogs to snap at the heels of sheep that wander from the flock or walk too slowly.

When Jesus spoke of Himself as a shepherd, He was confident in the fact that people do not need to be driven to follow Him. Only the insecure despot resorts to force. But there is something compellingly attractive about Jesus Christ. There is enticing beauty in His character, a drawing magnetism in His personality. He needs only to be lifted up on the horizon of our minds, lifted above the crowding distractions, to engage our attention.

But Jesus was talking specifically about the one event that, more than any other, would lift Him up before the people. That was the cross. Here the Shepherd becomes Himself the sacrificial Lamb, bearing in His own being the ugly death that should have been ours, since we are the rebels. On the cross, heaven channels every treasure of love that its infinity can hold, through one Man, to this plagued planet.

Oh, how much Satan fears to have us see Jesus willingly die on the cross. He did everything in his power, both in the wilderness and in Gethsemane, to turn Jesus from His mission of sacrifice. Failing that, however, the enemy has sought to nullify the cross, portraying it as a hostile event rather than a friendly one. The cross, he suggests, is Christ's way of turning away the Father's anger, rather than His way of revealing the Father's love.

Jesus is not lifted up on the cross in contrast to the Father, as One who is more gracious and accepting than the Father. As Jesus talked to His Father about His impending death on the cross, He said, "Father, glorify thy name." The Father immediately replied, "I have glorified it, and I will glorify it again" (John 12:28, N.E.B.). God, in Christ, was "reconciling the world unto himself" (2 Cor. 5:19).

THE POWER OF LOVE

Husbands, love your wives, as Christ also loved the church and gave himself up for it . . . so that he might present the church to himself all glorious, with no stain or wrinkle or anything of the sort, but holy and without blemish. Eph. 5:25-27, N.E.B.

In the spring of each year, on college campuses all over the land, the tempo quickens. Eligible young men and women, fearful of a dwindling supply, intensify their search for the perfect mate. Many of them later walk down the aisle blissfully content that they have indeed found the perfect partner.

But there is a dangerous flaw in the whole scenario. No one comes to the marriage altar as a whole and totally adequate person. In an ideal marriage, people do not *discover* the perfect mate, but they can *nurture* each other very nearly into perfectness. Something of immense power happens to people when they are loved by a giving person. It is so powerful that the apostle Paul could think of only one parallel that could describe it. While he is searching for words to tell husbands the manner in which they ought to love their wives, he says that it should be similar to the way Christ loves the church.

Paul cannot leave his favorite subject. Moving on from his advice to husbands, he pens a rhapsody of praise of what happens to the church when it is loved by Christ. What begins as a band of wounded and obscure people, comes forth without stain or wrinkle or blemish. Even Christ Himself counts them as holy and glorious. All this because they are loved by Jesus Christ!

How infinitely grateful we should be that Paul did *not* say, "Make yourself all spotless and wrinkle-free; *then* Christ will love you." He knew that Christ's love and acceptance are not the rewards for changed character; they are what causes the changes—which should encourage recently married persons who have discovered that they really haven't found the perfect spouse!

"UNFOLDED" SHEEP

But there are other sheep of mine, not belonging to this fold, whom I must bring in; and they too will listen to my voice. There will then be one flock, one shepherd. John 10:16, N.E.B.

According to the listings of some authorities, in America today more than 265 denominations identify themselves as Christian. Some are small and almost unknown; others are large and historically well established. Each makes claims of being more correct, more in line with God's will, than the others. Some denominations expend much energy pointing out the failings of other groups. For the newcomer to Christianity, it can be a bewildering array of options: Which "fold" should a young sheep join? Whichever way he decides, as many as 264 groups may say he has made the wrong choice!

At a time when there was essentially only one group claiming to be the unquestioned "people of God," Jesus Himself said that there were people He would claim as His own who were not in that group. While that thought was very disturbing to the guardians of the "in group," it left others wondering just how one might know how to identify that true flock. But Jesus clearly announced who they were: They were the people who would listen to His voice.

On the surface, that may not seem to help much. All of today's Christian groups claim to be listening to Jesus' voice, yet they still don't agree about what He is saying. It would be good, however, to remember what Jesus wanted to say more than anything else. He wanted to tell us about His Father. The common flock, the single fold, that Jesus foretold will be made up of people who have listened to His compelling messages about His Father.

When confronted with so many voices, so many competing claims to doctrinal rightness from today's varied groups, one issue rises to the top. Who is embracing and telling the truth about God? Who has the most integrated, sensible understanding of our heavenly Father? Whose portrayal of God is as warmly and intelligently inviting as was the message of Jesus? Considering that every doctrine is but a statement of how God goes about solving the sin problem, whose statement of beliefs casts God in the most winsome light?

Someday one single flock shall stand in the presence of our Father. Seeing Him face-to-face and hearing Him address them, they shall know that they are listening to a familiar voice!

THE DELUSION THAT BACKFIRES

By his cunning he shall make deceit prosper under his hand, and in his own mind he shall magnify himself. Without warning he shall destroy many; and he shall even rise up against the Prince of princes; but, by no human hand, he shall be broken. Dan. 8:25, R.S.V.

Experts say that a pathological liar is a terribly self-deceived person. That is, a person who constantly is telling lies in order to keep bolstering his sagging story ends up deceiving himself more than anyone else. Long after others have caught on that he is a big bluff, he still believes that he's the most incredible gift to the neighborhood.

If this principle holds true on a broader scale, then who do you suspect might be the most self-deceived person in the whole universe? Who has been telling the most outlandish lies to the most people for the longest period of time, with the most to lose when he gets found out? None other than the father of lies, Satan himself.

In today's text Daniel prophesies that Satan's campaign for an alternative to reality will, for a time, succeed marvelously. He will deceive many with the idea that he is indeed a great leader. He will portray himself as the source of life, wisdom, and happiness. The trouble is, after six thousand years of this line, "in his own mind" he apparently believes it. He really believes that he can overthrow Jesus, the Prince of princes. With a zeal born of conviction, he will press his campaign with increasing intensity. Yet it will backfire, for when the court shall sit in judgment and the books are opened (Dan. 7:10), the Big Lie shall be exposed. He will be broken, not by might nor by power, but by God's truth.

For all who despise the successes of the enemy, what better way to oppose his work than to "turn on the lights." Wouldn't it be thrilling if Satan were to throw a party in honor of his self-claimed greatness and no one showed up? How great if all we who claim loyalty to Jesus Christ were to cease showing any response to Satan's supposedly grand patterns for living. If we were to live the Christ life with joy, with the intelligent assent of our deepest loyalties, we could help expose the fraud for what he is. The beauty of God's truth will, in the end, destroy Satan's deceptions.

WHEN GOD CLAIMS HIS PEOPLE

But you are a chosen race, a royal priesthood, a dedicated nation, and a people claimed by God for his own, to proclaim the triumphs of him who has called you out of darkness into his marvellous light. 1 Peter 2:9, N.E.B.

Imagine that you are attending a great international festival where representatives from many nations have come to portray their native cultures. You watch as varied costumes pass the reviewing stand. You listen intently as the announcer highlights the unique features of each country. Suddenly a hush comes over the crowd as people of remarkable bearing step forward. In admiring tones the announcer explains that they come from a country where every citizen is counted as documented royalty. Furthermore, every one of them holds a high office in the dignified religion of the land. The citizenry is noted for the absence of crime and for its advanced social programs. Finally, there is clear evidence that the people of the country have special connections with the ruling powers of the universe.

If you suspect you might be impressed with such a scene, you have only to read today's text again and realize that it does not exist entirely in the realm of the imagination. For this is exactly what our Father desires each of us to be.

We are royalty, because we are even now in preparation to sit next to Jesus on His throne, entering with Him into consideration of the issues of vital interest to the universe. (See Rev. 3:21.)

We are priests, because we deal with the most sacred of all things: the character and reputation of our God. We have been entrusted with the immeasurable privilege of telling the world how God seeks their friendship. (See 2 Cor. 5:19.) We are spiritual ambassadors, representing the kingdom of God to people who don't yet know how much they would enjoy it. As priests, we stand between an alien world and a loving God, seeking to make Him known.

We are a dedicated nation—a people with a consuming spiritual purpose, set aside from all that is mundane to accomplish matters of eternal consequence.

Yet we are participants in any of these great privileges only because God, in His infinite graciousness, has claimed us. He alone can rescue, transform, and commission. And He alone has sole right to receive the honor and the praise, for when the universe is once again at-one with Him we shall all live in endless peace.

OUR FACE GIVES IT AWAY

So too when you fast, do not look gloomy like the hypocrites: they make their faces unsightly so that other people may see that they are fasting. I tell you this: they have their reward already. Matt. 6:16, N.E.B.

Really, now; with all the cosmic issues Jesus had on His agenda during the brief years of His earthly ministry, with all the crucially important things He had to say and do, what difference should it make how a certain group of people look when they choose to go without food? After all, if they want to smudge some ashes under their eyes to enhance the gaunt look, if they get some kind of kick out of standing on the street corners letting their stomachs growl in public, that's their problem! Why should such an incidental quirk be of concern to the Saviour of all mankind?

Fortunately, Jesus saw things far more clearly than our narrow vision usually allows. He knew that the Pharisees were not just some religious curiosity. They were the ones who, more than anyone else, claimed to be the spokesmen for God. In the eyes of most of Israel, they were on the inside track with Divinity. And as they dragged around the landscape in their regular sessions of exaggerated self-denial they were broadcasting that this is what God requires. The light-headed misery of systems drained of vitality, the sallow complexion and staggered step, the Pharisees claimed, were required of the devout as a means of impressing God.

But Jesus deflated the whole scheme. As these pallid figures staggered by, if any of their fellow humans wanted to stand for a moment in awe, that was all the reward they were going to get. He emphatically reported that His Father was not impressed. What is more, His Father was grieved that such gross misrepresentations of His character should be pawned off by the religious authorities. If they needed to fast for a time, perhaps to clear the mind for deeper spiritual understandings, then this should be a private matter. In public they should have their faces scrubbed, hair combed, and a touch of perfume to brighten the occasion.

Being in our Father's family is a joyous experience. All His paths are ways of brightness. The faces of His children can be as inviting as His own. Our eyes, as windows to our souls, may reveal an unmistakable inner joy. These are the ways of our Father.

SATAN'S OFFER TO HELP JESUS

And the tempter came and said to him, "If you are the Son of God, command these stones to become loaves of bread." Matt. 4:3, R.S.V.

Jesus did not come into this world with a fully developed memory of His previous existence. It was not because He could recall living in the presence of His Father that He knew He was the divine Son of God. His confidence was based instead upon His Spirit-led understandings of the prophecies and sacrificial system recorded in the Old Testament. He was ready to tell the world who He was, facing scorn from even His own family and eventually experiencing a cruel death, because He was certain of what He had read.

But what if He were wrong? What if He, like so many others, had misread Scripture? Or what if even the Scriptures were unreliable? Wouldn't it be comforting to know, right at the beginning of His earthly ministry, that He really did have innate divinity within Himself? He had worked no miracles prior to this time.

How "convenient," then, that Satan should arrive on the scene at that time and propose a simple little miracle that would not only satisfy Jesus' hunger following forty days of fasting but would also give Him an opportunity to prove His divinity to Himself. The drama was intensified the more by Satan's suggestion that certainly God would not leave His Son in such a bleak situation without providing a miraculous way of escape.

Yet Jesus saw the deeper issues. He discerned that the single underlying issue in all temptation is for one to break away from utter dependency upon God and to seek to solve one's own problems. For Jesus to have worked a miracle to meet His own needs—either for food or for verification of His divinity—would not have been fundamentally different from when Adam and Eve took the fruit in order to advance their own cause. In either case, the one who was dependent upon divinity would have broken that dependent relationship. And that, in the truest sense, is a denial of faith.

This temptation that Jesus faced was, in one important way, vastly more difficult than the temptations we face, because Jesus really did have divinity within Himself, which He could have relied upon to meet His needs. By contrast, when I am tempted to rely upon myself, it is a joke, a comical illusion. Trusting my Father makes vastly more sense.

FAITH IS BEING CONFIDENT

Do not then throw away your confidence, for it carries a great reward. Heb. 10:35, N.E.B.

Would you be willing to make a promise to do absolutely anything I asked you to do, without questioning? If you were to answer, "Yes! Of course!" then I would have some questions about *you*. Most likely you would respond with cautious questions such as "How can I know you won't ask me to do something foolish? Would you want to prove all that authority you have over me? Or abuse it?"

You probably would not be satisfied if I replied in soothing tones, "Just trust me. Take a blind leap in the dark, and just trust me." You would ask what basis you would have for trusting me, what evidence upon which to base your confidence.

It seems reasonable to relate to fellow human beings on this basis. We place our confidence in people only after we have come to have sufficient basis for doing so. We see no virtue in blind faith; we trust only the trustworthy. Why, then, do we feel so hesitant to relate to God in the same way? Why do we feel embarrassed about looking for evidence for trusting Him, when He has gone to such great lengths to give us so much of it? Why do we employ the highest mental capacities He has given us when making decisions of modest importance, but set them aside when making the most crucial decisions of our entire existence?

Through the ages, many Christians have felt that faith is simply a choice to believe religious convictions without any basis for doing so—that to ask for evidence is to undermine faith. Because the powers of intellect often have been perverted to the detriment of religious experience, it has seemed antireligious to bring careful mental discipline to one's informed trust in God.

But our God is not afraid of the evidence! He is not worried what people will find when they look closely in His direction. He knows that we turned from Him in the first place because we handled the evidence in a shoddy manner. He knows that through the centuries those who have been His best friends have always been those who understood Him most clearly and could speak most accurately about Him. He invites us to become acquainted with Him in Jesus, and then not to throw away our confidence.

HOW HOT IS HELL?

They will suffer the punishment of eternal destruction, separated from the presence of the Lord and from his glorious might. 2 Thess. 1:9, T.E.V.

If you have a table or desk lamp near you as you read this, let your eyes glance from the bulb down to the power cord at the base of the lamp. Then trace the cord across the floor to the wall plug. From there you will have to imagine electrical wires running through your house, across town, over the countryside, and finally ending at some huge generating plant. The little bulb in your lamp gives off light because it has an unbroken connection with the power plant. If the wires are broken at any point—by a tree falling across the power lines, or by you pulling the plug—the light will go out. The bulb cannot give light by itself.

In the same way, we live because we are in union with the Life-giver, our heavenly Father. Though we have broken connection with Him, God has been giving us the daily grace-gift of life that we might choose to renew our loyalties with Him. But He will not forever keep the whole planet on an emergency life-support system. God has great respect for our freedom; the day will come when those who refuse His gracious invitation for friendship will be given what they have chosen: separation from Him.

When you unplug your lamp, it doesn't explode. The light just goes out. Nor do you need to beat on the bulb in anger for its ceasing to give light. That's simply what happens when it is disconnected. By the same token, when one breaks union with God life ceases. God does not, in anger, need to crush it out. Nor does He need to work a miracle to keep a person alive so that He might at the same time inflict unending punishment on him. To be separated from the Life-giver is to be dead—eternally.

The people God was addressing in Biblical times did not always understand this cause-effect principle. It was difficult for them to appreciate the destructiveness of being out of harmony with God. And so the Bible writers employed the imagery of consuming flames to describe the sureness and completeness of the destruction of life apart from God. But being apart from God is in itself the worst thing that could ever happen to a person. God doesn't need to torch hellish fires to enhance what is already so terrible.

THE ROOTS OF UGLINESS

There is no fidelity, no tenderness, no knowledge of God in the country, only perjury and lies, slaughter, theft, adultery and violence, murder after murder. Hosea 4:1, 2, Jerusalem.

On a recent radio talk show various callers were expressing their firm opinions to the host about why there was so much crime in our country. One said, "It's the breakup of the family. That's why there is so much crime." So the host asked, "But why are there so many homes breaking up?" The caller didn't know.

The next caller did know. "It's because of television; that's what is breaking up our homes. They show such immoral stuff on TV that people just try to live that way too." Again the host responded, "The producers just give the people what they want. Why do people want to watch that stuff?" This caller wasn't sure.

Another caller wanted to blame the liberal courts, but when the host pointed out that juries and judges tend to reflect something of the prevailing morality of a society and asked where society was getting its values, the caller only mumbled that he didn't know. And so it went, each caller blaming what he thought was a prime cause, only to acknowledge that it also was just a symptom of a larger malaise.

Had Hosea been in the listening audience, however, we might have heard him say, "There is no knowledge of God in the land." The root cause of all the ugliness is that the people do not know their Father. He could have defended his position from any of several angles. Some might say, for example, that there really is a lot of religion in the country, so many professional clerics. To which he would have replied, "Let no one accuse the people or reprimand them—my complaint is against you priests" (Hosea 4:4, T.E.V.). The religious leaders, even though talking a great deal about God, have rejected a true understanding of Him (verse 6).

When a country claims to live by God's values, yet its people have no vital union with God to obtain the inner renewal to live by those values, the whole scheme becomes a frustrating mockery. There is neither a fixed point of certainty about what is right, nor the inner desire to live it. All the country's institutions suffer alike: the homes, the courts, the schools, and the media. The solution? "Let us know, let us press on to know the Lord" (chap. 6:3, R.S.V.).

THE LONGING IN GOD'S HEART

If you had responded to my rebuke, I would have poured out my heart to you and made my thoughts known to you. Prov. 1:23, N.I.V.

In our endeavors to please God, we often seek to know His will regarding what we should or should not do. Could it be that God is ultimately more concerned about our relationship with Him than with our actions? Could it be that His desire to deal with our actions is because He longs to promote, protect, and nurture that relationship?

Today's text speaks of a great longing in God's heart. It explains His intentions when He remonstrates with us. "If you had responded to my rebuke, I would have poured out my heart to you and made my thoughts known to you." It is plain that God not only wants to make His thoughts known to us; He desires to pour out His heart to us!

In human relationships, when we pour out our hearts to somebody, we trust that person with all our hopes and dreams. Can it be that our great God has hopes and dreams that He'd love to share with us? Have we been shortsighted in thinking that all He ever thinks about is our behavior? Before this world began, God had plans and dreams, and we may confidently know that we were a part of those dreams. Our companionship was something He envisioned long before sin entered the universe.

It is difficult for us to conceptualize eternity. I've heard people comment candidly that they are a little nervous about what we will find to *do* for a time as long as forever. Perhaps most of us will take a long time in getting past the relief we'll experience in not having any more trials. At this point I can picture God smiling broadly, because He can hardly wait to tell us what He's been thinking about!

The happiest times we know on earth are when we are sharing the rich companionship of trusted and loved friends. What we *do* together is almost inconsequential, though often stimulating and rewarding. It is the friendship that makes the experience worthwhile. In like manner, our friendship with God is what eternity is all about. Even now we may begin to enter into such a special relationship with Him that we will be eager to have anything and everything removed that would keep us from ever-deepening communion with Him. We will be just as eager as He is.

THE THEME OF JESUS' PRAYER

Oh, Simon, Simon, do you know that Satan has asked to have you all to sift like wheat?—But I have prayed for you that you may not lose your faith. Yes, when you have turned back to me, you must strengthen these brothers of yours. Luke 22:31, 32, Phillips.

How easy it is for us to pray amiss! We earnestly plead for God to bless the missionaries across the seas, while we neglect the needs of our neighbor next door. We ask for more money, while our prior need is to learn how to manage what money we have.

When Jesus prayed, however, His briefly stated concerns went right to the basic issues. The prayer for Peter that is recorded in today's text reveals such sensitive understanding. He knew that Peter would not make it through the night—that before the sun would rise on a new day, he would have vehemently denied his Lord three times. For Peter's sake, Jesus wanted to report the theme of His prayer; it contained the avenue of his recovery.

Peter was about to face an aspect of the Messiah's ministry that simply did not fit in his script. His vision of Jesus as the military conqueror and national deliverer was about to be nailed to an ugly cross. And Peter's narrowly based faith would die with Him. It is a crisis that all of Jesus' fragile-faithed friends will have to face eventually. All of us who have believed in Jesus because of what He can do for us, who have staked our confidence on our small vision of Him, will face a crash similar to Peter's.

Jesus knows better than to prevent that crash. He knows that immature, self-centered faith is too small for the great issues of life and salvation, and that it must die to give way to new understandings. So He tenderly walks with us through our Calvary, in order that when immature faith goes through its death throes, we can remember the heart of the One who looked Peter in the eye with great compassion even as he was swearing his denials. We can remember who He is and, remembering, we can return to Him.

The theme of Jesus' prayer was that Peter would return to *Him*. Rather than be disappointed that Jesus did not measure up to his own miniature expectations, Peter's faith needed to grow up. This is the kind of faith that Jesus prayed would not fail.

LET THERE BE LIGHT!

It is the same God that said, "Let there be light shining out of darkness," who has shone in our minds to radiate the light of the knowledge of God's glory, the glory on the face of Christ. 2 Cor. 4:6, Jerusalem.

One of my favorite fantasies is that we will get to watch Jesus do Creation week all over again. You know the setting: The earth will just have been cleaned up with a consuming fire, lying all barren and ready as it was six thousand years ago. The Father will announce, "Behold, I make all things new" (Rev. 21:5). Then Jesus' great voice will sweep across the landscape, creating in its wake green forests and blue lakes teeming with life. Perhaps it will take seven days, just as it did the first time, giving us twenty-four hours to celebrate each step.

Paul's favorite fantasy was only slightly different. He too pictured that great voice saying, "Let there be light!" But instead of suns and stars, he envisioned brilliant truth impacting the minds of men and women—truth about the glorious character of our Father as revealed in Jesus. He longed to see that bright, compelling truth sweeping aside every fragment of darkness—the darkness of Satan-sponsored misunderstanding.

Far from a fantasy, of course, this was Paul's life mission! Nothing meant more to him than that Jesus should be made known. His cherished definition of the gospel was the "Good News of the glory of Christ, who is the image of God" (2 Cor. 4:4, Jerusalem). To Paul, there could be no greater news than the discovery of the Father's true character as revealed in Jesus. There was nothing that would be of more benefit to the world, more valuable for mankind to know.

I'm so glad that Paul recognized this glory as being revealed on the face of Jesus. Far beyond words, there is so much that is revealed by one's face. The eyes, the gentle lines around the mouth, even the tilt of the head while listening intently to another speak, can reveal such winning qualities. What a delightful way to dispel the darkness.

The same creative power that could by a spoken word bring to life beings in God's own image could—by becoming the Word—fill their minds anew with truth that could reform their characters into His own likeness. In the final analysis, wouldn't that be even more thrilling to behold than Creation week? Fortunately, we can enjoy them both.

WHAT ELSE COULD HE DO?

The Lord was in the right; it was I who rebelled against his commands. Lam. 1:18, N.E.B.

What if God were to work miracles that made smokers healthy, adulterers happy, and cheaters wise? On the face of it, we know that these species of sins would suddenly become much more popular.

On the other hand, if smokers got healthy, then why would smoking be a sin? If adulterers truly became more happy, then why would God be against adultery? If people could cheat to gain genuine wisdom, wouldn't God be in favor of it?

This illustrates that God doesn't go around simply hanging the "sin" tag on various activities, then railing against all of the activities so labeled. Christian growth doesn't mean that we simply try to get all the tags right. There is nothing arbitrary about any of God's dealings with us. That which He rules out from our lives is that which in itself is hurtful to us. Christian growth, then, involves learning to walk within the patterns of inherent blessing. It means learning to avoid those patterns that will in themselves bring pain and grief.

In the Lamentations of Jeremiah, a man of God verbally weeps over the sorrows of his people. Their country has been invaded and badly damaged by foreign troops. The glorious Temple lies in ruins. The people are suffering from famine and disease. A nation that refused to listen to her God as He called her to repentance has come face-to-face with the consequences of her choices.

Yet there is no rancor in Jeremiah's voice, no bitterness that God has inflicted undue punishment upon His people. Instead, he is quick to acknowledge that God is absolutely in the right in allowing the nation to suffer. He knows that God does not work the kind of miracle that confuses people about reality; He does not step in to prevent a wandering people from feeling the pain of their wandering, lest they come to feel that wandering from God is a wholesome thing to do.

The pain that God's wandering people feel is portioned out to us with a loving hand. He allows enough to sober and instruct us, yet not so much as to crush us. He longs for us to feel His love, rather than to cower before His anger. The only enduring basis for true faith is admiration for the beauty of His character and the goodness of His ways.

November 28

MY DEFENDING COUNSEL

In my heart I know that my vindicator lives and that he will rise last to speak in court; and I shall discern my witness standing at my side and see my defending counsel, even God himself, whom I shall see with my own eyes, I myself and no other. Job 19:25-27, N.E.B.

There are few places in all of Scripture where one can find such a vivid, confident, and intensely personal portrait of God, wrapped into one sentence, than this expression by Job. All who have, like Job, felt accused, abandoned, and misunderstood will appreciate every nuance of this picture of our Father. It is particularly powerful when seen in contrast to Satan's portrait of God.

Satan has asserted that God relates to His people as an accuser. Being a perfect God who holds high standards, He can respond only with judgment against such obvious sinners as we are. But Job has a special title for Him. He speaks of God as "my vindicator," as one who not only announces forgiveness but who defends Job against all others who would accuse him.

Those who have had a case pending in court remember their apprehension about the summary arguments of the opposition. They worry that if their adversary has "the last word" they will have no chance for rebuttal and will lose the case. Job, however, is confident that his vindicator will have the last word, the final summary statement on his behalf. He knows that his accusers will have nothing more to say when God puts forth His final evidence.

As Job imagines the heavenly courtroom, he does not see himself standing alone and exposed before all the officials. With transparent warmth, he describes his heavenly advocate as "standing at my side." Of all the places God could position Himself, there is a touching message in His choice to show solidarity with His troubled friends.

No wonder, then, that Job could speak of God with the endearing term "my defending counsel." He did not regard God as though He were merely a court-appointed defense, going through the motions required by law in order to "make things proper." Job felt a deep, personal interest on God's part in a happy outcome for himself.

That's why God could speak so highly of Job, seeing him as one that could be counted on not to fail, even under the most trying circumstances. That's what happens to our faith when we know God as He is!

338

NO CONDEMNATION!

No condemnation now hangs over the head of those who are "in" Christ Jesus. For the new spiritual principle of life "in" Christ Jesus lifts me out of the old vicious circle of sin and death. Rom. 8:1, 2, Phillips.

"That's a tall list," the young man gasped. "Who could ever live up to all that?" He was studying the personal standards of his church; his youth pastor had been reviewing what the Bible requires in the areas of personal conduct, moral values, recreation, friendship, diet, dress, the media, use of time, and financial responsibilities. He was both bewildered and overwhelmed, because he was certain that until he had learned to embrace all these details he would be continually guilty of violating God's will.

He was expressing a familiar feeling: that we spend our life growing *toward* the security of freedom from guilt, rather than growing *within* that security. He shared the too-common perception that the only reason God could think of to get people to live by high standards was as an escape from condemnation. Therefore, in his mind, if God were to pronounce His people free from condemnation, they would start misbehaving all over again. At the same time, however, the thought of continually staggering under condemnation hardly seemed appealing.

So his pastor began to unfold to him the meaning of Romans 8:1. He pointed out that we bear a burden of guilt when we are outside of a relationship with Christ. Indeed, the broken relationship is itself the guilt-inducing sin, and being reunited with Christ is the desired remedy. The young man's eyes began to widen as he recognized that it is the union with Christ, not the dread of condemnation, that is the new motive power in the believer's life. Were Christ continually to hang the threat of condemnation over the growing believer's head, it would shift the focus away from Christ Himself. It would confuse the motives for obedience, offering self-centered escape from condemnation in the place of Christ-centered love for truth.

Oh, how much we need to grasp that guiltiness has no place in the life of one in union with Christ! Yes, we may stumble en route to wholeness in Christ. And we shall feel remorse for hurting others and for misrepresenting our Lord. But we must not let Satan push remorse into feeling condemned and rejected by God, for "there is therefore now no condemnation for those who are in Christ Jesus" (R.S.V.).

THE RIGHT USE OF AUTHORITY

When one rules over men in righteousness, when he rules in the fear of God, he is like the light of morning at sunrise on a cloudless morning, like the brightness after rain that brings the grass from the earth. 2 Sam. 23:3, 4, N.I.V.

"You're just trying to rule me!" pouted the defiant child. His sense of justice was wounded because his mother insisted that he perform a task in which he saw no meaning. When she scolded him for his unwillingness to obey, his countenance fell even further. His self-image was at stake. "I hate you!" he muttered as he left the room.

Before we take sides, let's consider today's scripture. "When one rules over men in righteousness, when he rules in the fear of God"—that is, when one who is in a position of authority is in right relationship with God, and finds His ways worth emulating—"he is like the light of morning at sunrise on a cloudless morning, like the brightness after rain that brings the grass from the earth."

The right use of authority is likened to the warm brightness of early-morning sunshine, which makes grass spring up from the earth. If authority, for whatever reason, blights the hearts of those over whom it is exercised, it is wrong. God Himself values the nurturing of our friendship more than He esteems mere correctness.

However, the attitude of altogether too many people who are in a position to order others around is "Get people in line first, then worry about their feelings!" Often the chief motivation is progress, not winning the respect of those who must answer to their demands. The need to avoid chaos is stressed. What they fail to realize is that people achieve far more when they are in an environment of trust. When there is respect for a supervisor because he respects the worth of the workers, camaraderie develops and production soars.

God has far more in mind than the production of good works. He has given us a glimpse of how He uses His infinite authority to warm frozen hearts into throbbing life. Tender as young blades of grass, our affections toward Him are nurtured by His commitment to respect and protect our individuality and freedom of conscience. He uses His power, not to whip us into line, but to enable us to respond to the high and lofty calling of walking as sons and daughters of the King.

MORE THAN AN EXAMPLE

And after you have borne these sufferings a very little while, the God of all grace, who has called you to share his eternal splendour through Christ, will himself make you whole and secure and strong. 1 Peter 5:10, Phillips.

I am an avid musician. Unfortunately, the only musical instrument I have ever learned to play is the phonograph. And so I have to content myself with being an appreciative listener as my wife lets Debussy flow through her fingertips on our piano. I listen with rapture on my stereo system as great orchestras play Vaughan Williams, Chopin, Rachmaninoff, and Copland. I have fantasized about being able to sit down at the keyboard of a massive organ and make the walls shake and the audience weep.

Would it work if I were simply to stand behind E. Power Biggs (or a similar great organist), and watch him play an organ for a time, then just "follow his example"? If he plays a Bach cantata perfectly, and I watch closely, shouldn't I also be able to play it perfectly? The idea is, of course, ludicrous—all the more so when you know how clumsy I am with my fingers!

The apostle Peter tells us that Jesus is an example for us, that we should follow in His steps (1 Peter 2:21). But I am so glad that he didn't stop there. Otherwise, I can imagine people simply looking at the life of Christ, watching closely as He behaved in such a flawless manner, with perfect spirit and tact, then saying, "All right; now I'll just do the same." The outcome is about as promising as my mimicking Biggs playing Bach.

Even more so than being a musician, being Christlike requires a movement within the soul. I can, in time, copy a C scale on the piano by rote memory and practice. But I can love an unlovely person only after my heart has been healed by Christ's divine love. I can care about the needs of others, even at my own expense and inconvenience, only after I have been made secure by Jesus' meeting of my needs. Though I may be able to say nice words to another person, I can succeed in imparting genuine strength to another struggling soul only when I am in bonded union with Him who is truly strong. Our Father Himself will make us whole, secure, and strong, not by waving some magic wand over us, but by drawing us into vital union with Himself.

RECONCILIATION IS REAL!

So if you are about to offer your gift to God at the altar and there you remember that your brother has something against you, leave your gift there in front of the altar, go at once and make peace with your brother, and then come back and offer your gift to God. Matt. 5:23, 24, T.E.V.

We parents have often watched our children go to church, sing "Jesus Loves Me," pray for their family members by name, then return home and fight with each other until the tears flow. We wonder just how we can get them to bridge the gap between the religious words and actions they perform at church, and the issues of their practical life. There are few things more deadly to true spirituality than for religion to become a round of mere formalism and ritual, cut off from conscious connection with the real world.

One of the greatest truths in salvation history is that God has gone to stunning lengths to win us back to Himself, to reconcile us wayward children to our Father. He sent His Son in human form to tell us that our warfare had ended, that the hostilities we felt toward Him, and perceived from Him, could be laid to rest. On the cross, all mankind could see the depths of divine love and the thoroughness with which God had dealt with sin.

Thousands of years earlier God had given His people an acted parable of the cross and its Sacrifice through the system of animal sacrifices. It was God's desire that it bring spiritual realities closer to the people, since they would actually participate in bringing the animals. As they watched innocent blood flowing because of their sins, it would draw their minds toward the great reconciling act of Christ on the cross.

Unfortunately, however, most of the people lost the message in the sacrifices. In the next deadly step, they came to believe that it was the animal sacrifice itself that God required—for *His* sake! They did not grasp that the sacrifice was intended to change *them,* not God.

Jesus tugged their thinking far beyond ritual; He carried it into their real lives. He said, in essence, "Don't come to celebrate God's reconciling act until the meaning of reconciliation has touched your own heart. When you have made peace with your alienated brother, you will know more of the reality of what God has done to win *you* back."

RESPECTING OUR FREEDOM

If anyone declares publicly that he belongs to me, I will do the same for him before my Father in heaven. But if anyone rejects me publicly, I will reject him before my Father in heaven. Matt. 10:32, 33, T.E.V.

Her eyes were wide and her voice was tense. "I wonder," she said, "what will be my destiny when my name comes up in the heavenly judgment? Will God declare me saved or lost?"

This young woman shared a widely held dread of the judgment, based on the assumption that the issues center on what God thinks about us. In her mind, she imagined scenes of God leafing through the books of record, as though to refresh His memory about her life's patterns. Perhaps He even keeps score in a small notebook. At some point, she feared, God will tally the score and make a decision about her. Her eternal destiny will be based on which way He votes: life, or death.

But Jesus' words suggest a distinctly different approach. He sets the focus, not around God's decision about us, but around our decision about God in Jesus Christ. Because heaven is rooted in reality, it can only acknowledge what we have in fact decided here on earth. Jesus simply states that He will be delighted to claim anyone who has claimed Him. Before the Father and all the interested angels (see Luke 12:8, 9), Jesus will announce that mutual friendship is there! On the other hand, because He does not force our free choices, when someone disowns Him before the world He will sadly have to report that no relationship exists between Himself and that person.

True, books of record are kept in the heavenly courts; but their purpose is not to enable God to make up His mind about His people, for "the Lord knows those who are his" (2 Tim. 2:19, T.E.V.). These records are kept to verify that God has nothing to hide. He is willing to open before the whole universe the life records of anyone, lost or saved. He does not need to erase the record of failures among those who are saved, because those same records document their repentance and their faith. Books of record prove that when God announces that certain people are ready for eternal life, it can be backed up by evidence.

Rather than us standing before God in puzzled anxiety, God is looking toward us with eager anticipation saying, "Won't you choose Me?"

December 4

THE OPPOSITE OF LEGALISM

Now, it is clear that no one is put right with God by means of the Law, because the scripture says, "Only the person who is put right with God through faith shall live." Gal. 3:11, T.E.V.

Ask most any first-year college theology major what is the opposite of legalism, and he will almost certainly answer, "Faith." When pressed a little further about what that might mean, he may explain, "Legalism means depending on the merits of human works; the opposite is to depend on the perfect merits of Jesus Christ."

It seems a good answer; it is one that would be accepted by many Christians from most denominations. Given the choice, which of us wouldn't rather depend upon the perfect and abundant merits of Jesus Christ than upon the miniature and sin-stained "merits" of faulty human attempts at lawkeeping. Certainly Paul wouldn't choose the latter!

But it raises another question. Where do we find in Scripture that the Father requires merit of any kind—ours or Christ's? Where do we read that He is impressed with merit? Do we have any evidence that the human sin problem stems from a lack of merit, to be made up from some other source?

When we turn to Paul's Galatian Epistle, the classic place in Scripture where reliance upon human works is most vigorously scorned, we find a surprising alternative. Paul does not suggest that we go in search of a better source of merit. In Paul's mind, the opposite of legalism is relationship. The alternative to frustrated human performance that attempts to please God is coming into fellowship with a God who is already pleased with us.

The second and third chapters of Galatians are so clear: those who have *faith* are in touch with eternal life. Faith is not simply reaching out to a larger store of merit; it is a union of the soul with Christ that is so vital and real that Paul can speak of Christ living *in* us (chap. 2:20). That blended life is lived by faith—that is, by an ongoing friendship with our divine Lord.

Faith involves having confidence in God. And that means trusting a God who is interested in matters more vital than the accumulation of merit. It means responding to One who is extremely interested in our love and loyalty, for He knows that when He is the center of our lives every other good thing comes as a result.

344

HE IS NOT SILENT

For the Lord God does nothing without giving to his servants the prophets knowledge of his plans. Amos 3:7, N.E.B.

In ancient Greece there developed an interesting form of religion known generally as mystery religions, which centered upon secret rites and esoteric sayings. Only the initiated were given access to the central core of worship and supposed benefit. Strict safeguards were imposed to prevent the privileged few from passing on the hidden doctrines to the general masses. Perhaps much of the appeal for its devotees was the sought-after thrill of finally being counted as part of the privileged inner circle.

Even to this day many people belong to secret orders, lodges, and fraternal organizations based on a similar mystique. But the religion of Jesus Christ has none of it! By contrast to the supposed deities of the mystery religions, our God is intensely eager to get all the accurate information He possibly can into the minds of His people. Indeed, it is the lack of truth, the scarcity of clear understanding about His character and kingdom, that has caused all the trouble in the first place. He is not stingy in passing on that precious truth.

Rather than communicating to us in a haphazard fashion, God has often followed the pattern of working through devout and teachable persons who are willing to carry His messages. The Bible refers to them as prophets, a word that means one who speaks on the behalf of God. Once their credentials have been established and the community of believers know that they are reliable channels of truth, God can work through them in increasingly effective ways to unfold His plans.

Throughout salvation history every critical turning point in God's dealings with His people has been marked by the ministry of a prophet. Moses led in the Exodus. Noah warned of, then survived, the great Flood. Isaiah comforted and guided during the great captivity by Babylon. And John the Baptist prepared the way for the coming of Christ. Isn't that just like our God not to leave His people in the dark at such crucial times?

How grateful we should be that, as Paul affirmed in Ephesians 4:11-13, the prophetic gift is still active, revealing the magnificent truths of God's character. God did not cut off all further communications at the time of John the revelator, but has given His last-day people a rich channel of reliable truth. In these dark hours, let's grasp all the light we can find!

WHAT MAKES OUR LOVE COMPLETE?

God is love. Whoever lives in love lives in God, and God in him. Love is made complete among us so that we will have confidence on the day of judgment, because in this world we are like him. 1 John 4:16, 17, N.I.V.

There is a progression that takes place as a believer first finds forgiveness, then newness of life and a growing relationship with the Father. To begin with, the most important thing for me, a sinner, to experience is God's unconditional love and forgiveness. When I learn that He fully accepts me, I become secure enough to welcome His counsel in making major adjustments in my outlook and lifestyle. In the process, I become increasingly appreciative of who He is—His wisdom is so good, His ways so appropriate, and His plans for me so exciting. I am drawn into communion with Him, for His own sake, because He is altogether lovely. Is there something more?

Our text says: "God is love. Whoever lives in love lives in God, and God in him. Love is made complete among us so that we will have confidence on the day of judgment, because in this world we are like him." What immediately grabs your attention when you read this passage? If you are still concerned about your standing on the day of judgment, you probably felt a surge of desire to have the confidence spoken of here. However, if you are confident that God loves and accepts you, you may have felt affirmed in your faith.

Actually, the apostle John is describing the relationship between God and His friends, the back-and-forthness of living His love. We come to know we are totally secure in the Father, who is the personification of love. *He* is our confidence on the day of judgment. But there is something more: "Love is made complete among us . . . because in this world we are like him." Now, this is very exciting! Our shared love with the Father is made complete as we interact with others in this world.Our friendship with God is reflected in all our earthly associations. Not only does this give unbelievers an opportunity to come to know God, but we also experience in a tangible way the validity of all that we have learned concerning Him. We are just like Him because we savor everything we know about Him.

And so our love is made complete.

THIS IS ETERNAL LIFE

Eternal life is this: to know you, the only true God, and Jesus Christ whom you have sent. I have glorified you on earth and finished the work that you gave me to do. John 17:3, 4, Jerusalem.

A popular series of television commercials depicts a respected businessman talking quietly to a friend in a busy and crowded room. He begins to quote the opinion of his stockbroker. A hush suddenly falls over the crowd as every ear strains to hear the advice of that respected firm. With important financial interests at stake, no one wants to miss such key information.

Place yourself in a setting with several serious-minded people, discussing what is essential for salvation. Some are suggesting that eternal life is found through a life of self-sacrifice and denial. Others are certain that eternal life is granted to those who accept certain legal provisions on their behalf. You are aware that the ultimate expert on eternal life, Jesus Christ Himself, has just entered the room. Though He seems to be in prayer to His Father, He is speaking so that others can hear.

"Eternal life," He says, "is this." Suddenly every other conversation stops. Every eye turns to His face; every ear strains to catch each word. Most expect a lengthy, complicated formula. They are stunned that it can be summarized in but three words. Eternal life is this: "To know you." To know the Father as He truly is, as He has been revealed through Jesus Christ—that is eternal life.

Some might object that it's too simple, that the Bible insists that no one is saved who does not do righteous works. But the only genuine works of righteousness are those that freely flow from a loving heart, and one's heart becomes loving only when it is bonded to the Father's great heart of love.

Others would urge the need for faith as the basis for salvation. Yet this is precisely what faith is. It is an informed friendship with God, leading to love and trust. Though faith may on occasion express itself in doing or believing something not fully understood, this is not its primary focus. Faith is built upon that which we *do* know and understand—the clear revelation of the Father in Jesus Christ.

Jesus looked back over His life mission and was able confidently to report, "Mission accomplished!" And what was that mission? "I have shown your glory on earth" (John 17:4, T.E.V.).

GOD IS FOR US

In face of all this, what is there left to say? If God is for us, who can be against us? Rom. 8:31, Phillips.

She had come for counseling, as do many students in their later adolescent years, because of troublesome home problems. I asked her about her feelings toward her father. "Oh, I love him," she quickly replied. Yet, as our conversation continued, I sensed that the word *love* wasn't adequate to describe the mixed bundle of feelings she held toward her father. Along with love, there were strong feelings of fear, of extreme apprehension lest she should fail to live up to his expectations and have to face his blistering rebukes. She assumed that since he was her father he had a right to act that way toward her. It was all part of the package.

In a similar vein, there are men who will quickly confess that they love God. Who could say otherwise, in view of all that He has done for us? Many of us have been singing songs about our love for God (or at least for Jesus) since we could first talk. Yet there is often, lurking below the surface in our hearts, a strong mixture of feelings toward God. The feelings of dread in the presence of such holy power; the feelings of being overmanaged by One whom we dare not question; the subtle fear of being manipulated by the price He has paid for us—we often learn to tuck all these feelings into the basements of our minds. After all, we conclude, it's all part of the package.

It was to people very much like ourselves that Paul was writing when he reached that resounding conclusion after paragraphs of argument: "What is there left to say? If God is for us, who can be against us?" With great earnestness, Paul wants us to know that God is every bit on our side. His every action is designed for the winning and healing of His hurting people.

We hear the words and smile warmly at their intent, but there is still that haunting fear that our failures will draw forth His coldness. We are in the habit of *creating God in man's image*. We remember too keenly the times that people, people whom we love, have used their rejection of us to get us to do what they wanted. But rather than controlling us with rejection, our Father heals us with His love!

"I NEVER DISOBEYED"

He answered his father, "Lo, these many years I have served you, and I never disobeyed your command; yet you never gave me a kid, that I might make merry with my friends." Luke 15:29, R.S.V.

What a pathetic sight! With sweat pouring down his cheeks from walking behind the oxen across a large field in the hot sun, a middle-aged man reports to his father that he has been doing this virtually every day for a lifetime, in order to gain a few rewards from his father—only to hear his father say, "Son, everything that I have is yours already!"

On the face of it, one could say, "Think of all that wasted effort—the years of plowing and planting and harvesting in the hot sun and reluctant soil—when he didn't need to. He already had the goods!"

But the real tragedy goes even deeper. Think of that son living on his father's estate all those years, and still thinking that his father shared his blessings only with those who merited them! Our mind pictures that older brother dutifully punching the time clock, grumbling under his breath about every moment of overtime, sullenly wishing that the "old man would kick off" so that he could rightfully inherit the estate. We watch him flash with rage as he recalls the father giving half the estate to that scoundrel brother who didn't play by the rules. He resents the homecoming celebration barbecue since it will deplete his inheritance by one goat.

The older brother's motives are so utterly narrow and petty that Jesus does not need to belabor that point. Instead, He turns (as always) to portray the Father. Even though he has every right to do a blistering exposé of his son's smallness, the father simply speaks gentle words of reassurance. He does not begrudge his son's anger. Amazingly, he reassures him that the wealth of the estate is already his!

I freely confess that this brings me a great comfort. When I recall how often I have resented God for passing by all my hard work to let His grace flow on one I regarded as unworthy, through my embarrassment I hear the Father's voice. He does not take issue with my claim never to have disobeyed, though He could. He doesn't let me pick a fight about the hours on my time card, though He knows it is irrelevant. He simply says, "Join your younger brother, and come home to your Father's heart."

FEAR MOTIVATES, BUT . . .

They put the altar in place first, because they lived in fear of the foreign population. Ezra 3:3, N.E.B.

It was the year America discovered that the Russians were placing nuclear missiles in Cuba. As a college student, I was a member of a large institutional church where a tiny percentage of the members showed up for the Wednesday night prayer meetings. President Kennedy told the Russians to take the missiles back home, "or else . . ." We all seemed to know what the "or else" meant, and we sensed that we were teetering on the very brink of that final nuclear death throe that could leave the world a poisoned cinder in about forty minutes.

Prayer meeting experienced a 600 percent increase. Voluntary prayer bands formed all around the campus, morning and evening. Conversation at the cafeteria tables became serious and very spiritual. The finest evangelist could not have worked a more sweeping revival.

And then the Russians took their missiles home. Everyone breathed easier, and life returned to normal. The busy routine crowded out the prayer bands. Football scores became vital table talk, and prayer meeting was once again attended by the faithful few.

Religion always seems to prosper in times of crisis. But the fact that its prosperity is so often short-lived raises questions about its genuineness. It is true that fear is a great motivator, but it is a very poor teacher. It moves people to action, but it fails to provide deep meaning and direction to that action. Fear drives many people to Christ, much as a fire drives people to a fire escape; but it fails to provide enduring reasons for people to stay with Christ.

The Jewish exiles, returning with Ezra to rebuild Jerusalem, were a frightened band. With an eye on the feisty local population, they hastened to build their sacrificial altar so that they might plead with God for safety. Morning and evening they brought their sacrifices, remembering their many years of having neglected these services prior to being taken captive. The situation had all the earmarks of a genuine religious revival.

But the years that followed revealed that the people had not been taught by their fears. Though they continued with great diligence to practice their religious forms, these became empty rituals, revealing no true knowledge of the character of the God they were worshiping. True faith is based not upon escape from the enemy's arrows or bombs, but upon an admiration for God because of who He is.

DO YOU LOVE YOUR NEIGHBOR?

The second most important commandment is like it: "Love your neighbor as you love yourself." Matt. 22:39, T.E.V.

What do you think would happen if all of us really did love our neighbors just as much, and in the same way, as we love ourselves? How would we act toward each other? Would we really take care to meet each other's needs?

Perhaps it would be useful to consider how most of us do love ourselves. At times it seems we border on a national epidemic of self-destruction, the way we badger ourselves with alcohol and drugs, overeating, lack of exercise, stress, loss of sleep, and a polluted environment. We take headache pills, tranquilizers, sleeping pills, and mood brighteners literally by the tons. We dull our minds with loud music, raunchy videos, and escapist games.

Though we are careful to defend ourselves, protect ourselves, and even lash out at others who might fault us, there is much evidence that we really aren't very fond of ourselves. Most of us are not enthralled with our weight, the color of our hair, or the shape of our nose. We are unsatisfied with our personalities, our style, and our personal past history. Our conversations reveal insecurities and self-put-downs.

How wise it was of Jesus that He should list loving our neighbors as ourselves as the second great commandment rather than the first. It is a fact that we cannot love ourselves until we first come into a loving relationship with our Father. Until we begin to absorb the truth of how God views us, we will continue to hold a very dim view of ourselves. In the light of the cross, we see the preciously high regard that He has placed upon us. And unless we want to argue that our opinion of ourselves is more accurate than that of the Creator, we have to accept that gracious message.

To see ourselves as persons created in the image of God, destined for fellowship with Him throughout eternity, is precisely how Jesus said we should see our neighbors. To love and care about all humanity is to include ourselves in that class. When Jesus said that we should forgive our enemies, we should consider whether we are holding any grudges against ourselves. Then we shall be set free from self-absorption to really care about others—and that most powerfully reflects the kind of love that Jesus expresses toward us.

A PURSE WITH HOLES IN IT

You earn wages, only to put them in a purse with holes in it. Haggai 1:6, N.I.V.

"Where does all the money go! You'd think there were holes in my pockets!" complained the young husband to his despairing wife. "We've got to learn to manage our finances better."

It's an area in which most of us could do better. However, all the techniques of the world will not bring budgetary success without God's blessings. Israel, in the days of King Darius, was having monetary problems. God spoke to them through the prophet Haggai, "Give careful thought to your ways. You have planted much, but have harvested little. You eat, but never have enough. You drink, but never have your fill. You put on clothes, but are not warm. You earn wages, only to put them in a purse with holes in it" (Haggai 1:5, 6, N.I.V.).

The house of the Lord was in ruins, but God's people were busy making nice homes for themselves and seeking financial gain. They kept saying, "The time has not yet come for the Lord's house to be built" (verse 2, N.I.V.). What they were really saying was that they did not want to part with any of their profits. They wanted to prosper themselves, even if it meant leaving their place of worship in shambles. Their selfishness revealed their lack of commitment to God. In leaving the Temple in ruins when repairs were possible, they were acting out their inner contentment with a broken relationship with the Almighty.

When we are out of relationship with God, we are out of tune with reality. Our lives cannot reap the results of right thinking because man, left on his own, is limited in his ability to make valid decisions. Consequently, the natural results of right thinking are thwarted. In Biblical language, God "withholds" His blessings. In actuality, God is committed to teaching us how to live accountably within the boundaries of cause and effect. This leads Him to allow us to experience deficit and need, rather than interfere as we might wish He would. Yet we hear His tender and earnest voice from heaven: "Give careful thought to your ways." Do not be irrational in your analysis of what is really happening.

When we make God the center of our lives, we have access to His vast wisdom. He speaks His mysteries to us personally. He "blesses" us; we experience the inherent benefits that surround an expanded reality, a reality of friendship with the Father.

IS THERE LIFE AFTER BIRTH?

Even though we were dead in our sins God, who is rich in mercy, because of the great love he had for us, gave us life together with Christ. Eph. 2:4, 5, Phillips.

As you push your way toward the checkout counter at most supermarkets, your eye is caught by the headlines of the pulp press as it hawks its latest piece of "earthshaking" trivia. At regular intervals you see minor variations on the theme: "Scientist Finds Shocking New Evidence for Life After Death!" If you venture to read the overstated stories, you find thirdhand reports of "out-of-body experiences" or other supposed sensations of those on the brink of death.

It is interesting that so many Christians are caught up in this concern about life after *death* when many of them have yet to figure out whether there is indeed life after *birth!* In other words, should it matter what happens when one dies unless one is certain that, as Christ has promised, eternal life has definitely begun at the new birth? If eternal life isn't genuine while we are alive, it doesn't offer much promise beyond the grave.

Jesus, Paul, and John all spoke repeatedly of the new birth. How else can you describe a change of values and life patterns and attitudes that is so radical that it seems as though life has begun all over again? Outside of Jesus Christ, one can be said to "live" only in the most basic, primitive sense. It is not much more than a biological existence, cut off from all the great issues and purposes of life. It is a narrow, self-centered, fear-ridden shuffle from the womb to the tomb.

But attachment to Christ changes everything! We receive new capacities for knowing and understanding spiritual truths. In place of scrambling to protect ourselves, we reach out to care about others. The cheap and temporary pleasures and treasures of this world are seen for the sham that they are. Greater themes and higher goals occupy our minds. Even our personalities, perhaps either flat or bluntly barbed outside of Christ, begin to reflect Christlike qualities of tenderness and poise.

"New life" means more than simply good behavior, for the sin problem is far greater than just bad behavior. Since the sin problem centers on alienation from Christ, then new life is, most fundamentally, an absorbing, spontaneous devotion to Christ as the natural focus of our life.

THE SWORD AS PROBLEM-SOLVER

Jesus said to him, "Put up your sword. All who take the sword die by the sword." Matt. 26:52, N.E.B.

It was a high-riding four-wheel-drive pickup truck, complete with rifle and shotgun mounted on the rack in the rear window. The driver appeared about as tough as the vehicle he drove. The sticker on the husky rear bumper seemed particularly appropriate: "Insured by Smith & Wesson." Rather than wait for theft to be repaid by his insurance agent, this driver wanted people to know that he would rely on the weapons of this well-known gunmaker to seek instant retribution on any thieves.

As I followed the truck down the freeway, my mind began imagining various scenarios. What if a would-be thief simply carried a larger Smith & Wesson, or was more skilled in its use? Then the driver would have to get his gun-toting friends to help him protect his truck. But if the thief also had armed friends . . .

Followed to its absurd conclusion—through armed gangs, extended feuds, border skirmishes, and major conflict—it is not all that different from the deadly arms race that threatens the very existence of humanity. Each party wants simply to protect what is his by being able to wound or destroy his opponents. No wonder Jesus warned Peter not even to get started down that path, for it has no rational ending place. The sons of Isaac and the sons of Ishmael have been trying to settle their differences by taking up the sword for almost four thousand years. Yet the Middle East is still in flames, with no reasonable peace in sight.

Jesus knew that no problem is solved because a person has been intimidated by force. Even though criminals need to be forcibly restrained, and the fear of a police officer's gun will lead some to outward compliance, we know that such force has not transformed the inner attitudes of the heart. In most cases, it even deepens the inner spirit of anger and hostility.

We can be certain that Jesus does not set a lower standard for Himself than He does for His creatures. If the truck owner is not ultimately secure with his Smith & Wesson, will eternal bliss be secured by the threat of wrathful destruction? Having told Peter to put away his sword, Jesus will not use it Himself. The wicked will die only because they have steadfastly chosen to remain separated from the Life-giver.

ARGUING WITH GOD

**Bear in mind that our Lord's patience with us is our salvation.
2 Peter 3:15, N.E.B.**

The devil is a great pendulum-swinger. He gloats over being able to
entice people into the fire on one side or the ice on the other. Some
Christians are too lax, caring little at all about their spiritual growth and
about the details of their lifestyle. Some swing the other way, constantly
uptight and bordering on the edges of despondency because they cannot
grow fast enough.

Peter's message in today's text is for this second group. To be fair,
their malady is an understandable one. They have caught a glimpse of the
beauties of Christ's character, and then contrasted them with their own
unflattering record. We can understand their desire to want to lunge into
wholeness and joy and to turn steadfastly away from every failing. They
are grief-stricken when their failings hurt others, misrepresent God, and
blunt their own peace of mind. They loathe having to deal again with the
same inner problems, and long to get on to higher ground.

The problem, however, is that Satan capitalizes on that very desire for
holiness, turning it into a cause for discouragement. He gets God's
children to become fruit inspectors rather than fruit trees. That is, we
become more engrossed with the fruits of righteousness than with the root
of righteousness. We measure our performance, comparing it with the
previous day's performance (or worse yet, someone else's performance),
then bow in discouragement. All this takes our attention off the real issue:
building a friendship with Christ through beholding His character.

Discouragement is the anesthesia the devil uses before he cuts your
heart out. For the perplexed Christian, failure to be Christlike seems to be
such a legitimate reason to be discouraged! Yet Peter tells us that when
the Lord looks at us He is not discouraged. Knowing even better than we
do the long way we have to go, He still looks upon us with patience. He
knows that we grow best with enticements rather than with pressures.

God remembers as well as we do how perplexed and distracted we
became when our parents disciplined us by expressing their impatience
with us. And He refuses to do it. If we are going to be impatient with
ourselves, we shall have to argue with God! We shall have to insist that
our opinion of ourselves is more accurate than God's. Fortunately, our
Father's opinion is what counts!

December 16

WHO BRUISED JESUS?

Yet it was the will of the Lord to bruise him; he has put him to grief. Isa. 53:10, R.S.V.

Sometime, when the setting is just right, open a modern-speech version of the Bible to Isaiah and read aloud the Suffering Servant passage. Start at Isaiah 52:13 and read thoughtfully and with emphasis through chapter 53. As you read this stunningly complete prophecy of the life and ministry of Jesus Christ, notice in particular the role that the Father played in the salvation drama.

Notice, and be amazed, that it was the Father who "laid upon him the iniquity of us all" (chap. 53:6, R.S.V.). The infinitely gracious arrangement by which the consequences of our wandering should be laid upon Jesus was a plan that the Father Himself endorsed and helped to carry out. This needs to be emphasized, clarified, and repeated anew, because the belief is so widespread that Jesus offered Himself as a means for appeasing the Father.

The great Reformation scholar John Calvin held that the perfect sacrifice of Christ resulted in us having "in heaven a propitious Father instead of a Judge." That is, Christ's ministry was to get the Father to change toward us, becoming loving rather than condemning. Calvin also taught that the Father "finds nothing in man which can incite Him to bless them." But Jesus' perfect life merits such blessing; and Jesus transfers that merit to us, that the Father might have cause to bless us. Once again, the Father is being coaxed, or entitled, to express a redemptive attitude toward us because of Jesus. The result, of course, is that we view Jesus as a refuge *from* the Father, rather than a pathway *to* the Father. Though I applaud much of the work of this great Reformer, I am dismayed that this view of our heavenly Father has gained such wide acceptance.

On the cross, the Father joined with Jesus in a united endeavor to reach the minds of men, that *we* might change toward *Him*. Equal to the pain of separation that Jesus suffered, the Father endured the pain of separation from His Son, as Jesus gave up the Spirit and slipped into the second death. Together, They revealed to the universe how deadly it is to rebel against the Source of all life. Together, They poured out upon mankind the greatest expression of love ever known. Together, They revealed that God always has been a loving Father! We love Jesus, not for appeasing God, but for revealing Him.

OUR GOD IS SENSIBLE

Whoever is wise, let him understand these things; whoever is discerning, let him know them; for the ways of the Lord are right. Hosea 14:9, R.S.V.

It is never quite satisfying when the editors of dictionaries make theological statements. Take, for example, this definition of the word *faith:* "unquestioning belief that does not require proof or evidence."

My concern, of course, is not with the dictionary editors, for they simply reflect how a word is being used among the general public. My perplexity is that so many people, including pastors and Bible scholars, insist on using this very definition of faith when it is applied to Christian experience. They believe that to ask for evidence, for intelligent understanding, is to undermine faith. They are content with a Christianity that is not required to make sense, and they think that it is a sign of one's devotion to God to believe what indeed is not appealing to one's intelligence. It has even led some to be suspicious of religious principles that require much thinking.

But Jesus would be unsatisfied with such a definition of faith. He who went to such lengths to give people abundant evidence upon which to base their faith would not wish them to set it all aside. Jesus held faith to be one's attitude of love and trust and admiration toward God. The only way one can ever come to see God in this way is to get to know Him. Jesus' ministry, then, is to provide evidence of who His Father really is. And this evidence appeals to that capacity to think and to reason that God Himself placed within us.

If God invites us to come and reason together with Him (Isa. 1:18), then shouldn't we expect that the lifestyle He offers us will also be reasonable? Once a person's mind has been enlightened by the Holy Spirit, expanded to include spiritual realities in one's reasoning process, then Christianity makes incredibly good sense. For example, to love one's enemy (as Jesus required of us) would not make any sense at all to a selfish person locked into getting all he can for himself. But to one who seeks the good of all humanity, loving one's enemy is the most innovative, disarming move one could make.

Hosea calls for the wise and the discerning to recognize that the ways of God are right—that they make incredibly good sense. Shouldn't we trust such a sensible, reasonable God?

THE MERCIFUL HANDS OF GOD

I am in deep distress. Let me fall into the hands of the Lord, for his mercy is very great; but do not let me fall into the hands of men. 1 Chron. 21:13, N.I.V.

David had gone against the explicit word of God; he had taken a census of Israel. Insecure about the military strength of the surrounding heathen nations, he numbered the fighting men of his own nation as if to assure himself that his army could withstand an onslaught from an enemy. Joab, general over all the armies, tried to dissuade David from taking this action. " 'May the Lord multiply his troops a hundred times over. My lord the king, are they not all my lord's subjects? Why does my lord want to do this? Why should he bring guilt on Israel?' The king's word, however, overruled Joab" (1 Chron. 21:3, 4, N.I.V.).

David knew God. He had spent many years trusting in Him for wisdom and strength. When he realized that he had done wickedly in looking to human armies for security instead of to the Lord, he immediately repented. "I have done a very foolish thing," he told God (verse 8, N.I.V.). Perhaps later, as he reminisced about this very time, he wrote, "The fool says in his heart, 'There is no God.' . . . There they were, overwhelmed with dread where there was nothing to dread. God scattered the bones of those who attacked you" (Ps. 53:1-5, N.I.V.).

God knew that David needed an opportunity to reexpress his faith in Him. He sent word to David: "I am giving you three options. Choose one of them for me to carry out against you. . . . Take your choice: three years of famine, three months of being swept away before your enemies, with their swords overtaking you, or three days of the sword of the Lord" (1 Chron. 21:10-12, N.I.V.). Because David *did* know God—that His justice is always flavored with fairness and mercy—he answered, "Let me fall into the hands of the Lord, for his mercy is very great; but do not let me fall into the hands of men" (verse 13, N.I.V.).

Seventy thousand of David's men died of a plague that swept through the land, yet God intervened and stopped its deadly onslaught. Had heathen warriors been slaughtering Israel, they might have continued until the nation no longer existed. David chose wisely to fall into God's hands, the hands He knew so well to be full of mercy.

WHAT DO YOU DO WITH TRUTH?

If I had not come and spoken to them, they would not be guilty of sin; but now they have no excuse for their sin. John 15:22, N.E.B.

"I don't attend prayer meeting," she admitted sheepishly, "because I don't want to hear more truth for which I will be held accountable. If I don't know what I am supposed to do, then I can't be counted as guilty for not doing it."

Though the honesty of her frank admission was commendable, her theology was tragically lacking. She held such an unfortunately dim view of God that she didn't want to hear what He had to say about the beautiful life He offers. She saw it all as heavy duties and obligations. Had she seen Jesus' lifestyle as it is, filled with high privileges and opportunities, she would have sought out every chance to learn more.

The people about whom Jesus was speaking in today's text were much the same as this woman. Having been raised in a steeply religious environment, they thought they knew all about God's requirements. From all the evidence, they didn't like it either. They would do the minimum in order to "squeak by" into the kingdom, but they had no interest in learning more. In fact, they were so closed to it all that they would choose to push Jesus off a cliff, drive Him out of town, or nail Him to a cross, rather than hear Him talk to them.

In an interesting way, Jesus didn't blame them. He understood how darkened their understanding was about religious things. He knew that their religious leaders had simply loaded their heads with burdens impossible to bear, threatened them with terrible consequences if they didn't perform, then walked away, offering no help in bearing their load. Jesus did not blame people for rejecting false religion. He would not hold them guilty for their attitudes had they not known otherwise.

But the people had heard Jesus. They had not heard Him stacking large burdens upon their weary shoulders; instead, they had heard Him unfolding gracious truths about a wise and loving Father, whom to know is to love. Many had listened for hours as Jesus explained a high and heart-oriented religion that could not be faulted.

Pilate asked the crucial question: "What shall I do with Jesus?" (Matt. 27:22, R.S.V.). To reject false religion is no cause for guilt, but to reject the gracious person of Jesus Christ is the ultimate sin.

DOES SATAN BEAR OUR SINS?

Aaron shall lay both his hands upon the head of the live goat, and confess over him all the iniquities of the people of Israel . . . and send him away into the wilderness by the hand of a man who is in readiness. Lev. 16:21, R.S.V.

Tucked away in the midst of this rather ponderous Old Testament book is a chapter that, if properly understood, would set the Christian world on its heels. The Lord has been teaching His people about the plan of salvation through the walk-in symbol of the sanctuary services. And He has given them many forms of animal sacrifices, all pointing forward to the sacrificial death of Christ on the cross. But in Leviticus 16 a surprising new element is introduced. The setting is the Day of Atonement ceremony that, coming at the end of the sacred calendar of events, symbolizes issues at the close of the great controversy. The surprise element is the use of *two* animals rather than one. Lots are cast, and one of the goats is designated as the Lord's goat. As has been done before, this goat is offered on the altar as a type of Christ.

But the other goat is designated as belonging to Azazel, which the people clearly understood to be a name for Satan. This goat is tied to a stake while the high priest enters into the Most Holy Place of the sanctuary. There he figuratively gathers up all the sins that have been transferred there during the previous year by repentant sinners. The priest then takes all those sins out to the Azazel goat and, as it were, dumps them on its head and sends it off into the wilderness, where it surely will die.

The mind-expanding perspective that this vital ceremony tells us is that in solving the cosmic sin problem, God is dealing with far more than the deadly consequences that individual sinners face. When Israel saw the priest (a type of Christ) place his hands on the Azazel goat's head, they were watching God's promise that someday everyone would know that Satan was ultimately accountable for sin.

Furthermore, when the people saw the goat being led away to die in the wilderness, cut off from every source of life, they knew that ultimately Satan and all who follow him will die the death of separation from God. Even the enemy will not be slaughtered by the hand of an angry God.

A PUZZLING MIRACLE

Now there was in Joppa a disciple named Tabitha, which means Dorcas or Gazelle. She was full of good works and acts of charity. Acts 9:36, R.S.V.

They say that it costs between $250,000 and $500,000 to replace a key corporate executive who has retired or become ill. This explains why large companies are putting so much emphasis on keeping their top men healthy. It makes good financial sense.

For reasons far greater than financial, the early church kept their key people working for the Lord for as long as possible. How could you ever replace the apostle Paul, or John the Beloved, even if you had large sums of money? Their wisdom, their spiritual maturity, was irreplaceable.

In this light, it seems that Peter came up with a rather novel approach to the problem of leadership attrition. When Tabitha, who was an important person in the church, became ill and died, he went into her home, prayed over her, and brought her back to life! As thrilling as this miracle was, I've often puzzled why it happened to this relatively unknown lady, yet no one returned the favor to Peter himself. Why didn't Peter bring some important preacher or gospel writer back to life to extend his service?

But Peter wasn't working alone; he was taking his instructions from God. And God sees things that we often miss. Perhaps the believers in Joppa needed some potent evidence of God's caring activity in their midst, but I suspect there may have been another reason why Tabitha was brought back to life. That reason is found in the description of the way she lived her life—a life filled with loving acts and caring deeds.

It is when people's lives flow with acted love that they become most effective in portraying the character of God. More than spoken words, the world has learned to trust what people do in the natural, acted patterns of daily living. Tabitha was making a powerful impact in favor of God's reputation throughout the whole town. Bringing her back to life so that her witness might continue to grace that early church was God's way of saying how vital her gift was to His cause. This should give all of us a new appreciation for those gentle, often unknown saints in the church whose passing may never make headlines but would cause the poor and needy to weep. They are telling vital truths about God!

WHO IS THE ACCUSER?

Then I heard a voice in heaven proclaiming aloud: "This is the hour of victory for our God . . . when his Christ comes to his rightful rule! For the accuser of our brothers is overthrown, who day and night accused them before our God." Rev. 12:10, 11, N.E.B.

Imagine that you have just made the acquaintance of two men. One is obviously a high-principled man who lives above reproach. You know that he would never stoop to doing anything wrong, nor knowingly tolerate anyone else's wrongdoing. The other man could best be described as a shady character. A man of questionable background and suspicious intent, he could be expected to be in trouble with the law.

Apart from your appraisal of their values, it would be interesting to consider this question: In whose presence would you most likely feel accused or condemned? Who would most likely project to you the impression that you had failed to live up to his expectations? Had you yourself lived a flawed and embarrassing past, in whose presence would you likely find the most acceptance and understanding?

It is hard for us to shake the image of righteous people as being very condemning, and of unrighteous people as looking for company in their misery. Most of us draw the same conclusions when we think of the two great adversaries in the great controversy. We suspect that our holy God would be very intolerant and accusing toward sinful people. By contrast, since Satan doesn't stand for anything good, our slim efforts at righteousness would not let him play one-upmanship with us. The very fact that we do not like to feel accused of wrongs that already have us smarting, drives many people away from God and toward Satan.

Satan has been woefully successful in coaxing some people to put together a theology that places God in the role of the accuser; he has gloated as people have squirmed away from God and toward himself. Meanwhile, he has continued to do the baleful work of crushing bruised sinners with accusations. The bony finger of condemnation and rejection is attached to the enemy's hand. But the Lord has much better plans for healing His people. Having persuaded them that they are out of relationship with Him (see John 16:9), He quickly offers to all who come home that He will never condemn them (Rom. 8:1) nor cast them out (John 6:37). That's the kind of good news that will topple Satan's kingdom.

WEARY IN WELL-DOING

Let us not grow weary in well-doing, for in due season we shall reap, if we do not lose heart. Gal. 6:9, R.S.V.

To the surprise of many of his classmates, a young man with a positive Christian character began keeping company with a rebellious and deceitful young woman. Before long, they were spiraling together into activities that violated their parents' trust and their own integrity. It seemed so out of character for him, in view of his spiritual commitments.

Several weeks later, when he once again stood on solid ground, he explained what had happened. "I just got tired of being the one with principles when so many others were enjoying a comfortable slide downhill. I got tired of saying No when everyone else was saying Yes. I got tired of being expected to live up to high ideals when it is so costly, so emotionally demanding. I just wanted to be with someone who didn't expect anything of me."

The Bible says that "the way of transgressors is hard" (Prov. 13:15) but that "the path of the righteous is like the light of dawn" (chap. 4:18, R.S.V.). Since that is true, then why is it so wearying to walk the paths of well-doing? Why does Paul need to warn against growing weary? Why can so many of us identify with the young man who simply claimed he was too tired to continue on? Should we fall into a fit of self-doubt, wondering if indeed we are even converted?

We will have to remember that Paul was a realist. Though he knew the grandeur of walking the high paths, he also knew that most people aren't instantly acclimatized to thin air. He knew that although the Christian has cast his steps toward a new and eternal country, he still walks in regular contact with entrenched earthlings. It takes time to learn the values of the new kingdom and to detach ourselves from the reference point of old friends' approval.

Some of the true joys of obedience are not as quick in coming as the temporary joys of indulgence; our minds must learn to reference to the larger picture. It was Jesus Himself who reminded us that the plant grows in stages, starting first with but a tiny blade. We shall indeed reap, Paul said, if we do not lose heart. Our God is not the kind of friend who leads His people down wearying, dead-end paths.

IS IT WRONG TO ASK FOR A SIGN?

He sighed deeply and said, "Why does this generation ask for a miraculous sign? I tell you the truth, no sign will be given it." Mark 8:12, N.I.V.

The young girl was filled with earnestness. She spoke of her pending engagement to a young man she'd met at college. "We're praying for a sign from God to let us know whether or not we should marry." As I pondered the significance of their request, something Jesus said came to my mind: "No sign will be given."

A large crowd of people had listened to the Master speak for three days. Many had come from long distances. Looking upon them, Jesus was moved with compassion. He knew that some would collapse if they were sent home hungry. He took a few loaves and fishes and fed several thousand people. Not long after that, the Pharisees came to question Him. "To test him, they asked him for a sign from heaven. He sighed deeply and said, 'Why does this generation ask for a miraculous sign? I tell you the truth, no sign will be given to it.'"

Why? Is it wrong to ask for a sign? Gideon did, twice, and God gave him exactly what he desired. Joshua and Hezekiah received the signs they asked for. When Ahaz was king of Judah, God spoke to him. "Ask the Lord your God for a sign, whether in the deepest depths or in the highest heights" (Isa. 7:11). When Ahaz refused, God volunteered the prophetic sign of the virgin birth that would herald the coming Messiah (see verse 14).

May I suggest that asking for signs can be an effort to shortcut the reasoning process that God so wisely desires us to develop. "Since we are surrounded by such a great cloud of witnesses" (Heb. 12:1, N.I.V.), there is less need today to seek supernatural manifestations of God's will. His desire is for us to "have [our] faculties trained by practice to distinguish good from evil" (chap. 5:14, R.S.V.). Couples contemplating marriage need to consider carefully their compatibility, their family backgrounds, individual temperaments and lifestyles, as well as stated goals for life—not to look for an occurrence of some extraneous event tagged as evidence of God's feelings in the matter.

It's not wrong to ask for a sign—but God would rather we come to know *Him* so thoroughly that we no longer feel the need to ask for one.

HOW TO RUIN A FRIENDSHIP

Those of you who try to be put right with God by obeying the Law have cut yourselves off from Christ. You are outside God's grace. Gal. 5:4, T.E.V.

You have received a personal request from a famous head of state that you share a meal with him. But he wants to come to your house. Your excitement turns quickly to dread as you think about your humble dress, your untrained manners, your small vocabulary, and narrow scope of conversational interests. You doubt that you would be a very satisfying dinner companion. Thinking that your host would be more satisfied with your presence if you could persuade him of your fitness, you request a postponement and begin a crash program of self-improvement.

Months stretch into years while, as on a treadmill, you doubt that you have sufficiently merited accepting the invitation. Your attention shifts entirely toward your performance until you lose track of the anticipated fellowship your host wanted to enjoy with you. Having become convinced that the friendship can happen only when you become fit for it, you ruin the friendship that itself would *make* you a fit companion.

The Bible speaks very sparingly about what it takes to commit "spiritual divorce." Jesus has courted our affection with such diligence, and offered us such security in union with Himself, that He sees little merit in giving large attention to how the relationship might die. We might stumble in our Christian walk, but His response is that He will forgive us "seventy times seven"—to start with! But He will not file for divorce on us.

In his Galatian letter, Paul spells it out: If you approach your friendship with Christ on the basis of your own merits, the relationship is ruined, not because Jesus will turn against you but because you will never open the door to His presence. Thinking that Jesus is one who requires merit rather than one who makes people whole through love, we have no common ground with Him. We remain perpetually cowering behind the door, fearing His searching, judgmental arrival.

But Jesus stands outside the door, gently knocking. If we listen with our hearts, we can hear Him telling us that He desires fellowship, not merit. He longs for union of the soul, not our credit list. Rather than our trying to prepare ourselves *for* His presence, He wants to prepare us *by* His presence. Who could close the door to such an appealing invitation?

THE GAMES GOD DOESN'T PLAY

Shall I bring to the point of birth and not deliver? Isa. 66:9, N.E.B.

"He never meant to marry me! He just wanted to see how far I would go!" The young woman spoke ruefully to her friend. Yet she herself had just "conned" her younger sister into doing a job for her by promising to take her to town when she was finished—a promise she never intended to keep.

We live in a world of disappointed hopes and broken promises. The "game of life" seems full of tricks and illusions. Many people become cynical, others despondent, still others doggedly cunning. This tragedy of broken and calloused hearts causes unspeakable grief to the heart of our faithful heavenly Father. He wants to assure us of His good intentions concerning us, but we have acquired through our relations with others a wariness that can render us faith-crippled.

Have you secretly wondered if God is ever going to come through with all that He has promised? Is He interested in an isolated experience called "unwavering faith" apart from the concrete benefits of being in an ongoing relationship with Him? As we come to know Him, we begin to understand that He is utterly trustworthy. He enters into no "game-playing" with us. His promises are as good as He Himself, because, in essence, in every promise He is offering to give us Himself.

Our text for today is one of my favorites, and speaks directly to this issue: "Shall I bring to the point of birth and not deliver?" Our Father is too kind to build up our hopes only to dash them to pieces just to see if we will still believe in Him! Though life's situations sometimes seem to support that He does just this, we may confidently know that this is not so. We have been living in a world distorted by separation from Him. Because of His regard for every man's freedom, often things happen as a result of other people's choices that are neither His will nor our own.

We may be sure, when disappointment comes, that the last chapter of this earth's history has yet to be written. We may remain undaunted in our aspirations, unthwarted as we stretch toward our goals. It is our privilege to know that someday all the restraints of this life, all the game-playing, will pass. Personally, I think God is just plain excited about the prospects!

FROM SERVANT TO FRIEND

I shall not call you servants any longer, for a servant does not share his master's confidence. No, I call you friends, now, because I have told you everything that I have heard from the Father. John 15:15, Phillips.

A servant is locked into a very distinct relationship with his master. And it is not an enviable one! The master bears final authority over the life of the servant, commanding his every action. The master has the power to reward obedience and to punish disobedience.

The servant, then, views his master primarily with fear and servile intimidation. He does not expect to share in the inner soul of the master—to know his thoughts or goals. He is sure that the master cares not one whit to share his own deepest thoughts with someone so insignificant as a servant.

The master/servant relationship exists entirely for the benefit of the master. It is not expected that the servant will grow or benefit from it. It is a dehumanizing, humiliating posture for the servant. One could hardly respect a master for imposing it upon another human. And yet, almost without exception, the people to whom Jesus was speaking viewed the Father as a stern master and themselves as the trifling servants. They saw themselves, by the very order of things, to be locked into the master/servant relationship, daring not even to question it for fear of the master's displeasure.

So Jesus dared to challenge them to break the grip of that misunderstood relationship. Though they could but barely grasp the meaning at the time, He invited them to enter into a friend/friend relationship. As proof of His serious intentions, He reminded them of how intimate and vulnerable He had been in sharing with them the richest treasures of His heart—something that would never happen in a master/servant relationship!

Friends look toward each other in mutual regard, each desiring the very best for the other. Remember, it is the Creator of the universe, speaking to His sin-damaged creatures, saying in effect, "I refuse to play one-upmanship with you. I do not want you groveling in front of Me as frightened servants. I want us to enjoy each other as friends, so that I can keep teaching you marvelous things about our Father."

Dear reader, do you hear our Father this day calling you from the oppression of servanthood to the joys of friendship?

GIVE FOR ONE ANOTHER

Forgive us the wrong we have done, as we have forgiven those who have wronged us. Matt. 6:12, N.E.B.

"Will you forgive me?" Countless times in a lifetime we hear these words and repeat them ourselves. They are spoken with the apparent intent of healing a relationship, yet seldom produce the expected results. There are an ever-increasing number of broken homes and fractured relationships. Why?

Could it be that most people want escape from the pain of another's judgment without dealing directly, healingly, with the issues that caused the pain or alienation? *Forgiveness* rightly means "giving for" the other, to heal and nurture the other's hurt and needs. When forgiveness is sought only as a method of clearing the offending party of guilt, it actually blocks healing. It is at this point that much human agony exists, captured in a sort of no-man's-land of issues rendered untouchable—"I asked you to forgive me, so don't bring up the subject again!"

Consequently, often the blame is shifted to the one who has suffered the hurt because he cannot respond readily to the offender who has "done his part." Listen: forgiveness is not something we grit our teeth and do. It is the product of a healed heart. And there are no self-healed hearts beating on Planet Earth! Only God's healing love can make us whole enough to forgive others even as they inflict hurt upon us.

Knowing that God does not expect us to muster up some kind of pious "OK" sets us free to bring to Him our incapacity to forgive our offenders. Sandwiched between the two clauses concerning forgiveness in the Lord's Prayer is the cry "Save us from the evil one!"

God wants us to recognize our dilemma—and the way out! We need saving from the devastating effects of sin in our lives—of our separation from the healing love of the Father. So God gives for us that we might be able to give for one another. If we reject the healing process that He has made available to us, we will never be able to give for others. Giving comes after we have received "our daily bread"—the provisions of our loving, caring Father for our own needs.

Giving for another can be an intensely sweet exercise of faith in who God is, whether we are asking for forgiveness or giving it. And as we help each other's healing processes, we ourselves find deeper healing.

"CHRISTIAN" CONFORMISTS

Do not be conformed to this world but be transformed by the renewal of your mind. Rom. 12:2, R.S.V.

Paul's admonition about not being conformed to this world is excellent sermon material. More preachers than I can recall have shaped their church service homilies around that warning against the evil enticements of this world.

More recently, however, I have sensed that Paul is concerned with something deeper than a contrast between the values of the world and the values of the kingdom of Christ. Something even more insidious rises to the surface as he contrasts those two words *con*formed and *trans*formed, for here he is dealing not just with the values one holds but with *how* he comes to hold them.

A person who is conformed is one who has no inner strength of conviction or purpose but who wishes above all to be accepted by other people. Rather than risk their rejection, he simply takes on their values or behaviors. He conforms to the values of the group that promises the most uncritical acceptance.

But this is not God's method for getting people to become Christians. It completely bypasses the deeper processes of the heart—the transformation of the most fundamental values and attitudes through one's union with Christ Jesus. It misses the fact that a true Christian is one who has been inwardly made secure through fellowship with his divine Friend. The conformist, by contrast, is the picture of insecurity.

We must honestly admit that all of us are subject to the tendency to be conformed Christians. Our lingering insecurities, our grasping desire to belong, our fears of rejection, set us up to embrace the "acceptable" behaviors and attitudes of our church-related friends. If we learn the games of "churchmanship" with adequate skill, we can appease ourselves that real Christian growth has happened.

As much as He values right behavior, our Father does not wish us to embrace it through fear of His rejection. For this reason, His first message to us assures us of His unconditional love and acceptance. He wants to set us free from the need to conform so that we can embrace the values of His kingdom for entirely proper reasons.

Only those who are *trans*formed Christians "will be able to discern the will of God, and to know what is good, acceptable, and perfect" (Rom. 12:2, N.E.B.). Our Father is one who desires that highly intelligent, inwardly free, peacefully harmonious approach to obedience!

THE END OF OUR CONFUSION

"Fallen, fallen is Babylon the great! . . . Come out of her, my people, lest you take part in her sins and share in her plagues." Rev. 18:2-4, N.E.B.

The crowd is large and the street unfamiliar. You have become separated from your friend. You decide to try to return to the place where you last were together. "Pardon me," you say as you stop someone who looks like he knows where he is going. "Could you tell me how to find my way?"

"Sure!" he answers. But in following his directions, you discover yourself still lost. Asking someone else, you become even more confused. Suddenly you hear a familiar voice calling your name. "Over here!" Together once again with your friend, you work your way through the crowd and home.

In this world, the crowd is large and the way through life uncertain. We hear conflicting reports about how to get where we want to go. Not only have we lost sight of our Best Friend; we aren't even sure He *is* our friend! The things we hear about Him greatly intensify our anxiety. When He calls to us, "Over here!" we are wary and distrustful. In the end, it is our own personal Babylon—confusion—that keeps us separated from Him. And as long as we remain apart from Him, our passage through this life remains hazardous and uncertain.

Does God fold His arms over His chest in disgust, saying, "Well, if they won't come when I call, it's their own fault if they stay lost"? No! He is not offended by our confusion. He does not condemn us for our wrong concepts about Him. He simply comes closer, mingling with us in the midst of the crowd, pacing Himself with us, going with us down one dark passage after another. Never does He try to force us to go His way, but quietly converses with us as we stumble along. Slowly we begin to realize that His commitment to us is genuine, His love unfailing. We sense that He is interested in *us*—not just getting us out of our predicament.

Our good Father calls us to come out of our Babylon confusion and into an understanding of who He is. We need not remain separated from Him. We need not experience the woeful effects of that separation—spiritual darkness, emotional starvation, atrophied capacities. We need not be plagued with guilt and remorse.

Well might we then shout with joy, "Fallen, fallen is Babylon the great!"

THE FINAL WORD

They sing the song of Moses, the servant of God, and the song of the Lamb, saying, "Great and wonderful are thy deeds, O Lord God the Almighty! Just and true are thy ways, O King of the ages!" Rev. 15:3, R.S.V.

On that great day when the saints receive the kingdom, there will be so much to sing about! The reunion with friends; the exhilaration of perfect bodies; the ending of all tension; the perfect harmony of all nature. How easy it would be to sing even about our own joy in being there—our blissful peace and our newfound capacities.

But the Scriptures record that one song shall swallow up every other. It is not a song written by some musically talented angel, published in large numbers, and distributed to the redeemed for them to memorize and rehearse. It is a free-flowing song, arising from the experience of the redeemed themselves. In fact, there are stanzas in the song that only the redeemed can ever fully appreciate.

It is an utterly God-ward song, inspired by and dedicated to the One who shall be known as alone worthy of our praise. It is called the song of Moses and the Lamb, because Jesus and Moses were the only ones in history ready to put their eternal lives on the line for the salvation of man and the honor of God (see Ex. 32:32). And it is sung by people who themselves would rather die than knowingly bring dishonor upon the One they have come to love and trust.

I was recently in conversation with a man who holds firmly to a belief in predestination—that God simply selects certain persons to be objects of His grace and others to be reprobates. "It's just one of the many dark pictures of God," he sighed, "and we simply have to learn to accept it. If God wills it, it is for that reason 'right.' Who are we to question?"

How grateful I am to worship a God who is someday soon going to open for review before the universe every act and every decision He has made in His six-thousand-year endeavor to win back His people. And the universal response will be "Who will not stand in awe of you, Lord? Who will refuse to declare your greatness? You alone are holy. All the nations will come and worship you, because your just actions are seen by all" (Rev. 15:4, T.E.V.).

Scripture Index

8:32	Apr. 3
8:37	Apr. 26
10:10	Mar. 23
11:32	Jan. 27
12:1	May 2
12:2	Dec. 29
13:10	Mar. 4
14:5	July 16
14:10	May 3

1 CORINTHIANS

3:14, 15	May 7
13:2	Aug. 20
13:5	Sept. 18
15:22	July 23
15:34	Mar. 30
15:53	July 2

2 CORINTHIANS

1:20	May 16
2:7	Sept. 19
3:6	Nov. 8
3:17	Jan. 1
4:2	Mar. 27
4:6	Nov. 26
5:15	Jan. 17, Sept. 25
5:19	Jan. 3
10:5	Oct. 6
13:5	Feb. 25

GALATIANS

2:16	Oct. 30
2:20	May 25
3:11	Dec. 4
3:23	Mar. 25
5:4	Dec. 25
5:6	June 6
5:22, 23	May 18
6:1	July 10
6:7	June 24
6:9	Dec. 23

EPHESIANS

1:6	Feb. 18
2:4, 5	Dec. 13
2:13	Oct. 16
3:12	Jan. 2, May 17
3:17-19	Jan. 10
3:20	Apr. 14
4:15	Apr. 12
5:25, 27	Nov. 15

| 6:4 | May 15 |
| 6:10 | Mar. 29 |

PHILIPPIANS

1:29	Aug. 11
2:9-11	July 20
2:12, 13	Feb. 12
3:8	Oct. 27
3:12	June 10

COLOSSIANS

1:21, 22	Jan. 7
2:12	Feb. 6
3:12, 13	July 8

1 THESSALONIANS

| 5:16, 17 | Sept. 24 |
| 5:20, 21 | June 9 |

2 THESSALONIANS

1:9	Nov. 22
2:8, 9	Mar. 26
5:18	Feb. 27

1 TIMOTHY

| 1:9 | Sept. 29 |
| 2:5 | Mar. 11 |

2 TIMOTHY

| 2:5 | July 6 |

TITUS

| 2:13 | Aug. 5 |
| 2:14 | Apr. 28 |

HEBREWS

1:1	Aug. 14
2:6, 7	July 17
2:17	Oct. 5
4:12	Aug. 12
8:9	Nov. 10
8:11	May 11
9:22	Apr. 1
10:35	Nov. 21
11:6	Mar. 6
11:37	Apr. 9
12:1	Mar. 1
12:2	Apr. 22
12:10	Mar. 16
13:8	July 29

JAMES

2:19	Aug. 28
4:2	Jan. 14
5:16	June 19, Nov. 13

1 PETER

2:9	Nov. 18
2:23	Sept. 13
3:3, 4	Mar. 28
3:15	Sept. 30
4:18	Sept. 14
5:10	Dec. 1

2 PETER

1:9	June 20
3:15	Dec. 15
3:17, 18	May 24

1 JOHN

2:27	June 28
3:2	Jan. 22
3:6	Jan. 11
4:8	Feb. 19
4:10	May 20
4:16, 17	Dec. 6
4:18	Apr. 27
5:13	Apr. 17

2 JOHN

| 4 | Nov. 5 |

JUDE

| 9 | Oct. 1 |
| 24 | Aug. 13 |

REVELATION

1:16	Nov. 11
3:18	May 26
3:21	Mar. 24
3:30	May 27
12:10	Dec. 22
13:3	Oct. 26
14:7	July 12
15:3	Dec. 31
18:2-4	Dec. 30
20:5	June 17
21:3	Sept. 20, Oct. 18
22:4	Aug. 25
22:11	Sept. 12
22:14	Feb. 14